The original and unique

Pets Welcome 2001

GW00504124

For Contents see Page 67
For Index of towns/counties see back of book

FHG

Part of IPC Media

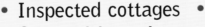
Please mention Pets Welcome when enquiring

Dalswinton

COUNTRY HOUSE HOTEL

A Victorian stone built Cornish house of character in a rural setting. Standing in 8 acres of secluded formal gardens and meadowland, the house overlooks the Vale of Lanherne and the village of St Mawgan with views to the sea at the dog friendly beach of Mawgan Porth. The Hotel is family run offering excellent food in a comfortable and friendly atmosphere. Please call 01637 860385 for more details and our colour brochure.

DINNER, BED AND BREAKFAST FROM £245.00 PER WEEK ● BED AND BREAKFAST FROM £165.00 PER WEEK ● SOLAR HEATED OUTDOOR SWIMMING POOL ● AMPLE CAR PARKING ● 8 ACRES OF PRIVATELY OWNED MEADOWLAND FOR DOG EXERCISE ● DOGS FREE OF CHARGE AND ALLOWED EVERYWHERE EXCEPT THE DINING ROOM ● TEA / COFFEE / COLOUR TV IN ALL ROOMS ● RESTAURANT AND BAR ● ONE FAMILY CHALET SELF CATERING/ROOM RATE ● OPEN ALL YEAR

STUART AND NICOLA BUSH,
DALSWINTON COUNTRY HOUSE HOTEL, ST MAWGAN-IN-PYDAR, NEWQUAY, CORNWALL TR8 4EZ. TEL/FAX: (01637) 860385
e-mail: dalswinton@bigwig.net

Cornish Dream

"For those who enjoy the comfort of a high quality hotel but prefer the freedom of a cottage" ...*The Good Holiday Cottage Guide*

Idyllic 18th Century Country Cottages for romantics and animal lovers, near the sea in the beautiful Looe River valley. Your own delightful private garden with roses around the door and breathtaking views.

Exclusively furnished, antiques, crackling log fires, candlelit meals, dishwashers, videos, four-poster beds, crisp white linen and towels. Riding & heated swimming pool. Wonderful walks from your cottage gate.

Golf, fishing, sea, coastal walks all nearby. Looe 3 miles. The cottages are heated and really warm and cosy in winter.

Pets are welcome.

Personal attention and colour brochure from:
B.Wright, Treworgey Cottages, Duloe,Liskeard, Cornwall PL14 4PP
Tel: 01503 262730 or 263757
Website: www.cornishdream.co.uk or www.treworgeycottages.co.uk
E-mail: treworgey@enterprise.net

Please mention Pets Welcome when enquiring

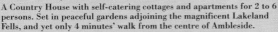

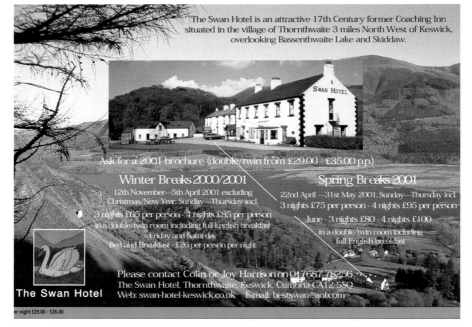

Derwent Manor

Portinscale, KESWICK, Cumbria, England, CA12 5RE

E-mail: info@derwentwater-hotel.co.uk Web: www.derwentwater-hotel.co.uk

Derwent Manor

Luxury Lakeland Holiday Cottages
and Apartments

This former gentleman's country residence now provides some of Lakeland's finest self-catering accommodation amid tranquil surroundings on the fringe of a picturesque village. Wander down to the shores of Lake Derwentwater through 16 acres of private, unspoilt meadows – a recognised conservation area, or stroll along footpaths and over the River into the village of Keswick.

Our tastefully converted one or two bedroomed self-catering apartments and cottages are all superbly appointed and offer a uniquely high standard of facilities. Fully fitted feature kitchens (many with dishwashers), independent central heating, remote control teletext colour televisions with video player, CD player and direct dial telephone, whilst the bedrooms are complete with hairdryer, trouser press and radio alarms.

Your accommodation comes complete with welcoming tea tray, bouquet of fresh flowers, fruit basket, beds made and towels supplied. Even fresh milk in the fridge, and to be sure your holiday starts with a sparkle, a bottle of chilled Champagne.

But that's not all.

On your first evening with our compliments, you may have dinner at the adjacent award winning and highly commended Derwentwater Hotel. Likewise, breakfast on your departure morning is also included, and there is more, ample free parking, takeaway meal and grocery delivery service, and a special welcome for pets.

For that really special occasion try our Glaramara Cottage, which is tucked away in the corner of the grounds and enjoys king size, half tester bed making an ideal romantic hideaway.

*Derwent Manor ...
an unrivalled location
with quality accommodation
and a range of
services and facilities
seldom matched.*

*Call us now for
our full colour brochure
on 01768772211.*

E-mail: info@derwentwater-hotel.co.uk
Web: www.derwentwater-hotel.co.uk

CUMBRIA

COTTAGE IN THE WOOD
Country House Hotel & Licensed Restaurant

Whinlatter Pass, Braithwaite, Keswick, Cumbria CA12 5TW

ETC
◆◆◆◆

- **Tel & Fax: 017687 78409**
- **E-mail: cottage@lake-district.net**
- **Web: www.lake-district.net/cottage**

This 17th century former Coaching Inn atop Whinlatter Pass has superb views of the Skiddaw mountain range. All seven en suite bedrooms are well appointed, two having four poster beds for the romantically inclined. Personally run by Barrie and Sandra

B&B £27.00 to £35.00
DB&B £46.50 to £51.50

Littlefair this NON-SMOKING hotel has a wide reputation for its excellent cuisine and fine wines. The convivial atmosphere assures guests of a memorable stay. Pets are welcome by arrangement and golf, bowls and tennis can be arranged locally.

Holbeck Ghyll Lodge
Tel: 01484 684605
Fax: 01484 689051
ETC ★★★

Extremely comfortable traditional Lakeland stone lodge with enclosed garden at rear. Two twin bedded bedrooms. Dining/living room with open fire and sofa bed. Fully equipped oak fitted kitchen. Bathroom with bath and shower. Second toilet. Antique pine furniture throughout. House situated for local walks, lake and pubs. Secure covered way for bikes. Parking for three cars. Available Easter to end of October. Saturday change over.

Mrs Kaye, Holmdene, Stoney Bank Road, Holmfirth HD7 2SL

Best Lakes Breaks

Stunning Offers *from* Stunning Hotels *in* Stunning Locations...

Rates from £99 per person for 3 nights DBB

Damson Dene Hotel & Leisure Centre
Perfectly situated in the tranquil Lyth Valley

Newby Bridge Hotel
Overlooking the Southern Shores of Lake Windermere

Lonsdale House Hotel
Conveniently located in a bustling market town

www.bestlakesbreaks.co.uk
Tel: 01539 568764

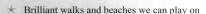

'Easily the best choice of cottages in Devon...'

...and comfortably the best value

Contact us now for a **free** colour guide and unbiased recommendation service to the 500 best value cottages around Devon's unspoilt National Trust Coast.

North Devon Holiday Homes

Barnstaple, Devon EX31 1BD

(01271) 376322

e mail: info@northdevonholidays.co.uk   www.northdevonholidays.co.uk

YOUR PET STAYS FREE

Your pet is welcome to stay FREE if you return this advert with your booking

ETC

THE EXMOOR SANDPIPER INN

A fine old coaching Inn, reputedly dating in part from the 13th and 15th centuries. It is in a beautiful setting amidst rolling moors, high above Lynmouth on the coastal road with the dramatic backdrop of Exmoor. Let us spoil you on arrival with a **free cream tea** and then be shown up to a beautiful character bedroom with tea making, colour TV and bathroom en suite, designed for your every comfort. A warm bath then a 5-course dinner including smoked salmon, seafood platters with lobster, steaks and a delicious selection of sweets. Sit in the character bars and sample our real ales or watch the late film in your bedroom.

After a traditional English breakfast set off to discover the magic of Exmoor whether in the car or on foot, along Doone Valley following the River to the majestic Watersmeet, or further to the Valley of the Rocks and up over to Glenthorne and beyond to the Devon/Somerset Borders. We have 7 circular walks around the area and the Inn can provide a packed lunch.

Please write or ring for FREE colour brochure to:-

The Exmoor Sandpiper Inn,
Countisbury, Lynmouth,
N.Devon EX35 6NE

Tel: 01598 741263
E-mail: exmoorsandpiper.demon.co.uk

YOUR PET STAYS FREE

ETC ★★★

Sandy Cove Hotel stands in 20 acres of cliff, coast and garden. The Hotel Restaurant overlooks the sea and cliffs with spectacular views of the bay. You will probably wonder how we can do it for the price when we offer a FIVE-COURSE MEAL including seafood platters with lobster, smoked salmon and steak. Every Saturday a Swedish Smorgasbord and Carvery carved by the Chef, and followed by dancing till late. Live entertainment weekly from Whitsun until September. All bedrooms have colour TV, telephone, teamaking and are en suite. The cocktail bar overlooks the bay and you have the use of the hotel's 80° heated indoor pool and recreation centre with sauna, sunbed, gym equipment and whirlpool, ALL FREE OF CHARGE.

Please return this advertisement to qualify for "Pets Stay Free" offer. Bargain Breaks and weekly rates available all year. Includes 5-course Evening Meal and coffee. Children – free accommodation. Please send for free brochure pack. Children under 5 years completely free, including meals.

Sandy Cove Hotel

Combe Martin Bay, Devon EX34 9SR
Tel: (01271) 882243 & 882888

Indoor pool heated to 80°F with roll-back sides to enjoy the sun

SAND PEBBLES HOTEL & RESTAURANT

Hope Cove, an idyllic fishing village set in National Trust countryside, with sandy beaches and cliff top walks. Our restaurant has an enviable reputation for serving superb food, so come and stay with us and

"Let Us Spoil You"

Telephone: 01548 561673

SEE OUR ENTRY UNDER DEVON – SALCOMBE

COUNTRY HOLIDAY PARK
FREE COLOUR BROCHURE
Tel: (01404) 841381 (Evgs to 8pm)
Fax: (01404) 841593
www.forestglade.mcmail.com
email: forestglade@cwcom.net

International Caravan & Camping Park

FOREST GLADE HOLIDAY PARK, CULLOMPTON, DEVON EX15 2DT

A small country estate surrounded by forest in which deer roam.
Situated in an area of outstanding natural beauty.
Large, flat, sheltered camping/touring pitches
Modern facilities building, luxury 2/6 berth full service holiday homes, also self contained flat for 2 persons.

OWNERS WELCOME TOO!

A holiday that's as enjoyable for your pets as it is for you

June and Roy Lewis would like to welcome you to Parkfield Luxury Apartments.
Parkfield Luxury Apartments are available for 12 months of the year including short winter breaks from 1st October to 1st April.
Our 1, 2 and 3 bedroom accommodation comes fully appointed, each with TV and video and its own patio.
Most have panoramic views over rolling Devonshire countryside.
Parkfield is set in an acre of landscaped grounds; children and dogs are most welcome.
It offers a children's play area, ample parking and kennels too. This tranquil setting nestles at the gateway to the 'English Riviera', so we're just a short drive from beaches, coastal walks, traditional pubs, steam railways and other family attractions aplenty.
For more information please phone/fax or write to June and Roy at:
Parkfield Luxury Apartments, Claddon lane, Maidencombe, Torquay TQ1 4TB Tel: 01803 328952

Where else would you rather walk your dog?

Well behaved dogs welcome free of charge

Prince Hall Hotel
Two Bridges
Dartmoor
Devon PL20 6SA

Winners of "Best Hotel Restaurant" West Country Food Awards 2000

Recommended in 2001 by
AA, Best Loved Hotels,
Good Hotel Guide, ETC,
Which? Hotel Guide

Tel: 01822 890 403
Fax: 01822 890 676
e-mail: info@princehall.co.uk
website: www.princehall.co.uk

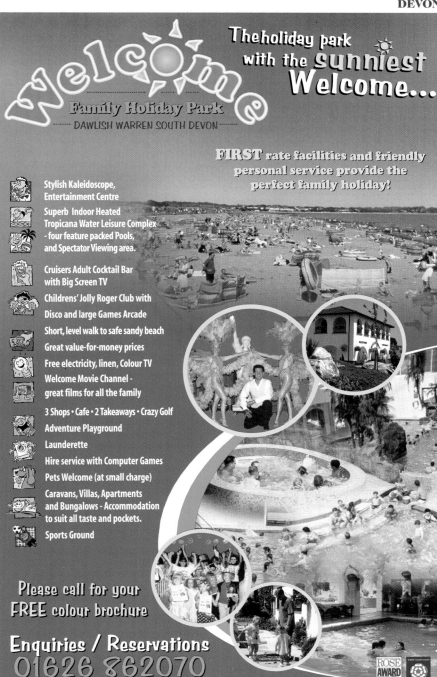

Welcome
Family Holiday Park
----- DAWLISH WARREN SOUTH DEVON -----

The holiday park with the sunniest Welcome...

FIRST rate facilities and friendly personal service provide the perfect family holiday!

- Stylish Kaleidoscope, Entertainment Centre
- Superb Indoor Heated Tropicana Water Leisure Complex - four feature packed Pools, and Spectator Viewing area.
- Cruisers Adult Cocktail Bar with Big Screen TV
- Childrens' Jolly Roger Club with Disco and large Games Arcade
- Short, level walk to safe sandy beach
- Great value-for-money prices
- Free electricity, linen, Colour TV Welcome Movie Channel - great films for all the family
- 3 Shops • Cafe • 2 Takeaways • Crazy Golf
- Adventure Playground
- Launderette
- Hire service with Computer Games
- Pets Welcome (at small charge)
- Caravans, Villas, Apartments and Bungalows - Accommodation to suit all taste and pockets.
- Sports Ground

Please call for your FREE colour brochure

Enquiries / Reservations
01626 862070
www.welcomefamily.co.uk

ROSE AWARD

HOLIDAY PARK

THE KNOLL HOUSE

STUDLAND BAY

A peaceful and relaxing holiday for all ages.
An independent country-house hotel, in an unrivalled position above three miles of golden beach. Dogs are especially welcome and may sleep in your room. Special diets arranged. Our 100 acre grounds offer nice walks; squirrels and rabbits!

Good food and a sensible wine list.
Tennis courts; nine acre golf course and outdoor heated pool.
Health spa with Jacuzzi, Sauna, Turkish room, plunge pool and gym.
Many ground-floor and single rooms for older guests.

Family suites, of connecting rooms with bathroom,
separate young children's dining room.
Playrooms and fabulous SAFE adventure playground.

Daily full board terms: £90-£115. Children less, according to age.

Open Easter - end October

STUDLAND BAY
DORSET

BH19 3AW

For Colour Brochure
TEL 01929 450450   FAX 01929 450423
Email: enquiries@knollhouse.co.uk
Website: www.knollhouse.co.uk

CHESTER HOUSE

—— Hotel ——

Bourton-on-the-Water

The Venice of the Cotswolds

A haven of peace and comfort tucked away in a quiet backwater of this famous village

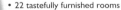

- 22 tastefully furnished rooms
- All with bathroom or shower room
- Four poster beds • Family rooms
- Ground floor rooms, wheelchair friendly, ETC approved
- Information centre • Enclosed parking • Colour TV and radio
- Free Tea and Coffee making facilities • Fully licensed
- Central heating • Creative, imaginative cooking
- Comprehensive wine list • Separate breakfast room with garden
- Friendly, helpful staff • Central base for touring the Cotswolds
- Quiet walled garden
- We welcome dogs free and well behaved owners

*Julian & Sue Davies welcome you to
Bourton-on-the-Water & the Cotswolds*

CHESTER HOUSE HOTEL

VICTORIA STREET, BOURTON-ON-THE-WATER, GLOUCESTERSHIRE GL54 2BU
TELEPHONE 01451 820286 • FAX 01451 820471
WEBSITE www.chesterhouse.u-net.com

FREEPHONE 0800 0199577

Carefree HOLIDAYS

A warm welcome for you and your pets. Inexpensive, 'live-as-you-please' self-catering holidays in beautiful Norfolk.

Chalets, Bungalows, Cottages and super Apartments near Great Yarmouth & Norfolk Broads.

SUPERB VALUE FOR 2001 SEASON

Booking Hotline Tel: 01493 732176 All calls personally answered

Short breaks available all season from £58.

1st pet £5; 2nd pet Free

Main Season Prices

Chalets from £85 to £295

Bungalows & Cottages from £105 to £365

Seadell Holiday Park, Beach Rd, Hemsby: Fully Detached.

The Laurels - Superb Bungalows close to beach. Private car park.

The Jasmines - Lovely cottages. 100 yards to golden sandy beach.

Belle-Aire - Family chalets, clubhouse. Free Electric and Linen.

Seadell - Fully detached. Park your car in front of chalet.

Winterton Valley - Chalets in pretty fishing village.

Fennside - Detached 3 bedroom bungalow. In residential Hemsby.

All accommodation is fully equipped for your holiday needs, including Free linen and entertainment at our club

1-6 The Laurels: Close to beach - Hemsby

1-9 The Jasmine Cottages: Close to sandy beach where you can take your pets, with access to lovely walks along Valley

For Free Colour Brochure:-

Write or phone to Carefree Holidays, Chapel Briers, Yarmouth Road, Hemsby, Norfolk NR29 4NJ (Tel: 01493 732176) Find us on the internet: www.carefree-holidays.co.uk

Johansens 'Inn of the Year' ✦ Egon Ronay 'Inn of the Year'

✦ Catey Award Winner "Bib Gourmand"

✦ Good Hotel Guide Cesar Awards 'Inn of the Year'

✦ Norfolk Dining Pub of the Year

✦ February 1999 – Voted by the Times as their second favourite Hotel in England, 27th favourite in the World

✦ June 1999 The Sunday Times 'Golden Pillow Award' for accommodation.

I have loved the North Norfolk coast since childhood and owning the Hoste is more than I could have wished for.

We now have 28 elegantly furnished bedrooms designed by my wife Jeanne. There are three air conditioned dining rooms serving an excellent and varied cuisine, as well as an outdoor restaurant in the gardens during summer. Recently refurbished residents' conservatory, lounge and Gallery Restaurant. There is also a beautiful 17th century bar, a favourite haunt for locals and visitors alike.

I have always adored dogs and have two black Labradors myself, Augustus and Sweep. Holkham and Brancaster beaches, both within three miles, provide wonderful lead free walking through sand and forest. Dogs are welcomed in all areas of the Hoste and insist on coming back time and time again.

I look forward to meeting you and your dogs at the Hoste.

Paul Whittome

Prices:
Bed and Breakfast, Doubles from £86.00 a night.
Low season Dinner, Bed & Breakfast available
selected months – amazing value.

The Hoste Arms Hotel, The Green, Burnham Market, Norfolk PE31 8HD
Tel: 01328 738777 • Fax: 01328 730103
E-mail: TheHosteArms@compuserve.com
Web: www.hostearms.co.uk

The Lifeboat Inn

16th Century
Smugglers' Ale House
Ship Lane, Thornham,
Norfolk PE36 6LT
Tel: 01485 512236
Fax: 01485 512323
e-mail: reception@lifeboatinn.co.uk

THE LIFEBOAT INN has been a welcome sight for the weary traveller for centuries – roaring open fires on a frosty night, real ales and a hearty meal awaiting. The Summer brings its own charm – a cool beer, gazing over open meadows to the harbour, and rolling white horses gently breaking upon Thornham's sandy beach.

Dogs are welcome in all our bars and we provide the sort of breakfast that will enable you to keep up with your four-legged friend on the way to the beach!

Guest arriving at reception are greeted by our grand old fireplace in the lounge – ideal for toasting your feet after a day walking the coastal path – if you can coax your sleeping dog out of prime position!

The restaurant (one AA rosette) opens every evening offering a varied selection of dishes to suit all tastes. Our extensive bar snack menu is also available if guests wish their pets to join them in the bar.

Bird watchers, walkers and nature lovers are spoilt for choice. A walk from our front door will take you to Thornham beach in no time at all and onto the Holme Nature Reserve. The Titchwell Marsh Nature Reserve is 2 miles away and Snettisham, Blakeney, Holkham and Cley Nature Reserves are all within short driving distance.

There are numerous and varied walks along miles of open beaches, across sweeping sand dunes, through pine woods or along chalk and sandstone cliff tops. It is truly a walker's paradise - especially if you're a dog.

We hope you will come and visit us. For our brochure and tariff which includes details of breaks please ring 01485 512236 or visit our website www.lifeboatinn.co.uk

Pictures of pets required!

We thank everyone who sent in pictures of their pets and regret that we were unable to include all of them. See page 60 for this year's selection.

If you would like to have a photo of your pet included in our next edition of *Pets Welcome!*, we would be grateful if you could forward it along with a brief note of the pet's name and any interesting anecdotes about them. Please remember to include your own name and address and let us know if you would like the pictures returned.

Everyone sending a photo can select a *FREE* copy of any of FHG's year 2001 guides from the list shown at the back of this book. If your picture is featured in the next issue we will also pay £10

We will be happy to receive prints, transparencies or pictures on disk or by e-mail to fhg@ipc.co.uk. All pictures should be forwarded by September 1st 2001.

Send to: FHG Publications, Abbey Mill Business Centre, Seedhill, Paisley PA1 1TJ.

YOUR PET STAYS FREE

THE EXMOOR WHITE HORSE INN

Exford
West Somerset
TA24 7PY

Tel: 01643 831229   Fax: 01643 831246
E-mail: exmoorwhitehorse@demon.co.uk

Managers: Peter and Linda Hendrie

INN: Situated in the delightful Exmoor village of Exford, overlooking the River Exe and surrounded by high moorland on almost every side, this family-run 16th Century Inn is an ideal spot for that well earned break. The public rooms are full of character with beams, log fires (Oct-April) and Exmoor stone throughout. There are 26 bedrooms, all of which have en suite facilities, colour TV, teamaking and central heating, and are furnished in keeping with the character of the Inn.

RESTAURANT: A variety of dishes to excite the palate served, including lobster, seafood platters, local venison & fish, whilst the bar has an extensive snack menu, with home made pies, local dishes and is renowned for its carvery. The menus change regularly with daily specials available.

NEARBY: Excellent walking country with a selection of circular walks from the Inn, plus many other local walks available. The village is also noted for its excellent riding facilities. Hunting, fishing & shooting can be arranged upon request. Open all year. Mini Breaks a speciality.

★ *Remember that your pet is FREE providing that you* ★
return this advert with your booking

THE PERFECT RETREAT FOR YOU AND YOUR DOG

Please mention Pets Welcome when enquiring

CLEAVERS LYNG

16th Century Country Hotel & Restaurant

C **LEAVERS LYNG** is a privately owned family-run hotel with a history dating back to the reign of Queen Elizabeth 1.

Set amidst elegant secluded gardens, Cleavers Lyng offers panoramic views across unspoilt Sussex countryside.

A perfect retreat in the heart of beautiful & historic East Sussex

Good traditional English cooking is enjoyed in the intimate restaurant, and the spacious lounge bar offers a wide selection of spirits, liqueurs and draught beers in a relaxed and friendly atmosphere.

All our en suite bedrooms are extremely comfortable and are centrally heated with tea/coffee making facilities and direct dial telephones. Lots of excellent walks

**Church Road, Herstmonceux,
Hailsham, East Sussex BN27 1QJ**
Telephone: 01323 833131 • Fax: 01323 833617
E-Mail: SCIL@supanet.com

RYE LODGE

Hilder's Cliff, Rye,
East Sussex TN31 7LD

Estuary views yet adjacent High Street, monastery and historical 14th century Landgate. Elegant de luxe rooms named after French wine regions, tastefully furnished. Delicious food, candlelit dinners, fine wines, room service, breakfast in bed as late as you like! Indoor swimming pool, sauna, and jacuzzi. Private car park. The stylish place to stay at this ancient Cinque Ports town.

Tel: 01797 223838 ✦ Fax: 01797 223585
Website: www.ryelodge.co.uk

**Short Break package: 2 nights inc. 3 course dinner
and coffee, room and full English breakfast from £120.00**

ETC ★★★ Silver Award

PUBLISHER'S NOTE

While every effort is made to ensure accuracy, we regret that FHG Publications cannot accept responsibility for errors, omissions or misrepresentations in our entries or any consequences thereof. Prices in particular should be checked because we go to press early. We will follow up complaints but cannot act as arbiters or agents for either party.

 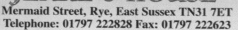

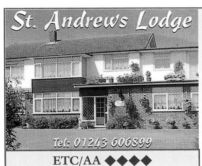

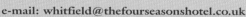

DON'T DELAY, SEND, PHONE OR FAX FOR FREE COLOUR BROCHURE.

TYGLYN HOLIDAY ESTATE

**CILIAU AERON,
NEAR LAMPETER,
CEREDIGION,
WALES SA48 8DD
TEL & FAX:
01570 470684**

**FOR THE MORE ACTIVE
HOLIDAYMAKER**

- horseriding
- golf
- tennis
- bowls
- walking
- swimming
- ten-pin bowling
- cycling
- quad-biking

  a number of leisure
  centres are all within
  easy reach.

A chance to spend a relaxing time amidst beautiful, unspoilt Welsh countryside yet within easy reach of the renowned coastal towns and beaches of New Quay and Aberystwyth with the nearest being the picturesque Aberaeron.

The bungalows are set within seventeen acres of the awe-inspiring Aeron Valley which is home to some magnificent wildlife with Buzzards, Kestrels and the re-established Red Kites being a main attraction, with fishing available on the River Aeron which runs through the estate.

Each bungalow is semi-detached, self-catering, ideal for four people but will accomodate six, with two bedrooms, lounge, kitchen and bathroom. Bed linen and Electricity are provided.

Your evenings can be spent happily at the adjacent Tyglyn Aeron Hotel, whose bars and restaurants are available to all our visitors.

Don't forget your dogs are always welcome with a nine acre field for their exercise and freedom. Short breaks available on request.

www.tyglynholidaybungalows.co.uk

WTB ★★ Hotel — Hen Dŷ Hotel

10 North Parade, Llandudno LL30 2LP   Tel: 01492 876184

TOM & CAROL LONG welcome you to the Hen Dŷ Hotel, set on the promenade, opposite the Pier. Wonderful panoramic views over the Bay. All our bedrooms have radio, TV, teamakers, central heating; all en suite. Enjoy the Chef/Proprietor's menu and the cosy Residents' Bar. Pets welcome by arrangement. We are close to shops, Happy Valley, Dry Ski Slope, Great Orme Summit. Our priority is YOUR comfort and enjoyment.   **Tariff on request.**

DOGS' PARADISE
– PEOPLE LOVE IT TOO!

RAC ◆◆◆◆   AA ◆◆◆◆
WTB ★★★★ Guest House

* En suite rooms * Exclusively for adults (and dogs!)
* Imaginative Welsh cooking * Licensed Bar
* Non-Smoking * Private Parking * Quiet, convenient location for Cathedral, coastal walks and sandy beaches
* Dinner, B&B from £44.00 to £48.00 p.p.p.n. 7 nights for the price of 6

RAMSEY HOUSE • ST DAVIDS, PEMBROKESHIRE SA62 6RP • (01437) 720321

Cwrt-y-Gaer in the Vale of Usk and Wye Valley

One, four or more dogs welcome FREE.
Three self catering units in well converted stone
Welsh Longhouse, set in old hilltop fort in
20 acres with fine views across to mountains.
Quiet area with good access to many places of
interest. Good walking. Open all year.

Brochure from Sue & John Llewellyn,
Cwrt-y-Gaer, Wolvesnewton,
Chepstow, Monmouthshire NP16 6PR
Tel: (01291) 650700
E-mail: <john.ll@talk21.com>

All units are WTB ★★★★
One unit is Grade 1 access for the disabled.

Recommended SHORT BREAK HOLIDAYS IN BRITAIN

Introduced by John Carter, TV Holiday Expert and Journalist
Specifically designed to cater for the most rapidly growing sector of the
holiday market in the UK. Illustrated details of hotels offering special
"Bargain Breaks" throughout the year.

*Available from newsagents and bookshops for £4.99 or direct from
the publishers for £5.50 including postage (UK only)*

FHG PUBLICATIONS LTD
Abbey Mill Business Centre, Seedhill, Paisley,
Renfrewshire, Scotland PAI 1TJ

LOCHMEYLER FARM

Tel: 01348 837724
Fax: 01348 837622
E-mail: stay@lochmeyler.co.uk
Web: www.lochmeyler.co.uk

Mrs Morfydd Jones
Llandeloy,
Pen-y-Cwm,
Near Solva,
St. Davids,
Pembrokeshire
SA62 6LL

A warm welcome awaits you at Lochmeyler, a 220 acre dairy farm in the centre of the St David's Peninsula. It is an ideal location for exploring the beauty of the coast and countryside.

There are 16 bedrooms, eight of them in the adjacent cottage suites. All are en-suite, non-smoking, luxury rooms with colour TV, video and refreshment facilities. Optional evening dinner with choice of menu including vegetarian. Children are welcome and there is a children's play area. Dogs free. Kennel facilities are free for owners wishing to leave their dogs during the day. Well behaved dogs can

sleep in bedrooms providing they have their own bedding on the floor.

Open all year. Credit cards accepted. Colour brochure on request.

 AA/RAC
♦♦♦♦♦ WTB FARM GOLD

DAILY RATES
Bed & Breakfast per person per night • min £20 - max £25
Optional evening dinner £12.50
Children half price sharing family room.

BOARDING YOUR PET by Kenn Oultram

The remarkable growth of travel and tourism has provided satellite industries like Animal Boarding Establishments (ABE) with year-round financial benefits, though ABE owners will reveal they were never entirely dependent on the holiday-maker. For this is very much a service industry in its own right; greatly appreciated by, for example, pet owners who may be moving house...entering hospital...taking a work assignment abroad...having the builders in...throwing a fireworks party...coping with a bitch in season or, perhaps, a cat recuperating from surgery. As looking after pets is an awesome responsibility and a job for the professional, is it reasonable to expect a neighbour or pet-sitter to take this on?

Staff at an ABE must be alert for blood, constipation, diarrhoea, lethargy, coughing, fleas, incontinence, sneezing, worms and vomit! It is taken for granted that an ABE will accept the allergic, the arthritic, the diabetic, the epileptic, the hyper-active and the neurotic...and administer pills, drops and injections. Most of all they will be expected to guarantee the safe-keeping of your pet during your absence. Postmen may claim they face the risk of dog bites, but try opening the kennel door of an outsize hound with a 30 inch neck and two cute rows of flashing stained teeth.

Early advance booking at an ABE for your pet's boarding card is now essential as the equation of 5,000 kennels/catteries to cope with a potential 11 million UK dogs and cats simply doesn't balance and, at peak times, you'll discover there's no room at the inn.

All ABEs are inspected annually by an officer from the Environmental Health Department of the Local Authority which issues a licence to operate. It is illegal to run an ABE without a licence and this must be displayed for all to see (usually in the reception area).

Some general guidelines:

● A brochure indicates a professional approach. Ring round requesting these.

● Do NOT book if the ABE will not permit you to inspect the facilities. On arrival ask to see the exercise area for dogs (leaving dogs to their own devices all day in outside runs is NOT exercise). In catteries check that sneeze barriers are installed.

● If vaccinations are not necessary do NOT book; especially if dogs are not required to be vaccinated against kennel cough.

● Ask if the ABE's insurance covers your pet's stay; otherwise a nasty vet's bill could be awaiting your return.

● Many pet owners have more than one dog or cat. Look for family-sized units and check heating facilities (after all, our winters are twice the duration of our summers...and the ABE staff need to be kept warm too!)

● Check that your pet will not come into contact with another client's pet.

● On arrival – your ears, eyes and nose will tell all! You are looking for cleanliness, contented boarders and an experienced, caring staff.

● If apprehensive ask if you may send someone to visit your pet during its stay. You could also try your pet for a day (or a night) prior to the planned lengthy stay.

Please mention Pets Welcome when enquiring

- If your pet is taken ill, ensure that the ABE is advised whether to call its own veterinarian or your own. Leave a contact number.
- If the ABE does not stock your pet's favourite food, offer to supply this, though there may not be any discount off your bill by doing so.
- Ask if a grooming service is offered. Some ABEs do. Others provide a collection and delivery service.

Finally, the time has surely come for an exhaustive, independent survey of British kennels and catteries with a one-to-four star ratings assessment. Perhaps one of the major motoring organisations should attempt this.... after all, 99% of ABE clients arrive on four wheels.

For advice and addresses call the Animal Boarding Advisory Bureau on 01606 891303 or the Feline Advisory Bureau on 01747 871872 during office hours. For the boarding of house rabbits write to The British House Rabbit Association, Box 346, Newcastle-upon-Tyne NE99 1FA. You may even wish to recommend your own ABE!

Pets Pictures

We would like to thank readers of Pets Welcome 2000 for the wonderful response to our request for pictures, and we really enjoyed seeing them.

We are unable to use all of them but are pleased to publish the following selection.

Also see front cover for picture of **Darcy** and **Merlin** *sent by Mrs Thacker of Chesterfield.*

▼ Good friends **Jack, Oban,** and **Gemma-Kelly** in the garden *sent by Elizabeth Walker of Saffron Walden.*

▲ **Shanie** makes a new friend *from Miss S. Watson, East Ham.*

▲ **Kirsty** in the country *sent in by P.M. Williams, Edinburgh.*

▼ Ship ahoy! **Sophie** waits patiently for the crew *from Miss M.R. Thomson from Enfield.*

▲ **Millie** watching the waves *sent in by Margaret Litchfield of Wimborne.*

▲ **Blaze** by the seaside *sent by C.M. Billington, Lancashire.*

▲ **Murray** enjoys the Scottish scenery *sent by Martin Hoban and Wendy Aitkinson of Birmingham.*

▲**The Dobson gang** on the beach at Booby's Bay, Cornwall *from Ros & Chris Dobson, Stratford-upon-Avon.*

▲ Which way next? **Bonnie** and **Gemma** on holiday at Woolacombe *sent by Ms Lisa Breckin of Leeds.*

▶ **Snowy** the horticultural expert *sent in by Mr A. Willis from Doncaster.*

▲ **Badger** and **Freddy** explore Kielder Forest *from Jenny Prescott, Desborough.*

▼ When's the next train? ask **Kerry** and **Cassie** *from Mrs M. Devaney of Northwich.*

◀ **Josie** exploring her holiday home *sent by Mrs J. Aldridge of Horsham.*

▶ **Hatti** and her friend **Jasper** relax in the garden *sent by Mrs Adams of Hinckley.*

Nico scales the heights in the Lake District *sent by Mrs L.M. Sarjeant of Belper.*

▲ The water's fine says **Pluto** *sent by Mrs J.F. Owens of Ferryhill.*

Please mention Pets Welcome when enquiring

▲ **Brodie** loves the outdoor life from *Mr & Mrs White of Peterlee.*

▲ **Pheobe** smiles for the camera *from Joanne Downs of Worcester Park..*

▲ **Bear** – mistress of all she surveys *from M.K. Duffy of London.*

▲ **Mabel's** Happy Christmas *sent in by Julie Hirons, Brentford.*

◀ **Tilly** goes crab hunting in Devon *from Mr and Mrs Vallance, Basingstoke.*

Ratings You Can Trust

ENGLAND

The *English Tourism Council* (formerly the English Tourist Board) has joined with the *AA* and *RAC* to create a new, easily understood quality rating for serviced accommodation, giving a clear guide of what to expect.

HOTELS are given a rating from One to Five *Stars* – the more Stars, the higher the quality and the greater the range of facilities and level of services provided.

GUEST ACCOMMODATION, which includes guest houses, bed and breakfasts, inns and farmhouses, is rated from One to Five *Diamonds*. Progressively higher levels of quality and customer care must be provided for each one of the One to Five Diamond ratings.

HOLIDAY PARKS, TOURING PARKS and CAMPING PARKS are now also assessed using *Stars*. Standards of quality range from a One Star (acceptable) to a Five Star (exceptional) park.

Look out also for the new *SELF-CATERING* Star ratings. The more *Stars* (from One to Five) awarded to an establishment, the higher the levels of quality you can expect. Establishments at higher rating levels also have to meet some additional requirements for facilities.

NB Some self-catering properties had not been assessed at the time of going to press and in these cases the old-style KEY symbols will still be shown.

SCOTLAND

Star Quality Grades will reflect the most important aspects of a visit, such as the warmth of welcome, efficiency and friendliness of service, the quality of the food and the cleanliness and condition of the furnishings, fittings and decor.

THE MORE STARS, THE HIGHER THE STANDARDS.

The description, such as Hotel, Guest House, Bed and Breakfast, Lodge, Holiday Park, Self-catering etc tells you the type of property and style of operation.

In England, Scotland and Wales, all graded properties are inspected annually by Tourist Authority trained Assessors.

WALES

Places which score highly will have an especially welcoming atmosphere and pleasing ambience, high levels of comfort and guest care, and attractive surroundings enhanced by thoughtful design and attention to detail

STAR QUALITY GUIDE FOR SERVICED ACCOMMODATION AND HOLIDAY PARKS

★★★★★	*Exceptional quality*
★★★★	*Excellent quality*
★★★	*Very good quality*
★★	*Good quality*
★	*Fair to good quality*

SELF-CATERING ACCOMMODATION

The *DRAGON GRADES* spell out the quality. They range from Grade 1 (simple and reasonable) to Grade 5 (excellent quality). The grades reflect the overall quality, not the range of facilities.

Please mention Pets Welcome when enquiring

The original and unique
Pets Welcome 2001

Foreword

Pets Welcome!, with its varied choice of holiday accommodation, remains as popular as ever, and this 40th edition is packed with features old and new.

In the year 2000 edition of the guide we asked readers to send in pictures of their pets and were pleased, though not surprised, at the response. We have shown a super selection of these pictures on page 60 and hope to include others in future editions. Our Kennels and Catteries supplement has been replaced by a useful article on Boarding your Pet (page 58) and, with 'Pet Passports' looming on the horizon, we have included some details (page 84) on the requirements for this.

Pet-Friendly Pubs and Holidays with Horses supplements are now well established and this year's selections appear on pages 441 and 445 respectively while our Readers' Offer Vouchers, plus a selection of other attractions which welcome pets, start on page 69.

Most of our entries are of long standing and are tried and tested favourites with animal lovers. However as publishers we do not inspect the accommodation advertised in Pets Welcome! and an entry does not imply our recommendation. Some proprietors offer fuller facilities for pets than others, and in the classified entry which we give each advertiser we try to indicate by symbols whether or not there are any special facilities and if additional charges are involved. However, we suggest that you raise any queries or particular requirements when you make enquiries and bookings.

If you have any problems or complaints, please raise them on the spot with the owner or his representative in the first place. We will follow up complaints if necessary, but we regret that we cannot act as intermediaries nor can we accept responsibility for details of accommodation and/or services described here. Happily, serious complaints are few. Finally, if you have to cancel or postpone a holiday booking, please give as much notice as possible. This courtesy will be appreciated and it could save later difficulties.

We would be happy to receive readers' suggestions on any other useful features. Please also let us know if you have had any unusual or humorous experiences with your pet on holiday. This always makes interesting reading! And we hope that you will mention Pets Welcome when you make your holiday inquiries or bookings.

Anne Cuthbertson, Editor

40th Edition © IPC Media Ltd 2001
ISBN 1 85055 318 1

Cover design: Oliver Dunster, Focus Network
Cover Pictures: IPN
and Mrs Thacker, Chesterfield

Cartography by GEO Projects, Reading

Maps are based on Ordnance Survey Maps with the permission
of the Controller of Her Majesty's Stationery Office,
Crown Copyright reserved.

Typeset by FHG Publications Ltd, Paisley.
Printed and bound in Great Britain by William Clowes, Beccles, Suffolk.

Distribution. Book Trade: WLM, Unit 11, Newmarket Court, Newmarket Drive, Derby DE24 8NW
(Tel: 01332 573737. Fax: 01332 573399).
News Trade: Market Force (UK) Ltd, 247 Tottenham Court Road, London WIP 0AU
(Tel: 020 7261 6809; Fax: 020 7261 7227).

Published by FHG Publications Ltd., Abbey Mill Business Centre,
Seedhill, Paisley, Scotland PA1 ITJ
(Tel: 0141-887 0428 • Fax: 0141-889 7204).
e-mail: fhg@ipcmedia.com

Pets Welcome is an FHG publication, published by
IPC Country & Leisure Media Ltd, part of IPC Media °Group of Companies.

All the advertisers in PETS WELCOME! have an entry in the appropriate classified section and each classified entry may carry one or more of the following symbols:

ħ   This symbol indicates that pets are welcome free of charge.

£   The £ indicates that a charge is made for pets. We quote the amount where possible, either per night or per week.

pw!   This symbol shows that the establishment has some special provision for pets; perhaps an exercise facility or some special feeding or accommodation arrangements.

◻   Indicates separate pets accommodation.

PLEASE NOTE that all the advertisers in PETS WELCOME! extend a welcome to pets and their owners but they may attach conditions. The interests of other guests have to be considered and it is usually assumed that pets will be well trained, obedient and under the control of their owner.

CONTENTS

ENGLAND

SCOTLAND

WALES

Ratings You Can Trust

ENGLAND

The *English Tourism Council* (formerly the English Tourist Board) has joined with the *AA* and *RAC* to create a new, easily understood quality rating for serviced accommodation, giving a clear guide of what to expect.

HOTELS are given a rating from One to Five *Stars* – the more Stars, the higher the quality and the greater the range of facilities and level of services provided.

GUEST ACCOMMODATION, which includes guest houses, bed and breakfasts, inns and farmhouses, is rated from One to Five *Diamonds*. Progressively higher levels of quality and customer care must be provided for each one of the One to Five Diamond ratings.

HOLIDAY PARKS, TOURING PARKS and CAMPING PARKS are now also assessed using *Stars*. Standards of quality range from a One Star (acceptable) to a Five Star (exceptional) park.

Look out also for the new *SELF-CATERING* Star ratings. The more *Stars* (from One to Five) awarded to an establishment, the higher the levels of quality you can expect. Establishments at higher rating levels also have to meet some additional requirements for facilities.

NB Some self-catering properties had not been assessed at the time of going to press and in these cases the old-style KEY symbols will still be shown.

SCOTLAND

Star Quality Grades will reflect the most important aspects of a visit, such as the warmth of welcome, efficiency and friendliness of service, the quality of the food and the cleanliness and condition of the furnishings, fittings and decor.

THE MORE STARS, THE HIGHER THE STANDARDS.

The description, such as Hotel, Guest House, Bed and Breakfast, Lodge, Holiday Park, Self-catering etc tells you the type of property and style of operation.

In England, Scotland and Wales, all graded properties are inspected annually by Tourist Authority trained Assessors.

WALES

Places which score highly will have an especially welcoming atmosphere and pleasing ambience, high levels of comfort and guest care, and attractive surroundings enhanced by thoughtful design and attention to detail

STAR QUALITY GUIDE FOR SERVICED ACCOMMODATION AND HOLIDAY PARKS

★★★★★	*Exceptional quality*
★★★★	*Excellent quality*
★★★	*Very good quality*
★★	*Good quality*
★	*Fair to good quality*

SELF-CATERING ACCOMMODATION

The *DRAGON GRADES* spell out the quality. They range from Grade 1 (simple and reasonable) to Grade 5 (excellent quality). The grades reflect the overall quality, not the range of facilities.

FHG Pets Welcome! and Petplan have joined together to offer you specially negotiated insurance for your pet, including the first month of your plan free, AND lifetime Petsafe membership which uses a unique tag system to return your pet should he or she get lost.

A 65-minute journey into the lost world of the English narrow gauge light railway. Features historic steam locomotives from many countries.

PETS MUST BE KEPT UNDER CONTROL AND NOT ALLOWED ON TRACKS

Open: Sundays and Bank Holiday weekends 25 March to 28 October. Additional days in summer.

Directions: On A4146 towards Hemel Hempstead, close to roundabout junction with A505.

The world's leading collection of lighthouse equipment. AV theatre and reconstructed living quarters.

DOGS ON LEADS

Open: Sunday to Friday 10.30am to 4.30pm Easter to 31st October 2001

Directions: A30 into Penzance

World's finest steamboat collection and premier all-weather attraction. Swallows and Amazons exhibition, model boat pond, tea shop, souvenir shop. Free guided tours "Dolly": 1850-2000 Exhibition.

Open: 10am to 5pm 3rd weekend in March to last weekend October

Directions: on A592 between Windermere and Bowness-on-Windermere

---

A collection of cars from film and TV, including Chitty Chitty Bang Bang, James Bond cars, Del Boy's van, Fab1 and many more.

PETS MUST BE KEPT ON LEAD

Open: Daily 10am-5pm. Closed February half term. Weekends only in December.

Directions: In centre of Keswick close to car park

FHG READERS' OFFER 2001

Eskdale Historic Water Mill

Mill Cottage, Boot, Eskdale, Cumbria CA19 1TG

Tel: 019467 23335

Free child with two adults

valid during 2001

NOT TO BE USED IN CONJUNCTION WITH ANY OTHER OFFER

FHG READERS' OFFER 2001

Blue-John Cavern

Castleton, Hope Valley, Derbyshire S30 2WP

Tel: 01433 620642

One child free with every paying adult

Valid until end 2001

NOT TO BE USED IN CONJUNCTION WITH ANY OTHER OFFER

FHG READERS' OFFER 2001

National Tramway Museum

Crich, Matlock, Derbyshire DE4 5DP

Tel: 01773 852565 e-mail: ntm-photos@online.rednet.co.uk
website: www.tramway.co.uk

One child free with every full-paying adult

Valid to end October 2001

NOT TO BE USED IN CONJUNCTION WITH ANY OTHER OFFER

FHG READERS' OFFER 2001

Treak Cliff Cavern

HOME OF BLUE JOHN STONE

Castleton, Hope Valley, Derbyshire S33 8WP

Tel: 01433 620571

10% discount

valid during 2001

NOT TO BE USED IN CONJUNCTION WITH ANY OTHER OFFER

FHG READERS' OFFER 2001

The Gnome Reserve & Wild Flower Garden

West Putford, Near Bradworthy, Devon EX22 7XE

Tel: 01409 241435 e-mail: info@gnomereserve.co.uk
website: www.gnomereserve.co.uk

One free child with full paying adult

Valid during 2001

NOT TO BE USED IN CONJUNCTION WITH ANY OTHER OFFER

England's oldest working watermill, milling oatmeal daily

DOGS ON LEADS

Open: 11am to 5pm April to October (may be closed Mondays)

Directions: Near inland terminus of Ravenglass & Eskdale Railway or over Hardknott Pass

FHG PUBLICATIONS, ABBEY MILL BUSINESS CENTRE, PAISLEY PA1 1TJ

Large range of natural water worn caverns featuring mining equipment, stalactites and stalagmites, and fine deposits of Blue-John stone, Britain's rarest semi-precious stone.

DOGS MUST BE KEPT ON LEAD

Open: 9.30am to 5.30pm

Directions: Situated 2 miles west of Castleton; follow brown tourist signs

FHG PUBLICATIONS, ABBEY MILL BUSINESS CENTRE, PAISLEY PA1 1TJ

Ride vintage trams from all over the world using genuine old pennies and halfpennies given on arrival. Plus over 30, 000 square feet of indoor attractions. Tea rooms, shops, picnic areas, playgrounds. Braille guide books, specially converted tram to lift and carry wheelchairs. Free car and coach parking.

DOGS MUST BE KEPT ON LEAD

Open: April to Oct, Daily 10am - 5.30pm. Phone for details of winter opening times

Directions: Follow brown tourist signs from A6 and A38

FHG PUBLICATIONS, ABBEY MILL BUSINESS CENTRE, PAISLEY PA1 1TJ

An underground wonderland of stalactites, stalagmites, rocks, minerals and fossils. Home of the unique Blue John stone – see the largest single piece ever found. Suitable for all ages.

Open: March to October opens 9.30am, November to February opens 10am. Enquire for last tour of day and closed days.

Directions: ½ mile west of Castleton on A6187 (old A625)

FHG PUBLICATIONS, ABBEY MILL BUSINESS CENTRE, PAISLEY PA1 1TJ

Visit 1000+ gnomes and pixies in two acre beech wood. Gnome hats are loaned free of charge - so the gnomes think you are one of them - don't forget your camera! Also 2-acre wild flower garden with 250 labelled species.

Open: daily 10am to 6pm 21st March to 31st October

Directions: Between Bideford and Bude; follow brown tourist signs from A39/A388/A386

FHG PUBLICATIONS, ABBEY MILL BUSINESS CENTRE, PAISLEY PA1 1TJ

READERS'
OFFER
2001

Killhope Lead Mining Museum

Cowshill, Upper Weardale, Co. Durham DL13 1AR

Tel: 01388 537505

One child FREE with full-paying adult (not valid for Park Level Mine)

valid April to
October 2001

NOT TO BE USED IN CONJUNCTION WITH ANY OTHER OFFER

READERS'
OFFER
2001

BARLEYLANDS FARM

Barleylands Road, Billericay, Essex CM11 2UD

Tel: 01268 290229   e-mail: barleyfarm@aol.com

Free adult ticket when accompanied by two children

Valid 1st March to 31st
October. Not special event days

NOT TO BE USED IN CONJUNCTION WITH ANY OTHER OFFER

FHG

READERS'
OFFER
2001

Museum of Kent Life

Sandling, Maidstone, Kent ME14 3AU

Tel: 01622 763936 e-mail: enquiries@museum-kentlife.co.uk website: www.museum-kentlife.co.uk

Free entry for child when accompanied by full-paying adult

Valid 1/3/01 to 31/10/01

NOT TO BE USED IN CONJUNCTION WITH ANY OTHER OFFER

FHG

READERS'
OFFER
2001

Skegness Natureland Seal Sanctuary

North Parade, Skegness, Lincolnshire PE25 1DB

Tel: 01754 764345 e-mail: natureland@fsbdial.co.uk
website: www.skegnessnatureland.co.uk

Free entry for one child when accompanied by full-paying adult.

Valid during 2001

NOT TO BE USED IN CONJUNCTION WITH ANY OTHER OFFER

FHG

READERS'
OFFER
2001

Southport Zoo and Conservation Trust

Princes Park, Southport, Merseyside PR8 1RX

Tel: 01704 538102

FREE Zoo Pack per family

valid during 2001
except Bank Holidays

NOT TO BE USED IN CONJUNCTION WITH ANY OTHER OFFER

Britain's best preserved lead mining site – and a great day out for all the family, with lots to see and do. Underground Experience – Park Level Mine now open.

Open: April 1st to October 31st 10.30am to 5pm daily

Directions: alongside A689, midway between Stanhope and Alston in the heart of the North Pennines.

FHG PUBLICATIONS, ABBEY MILL BUSINESS CENTRE, PAISLEY PA1 1TJ

Farm Centre with animals, museum, blacksmith, glassblowing, miniature railway (Sundays and August), craft shops, tea room and licensed restaurant.

DOGS MUST BE KEPT ON LEAD

Open: 1st March to 31st October

Directions: M25, A127 towards Southend. Take A176 junction off A127, 3rd exit Wash Road, 2nd left Barleylands Road.

FHG PUBLICATIONS, ABBEY MILL BUSINESS CENTRE, PAISLEY PA1 1TJ

Open-air museum with historic buildings housing exhibitions on Kent life over past 100 years. Sample Kentish fare in the tearoom. Medway boat trip, adventure playground, free parking.

DOGS MUST BE KEPT ON LEAD

Open: daily March to November 4th 10am to 5.30pm

Directions: just off Junction 6 M20, A229 to Maidstone

FHG PUBLICATIONS, ABBEY MILL BUSINESS CENTRE, PAISLEY PA1 1TJ

Well known for rescuing and rehabilitating orphaned and injured seal pups found washed ashore on Lincolnshire beaches. Also: penguins, aquarium, pets' corner, reptiles, Floral Palace (tropical birds and butterflies etc).

Open: Daily from 10am. Closed Christmas/Boxing/New Years Days.

Directions: At the north end of Skegness seafront

FHG PUBLICATIONS, ABBEY MILL BUSINESS CENTRE, PAISLEY PA1 1TJ

Lions, snow leopards, chimpanzees, penguins, reptiles, aquarium and lots more, set amidst landscaped gardens. Gift shop, cafe and picnic areas.

Open: all year round from 10am

Directions: on the coast 16 miles north of Liverpool; follow the brown and white tourist signs

FHG PUBLICATIONS, ABBEY MILL BUSINESS CENTRE, PAISLEY PA1 1TJ

FHG READERS' OFFER 2001

Newark Air Museum

The Airfield, Winthorpe, Newark, Nottinghamshire NG24 2NY

Tel: 01636 707170   e-mail: newarkair@lineone.net

Party rate discount for every voucher
(50p per person off normal admission).

Valid during 2001

NOT TO BE USED IN CONJUNCTION WITH ANY OTHER OFFER

FHG READERS' OFFER 2001

Cogges Manor Farm Museum

Church Lane, Witney, Oxfordshire OX8 6LA

Tel: 01993 772602

Two for the price of one

Valid April to end of October 2001

NOT TO BE USED IN CONJUNCTION WITH ANY OTHER OFFER

FHG READERS' OFFER 2001

Avon Valley Railway

Bilton Station, Bath Road, Willsbridge, Bristol, Somerset BS30 6ED

Tel: 0117 932 5538   website: www.avonvalleyrailway.co.uk

One free ticket with every fare-paying adult
(Not valid for "Day out with Thomas Events")

valid from May to September 2001

NOT TO BE USED IN CONJUNCTION WITH ANY OTHER OFFER

FHG READERS' OFFER 2001

Exmoor Falconry & Animal Farm

Allerford, Near Porlock, Minehead, Somerset TA24 8HJ

Tel: 01643 862816   e-mail: exmoorfalcon@freenet.co.uk
website: www.exmoorfalconry.co.uk
10% off entry to Falconry Centre

Valid during 2001

NOT TO BE USED IN CONJUNCTION WITH ANY OTHER OFFER

FHG READERS' OFFER 2001

Museum of East Anglian Life

Crowe Street, Stowmarket, Suffolk IP14 1DL

Tel: 01449 612229
website: www.suffolkcc.gov.uk/central/meal

Free entry for child accompanied by adult

Valid April to October 2001

NOT TO BE USED IN CONJUNCTION WITH ANY OTHER OFFER

A collection of 55 aircraft and cockpit sections from across the history of aviation. Extensive aero engine and artefact displays.

Open: daily from 10am (closed Christmas period).

Directions: Follow brown and white signs from A1, A46, A17 and A1133

Historic manor house and farm with traditional animals. Baking in the Victorian kitchen every afternoon.

PETS MUST BE KEPT ON LEAD; NOT ALLOWED IN BUILDINGS

Open: April to end October: Tuesday to Friday 10.30am to 5.30pm. Saturday and Sunday 12-5.30pm

Directions: Just off A40 Oxford to Cheltenham road at Witney

The Avon Valley Railway is more than just a train ride, offering a whole new experience for some, or a nostalgic memory for others.
Steam trains operate every Sunday May to September, plus Bank Holidays and Christmas.

PETS MUST BE KEPT ON LEADS AND OFF TRAIN SEATS

Open: Steam trains operate every Sunday May to Sept plus Bank Holidays and Christmas

Directions: On the A431 midway between Bristol and Bath at Willsbridge

---

Falconry centre with animals - flying displays, animal handling, feeding and bottle feeding - in 15th century NT farmyard setting on Exmoor. Also falconry and outdoor activities, hawk walks and riding

Open: 10.30am to 4.30pm

Directions: A39 west of Minehead, turn right at Allerford, half-mile along lane on left

---

Lush 70-acre site with wonderful collection of artefacts. Farmyard animals, adventure playground, cafe and shop. Something for everyone

ANIMALS WELCOME , MUST BE KEPT ON LEAD

Open: April to November. Mon-Sat 10am to 5pm, Sun 11am to 5pm

Directions: A14 adjacent to Asda

Lots of baby animals. pony rides, face painting, green trail, watch the cows being milked, children's battery tractors; gift shop, tearoom, pets' paddocks

DOGS MUST BE KEPT ON LEADS

Open: March to October 10.30am to 6pm

Directions: Follow brown tourist signs off A12 and other roads

---

Experience history and nostalgia at its very best at one of the South of England's favourite attractions. Over 30 room and shop displays bring the park to life

PETS NOT ALLOWED IN CHILDRENS PLAY AREA

Open: 10am to 6pm (last admission 4.45pm, one hour earlier in winter)

Directions: Just off A21 in Battle High Street opposite the Abbey

---

Steam train operate over a 4½ mile line from Bolton Abbey Station to Embsay Station. Many family events including Thomas the Tank Engine take place during major Bank Holidays.

Open: steam trains run every Sunday throughout the year and up to 7 days a week in summer. 11am to 4.15pm

Directions: Embsay Station signposted from the A59 Skipton by-pass; Bolton Abbey Station signposted from the A59 at Bolton Abbey.

A fascinating display of railway carriages and a wide range of railway items telling the story of rail travel over the years.

ALL PETS MUST BE KEPT ON LEADS

Open: daily 11am to 4.30pm

Directions: Approximately one mile from Keighley on A629 Halifax road. Follow brown tourist signs

---

45-acre natural wildlife park, with nature trails. On view are fallow deer, raccoons, wallabies, pigs, Scottish wild cats, foxes, monkeys, birds of prey, deer and much more. Small cafe and gift shop

ALL PETS MUST BE KEPT ON LEADS

Open: Easter weekend to October 31st. Open 10am, last admission 5pm

Directions: A82 Glasgow-Tarbet, then A83 Campbeltown. One mile south of Inveraray village

Dunaskin Open Air Museum

Waterside, Patna, Ayrshire KA6 7JF

Tel: 01292 531144 e-mail: dunaskin@btconnect.com
website: www.dunaskin.org

Two for the price of one

READERS' OFFER 2001

valid from 1st May to 31st October 2001

NOT TO BE USED IN CONJUNCTION WITH ANY OTHER OFFER

Kelburn Castle & Country Centre

Fairlie, Near Largs, Ayrshire KA29 0BE

Tel: 01475 568685 e-mail: info@kelburncountrycentre.com
website: www.kelburncountrycentre.com

One child free for each full paying adult

READERS' OFFER 2001

Valid until October 2001

NOT TO BE USED IN CONJUNCTION WITH ANY OTHER OFFER

MYRETON MOTOR MUSEUM

Aberlady, East Lothian EH32 0PZ

Tel: 01875 870288

One child FREE with each paying adult

READERS' OFFER 2001

valid during 2001

NOT TO BE USED IN CONJUNCTION WITH ANY OTHER OFFER

Landmark Forest Heritage Park

Carrbridge, Inverness-shire PH23 3AJ

Tel: 01479 841613 Freephone 0800 731 3446

10% discount for pet owners. Free admission for pets!

READERS' OFFER 2001

Valid during 2001

NOT TO BE USED IN CONJUNCTION WITH ANY OTHER OFFER

Bala Lake Railway

The Station, Llanuwchllyn, Bala, Gwynedd LL23 7DD

Tel: 01678 540666 website: www.bala-lake-railway.co.uk

Two adults for the price of one with voucher. Dogs are free!

READERS' OFFER 2001

Valid during 2001 season

NOT TO BE USED IN CONJUNCTION WITH ANY OTHER OFFER

Set in the rolling hills of Ayrshire, Europe's best preserved ironworks. Guided tours, audio-visuals, walks with electronic wands. Restaurant/coffee shop

Open: April to October daily 10am to 5pm

Directions: A713 Ayr to Castle Douglas road, 12 miles from Ayr, 3 miles from Dalmellington

---

The historic home of the Earls of Glasgow. Waterfalls, gardens, famous Glen, unusual trees. Riding school, stockade, play areas, exhibitions, shop, cafe and The Secret Forest.

PETS MUST BE KEPT ON LEAD

Open: daily 10am to 6pm Easter to October

Directions: On A78 between Largs and Fairlie, 45 mins drive from Glasgow

---

Motor cars from 1896, motorcycles from 1902, commercial vehicles from 1919, cycles from 1880, British WWII military vehicles, ephemera, period advertising etc

Open: daily October to Easter 10am to 5pm; Easter to October 10am to 6pm. Closed Christmas Day and New Year's Day

Directions: off A198 near Aberlady. two miles from A1

Great day out for all the family. Forest trails, Clydesdale Horse, Steam powered saw mill; Try a 2 man saw. Wild Water Coaster (April to Oct), Microworld - an expedition into inner space. Meals and snacks, shop.

DOGS MUST BE KEPT ON LEADS

Open: daily except Christmas Day

Directions: 20 miles south of Inverness at Carrbridge, just off the A9

A delightful ride by narrow gauge steam train along the shore of Wales largest natural lake through the beautiful scenery of Snowdonia National Park

Open: Easter to end September; daily except some Mondays and Fridays early/late season

Directions: Easily accessible via A55 and A494

FHG READERS' OFFER 2001

Llanberis Lake Railway

Gilfach Ddu, Llanberis, Gwynedd LL55 4TY

Tel: 01286 870549   e-mail: info@lake-railway.co.uk
website: www.lake-railway.co.uk

One pet travels free with each full fare paying adult

Valid Easter to October 2001

NOT TO BE USED IN CONJUNCTION WITH ANY OTHER OFFER

FHG READERS' OFFER 2001

National Cycle Collection

Automobile Palace, Temple Street, Llandrindod Wells, Powys LD1 5DL

Tel: 01597 825531

Two for the price of one

Valid during 2001 except Special Event days

NOT TO BE USED IN CONJUNCTION WITH ANY OTHER OFFER

FHG Pets Welcome! Pet Insurance in association with *Petplan*®

As a pet owner and animal lover, I know that you will want the very best in veterinary treatment should anything happen to your pet, whilst at home or on holiday.
FHG Pets Welcome! and **Petplan**, the UK's most popular pet insurance provider have joined together to offer you specially negotiated insurance for your pet.
And here are just a few of the excellent benefits...

- It takes the worry out of paying for veterinary treatment.
- Petplan covers each illness and injury for life - not just for the first 12 months like most plans.
- Generous maximum amounts you can claim for the cost of treatment each year and every year you renew.
- Claims settled quickly and fairly by Petplan, normally within 3 days and there's no limit to the number of claims you can make each year
- You are far more likely to claim on your Petplan insurance than other forms of insurance. In fact, 3 out of 10 Petplan members do so every year.

As a special offer, you will receive the first month of your Pet Insurance plan free of charge. Another bonus is that Petplan will give you free lifetime Petsafe membership when you insure your pet. Petsafe is a 24-hour national pet monitoring service that returns lost cats and dogs to their owners using a unique tag system.

If you would like more information about this special Petplan offer or to arrange cover for your pet you can call us free on 0800 072 6090.

Anne Cuthbertson, Editor

1st month free, free lifetime Petsafe membership, call today - 0800 072 6090

Valid until December 31st 2001

A 40-minute ride along the shores of beautiful Padarn Lake behind a quaint historic steam engine. Magnificent views of the mountains from lakeside picnic spots

DOGS MUST BE KEPT ON LEAD AT ALL TIMES ON TRAIN

Open: Most days Easter to October. Free timetable leaflet on request

Directions: just off A4086 Caernarfon to Capel Curig road at Llanberis; follow 'Country Park' signs

Journey through the lanes of cycle history and see bicycles from Boneshakers and Penny Farthings up to modern Raleigh cycles. Over 200 machines on display

PETS MUST BE KEPT ON LEADS

Open: daily 10am onwards

Directions: AA signs to car park. Town centre attraction

If you are planning a family day out and don't want to leave your pet behind, then check out the attractions listed below which allow pets (in most cases they must be kept on leads).

Bucks Goat Centre, Layby Farm, Stoke Mandeville, Buckinghamshire HP22 5XJ
Tel: 01296 612983
The most comprehensive collection of goat breeds in Britain; other animals, shops and cafe.
Dogs must be kept on leads.

Chiltern Open Air Museum, Gorelands Lane, Chalfont St Giles, Bucks HP8 4AD
Tel: 01494 871117
Museum of historic buildings set in beautiful parkland.
Dogs welcome but must be kept on leads. Owners responsible for clearing up their dog's mess!

Wheal Martyn Discovery Centre, Carthew, St Austell, Cornwall PL26 8XG
Tel: 01726 850362
Industrial museum of the china clay industry. Historic trail with working water wheels; nature trail.
Dogs on leads welcome

Launceston Steam Railway, St Thomas Hill, Launceston, Cornwall PL15 8DA
Tel: 01566 775665
Victorian locomotives haul from Launceston (buffet, museum, workshops, souvenirs, books) to Newmills (picnic, play area, riverside walk).
Dogs on lead at all times. They are charged 50p but get a ticket!

Trebah Garden, Mawnan Smith, Falmouth, Cornwall TR11 5JZ
Tel: 01326 250448
A magnificent Cornish ravine garden of 25 acres which falls 200ft to a private beach.
Dogs must be kept on lead and away from children's play areas.

Peak Cavern, Castleton, Hope Valley, Derbyshire S33 8WS
Tel: 01433 620285
Guided tours of this vast limestone cave, whose entrance is so large it once contained a village and rope works.
Dogs must be kept on lead in the cave

The Milky Way Adventure Park, Downland Farm, Clovelly, Bideford, Devon EX39 5RY
Tel: 01237 431255
The largest all-weather facilities in North Devon including the Time Warp, a huge indoor play area, archery, birds of prey and dog shows.
Dogs must be kept on leads and not taken to live shows (dog shows and birds of prey).

South Devon Railway, The Station, Buckfastleigh, Devon TQ11 0DZ
Tel: 01364 642338
GWR steam-operated branch line from Buckfastleigh to Totnes beside the River Dart.
Dogs must be kept on lead

Beamish, The North of England Open Air Museum, Beamish, Durham DH9 0RG
Tel: 01207 231811
An open-air museum illustrating life in the 1800s and 1900s, set in 200 acres of beautiful countryside.
Dogs must be kept on lead at all times.

Robin Hill Country Park, Downend, Near Arreton, Newport, Isle of Wight PO30 2NU
Tel: 01983 527352
The only park on the island with three major rides. 88-acre park with over 20 other attractions; catering and gift shop.
Dogs must be kept on leads at all times.

Hever Castle & Gardens, Edenbridge, Kent TN8 7NG
Tel: 01732 865224
Romantic 13th century castle, childhood home of Anne Boleyn, set in award-winning gardens.
Dogs must be kept on leads; not admitted into castle.

Didcot Railway Centre, Didcot, Oxfordshire OX11 7NJ
Tel: 01235 817200
Recreating the golden age of the Great Western Railway, with steam trains, and much more.
Dogs allowed on leads.

Forde Abbey Gardens, Chard, Somerset TA20 4LU
Tel: 01460 221290
30 acres of award-winning gardens surrounding the 12th century former abbey.
Dogs on short leads please.

Secret World, East Huntspill, Highbridge, Somerset TA9 3PZ
Tel: 01278 783250
Visit this Badger and Wildlife Centre for a fun-filled day packed with animals.
Dogs must be kept on leads

Rede Hall Farm Park, Rede, Bury St Edmunds, Suffolk IP29 4UG
Tel: 01284 850695
Open farm with heavy horses and vintage tractors. Farm walks, feed the animals, gift shop and tearooms.
Dogs must be kept on lead round main farm area.

Stratford-upon-Avon Shire Horse Centre, Clifford Road, Stratford-upon-Avon, Warwickshire CV37 8HW
Tel: 01789 415274
Shire horses and rare breeds of farm animals; country village exhibition.
Dogs must be kept on leads at all times.

National Trust Gibside, Burnopfield, Newcastle-upon-Tyne, Tyne & Wear NE16 6BG
Tel: 01207 542255
One of the finest designed landscapes in the North; miles of woodland and river walks.
Dogs must be kept on leads and owners must clean up after their pets.

Cholderton Rare Breeds Farm, Amesbury Road, Cholderton, Salisbury, Wilts. SP4 0EW
Tel: 01980 629438
Lots of friendly rare farm animals in beautiful parkland with gardens and woodland.
Dogs must be kept on lead at all times.

Avoncroft Museum of Historic Buildings, Stoke Heath, Bromsgrove, Worcs B60 4JR
Tel: 01527 831363/831886
A fascinating world of historic buildings on open-air site in heart of countryside
Dogs must be kept on lead.

SCOTLAND

Bo'ness & Kinneil Railway, The Station, Bo'ness, West Lothian EH51 9AQ
Tel: 01506 822298
A living museum of steam and diesel locomotives, carriages and historic buildings.
Pets welcome on lead (not restaurant or museum).

Oban Rare Breeds Farm Park, New Barran, Oban, Argyll PA34 4QB
Tel: 01631 770604/608
Farm park with rare breeds; pets' corner, tearoom, woodland walk and beautiful views.
Dogs must be kept on leads.

Auchindrain Township, By Inveraray, Argyll PA32 8XN
Tel: 01499 500235
Original Highland township, restored, furnished and equipped, gives fascinating glimpse of past.
Dogs must be on lead.

Bowhill House and Country Park, Bowhill, Selkirk, Scottish Borders TD7 5ET
Tel: 01750 22204
Home of the Duke & Duchess of Buccleuch, with outstanding collections of art, silverware and porcelain.
Dogs must be kept on lead and stick to main tracks.

Mull Railway, Craignure, Isle of Mull PA65 6AY
Tel: 01680 812494
A 20-minute journey through beautiful coastal scenery and woodland.
Pets travel free!

WALES

Welsh Highland Railway, c/o Ffestioniog Railway, Porthmadog, Gwynedd LL49 9NF
Tel: 01766 512340
The railway climbs gently past streams and woodland to Waunfawr, one of the gateways to Snowdonia.
Dogs must be kept under control; other animals in suitable containers.

Join Us –
Preparing your Dogs and Cats for travel

Your pet must be injected with a harmless identification ISO (International Standards Organisation) approved microchip. This chip will be read by a handheld scanning device.

From and back to the UK.

Ask your vet to implant an ISO (International Standards Organisation) approved microchip - then to vaccinate against rabies recording the batch number of the vaccine on a veterinary certificate together with the microchip number.

Approximately 30 days later your vet should take a blood sample and send it to one of the approved Ministry of Agriculture laboratories (list attached) to check that the vaccine has provided the correct level of protection. * If the test is OK a certificate will then be issued. Your dog/cat will then be ready to travel immediately once the date of the pilot scheme is announced.

* Once the date of the pilot scheme is announced UK based cats and dogs which have been tested after that date will have to wait SIX MONTHS before they re-enter the UK – this is to comply with the regulations applying from Europe.

Shortly before returning to the UK the dog/cat will need treatment for ticks and one particular parasite (echinooccocus multilocularis) - but we are still battling with the Ministry over the timing for this treatment. On embarkation (land, sea, air, rail) you will have to present 2 certificates from a vet. One recording details of microchips, vaccine and blood test, the other confirming treatment for ticks and parasites.

From Europe to the UK

As above, you must microchip your pet, vaccinate against rabies and approximately 30 days later your vet will take a blood test sending it to one of the laboratories from the list of those approved by MAFF. SIX MONTHS after a successful blood test your pet will be allowed to travel to the UK providing it has been treated against ticks and worms.

This is how the microchips will be read

Costs:

- Microchip: Should be in the region of £25.00

- Vaccine: Varies according to vet but again approximately £30.00

- Blood test: We know that the blood testing laboratory at Weybridge (VLA) charge £49.50 per test.

Therefore anything in addition is that levied by the vet. Providing the rabies vaccination is kept up to date the blood test will not have to be repeated. Should there be a break between rabies vaccines a further blood test would have to be taken and then a period of 6 months allowed before re-entry to the UK would be permitted.

Therefore: Microchip and blood-test are one-off costs but the rabies vaccination is a yearly or 2 yearly cost depending on the vaccine used.

MAFF Help line Telephone Number is: 0181 330 6835

Lady Mary Fretwell and the supporters of Passports For Pets have argued that for far too long dogs and cats have suffered and died in quarantine when a modern scientific alternative to quarantine was available.

The laboratories approved by MAFF for blood testing:

Veterinary Laboratory Agency	Tel: (+44) 01932 357 345
New Haw, Addlestone	Fax:(+44) 01 932 357 856
Surrey KT15 3NB	
UNITED KINGDOM	*Costs: £49.50*
Agence Francaise De Securite	Tel: (+33) 3 83 298950
Sanitare des Aliments	Fax:(+33) 3 83 298959
Nancy	
Domaine de Pixerecourt	
B.P. 9F-54220	
Maizeville, FRANCE	*Costs: 425ff = approx £42*
National Veterinary Institute	Tel: (+46) 1867 4000
Commission of Diagnosites	Fax:(+46) 1847 14517
Section of Diagnostics	
Department of Virology	
P.O. Box 585, BMCS-751 23	
Uppsala	
SWEDEN	*Costs: 500K=approx £40*
Danish Veterinary Institute for	Tel: (+45) 55 8602 00
Virus Research	Fax:(45) 55 8603 00
Lindholm	
DK-4771 Kalvehave	
DENMARK	*Costs: 252K=approx £25*
National Veterinary and Food	Tel: (35) 89393 1901
Research Institute	Fax:(35) 89393 1811
PL 368 (Heimmeentie 57)	
00231 Helsinki	
FINLAND	*Costs: 396.50 Fmark = approx £26.00*

Instut fur Virologie
Frankfurter Strasse 107
D35392 Giessen
GERMANY

Tel: (49) 641 99 38350
Fax: (+49) 641 9938359

Costs: 72.60DM= approx £25

Dept. for Equine, Pets and
Vaccine Control Virology Unit
Federal Institute for the Control
of Viral Infection in Animals
Robert Kochgasse 17
2340 Modling
AUSTRIA

Tel: (43) 2236 46 640 902 or 906
Fax:(43) 2236 46 640 941

Costs: 600 shillings= approx £30

Instituto Zooprotilattico
Sperimentale delle Venezie
Via Romea 14/A
1-35020 Legonaro (PD)
ITALY

Tel: (+39) 04980 70 306
Fax:(+39 04988 30

Costs: Price Unknown

Direccion General de Sanidad
de la Produccion Agaria,
Laboratono de Sanidad y
Produccion Animal del
Estado,
Camino del Jau, S/N
E-18320 Santa Fe (Granada)
SPAIN

Tel: (+34) 958 44 03 75
Fax:(+34) 95844 1200

Costs: FREE

Institute Pasteur of Brussels
Rue Engeland 642
B-i 180 Brussels
BELGIUM

Tel: (+32) 2 373 31 58
Fax:(+32) 2 373 31 74

Costs: 1,500BF- approx £25

Institute of Veterinary Virology
Schweizerische Tollwutzentrale
Langgass-Strasse 122
CH-3012 Bern
SWITZERLAND

Tel: (+41) 31 631 2378
Fax:(+41) 31 631 2534

Costs: 96.75 SF= approx £40

You can e-mail us at

passports.forpets@virgin.net

or write to our London address:

PASSPORTS FOR PETS

Please mention *Pets Welcome*
when enquiring about accommodation featured in these pages.

BERKSHIRE

The Compton Swan Hotel, High Street, Near Newbury, Berkshire RG20 6NJ
In the Berkshire Downlands, the Hotel has 5 en suite bedrooms, TV, beverages and telephones. An extensive menu with traditional, exotic, vegetarian and special diets catered for. Home-cooked meals a speciality. Downlands Healthy Eating Award winner. Walled garden where we have *al fresco* eating; BBQs. Near the Ridgeway National Trail, an ideal base for walking, horse-riding and golf. Stabling and horsebox. Real Ales, Bar Meals available. CAMRA Good Beer Guide and Good Pub Guide. ETB.
Phone Garry Mitchell F.B.I.I. on 01635 578269   Fax: 01635 578765

See also Colour Advertisement on page 3

Compton

Village 5 miles/7 km west of Streatley where Georgian houses are one of the notable sights on the banks of the Thames.

COMPTON SWAN HOTEL, HIGH STREET, COMPTON, NEAR NEWBURY RG20 6NJ (01635 578269; Fax: 01635 578765). Situated in the heart of the Berkshire Downlands; 5 rooms en suite with TV, beverage facilities and telephones. Extensive menu with special diets catered for. Large walled garden. [🐾]

BUCKINGHAMSHIRE

Chesham

Town on south side of Chiltern Hills. Ideal walking area.

PAT & GEORGE ORME, 49 LOWNDES AVENUE, CHESHAM HP5 2HH (01494 792647). B&B detached house. 10 minutes from underground. Private bathroom, Tea/coffee. TV. Good walking country - Chiltern Hills (3 minutes). ETC ◆◆.[🐾]

CAMBRIDGESHIRE

Ely

Magnificent Norman Cathedral dating from 1083. Ideal base for touring the fen country of East Anglia.

MRS C. H. BENNETT, STOCKYARD FARM, WISBECH ROAD, WELNEY PE14 9RQ (01354 610433). Comfortable converted farmhouse, rurally situated between Ely and Wisbech. Conservatory breakfast room, TV lounge. Free range produce. Miles of riverside walks. No smoking. B&B £14–£21. [🐾 pw!]

St Ives

Town on the River Ouse 5 miles east of Huntingdon.

ST IVES MOTEL, LONDON ROAD, ST IVES, HUNTINGDON PE17 4EX (Tel & Fax: 01480 463857). RAC & AA 2 Stars. 16 rooms, all en suite, overlooking orchards and garden. Close to Cambridge and A14. Licensed bar and restaurant. [Pets £2-£5 per night depending on type of animal].

CHESHIRE

BALTERLEY

Small village two miles west of Audley.

MR & MRS HOLLINS, BALTERLEY GREEN FARM, DEANS LANE, BALTERLEY, NEAR CREWE CW2 5QJ (01270 820214). 145-acre dairy farm in quiet and peaceful surroundings. Within easy reach of Junction 16 on the M6. Bed and Breakfast from £19pp. ETC ◆◆◆◆. Caravans and tents welcome. [pw! Pets £1 per night]

CHESTER

Former Roman city on the River Dee, with well-preserved walls and beautiful 14th century Cathedral. Liverpool 25 miles

THE EATON HOTEL, CITY ROAD, CHESTER CH1 3AE (01244 320840; Fax: 01244 320850). In a perfect central location. All rooms have bath or shower, colour TV, radio, telephone, hair dryer and tea making facilities. [🐕]

NANTWICH

Old town on River Weaver 4 miles south west of Crewe. Former centre of salt industry.

THE RED COW, NANTWICH CW5 5NF (01270 628581). Recommended by CAMRA Good Pub Guide, Manchester Evening News, Sunday Observer, Good Pub Guide, Rough Guide to England and Vegan Travel Guide. Bed and Breakfast. Dogs welcome. [🐕]

MACCLESFIELD

Old silk town nestling between the tranquil farmland of the Cheshire Plain and the dramatic rugged hills of the Peak District National Park and Buxton.

MOORHAYES HOUSE HOTEL, MANCHESTER ROAD, TYTHERINGTON, MACCLESFIELD SK10 2JJ. Comfortable en suite accommodation, tea/coffee making facilities, colour TVs, telephones. Ample parking, hearty breakfast, friendly atmosphere. Dogs welcome - enclosed garden, river walk nearby. B&B from £26 per person. ETC/RAC ◆◆◆. Ring HELEN WOOD on 01625 433228. [🐴 pw!].
e–mail: helen@moorhayeshouse.freeserve.co.uk

CORNWALL

Cornish Home Holidays - West Cornwall
Coastal & Country Cottages, Town Houses & Apartments
Pets with well behaved owners welcome in many of our properties!
Colour Brochure: 01736 368575   Website: www.chh.co.uk

Cornish Traditional Cottages

400 Quality self catering cottages in Cornwall.

Pets welcome in many.

For your FREE brochure

Phone: 01208 821666
Fax: 01208 821766
www.corncott.com

Holiday Homes and Cottages S.W.
Dept 10. 365A Torquay Rd, Paignton TQ3 2BT

Large choice of cottages in Devon and Cornwall. Coastal and rural locations. Pets very welcome. Many ETC rated

Tel (01803) 663650
E-mail: holcotts@aol.com
website: www.swcottages.co.uk

01756 702201

IN CORNWALL. QUALITY PROPERTIES IN WONDERFUL LOCATIONS AT WELCOMING LOW PRICES. MANY LESS THAN £170 PER WEEK FROM OCTOBER TO APRIL. LOTS AT LESS THAN £350 PER WEEK FROM MAY TO SEPTEMBER. PETS, LINEN AND FUEL MOSTLY INCLUDED. **PHONE FOR FREE 2001 FULL COLOUR BROCHURE**

FHG PUBLICATIONS

publish a large range of well-known accommodation guides. We will be happy to send you details or you can use the order form at the back of this book.

Coombe Mill

ETB ♀♀♀♀
and ♀♀♀♀♀

A picturesque hamlet of secluded cottages and quiet riverside lodges set amidst an idyllic 30 acre private estate.

Cottages to sleep 2-6/7 with four posters and log burners. Lodges for 2-5, each with its own verandah.

Farm animals and wildlife in abundance. Special morning tractor run for children to feed the animals.

Trout and Carp fishing lakes, private river fishing. Grocery and home cooking to order.

Beaches, coastal walking, rugged moorland nearby. Indoor pool 5 minutes away.

Open All Year.

PETS VERY WELCOME

St Breward, Bodmin
Cornwall PL30 4LZ

Tel: 01208 850344

See our brochure and more at:
www.coombemill.com

The Old Ferry Inn

Bodinnick-by-Fowey
Cornwall PL23 1LX

Telephone: (01726) 870237 Fax: (01726) 870116

Why not bring your dog for its well deserved holiday to the family-run Old Ferry Inn, close to the edge of the beautiful River Fowey.

There are many varied walks from country and riverside to breathtaking views along the Cornwall Coastal Path.

The 400-year-old hotel has an excellent à la carte restaurant for evening meals and a comprehensive bar menu for lunch and evening. The Inn has 12 letting rooms with tea and coffee making facilities, colour TVs and telephones, most rooms being en suite, some with views of the Fowey river.

Prices are from £22.50 per person, per night
including Full English Breakfast.

PUBLISHER'S NOTE

While every effort is made to ensure accuracy, we regret that FHG Publications cannot accept responsibility for errors, omissions or misrepresentations in our entries or any consequences thereof. Prices in particular should be checked because we go to press early. We will follow up complaints but cannot act as arbiters or agents for either party.

Please mention *Pets Welcome*
when enquiring about accommodation featured in these pages.

FOR THE MUTUAL GUIDANCE OF GUEST AND HOST

Every year literally thousands of holidays, short breaks and overnight stops are arranged through our guides, the vast majority without any problems at all. In a handful of cases, however, difficulties do arise about bookings, which often could have been prevented from the outset.

It is important to remember that when accommodation has been booked, both parties – guests and hosts – have entered into a form of contract. We hope that the following points will provide helpful guidance.

GUESTS: When enquiring about accommodation, be as precise as possible. Give exact dates, numbers in your party and the ages of any children. State the number and type of rooms wanted and also what catering you require – bed and breakfast, full board etc. Make sure that the position about evening meals is clear – and about pets, reductions for children or any other special points.

Read our reviews carefully to ensure that the proprietors you are going to contact can supply what you want. Ask for a letter confirming all arrangements, if possible.

If you have to cancel, do so as soon as possible. Proprietors do have the right to retain deposits and under certain circumstances to charge for cancelled holidays if adequate notice is not given and they cannot re-let the accommodation.

HOSTS: Give details about your facilities and about any special conditions. Explain your deposit system clearly and arrangements for cancellations, charges etc. and whether or not your terms include VAT.

If for any reason you are unable to fulfil an agreed booking without adequate notice, you may be under an obligation to arrange suitable alternative accommodation or to make some form of compensation.

While every effort is made to ensure accuracy, we regret that FHG Publications cannot accept responsibility for errors, omissions or misrepresentations in our entries or any consequences thereof.
Prices in particular should be checked because we go to press early. We will follow up complaints but cannot act as arbiters or agents for either party.

White Lodge Hotel

Mawgan Porth Bay, Near Newquay, Cornwall TR8 4BN
Tel: St. Mawgan (STD 01637) 860512
E-mail: dogfriendlyhotel@redhotant.com Website: www.dogfriendlyhotel.co.uk

GIVE YOURSELVES & YOUR DOGS A BREAK

at our family-run White Lodge Hotel overlooking beautiful
Mawgan Porth Bay, near Newquay, Cornwall

*Dogs most welcome-
FREE OF CHARGE

*Your dogs sleep with you in your
bedroom.

*Direct access to sandy beach and
coastal path.

*Dog loving proprietors with 18
years' experience in catering for dog
owners on holiday with their dogs

*ALL bedrooms with colour TV,
tea/coffee makers, alarm clocks,
radios, intercoms, heaters etc.

*Some en suite bedrooms

*Fantastic sea views from most rooms.

*Well-stocked residents' lounge bar,
dining room & sun patio with
outstanding sea views across the bay.

*Games room with pool table and dart
board etc.

* Large free car park within hotel
grounds

SPECIAL 6 DAYS (5 NIGHTS) CHRISTMAS HOUSE PARTY **ONLY £250** *Full Board*	SPECIAL 6 DAYS (5 NIGHTS) NEW YEAR (HOGMANAY) BREAK **ONLY £210** *Half Board*	SPECIAL 6 DAYS (5 NIGHTS) BREAKS **ONLY £160-£175** *BB&EM*	WEEKLY TERMS **FROM £210-£230** FOR 5-COURSE EVENING DINNER, BED AND 4-COURSE BREAKFAST WITH CHOICE OF MENU

Phone 01637 860512 John or Diane Parry
for free colour brochure

ALL PRICES INCLUDE
VAT AT $17\frac{1}{2}\%$

See also Colour Advertisement on page 10

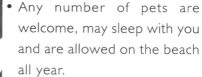
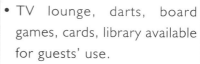

BUCKINGHAM HOUSE

17 Tregoney Hill, Mevagissey, Cornwall PL26 6RD

Buckingham House is a charming Grade II Listed property in the heart of the quaint Cornish fishing village of Mevagissey. All rooms are en suite and many have fine sea views, including the most wonderfully well-appointed family room. For longer stays, complimentary tickets are available to the nearby "Lost Gardens of Heligan" (July and August excluded). Bed and Breakfast from £17 per person per night. Facilities include guest lounge, Sky TV, tea and coffee making facilities and licensed bar. The friendly family atmosphere makes for a most enjoyable and relaxed holiday.

Telephone: 01726 843375

Golden Bay Hotel

Unwind and relax in this small and surprisingly affordable quality hotel. Overlooking Fistral beach with the Gannel River and National Trust countryside at the rear. All rooms private facilities, some deluxe four poster rooms. Lovely coastal and countryside walks, also close to golf. B&B £18-£30 E.M. optional. Good doggies very welcome and free of charge. **ETC ◆◆◆**

Pentire, Newquay, TR7 1PD Tel: 01637 873318
E-mail: enquiries@goldenbayhotel.co.uk Website: www.goldenbayhotel.co.uk

---

Trethiggey Touring Park, Quintrell Downs, Newquay TR8 4LG
Tel: 01637 877672　　Website: www.trethiggey.co.uk

Two miles from Newquay and sandy surfing beaches. Beautiful and secluded, landscaped park with panoramic views over countryside. Family owned site open from March to Jan 2nd. Christmas breaks. Shop and off-licence on park (take away food peak season). Children's play area. Games room, laundry facilities and modern toilet and shower block. Large recreation field. Three pubs and restaurants within walking distance. Park runs evening minibus service to and from Newquay. **ETC ★★★★**

Retorrick Mill, St Mawgan, Newquay TR8 4BH (01637 860460).

Retorrick Mill is situated in the beautiful Lanherne Valley, within walking distance of the sea at Mawgan Porth, its sandy beach and eating places. 1 mile from St Mawgan picturesque village, shop, pub and Post Office. Halfway between Newquay and old port of Padstow. Activites include: surfing, golf, riding, fishing and walking, with coastal path only one mile away. Mill cottage has its own garden onto a stream, sleeping 5. The bungalows are bright and well-furnished with own parking. Gardens of 9 acres including duck pond and rare sheep. Pets welcome. Brochure on request.

Contact: Mrs Bertoli. Cottage and Bungalows ETC ★★ SELF-CATERING

CLEARWATER LODGE HOTEL Tel: 01637 873151

A warm welcome awaits your best friend and yourselves. Lovely cliff-top walks. Near beach. All rooms ground floor with private facilities, colourTV, etc Children's Discounts, 1 Dog Free B&B from £18 pppn

30 LEWARNE ROAD, PORTH, NEWQUAY, CORNWALL, TR7 3JS

FHG

PLEASE MENTION THIS GUIDE WHEN YOU WRITE

OR PHONE TO ENQUIRE ABOUT ACCOMMODATION

IF YOU ARE WRITING, A STAMPED, ADDRESSED

ENVELOPE IS ALWAYS APPRECIATED

Please mention *Pets Welcome*
when enquiring about accommodation featured in these pages.

Penkerris

An enchanting Edwardian residence, with large lawn in unspoilt Cornish village. AA, RAC and Les Routiers Recommended. Penkerris has fields on one side yet there are pubs, shops, etc; only 150 yards away on the other. Attractive dining room, lounge with colour TV, video, piano and log fires in Winter. Bedrooms with washbasins, TV, kettles, shaver points, radios; en suite if required. There is a shower room as well as bathrooms. Bed and breakfast. Dinner, with superb home-cooking, by arrangement.

Beaches, swimming, surfing and dramatic cliff walks nearby.

Licensed. Ample parking. Open all year. From £15.00 to £22.50 B&B. Dinner £10.   ETC ◆◆

Contact Dorothy Gill-Carey, Penkerris, Penwinnick Road, St. Agnes TR5 0PA Telephone: 01872 552262

BOSINVER HOLIDAY COTTAGES

Nestling in a hidden valley near the sea, the Eden Project and Lost Gardens of Heligan, our small farm has friendly animals and ponies. Choose from our 16th century thatched farmhouse or cottages privately set in their own gardens surrounded by wildflower meadows. Wander down to the fishing lake or village pub, swim in the pool, play tennis, or relax and listen to the birdsong. ETC ★★★★ **Brochure from Pat Smith, Bosinver Farm, St Austell, Cornwall** **Tel: 01726 72128 • E-mail: Bosinver@Holidays2000.freeserve.co.uk • Internet: www.bosinver.co.uk**

See also colour advertisement on page 5

ST MARGARET'S PARK HOLIDAY BUNGALOWS
Polgooth, St Austell PL26 7AX

Family-owned and run with 27 timber bungalows set in 6 acre sun trap wooded valley $2\frac{1}{2}$ miles from safe sandy beaches.

500 yards to Golf, Village Inn and Shop.

Children and pets welcome.

We have a playing field and separate dog walking area.

From £95 to £480 weekly.

For **FREE** brochure:

Tel: (01726) 74283 • Fax: (01726) 71680

e-mail: reception@stmargaretsholidays.co.uk

website: www.stmargaretsholidays.co.uk

RIVER VALLEY HOLIDAY PARK
London Apprentice, St Austell, Cornwall PL26 7DS Tel: 01726 73533

Friendly Family Park in The Pentewan Valley where pets are welcome, either in our caravans or on the large touring pitches. Lots of woodland walks. Off road cycle trail. Indoor heated swimming pool or relax where peace and tranquillity prevails. ETB ★★★★

Visit our web page: www.river-valley.co.uk

Please mention *Pets Welcome*

when enquiring about accommodation featured in these pages.

Willapark Manor Hotel
Bossiney, Near Tintagel,
Cornwall PL34 0BA
Telephone: 01840 770782

ETC ★★

One of the most beautifully situated Country House Hotels in England

See also Colour Advertisement on page 6

TRETHEVY MANOR - TINTAGEL

Mrs Lynda Spring, Trethevy Manor, Trethevy Tintagel, Cornwall PL34 0BG * Tel/Fax: 01840 770636
E-mail: manor1151@talk21.com * Website: www.cornwall-online.co.uk/trethevy-manor

Tucked away in the rural hamlet of Trethevy, two 14th century Stone-built Cottages adjoining 12th century Manor House. Cleverly converted with exposed beams. Cosy, comfortable well-equipped, self-contained accommodation within the walled garden of the Manor. 1.5 miles from Tintagel, 2 miles from Boscastle. Spectacular coastal walks. Perfect all year round retreat.

RAC ★★   *Whitsand Bay Hotel*   **AA** ★★

Magnificent Country Manor Hotel on cliff top at edge of beach. ★ Safe sandy beach.
★ **Own 18-hole Golf Course.** ★ Indoor heated swimming pool and leisure complex.
★ Fine food. ★ Family -sized en suite rooms.★ Many walks
Children welcome. Cots, high chairs. Children's menu. Children's budget-type rooms.
Near the Eden Project and Lost Gardens of Heligan
Whitsand Bay Hotel Golf & Country Club
Portwrinkle, by Torpoint, Plymouth, Cornwall PL11 3BU
Tel: (01503) 230276 Fax: (01503) 230297
Website: www.cornish-golf-hotels.co.uk   E-mail: earlehotels.btconnect.com

FHG PUBLICATIONS LIMITED publish a large range of well-known accommodation guides. We will be happy to send you details or you can use the order form at the back of this book.

MARCORRIE HOTEL

20 FALMOUTH ROAD, TRURO TR1 2HX

Victorian town house in conservation area, five minutes' walk
from the city centre and cathedral. Centrally situated for
visiting country houses, gardens and coastal resorts.
All rooms are en suite and have central heating, colour TV,
telephone, tea-making facilities. Ample parking. Credit cards:
Visa, Access, Amex. Open all year. B&B from £24.00 pppn.

Tel: 01872 277374 Fax: 01872 241666

See also Colour Advertisement on page 8

Lemain Garden Apartments

Quality self-contained holiday apartments in converted Victorian Villa.
Sleeps 2 to 6 people. All with magnificent sea views across Looe Bay.
Open all year (reduced rates for early and late season).

• Central Heating in Winter • Teletext CTV/ Video in lounges
• CTV in bedrooms • IDD Telephones • Microwave • Freshly laundered bed
linen included • Launderette • Balconies, terraces, barbeque
• Individual off-street parking • Beach 2 minutes • Shops and harbour 10
minutes' walk • Tennis, Bowls, Putting and coastal path within easy walk •
Watersports and other leisure activities readily accessible • Pets welcome
Personally supervised by owners Alan and Dee Palin
Lemain Garden Apartments, Portuan Road, Hannafore, West Looe, Cornwall PL13 2DR
• Tel: 01503 262073 • Fax: 01503 265288 • E-Mail: sales@lemain.com • Website: www.lemain.com

See also Colour Advertisement on page 8

POWELLS COTTAGE HOLIDAYS, HIGH STREET, SAUNDERSFOOT, PEMBROKESHIRE SA69 9EJ.
Many of our top quality holiday properties accept pets. Cottages in Devon, Cornwall, Cotswolds,
Pembrokeshire and Heart of England. For colour brochure FREEPHONE 0800 378771 (24 hours).

CLASSIC COTTAGES, HELSTON, CORNWALL TR13 8NA (01326 565555). Choose your cottage from
400 of the finest coastal and country cottages throughout the West Country. Many welcome pets.

A fine selection of Self-catering and similar Cottages on both coasts of Cornwall and on Scilly. Pets
welcome in many cottages. Free colour brochure from: CORNISH TRADITIONAL COTTAGES,
BLISLAND, BODMIN PL30 4HS (01208 821666; Fax: 01208 821766).
website: www.corncott.com

HOLIDAY HOMES & COTTAGES S.W, 365A TORQUAY ROAD, PAIGNTON TQ3 2BT (01803 663650;
Fax: 01803 664037). Hundreds of Self-Catering Holiday Cottages, Houses, Bungalows, Apartments,
Chalets and Caravans in Devon and Cornwall. Please write or phone for free colour brochure. [˙]
e–mail: holcotts@aol.com
website: www.swcottages.co.uk

SYMBOLS

🐾 Indicates that pets are welcome free of charge.

£   Indicates that a charge is made for pets: nightly or weekly.

pw! Shows some special provision for pets; exercise facility, feeding or accommodation arrangement.

⌂   Indicates separate pets accommodation.

WELCOME COTTAGE HOLIDAYS. Quality Cottages in wonderful locations at welcomi
Pets, linen and fuel mostly included. PHONE FOR FREE 2001 FULL COLOUR BROC
702201.

CLASSY COTTAGES – Three superb coastal cottage locations between Polperro and i uwey. Willy
Wilcox cottage is just 11 feet from beach over smugglers' cave. Log fires, dishwashers, washing
machines etc. Indoor Private Swimming Pool. Contact FIONA & MARTIN NICOLLE (07000 423000).
[Pets £12 per week]

CORNISH HOME HOLIDAYS, WEST CORNWALL (01736 368575). Coastal and country cottages,
town houses and apartments. Pets with well behaved owners welcome in many of our properties.
website: www.chh.co.uk

Bodmin

Quaint county town of Cornwall, standing steeply on the edge of Bodmin Moor. Pretty market town and touring centre.
Plymouth 31 miles, Newquay 20, Wadebridge 7.

COOMBE MILL, ST BREWARD, BODMIN PL30 4LZ (01208 850344). A picturesque private hamlet
of cottages and quiet riverside lodges. 30 acres of glorious grounds. Carp and Trout lakes and
private river fishing. Four-posters, log burners, grocery and home cooking to order. ETC 4/5 KEYS.
Pets very welcome. [First Pet £18 per week, others £5 per week]
website: www.coombemill.com

TREDETHY COUNTRY HOTEL, HELLANBRIDGE, BODMIN PL30 4QS (01208 841262). Excellent
walking with access to Camel Trail, on edge of Bodmin Moor. Spacious courtyard suites ideal for
dogs. Blankets/throws and dogs meals provided on request. Restaurant specialising in freshly
produced good quality cuisine, all meals including packed lunches/hampers. [pw!]

PENROSE BURDEN, ST BREWARD, BODMIN PL30 4LZ (01208 850277 & 850617). Holiday Care
Award Winning Cottages featured on TV. Open all year. Outstanding views over wooded valley. Free
Salmon and Trout fishing. Daily meal service. Superb walking area. Dogs welcome, wheelchair
accessible.[Pets £15 per week]
website: www.saqnet.co.uk/users/penrose_burden/

MRS JOAN HARRISON, WILBURY, SUNNYBANKS LANE, FLETCHERS BRIDGE, BODMIN PL30
4AN (01208 74001). Spacious house, centrally situated. Three double bedrooms. Optional evening
meal. The surrounding area is breathtakingly beautiful, especially in springtime. Short walks from
the house will take you to some of the county's best beauty spots like Cardinham Woods which is
ideal for dog walking. B&B £15, BB&EM £21. [🐾]

Bodmin Moor

Superb walking area attaining a height of 1375 feet at Brown Willy, the highest point in the country.

DARRYNANE COTTAGES, DARRYNANE, ST BREWARD, BODMIN MOOR PL3O 4LZ (Tel & Fax: 01208
850885). Absolutely fabulous detached cottages. Set in private gardens. Unique moorland valley
setting. Waterfalls, woods, river. Wood-burning stoves, four-poster bed. Excellent walking. Camel
Trail close by. ♕♕♕♕ Commended.
e–mail: alegna@eclipse.co.uk
website: www.chycor.co.uk/cottages/darrynane

JENNY LUCAS, MENNABROOM FARM, WARLEGGAN, BODMIN PL30 4HE (Tel:01208 821272;
Fax: 01208 821555). Immaculate cosy cottages on mediaeval farm, Bodmin Moor. Superb walks
for dogs and owners on farm moor, and both Cornish coasts. Peace, beauty and seclusion.
ETC/WCTB ★★★.
e–mail: lucas@avnet.co.uk
website: www.dorsetweb.co.uk/business/mennabroom

Please mention *Pets Welcome*

when enquiring about accommodation featured in these pages.

CORNWALL

Boscastle

Picturesque village in tiny harbour, with rocky beach, some sand, and fine scenery. Tintagel 4 miles.

THE WELLINGTON HOTEL, THE HARBOUR, BOSCASTLE PL35 0AG (01840 250202). Historic 16th-Century Coaching Inn by Elizabethan harbour and National Trust countryside. Fine Anglo-French restaurant, specialising in regional cuisine and seafood. Freehouse with real ales, pub grub, open fires and beams. 10 acres of private woodland walks. [🐾]
e–mail: vtobutt@enterprise.net
website: www.wellingtonboscastle.co.uk

BOSCASTLE/CRACKINGTON-HAVEN AREA. Modern bungalow sleeping 2-6, heating; microwave; Near sandy beaches, cliff and valley walks. Beautiful scenery, walking distance local store and Inn. Just off A39 and central to most tourist attractions. Spring and Autumn £90-£200 per week. Pets welcome. ETC ♙♙♙ Approved. MRS PROUT (01840 250289). [🐾]

RINGFORD FARM, ST JULIOT, BOSCASTLE PL35 0BX. Stay on a farm, join in, look around. Two bed-roomed converted barn, fully equipped, centrally heated. Very peaceful, sea views. Spring water. Many coastal walks. Local pub one mile. Near many sandy beaches, horse riding, fishing, golf. Pets welcome. MRS HARDING (01840 250306).

Bude

Popular seaside resort overlooking a wide bay of golden sand and flanked by spectacular cliffs. Ideal for surfing; sea water swimming pool for safe bathing.

HEDLEY WOOD CARAVAN & CAMPING PARK, BRIDGERULE, (NR BUDE), HOLSWORTHY EX22 7ED (01288 381404). 16 acre woodland family run site; childrens adventure areas, bar, clubroom, shop, laundry, meals & all amanities. Static caravans for hire, Caravan Storage available. [pw!🐾]
website: www.hedleywood .co.uk

Two cottages in an area of outstanding natural beauty. Sleep 6 and 8. 100 yards from unspoilt beach. Open all year. Pets and children welcome. APPLY – MR AND MRS H. CUMMINS, MINESHOP, CRACKINGTON HAVEN, BUDE EX23 0NR (01840 230338). [£10 per pet per week.]
website: www.cornwall-online.co.uk/mineshop

STAMFORD HILL HOTEL, STRATTON, NEAR BUDE EX23 9AY (01288 352709). Elegant Georgian manor, 5 mins from beaches, 15 en suite rooms, all with colour TV, tea/coffee makers. Heated pool, tennis court, badminton etc. Ideal for golf, fishing, walking. ETC ◆◆◆◆ AA ★★. [£2 per night.]

BROCKSMOOR HOTEL, WIDEMOUTH BAY, BUDE EX23 0AF (01288 361207). Unique bungalow hotel set in four acres of beautiful gardens. All rooms en suite with colour TV and hospitality tray. Only five minutes' walk to coastal paths and beach.

Cawsand

Quaint fishing village with bathing beach; sand at low tide. Ideal for watersports. Plymouth (car ferry) 11 miles, (foot ferr) 3.

MR AND MRS A. FIDLER, RAME BARTON, RAME, CAWSAND PL10 1LG (01752 822789). Two self contained holiday flats in old farmhouse on the beautiful Rame peninsula. Lovely coastline, beaches, country park. Children and pets welcome.

Crackington Haven

Small coastal village in North Cornwall set amidst fine cliff scenery. Small sandy beach, Launceston 18 miles, Bude 10, Camelford 10.

TRELAY FARM COTTAGES ST, GENNYS, BUDE EX23 0NJ (01840 230378). Lovely stone cottages on tranquil farm. Accommodates 2/4/6/8. Log fires, linen, fenced gardens/patios, woodland walk. Sandy beach and spectacular National Trust cliffs nearby. [£8 per pet per week]
e-mail: trelay@talk21.com

5 beautiful cottages in lovely rural setting 5 miles from Crackington Haven. Log fires, every comfort, furnished and equipped to a very high standard. Dogs welcome by arrangement. Open all year. From £130 per week. Cornwall Tourist Board Inspected. APPLY: LORRAINE HARRISON, TRENANNICK COTTAGES, TRENANNICK, WARBSTOW, LAUNCESTON PL15 8RP (01566 781443). [Pets £10 per stay] [PW!]

HENTERVENE PINE LODGE CARAVAN AND CAMPING PARK, CRACKINGTON HAVEN, NEAR BUDE EX23 0LF (01840 230365). 1½ miles unspoilt sandy beach. Area of outstanding natural beauty. Luxury caravans to let. First-class facilities for families and pets. Caravans for sale. Open all year. Short breaks. Camping £4.50 pppn, child Half 4-14 years. Caravan Sales and Tourer Storage. AA 3 Pennants. [Pets £15 per week, £1 per night camping]

Crafthole

Village near sea at Portwrinkle. Fine views over Whitsand Bay and River Lynner. Golf course nearby. Torpoint 6 miles.

THE LISCAWN INN, CRAFTHOLE, NEAR TORPOINT PL11 3BD (01503 230863). Charming, Family-run 14th Century Hotel. Close to Coastal Path in the forgotten corner of Cornwall. En suite accommodation; bar meals available; cask ales a speciality. Open all year. Self-catering now available in newly converted Barn. [🐾]

Cusgarne

Located four miles east of Redruth.

CUSGARNE (NEAR TRURO), JOYCE AND GEORGE CLENCH, SAFFRON MEADOW, CUSGARNE, TRURO TR4 8RW (01872 863171). A cosy single storey clean detached dwelling within grounds of Saffron Meadow. Own enclosed garden, secluded and surrounded by wooded pastureland. Central to Truro, Falmouth and North Coast. £110 to £200 per week. [Pets £5 per week]

Delabole

Village two miles west of Camelford.

JOHN AND SUE THEOBALD, TOLCARNE, TREBARWITH ROAD, DELABOLE PL33 9DB. Quiet, comfortable guesthouse in beautiful North Cornwall close to coast path, beaches and surfing. Private bathroom, TV lounge. Kennel and covered run for pets left home during the day. Woodturning courses available. Ample parking. For free brochure call 01840 213558. [pw! 🐾]

Falmouth

Well-known port and resort on Fal esturay, ideal for boating, sailing and fishing; safe bathing from sandy beaches. Of interest is Pendennis Castle (18th century). Newquay 26, Penzance 26, Truro 11.

Ideally situated for touring Cornwall. First floor apartment with 3 bedrooms, lounge with colour TV, kitchen/diner; bathroom, shower room with toilet. Hot water, electricity, bed linen incl. Garden. Open all year. MRS B. NEWING, GLENGARTH, BURNTHOUSE, ST GLUVIAS, PENRYN TR10 9AS (01872 863209). [🐾]

HOLIDAY BUNGALOW ~ FALMOUTH. Magnificent river, sea, countryside views. Spacious detached bungalow and gardens. Shower room. bathroom and separate WC. Sleeps two to six plus cot. Garage and parking. From £100 to £490 per week including unlimited electricity and hot water. Booking Office: CREATION ACCOMMODATION, 96 MARKET STREET, PENRYN TR10 8BH (Tel: 0800 298 65 65 (Voice/Minicom) Fax: 01326 375088) e–mail: Falmouth@Encompasstravel.com

TREVAYLOR, 8 PENNANCE ROAD, FALMOUTH TR11 4EA (01326 313041; FAX: 01326 316899). Between town and beaches, with sea views. Non-smoking, en suite rooms with tea. coffee and TV. Evening meals available, special diets catered for, vegetarian options. Walking, sailing and fishing nearby. open all year. B&B from £18. [Pets £2 per night]. e-mail: stay@trevaylor.co.uk

SELF-CATERING BUNGALOW. Sleeps 6. Walking distance of harbour and town, One and a half miles from coast. Dogs welcome. Low Season: £160 to £205; High Season: £240 to £350. Apply MRS J. A. SIMMONS, 215A PERRY STREET, BILLERICAY, ESSEX CM12 0NZ (01277 654425). [Pets £5 weekly.]

PETER WATSON, CREEKSIDE HOLIDAY HOUSES, RESTRONGUET, FALMOUTH TR11 5ST (Tel & Fax: 01326 372722). Spacious houses sleep 2/4/6/8. Peaceful, picturesque waters edge hamlet. Boating facilities. Use of boat. Own quay, beach. Secluded gardens. Near Pandora Inn. Friday bookings. Dogs welcome. [£10 per week]

Fowey

Historic town, now a busy harbour, Regatta and Carnival Week in August.

OLD FERRY INN, BODINNICK-BY-FOWEY PL23 1LX (01726 870237 Fax: 01726 870116). Family-run Inn, ideal for many varied walks. Excellent à la carte restaurant; bar meals available. Comfortable bedrooms with colour TV and tea/coffee. B&B from £22.50pppn. [Pets £2 per night]

Gorran Haven

Coastal village, 3 miles from Mevagissey.

Self-catering apartments sleeping 2–6. Beautiful rural area, 600 yards from sandy beach and harbour. Near the Lost Gardens of Heligan. Colour TV, cooker, microwave, fridge freezer. Secluded garden, private parking. Open all year. Registered and inspected by the English and Cornwall Tourist Boards. KEN AND SALLY PIKE, TREGILLAN, TREWOLLOCK LANE, GORRAN HAVEN, NEAR MEVAGISSEY PL26 6NT (01726 842452). [Pets £15 per week]
e-mail: tregillan-hol-apts@talk21.com.

MS M.R. BULLED, MENAGWINS, GORRAN, ST AUSTELL PL26 6HP (01726 843517). Traditional cottage, sleeps five. Linen, towels, electricity supplied. Beach one mile. Large garden. Central for touring/walking. Near coastal footpath. Pets welcome. [🐾]

Hayle

Resort, shopping centre and seaport with excellent sands and dunes. Helston 10 miles, Redruth 10, Penzance 8, Cambourne 5.

MR A. JAMES, ST IVES BAY HOLIDAY PARK, 73 LOGGANS ROAD, UPTON TOWANS, HAYLE TR27 5BH (24hr Brochure Line 0800 317713). Park in sand dunes adjoining huge sandy beach. Choice of bars, free entertainment. Chalets, Caravan and Camping. Large indoor pool. [Pets £20 per week.]

Helston

Ancient Stannary town and excellent touring centre, noted for the annual "Furry Dance". Nearby is Loe Pool, separated from the sea by a bar. Truro 17 miles, St Ives 15, Redruth 11.

TREGILDRY HOTEL, GILLAN, MANACCAN, CORNWALL TR12 6HG (01326 231378). Spectacular seaviews, 10 pretty en suite rooms. Excellent cuisine, uncrowded coastal path walks. AA ★★ 80%. "Courtesy & Care Award", 2 Rosettes for Food. Good Food Guide. [🐾]
e-mail: trgildry@globalnet.co.uk
website:www.tregildryhotel.co.uk

GILLAN, HELFORD RIVER. Sleeps 2/4. Four warm and comfortable cottages converted from old stone farm buildings set in five acres of paddocks and gardens. Magnificent far-reaching views towards Falmouth Bay. Footpath to Porthallow Cove, pub, restaurant and cream teas. WENDY BAXTER, 'MENIFTERS', GILLAN, MANACCAN, HELSTON, CORNWALL TR12 6ER (01326 280711). [Pets £10 per week, pw!].
website: www.menifterscottages.co.uk

GREYSTONES GUEST HOUSE, 40 WEST END, PORTHLEVEN, HELSTON TR13 9JL (Tel & Fax: 01326 565583). Picturesque fishing village, ideal for touring. Dogs/children welcome. Overlooking sea, near harbour, beaches, shops, pubs and restaurants. Tea and coffee facilities, colour TV. From £15.00 pppn. [🐕]

MRS MOIRA BEVAN, THE MANSE, ST KEVERNE, HELSTON, CORWALL TR12 6LY (Tel & Fax: 01326 281025). Victorian house in friendly village. Ideal base for walking, diving, fishing and exploring the beautiful Lizard Peninsula. En suite available. Home-cooked food, vegetarian options, Evening Meal available. Non-smoking, children over 12 and well behaved dogs welcome. Brochure on request. [🐕]
e-mail: themanse@classicfm.net

Launceston

Town on hill above River Kensey Valley, 20 miles north west of Plymouth. Remains of Norman Castle.

LOWER DUTSON FARM, LAUNCESTON, CORNWALL PL15 9SP (01566 776456). Launceston with its Norman Castle is two miles. Centrally situated for touring both coasts, Dartmoor and Bodmin Moor. Salmon and trout fishing on River Tamar. Well-equipped cottage with 2 bathrooms. ETC ★★★ [Pets £10 per week]
e-mail:francis.broad@btclick.com

Liskeard

Pleasant market town and good centre for exploring East Cornwall. Bodmin Moor and the quaint fishing villages of Looe and Polperro are near at hand. plymouth 19 miles, St Austell 19 miles, Launceston 16, Fowey (via ferry) 15, Bodmin 13, Looe 9.

CELIA HUTCHINSON, CARADON COUNTRY COTTAGES, EAST TAPHOUSE, NEAR LISKEARD, CORNWALL PL14 4NH (TEL & Fax: 01579 320355). Luxury cottages in the heart of the Cornish countryside. Ideal centre for exploring Devon and Cornwall, coast and moor. Central heating and log burners for cosy off-season breaks. [pw! Pets £10 per week]

ROSECRADDOC LODGE, LISKEARD PL14 5BU Tel or Fax: 01579 346768. Modern two/three bedroom bungalows set in lawned gardens and woodland, in countryside at the foot of Bodmin Moor. Many have microwave ovens and videos. Suitable for disabled visitors. Terms: £135 - £375 per week. [Pets £12 per week]

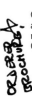

HENWOOD BARNS HOLIDAY COTTAGES, HENWOOD BARNS, HENWOOD, LISKEARD PL14 5BP 01579 363576; Fax: 01579 363101). Situated on Bodmin Moor, a perfect area to holiday with pets. Three converted barns sleeping 2/4/6 offer high quality self-catering accommodation in a beautiful, peaceful setting with wonderful views. [🐕]
e–mail: henwood.barns@internet-today.co.uk

MRS E. COLES, CUTKIVE WOOD HOLIDAY LODGES, ST. IVE, LISKEARD PL14 3ND (01579 362216). Self-catering Chalets in 41 acres of woodland. 2/3 bedrooms; fully equipped inc. linen, colour TV, fridge, cooker and microwave. Pets corner for children. Dogs welcome. [🐕 pw!]

MRS V.M. NORTHCOTT, "PENDOWER HOUSE", EAST TAPHOUSE, LISKEARD PL14 4NH (01579 320332). All comforts. Open all year. Main road, Good food. Moderate terms. Ground floor suite available. Central for Cornwall. [🐕]

MR AND MRS HUNSTONE, RIVERMEAD FARM, TWOWATERSFOOT, LISKEARD PL14 6HT (01208 821464). Self-catering Apartments and Farm Cottage convenient for both coasts and moors. Fishing on River Fowey. Pets welcome at a charge.
website: www.zednet.co.uk/rivermead

Gorgeous old world country cottages dating back to 15th century. Open all year. Log fires, antiques and lovely country furnishings, fresh linen, flowers and all comforts of home. Heated pool, meals service, private garden, plenty of country walks. A paradise for dogs and their owners. O. SLAUGHTER, TREFANNY HILL, DULOE, LISKEARD PL14 4QF (01503 220622).

Lizard

The most southerly point in England, with fine coastal scenery and secluded coves. Sandy beach at Housel Bay. Truro 28 miles, Helston 11.

PARC BRAWSE HOUSE, PENMENNER ROAD, THE LIZARD TR12 7NR (01326 290466). Lovely old Cornish house overlooking Lizard Point. Comfortable rooms with sea views, colour TV and teamakers; most en suite. Home cooking (including vegetarian). Licensed. Open all year. ETC ◆◆◆, RAC Acclaimed. [Pets £1 per dog per night.]

MULLION HOLIDAY PARK. A very special place! Situated in an area of outstanding natural beauty close to glorious sandy beaches. ◆◆◆. Phone WESTSTAR HOLIDAY PARK on 01326 240000.

Looe

Twin towns linked by a bridge over the River Looe. Capital of the shark fishing industry; nearby Monkey Sanctuary is well worth a visit.

NEAR LOOE. Spectacularly situated holiday cottages in picturesque Cornish fishing village - one of the finest on the Cornish coast. Sleeping from two to eight persons at a charge of £100 to £395 per cottage per week. Either with terraced gardens and fabulous outlook over harbour encompassing 15 mile sea views, or conveniently positioned by river in older part of village. Excellent selection of quality restaurants and olde worlde pubs nearby, and on offer delicious pasties and locally made ice-cream. Private parking or garaging, two minutes shops, beach, quay and National Trust cliff walks. Open all year, children and pets most welcome. All cottages are fully furnished and equipped, to include a colour television, microwave, electric oven, refrigerator, duvets and pillows. Ring GRAHAM WRIGHT ON 01579 344080, GUARDIAN HOUSE, LISKEARD, CORNWALL PL14 6AD. [🐾]

CLASSY COTTAGES – Three superb coastal cottage locations between Polperro and Fowey. Willy Wilcox cottage is just 11 feet from beach over smugglers' cave. Log fires, dishwashers, washing machines etc. Indoor Private Swimming Pool. Contact FIONA & MARTIN NICOLLE (01720 423000). [Pets £12 per week].

MRS ANN BRUMPTON, TALEHAY HOLIDAY COTTAGES, PELYNT NR LOOE PL13 2LT (Tel & Fax: 01503 220252). Cosy, traditional cottages set in four acres of unspoilt countryside offering peace and tranquillity Breathtaking coastal and country walks. An ideal location for dogs and their owners. C.T.B. approved. Non smoking. [Pets £2 per night, £10 per week]
e–mail: pr.brumpton@ukonline.co.uk
website: www.cornwallexplore.co.uk/talehay

Idyllic 18th century country cottages for romantics and animal lovers. Looe three miles. Wonderful walks from your gate. Cottages warm and cosy in winter. Personal attention and colour brochure from: B. WRIGHT, TREWORGEY COTTAGES, DULOE, LISKEARD PL14 4PP (01503 262730).
e-mail: treworgey@enterprise.net
website: www.cornishdream.co.uk or www.treworgeycottages.co.uk

TRENANT PARK COTTAGES. Four delightful cottages sleep from 2 to 7 persons. Each has spacious lounge with colour TV, fully equipped kitchen, private garden. Ample room to relax. APPLY: MRS E. CHAPMAN, TRENANT LODGE, SANDPLACE, LOOE PL13 1PH (01503 263639/262241). [Pets £12.50 per week.]
e–mail: Liz@holiday-cottage.com
website: www.holiday-cottage.com

Gorgeous old world country cottages dating back to 15th century. Open all year. Log fires, antiques and lovely country furnishings, fresh linen, flowers and all comforts of home. Heated pool, meals service, private garden, plenty of country walks. A paradise for dogs and their owners. O. SLAUGHTER, TREFANNY HILL, DULOE, LISKEARD PL14 4QF (01503 220622).

LOOE VALLEY TOURING PARK, LOOE, CORNWALL. (01503 262425). Tour and Explore the Looe Valley. Set in glorious countryside, Looe Valley is ideally situated for touring beautiful South East Cornwall. Close to beautiful, safe, sandy beaches, secluded coves and picturesque villages.

LOOE BAY. A very special place! Award Winning Holiday Park situated in an area of outstanding natural beauty close to glorious sandy beaches. ◆◆◆◆. Phone WESTSTAR HOLIDAY PARKS on 01392 447447.

TALLAND BARTON CARAVAN PARK, TALLAND BAY, LOOE PL13 2JA (01503 272715). Fully equipped two and three bedroom caravans. Direct access to coastal path and beach. Shop, clubroom, laundry, play area and swimming pool. Short Breaks off-season. Pets welcome. [Pets £20.00 per week.]

MRS KEILTHY, CARDWEN FARM, PELYNT, LOOE PL13 2LU (Tel & Fax: 01503 220213). Cardwen is a 17th century Grade II Listed Farmhouse set in three acres of notable gardens with a stream and pond. We have two en suite double bedrooms and one twin room, all overlooking the garden and surrounding fields. [🐾]

VALLEYBROOK, PEAKSWATER, LANSALLOS, LOOE, CORNWALL. PL13 2QE (01503 220493). Self-catering quality pine lodges and caravans in peaceful setting near Polperro. Open all year. Short breaks. Phone for brochure. [Dogs £1.50 per day, £10.50 per week].

TRELAWNE LODGE, LOOE. Delightful detached period lodge. Lovely secluded wooded gardens. Summer house. Barbecue. Woodland and coastal walks. Beaches one mile. Comfortably furnished, well equipped. Two bedrooms. Sleeps five. ENQUIRIES: BARTERS OLD FARMHOUSE, NORTH WHILBOROUGH, NEWTON ABBOT TQ12 5LP (Tel: 01803 873213; Fax: 01803 875096) [Pets £8 per week] e–mail: holcot@eclipse.co.uk

WELL MEADOW COTTAGE, DULOE, NEAR LISKEARD. Attractively converted barn set in a large secluded garden. Excellent locality for walking and relaxing. Sleeps 2/4 people. Ideal place for families and dogs alike. For a brochue contact BILL AND KAYE CHAPMAN, COLDRINNICK FARM, DULOE, LISKEARD PL14 4QF (01503 220251).

HENDRA FARM COTTAGES, PELYNT, LOOE PL13 2LU (Tel & Fax: 01503 220701). Three quality cottages peacefully set in 250 acres of beautiful countryside on working farm. A hidden retreat only four miles from Looe, Polperro, Coastal Path and coves. Excellent locality for walking. Cottages sleep 2 to 5 persons. Heating, electricity and bed linen included in price. ♔♔♔♔ Highly Commended. [Pets £5 per week], e–mail: Roderick.J.Farrelly@farmline.com

TREMAINE GREEN COUNTRY COTTAGES, PELYNT, NEAR LOOE, CORNWALL PL13 2LT (Tel: 01503 220333). A beautiful Hamlet of 11 traditional cosy craftsmen's cottages. Clean, comfortable and well equipped. Set in lovely grounds with country and coastal walks. e-mail: j7p@tremaine.sagehost.co.uk

Mawgan Porth

Modern village on small sandy bay. Good surfing. Inland stretches the beautiful Vale of Lanherne. Rock formation of Bedruthan Steps is nearby. Newquay 6 miles west.

SEA VISTA HOTEL, MAWGAN PORTH, NEAR NEWQUAY TR8 4AL (01637 860276). Licensed family run Hotel, 9 bedrooms all with shower, washbasins, colour TV, tea/coffee making facilities. Car park, residents' lounge, TV lounge, pool table, darts and garden. Christmas and New Year Breaks available.[🐾] e-mail: crossd@supanet.com website: www.seavistahotel.co.uk

---

SYMBOLS

🐾   **Indicates that pets are welcome free of charge.**

£   **Indicates that a charge is made for pets: nightly or weekly.**

pw!   **Shows some special provision for pets; exercise facility, feeding or accommodation arrangement.**

◻   **Indicates separate pets accommodation.**

WHITE LODGE HOTEL, MAWGAN PORTH BAY, NEAR NEWQUAY TR8 4BN (01637 860512). Give yourselves and your dogs a quality holiday break at this family-run hotel overlooking beautiful Mawgan Porth Bay. Bedrooms en suite, all rooms with washbasins, shaver points, heaters etc. Lounge bar, games room, sun patio, dining room. Car park. 18 years experience. Phone for free brochure. [🐾 pw!]
e-mail: dogfriendlyhotel@redhotant.com
website: www.dogfriendlyhotel.co.uk

THE MALMAR HOTEL, TRENANCE, MAWGAN PORTH, CORNWALL TR8 4DA (01637 860324). Small Licensed Hotel. Close to beach and coastal path. Two good golf courses nearby. Good English cooking. Rooms with tea making facilities, most ground floor/en suite. [🐾]

Mevagissey

Small town on Mevagissey Bay 5 miles south of St Austell.

BUCKINGHAM HOUSE, 17 TREGONEY HILL, MEVAGISSEY PL26 6RD (01726 843375) Charming Grade II Listed property in quaint fishing village. All rooms en suite many with fine views. Facilities include guest lounge, Sky TV, tea and coffee making facilities and licensed bar.

Mousehole

Picturesque fishing village with sand and shingle beach. Penzance 3 miles.

At the entrance to an unspoilt fishing village are four fully equipped S/C flats. Two with full sea view. All bedding and towels provided. Colour TV. Open all year from £80.00 per week. Special out of season short break terms. MR A. G. WRIGHT, 100 WENSLEY ROAD, WOODTHORPE, NOTTINGHAM NG5 4JU (Tel and Fax: 0115 963 9279 or 01736 731563). [🐾]

Newquay

Popular family holiday resort surrounded by miles of golden beaches. Semi-tropical gardens, zoo and museum. Ideal for exploring all of Cornwall.

GOLDEN BAY HOTEL, PENTIRE, NEWQUAY TR7 1PD (01637 873318). ETC ◆◆◆. Affordable quality hotel. Overlooking Fistral beach with the Gannel River and National Trust countryside at rear. All rooms private facilities, some deluxe four poster rooms. Lovely coastal and countryside walks, also close to golf. B&B £18-£30 E.M. optional. [🐾]
e-mail: enquiries@goldenbayhotel.co.uk website: www.goldenbayhotel.co.uk

TRETHIGGEY TOURING PARK, QUINTRELL DOWNS, NEWQUAY TR8 4LG (01637 877672). Open 1st March to 2nd January. Toilets, hot showers, disabled toilet, shaver points, hairdryers, dishwashing facilities, launderette, shop, freezer packs, telephone, chemical toilet disposal point, electric hook-ups, games room, TV/off-licence. Touring caravans to let. ETC ★★★★ [Pets £1.30 per night, pw!]
website: www.trethiggey.co.uk

RETORRICK MILL, ST MAWGAN, NEWQUAY TR8 4BH (01637 860460). Cottage and Bungalows Old cottage and comfortable bungalows, within walking distance of picturesque village of St Mawgan and sandy beach at Mawgan Porth. Set in nine acres of beautiful gardens with ducks and sheep, halfway between Newquay and the fishing village of Padstow. From £120 to £380 weekly. Pets welcome. ETC ★★ SELF-CATERING.

CLEARWATER LODGE HOTEL 30 LEWARNE ROAD PORTH NEWQUAY TR7 3JS (01637 873151). Warm welcome awaits. Lovely cliff-top walks. Near beach. All rooms are ground floor with private facilities. Childrens discounts. [First pet free, second £1 per night].

ROSEMERE HOTEL, WATERGATE BAY, NEWQUAY TR8 4AB (01637 860 238). Family-run hotel overlooking the beautiful Watergate Beach and Coastal Footpath. 38 en suite rooms, many with sea views. Heated outdoor pool. Dogs welcome to sleep in your room. [🐾]

WHITE LODGE HOTEL, MAWGAN PORTH BAY, NEAR NEWQUAY TR8 4BN (01637 860512). Give yourselves and your dogs a quality holiday break at this family-run hotel overlooking beautiful Mawgan Porth Bay. Bedrooms en suite, all rooms with washbasins, shaver points, heaters etc. Lounge bar, games room, sun patio, dining room. Car park. 18 years experience. Phone for free brochure. [🅃 pw!]
e-mail: dogfriendlyhotel@redhotant.com
website: www.dogfriendlyhotel.co.uk

Padstow

Bright little resort with pretty harbour on Camel estuary. Extensive sands. Nearby is Elizabethan Prideaux Place. Newquay 15 miles, Wadebridge 8.

RAINTREE HOUSE HOLIDAYS, WHISTLERS, TREYARNON BAY, PADSTOW PL28 8JR (01841 520228; Fax:01841 520130). We have a varied selection of accommodation. Small or large, houses and apartments, some by the sea. All in easy reach of our lovely beaches. Please write or phone for brochure. [🅃]

Penzance

Well-known resort and port for Scilly Isles, with sand and shingle beaches. Truro 27 miles, Helston 13, Land's End 10, St Ives 8.

EDNOVEAN HOUSE PERRANUTHNOE, PENZANCE TR20 9LZ. Tel: 01736 711071. Pictures cannot do justice to our fabulous views. See for yourself by staying with us in our Victorian Country House overlooking St. Michael's Mount. [Pets £2.50 per night]

GLENCREE PRIVATE HOTEL, 2 MENNAYE ROAD, PENZANCE TR18 4NG (01736 362026). Just off seafront with comfortable friendly atmosphere. Spacious rooms with colour TV and tea-making. Most rooms are en suite, some with good sea views. Unrestricted parking. Good home cooking. All well-behaved pets welcome and their owners too! Open all year including Christmas and New Year. B&B from £18 nightly, £108 weekly. ETC ◆◆◆. Mike and Rosemary Tedaldi. [🅃]

Modern, well-equipped two bedroom apartment, set in charming Chapel Street, overlooking harbour. Conveniently located near an excellent range of restaurants. Five minutes to beach, promenade, main station, shops and ferry to Scilly Isles. Panoramic views, including St. Michaels Mount. Private parking one car. Pets welcome. THE OLD LIBRARY, CORPORATION STREET PENZANCE TA1 4AJ. PHONE SIOBHAN (01823 350104/07968 595138; Fax: 01823 354755).

Polperro

Picturesque and quaint little fishing village and harbour. Of interest is the "House of the Props". Fowey 9 miles, Looe 5.

POLPERRO. Spectacularly situated holiday cottages in picturesque Cornish fishing village - one of the finest on the Cornish coast. Sleeping from two to eight persons at a charge of £100 to £395 per cottage per week. Either with terraced gardens and fabulous outlook over harbour encompassing 15 mile sea views, or conveniently positioned by river in older part of village. Excellent selection of quality restaurants and olde worlde pubs nearby, and on offer delicious pasties and locally made ice-cream. Private parking or garaging, two minutes shops, beach, quay and National Trust cliff walks. Open all year, children and pets most welcome. All cottages are fully furnished and equipped, to include a colour television, microwave, electric oven, refrigerator, duvets and pillows. Ring GRAHAM WRIGHT ON 01579 344080. GUARDIAN HOUSE, LISKEARD, CORNWALL PL14 6AD. [🅃]

CLASSY COTTAGES – Three superb coastal cottage locations between Polperro and Fowey. Willy Wilcox cottage is just 11 feet from beach over smugglers' cave. Log fires, dishwashers, washing machines etc. Indoor Private Swimming Pool. Contact FIONA & MARTIN NICOLLE (01720 423000). [Pets £12 per week].

SYMBOLS

🅃   Indicates that pets are welcome free of charge.

£   Indicates that a charge is made for pets: nightly or weekly.

pw!   Shows some special provision for pets; exercise facility, feeding or accommodation arrangement.

⌂   Indicates separate pets accommodation.

CHARACTER & LUXURY - POLPERRO. (Telephone: 01753 882482) 2 stunningly refurbished and furnished stone cottages. Central old village location close to enchanting harbour, pubs, restaurants and cliff walks. Sleep 2-16. Each has 2 baths, one has roof terrace. Open fires, beams plus every modern facility. [Pets £10 per week]

Polzeath

Small, friendly resort on cliffs near Padstow. Fine sands, good bathing, surfing. Sheltered by Pentire Head to the north. Wadebridge 8 miles.

D. & L. SHARPE, PINEWOOD FLATS, POLZEATH PL27 6TQ (01208 862269). Flats, Chalets and Cottage. Tabletennis, launderette, baby-sitting. Superb touring centre. [🐾]

Port Gaverne

Hamlet on east side of Port Isaac, near Camel Estuary.

CHIMNEYS, PORT GAVERNE, PORT ISAAC PL29 3SQ (Tel & Fax: 01208 880254). A charming 18th Century Cottage only 10 metres from beach. Four bedrooms, two bathrooms, lounge, dining room and kitchen. Good size garden. Brochure from Mrs. Holmes. [🐾]

Port Isaac

Attractive fishing village with harbour. Much of the attractive coastline is protected by the National Trust. Camelford 9 miles. Wadebridge 9.

PORT GAVERNE INN AND GREEN DOOR COTTAGES, NEAR PORT ISAAC PL29 3SQ (01208 880244; Fax: 01208 880151). Comfortably renovated character cottages, sleep 2/6, fully equipped, no meters, all inclusive price. Convenient for the Port Gaverne Inn. Open all year. ♕♕♕♕ Commended. [Pets £3 per night (hotel)].
e-mail: pghotel@telinco.co.uk

Homes from home around our peaceful courtyard garden 100 yds from sea in bygone fishing hamlet. Each sleeps six and has full CH, fridge-freezer, washer-dryer, dishwasher, microwave, video. £160 (February), £600 (August) weekly. Daily rates off-season. Resident owners APPLY:- CAROLE & MALCOLM LEE, GULLROCK, PORT GAVERNE, PORT ISAAC PL29 3SQ (01208 880106).[🐾]

LONG CROSS HOTEL & VICTORIAN GARDENS, TRELIGHTS, PORT ISAAC PL29 3TF (01208 880243). Set in magnificent public gardens with tavern in the grounds. Pets' corner. Perfect base for touring. Excellent food served all day. Bargain Spring/Autumn Breaks. [Pets £2.00 per night.]

CARN AWN, PORT GAVERNE, PORT ISAAC. Fishing, swimming, boating and delightful rock pools for the children. Many beaches within reach. Car essential. Fully fitted kitchen. Cot available. All electric, coal fire. Open all year. Well behaved dogs welcome. For terms contact: MRS S.A. MAY, ORCADES HOUSE, PORT GAVERNE, PORT ISAAC, CORNWALL PL29 3SQ (Tel & Fax: 01208 880716). [🐾]

Portreath

Coastal village 4 miles north west of Redruth.

Charming elegantly furnished self catering cottages between Newquay and St Ives. Sleep 2 to 6. Fully equipped including linen. Beautiful beaches. Laundry and games room plus bar. Ample parking. Colour brochure – FRIESIAN VALLEY COTTAGES, MAWLA, CORNWALL TR16 5DW (01209 890901) [🐾]

FHG PUBLICATION LIMITED publish a large range of well-known accommodation guides. We will be happy to send you details or you can use the order form at the back of this book.

Portscatho

Tiny cliff-top resort on Roseland Peninsula overlooking beach of rocks and sand. Harbour and splendid views. Falmouth 5 miles.

PETER AND LIZ HEYWOOD, TREWINCE MANOR, PORTSCATHO, NEAR TRURO TR2 5ET (FREEP-HONE 0800 0190289). Georgian Manor house estate with luxury lodges, cedarwood cabins, cottage, manor house apartment. Lounge bar and restaurant. Superb walking and sailing. Dogs welcome. [pw! Pets £21 per week]
e–mail: bookings@trewince.co.uk

Praa Sands

Magnificent stretch of sands and dunes. Nearby is picturesque Prussia Cove. Penzance 7½ miles. Helston 6.

Well appointed Bungalows. One chalet bungalow sleeps 9+ in 4 bedrooms. Lovely peaceful countryside with large garden not overlooked. 2 miles inland. One 3 bedroomed sleeps 6+. Overlooking sea. Large garden. Both fully equipped. Dogs very welcome. APPLY – MRS J. LAITY, CHYRASE FARM, GOLDSITHNEY, PENZANCE TR20 9JD (01736 763301). [Pets £14 per week]

BLUE BURROW COTTAGES, PERRANUTHNOE, PENZANCE TR20 9NF. Sleeps 4. Ground floor self-contained flat with enclosed garden and garage. Warm, roomy, comfortable and fully equipped. Located close to sandy beach; good touring centre. Coastal path walks nearby. Children and pets welcome. Available all year; Short Breaks in Winter. Weekly terms from £80. Contact: AUDREY G. HOLLAND, FLAT 1, 19 TREWARTHA ROAD, PRAA SANDS, PENZANCE. (01736 711108/01736 763799).

Redruth

Market town 8 miles west of Truro.

GLOBE VALE HOLIDAY PARK, RADNOR, REDRUTH TR16 4BH (01209 891183). "In the Countryside, near the Sea." Perfect for pets and owners, with unlimited trails to explore and near "Dogs Allowed" beaches. Shop, play area, launderette, bar and games room. Caravans, static caravans, tourers and tents welcome. [Pets £7.50 per week]

Ruanhighlanes

Picturesque hamlet convenient for Veryan and Philleigh. Beautiful surrounding countryside.

POLSUE MANOR, RUANHIGHLANES, NEAR ST. MAWES TR2 5LU (Tel: 01872 501270; Fax: 01872 501177). Tranquil secluded Manor House in 8 acres. En suite bedrooms. Close to sandy coves, coastal paths, country walks and Eden Project. Pets very welcome. AA ◆◆◆◆. [Pets £3.50 per night]

St Agnes

Patchwork of fields dotted with remains of local mining industry. Watch for grey seals swimming off St. Agnes Head.

CHIVERTON PARK, NEAR ST. AGNES. Caravan and touring holidays only a short drive from magnificent beaches. Quiet, spacious, laundry, shop, play area and games room. All amenities. No club, no bar, no disco. [🐾]

THE DRIFTWOOD SPARS HOTEL, TREVAUNANCE COVE, ST AGNES TR5 0RT (01872 552428/553323). Take a deep breath of Cornish fresh air at this comfortable Hotel ideally situated for a perfect seaside holiday. Wonderful food, traditional Cornish home cooking. Children and pets welcome. [Pets £1.50 per night]

SUNHOLME HOTEL, GOONVREA ROAD, ST AGNES TR5 0NW (01872 552318). Enjoy some of the finest views in the South West. Ideal for touring; cliff walks and beaches. Good food and service. All bedrooms en suite. Write or phone for brochure. [Pets £1.50 per night.]

PENKERRIS, PENWINNICK ROAD, ST. AGNES TR5 0PA (01872 552262). Enchanting Edwardian licensed residence. Lounge with TV, video, piano, and log fires in Winter. Open all year. ETC ◆◆. AA, RAC Listed. Les Routiers recommended. [🦮 One dog free]

St Austell

Old Cornish town and china clay centre with small port at Charlestown (1½ miles). Excellent touring centre. Newquay 16 miles, Truro 14, Bodmin 12, Fowey 9, Mevagissey 6.

BOSINVER HOLIDAY COTTAGES. Individual cottages and lodges in peaceful garden surroundings. Close to major holiday attractions. Short walk to shop and pub. Phone 01726 72128 for brochure. [Pets £15 per week].
e–mail: Bosinver@Holidays2000.freeserve.co.uk
website: www.bosinver.co.uk

ST MARGARET'S PARK HOLIDAY BUNGALOWS, POLGOOTH, ST AUSTELL PL26 7AX (01726 74283; Fax: 01726 71680). Family-run timber Bungalows in sunny wooded valley. Village Inn, shop, golf 500 yards. Children and pets welcome. From £95 per week. [pw! £20 per week.]

RIVER VALLEY HOLIDAY PARK, LONDON APPRENTICE, ST AUSTELL, CORNWALL PL26 7DS (01726 73533) Friendly family park in the Pentewan Valley. Woodland walks, off road cycle trail and indoor heated swimming pool. Pets Welcome. ETC ★★★★ [£20 per week].
e-mail: johnclemo@aol.com
website: www.river-valley.co.uk

CROFT FARM HOLIDAY PARK, LUXULYAN, BODMIN PL30 5EQ (01726 850228). Gold David Bellamy Conservation Award. Secluded, picturesque and three miles from St Austell Bay. Dog exercise area and woodland walk. On the doorstep of Eden!

St Ives

Picturesque resort, popular with artists, with cobbled streets and intriging little shops. Wide stretches of sand.

SANDBANK HOLIDAYS, ST IVES BAY, HAYLE (01736 752594). High quality Apartments and Bungalows for 2-6 persons. Heated, Colour TV, Microwave etc. Open all year. Short Breaks and weekly rates. Dogs welcome. [Pets £15 p.w]
website: www.sandbank-holiday.co.uk

MRS PAPWORTH, CARLYON GUEST HOUSE, 18 THE TERRACE, ST IVES TR26 3BP (01736 795317). Warm, friendly atmosphere with good English cooking. All bedrooms with TV and tea/coffee facilities; most with showers. Bed and Breakfast, with Evening Meal optional.

St Just in Penwith

Small town 4 miles north of Land's End

"MEANDER" - charming stone cottage to let, two bedrooms, sea views to Scilly Isles. Lovely walks, beaches. Central heating, fitted kitchen, colour TV, microwave, dishwasher, garden. MRS P. MORRIS, FARM LODGE, 62A WEST HILL, PORTISHEAD, NORTH SOMERSET BS20 6LR. (Tel and Fax: 01275 843420). [🦮]

St Mawes

Friendly little harbour town on north bank of Percuil River.

THE ROSEVINE HOTEL, PORTHCURNICK BEACH, PORTSCATHO, ST MAWES TR2 5EW (01872 580206; Fax: 01872 580230). Cornwall's new luxury hotel. De luxe bedrooms and suites. Award-winning cuisine. Beautiful sub-tropical gardens facing directly over the safe sandy beach fronting the National Trust coastline. Warm heated indoor pool. AA/RAC ★★★ [🦮]
e-mail: info@makepeacehotels.co.uk
website: www.makepeacehotels.co.uk

St Mawgan

Delightful village in wooded river valley. Ancient church has fine carvings.

DALSWINTON COUNTRY HOUSE HOTEL, ST MAWGAN, NEAR NEWQUAY TR8 4EZ (01637 860385). Old Cornish house standing in eight acres of secluded grounds. All rooms en suite, colour TV, tea/coffee facilities. Solar heated outdoor swimming pool. Restaurant and bar. Out-of-season breaks. [🐕]

Sennen

Situated east of Land's End.

HOMEFIELDS LICENSED GUEST HOUSE, SENNEN, NEAR PENZANCE, CORNWALL TR19 7AD (01736 871418 Fax: 01736 871666). A small and friendly place to stay. Near Lands End. All rooms have TV, heating, tea/coffee. En suite rooms, sea views, four posters. Prices from £15.00 - £19.00. Pets Welcome. [🐕]
e-mail: homefields1bandb@aol.com

Tintagel

Attractively situated amidst fine cliff scenery; small rocky beach. Famous for associations with King Arthur, whose ruined castle on Tintagel Head is of interest. Bude 19 miles, Camelford 6.

BOSSINEY FARM CARAVAN AND CAMPING PARK, TINTAGEL PL34 0AY (01840 770481). Family-run Park. 19 Luxury Letting Vans; fully serviced, H&C with shower, room heater, TV. On the coast at Tintagel. Colour brochure available. BGHP ★★★★ [🐕]

WILLAPARK MANOR HOTEL, BOSSINEY, TINTAGEL PL34 0BA (01840 770782). Beautiful character house amidst 14 acres and only minutes from the beach. All en suite rooms. Children and pets welcome. Open all year. SAE for brochure. ETC ★★. [🐕]

MS W. KEATING, CHYLEAN, PENPETHY, TINTAGEL, CORNWALL PL34 0XH (01840 212262). Peace, quiet in hamlet near Tintagel. Self-catering chalet sleeps 2/4. Elevated rural position with coastal view. £95 - £205 per week including electricity and bed linen.

PENPETHY HOLIDAY COTTAGES, set in large sheltered courtyard with ample parking. Peaceful, relaxing location, ideal for exploring coast, moors. Phone for brochure/tariff 01840 213903.

SANDY AND DAVE WILSON, SALUTATIONS, ATLANTIC ROAD, TINTAGEL PL34 0DE (01840 770287). Comfortable, well-equipped, centrally heated cottages sleeping two. Ideal for touring, walking and relaxing. Close to coastal path and village amenities. Private parking. Ring for brochure. Pets Free. [🐕]

MRS LYNDA SPRING, TRETHEVY MANOR, TRETHEVY, TINTAGEL, CORNWALL PL34 0BG (Tel/Fax: 01840 770636). Two comfortable, well-equipped, Self-contained Cottages adjoining historical 12th Century Manor House. One-and-a-half miles from Tintagel. Sandy beaches, spectacular coastal and country walks. [🐕]

Torpoint

Busy and pleasant little town on the Hamoaze facing Devonport from and to which runs a car ferry. Plymouth (via ferry) 3 miles.

WHITSAND BAY HOTEL, PORTWRINKLE, BY TORPOINT, PLYMOUTH PL11 3BU (01503 230276; Fax: 01503 230297). Magnificent Country Manor Hotel on cliff top at edge of beach. Own 18 hole golf course, indoor heated swimming pool. Family-sized en suite rooms. AA/RAC ★★. [Pets £3.50 per night, £24.50 per week] ,
website: www.cornish-golf-hotels.co.uk ,
e–mail: earlehotels.btconnect.com

Truro

Pleasant cathedral city. An excellent touring centre with both north and south coasts within easy reach. There are numerous creeks to explore and boat trips may be made across the estuary to Falmouth. Penzance 27 miles, Bodmin 25, Helston 17, St. Austell 14, Redruth 8.

MARCORRIE HOTEL, 20 FALMOUTH ROAD, TRURO TR1 2HX (01872 277374 Fax: 01872 241666) Victorian town house 5 minutes' walk from the city centre and cathedral. All rooms are en suite with central heating, colour TV, telephone, tea-making facilities. Ample parking. ETC Four Diamonds, Les Routiers. [Pets £2.50 per night].

Wadebridge

Town on River Camel, 6 miles north-west of Bodmin

Peaceful farm cottages with superb views of Camel Valley. Ideal for walking, cycling, beaches and touring all Cornwall and North Devon. These fully equipped cottages have cosy log fires, private gardens and parking. Heating and linen included. Personally supervised. Sleeps 2 to 7 plus cot. Dogs by arrangement. ETC ꝑꝑꝑ Commended. MRS SUE ZAMARIA, COLESENT COTTAGES, ST TUDY, WADEBRIDGE, CORNWALL PL30 4QX (Tel/Fax: 01208 850112). [🐾]

West Looe

Linked to East Looe by bridge over River Looe. Nearby monkey Sanctuary worth a visit. Capital of shark fishing industry.

LEMAIN GARDEN APARTMENTS, PORTUAN RD, HANNAFORE, WEST LOOE, CORNWALL PL13 2DR (01503 262073 Fax: 01503 265288) Self-contained holiday apartments in converted Victorian Villa. Sleeps 2-6 people. Magnificent views over Looe Bay. Beach in two minutes. Pets Welcome. Alan & Dee Palin.
e-mail: sales@lemain.com
website: www.lemain.com

ISLES OF SCILLY

SALLAKEE FARM ꝑꝑꝑ

Mrs P. Mumford, St. Mary's, Isles of Scilly TR21 0NZ Telephone: 01720 422391

Self catering farm cottage, available all year round. Sleeps 5. Woodburner. Near beach and coastal paths. Visit self-catering cottage, typical Scillonian cottage. Try Golf, Tennis or Wind Surfing. Pets welcome. Write or phone for details.

St. Mary's

Largest of group of granite islands and islets off Cornish Coast. Terminus for air and sea services from mainland. Main income from flower-growing. Seabirds, dolphins and seals abound.

MRS PAMELA MUMFORD, SALLAKEE FARM, ST. MARY'S TR21 0NZ (01720 422391). Self catering farm cottage, available all year round. Sleeps 5. Woodburner. Near beach and coastal paths. Pets welcome. Write or phone for details. ꝑꝑꝑ.

FHG

Visit the website

www.holidayguides.com

for details of the wide choice of accommodation featured in the full range of FHG titles

Please mention *Pets Welcome*
when enquiring about accommodation featured in these pages.

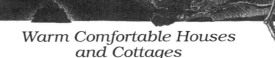

IRTON HOUSE FARM

Farm location with superb views over lake and mountains. Sleeps 2/6. Family accommodation (wheelchair accessible). Children and dogs welcome! Interesting walking area and comfortable motoring. Convenient restaurant nearby - also facilities for fishing, riding, swimming and golf. Ample parking. Please telephone for colour brochure.

Isel, Cockermouth, Near Keswick CA13 9ST Tel: 017687 76380
See our website: www.almondirtonhousefarm.com
E-mail:almond@farmersweekly.net

Royal Oak Hotel　　Rosthwaite, Keswick CA12 5XB

Traditional Lakeland Hotel with friendly atmosphere, home cooking, cosy bar, comfortable lounge and some riverside rooms. Ideally situated in the heart of Borrowdale. 6 miles south of Keswick. dinner, bed and breakfast £30 - £46. Brochure and Tariff available.

Tel: 017687 77214　　　　　　　　　　　　　*AA* ★ Hotel
Website: www.royaloakhotel.co.uk

Cragside　A quiet, comfortable guest house with beautiful views of the surrounding fells **AA**
yet close to the centre of Keswick. All rooms are tastefully decorated, centrally ◆◆◆
heated and have clock radio, colour TV and tea/coffee making facilities. En suite rooms available. Rest assured you will have a comfortable and relaxed stay with us. Bed and Breakfast from £18.50. £150 per week en suite, from £125 per week standard. Children from three years welcome. Pets welcome.

39 Blencathra Street, Keswick CA12 4HX Tel: 017687 73344

THORNTHWAITE HALL　　ETC

THORNTHWAITE, NEAR KESWICK CA12 5SA　◆◆◆◆

17th century farmhouse converted into comfortable country house accommodation set in an acre of landscaped garden and grounds. Rooms en-suite with TV. We offer an extensive menu providing a variety of delicious food with residential license. Ideally located in peaceful hamlet with magnificent views of forest and fells. Dogs welcome at no charge. Telephone for further information and brochure.

Bed & Breakfast £23.50-£26.50, Dinner, Bed & Breakfast from £33. Weekly terms from £234.
Major credit cards accepted.

Maureen & Roy Butcher　　　　　　　**Tel: 017687 78424 • Fax 017687 78122**
E-mail thornthwaite@msn.com • Website: www.cumbria-the-lake-district.co.uk/

The **FHG**
GOLF GUIDE
Where to Play
Where to Stay
2001

Available from most bookshops, the 2001 edition of **THE GOLF GUIDE** covers details of every UK golf course – well over 2500 entries – for holiday or business golf. Hundreds of hotel entries offer convenient accommodation, accompanying details of the courses – the 'pro', par score, length etc.

In association with 'Golf Monthly' and including the Ryder Cup Report as well as Holiday Golf in Ireland, France, Portugal, Spain, The USA, South Africa and Thailand .

£9.99 from bookshops or £10.50 including postage (UK only) from FHG Publications, Abbey Mill Business Centre, Paisley PA1 ITJ

**OVERWATER, NR IREBY,
KESWICK
CUMBRIA CA7 1HH
Tel: (017687) 76566**

Elegant 18th century Country House Hotel. Family run and cared for, offering the best in traditional comforts and service. Award winning restaurant. Peacefully secluded location yet within only a short drive of the popular centres of Lakeland.
Dogs very welcome in your room. 18 acres of gardens for your dog to enjoy unleashed.
Any 4 nights from £180 per person, Inclusive of Dinner, Room and Breakfast.
Please Telephone for brochure.

Rickerby Grange

AA/ETC◆◆◆◆
RAC ◆◆◆◆ SPARKLING AWARD

Portinscale, Keswick, Cumbria CA12 5RH

Set within its own garden with private car parking, in the picturesque village of Portinscale near the shores of Lake Derwentwater within walking distance of the market town of Keswick, ideally situated for exploring all parts of the Lakes. Offering comfort, friendly service, these being the essential qualities provided by the resident proprietor. A well stocked bar, comfortable lounge and elegant dining room where a five course dinner can be enjoyed, with a varied selection of fine wines. Three ground floor bedrooms, all rooms en suite with tea and coffee making facilities, colour TV, direct dial telephone.

B&B from £28, DB&B from £41, Winter Rates Available (Special Breaks) Open all Year, including Christmas and New Year.

Brochure on request, Contact Val Bradley on 017687 72344
E-MAIL: val@ricor.demon.co.uk WEB: www.ricor.demon.co.uk

Thwaite Howe Hotel

Small friendly country house hotel situated in its own grounds, with magnificent mountain views to Skiddaw. Within easy reach of all the Lake District's attractions and also the Cumbrian coast. Specialising in delicious home cooking, complemented by an excellent selection of fine wines. All eight bedrooms have en suite bathrooms. Residents lounge and well stocked bar. Well behaved dogs welcome. Non-smoking rooms. ETC ★★ AA ★★.

Thornthwaite, Near Keswick CA12 5SA Tel: 017687 78281; Fax: 017687 78529

See also Colour Advertisement on page 15

Derwent Lodge Luxury Executive Apartments

Situated in one of the Lake Districts most unspoilt locations

Derwent Lodge, originally a 17th Century Lakeland farm, has been converted into exclusive time ownership apartments. Each apartment has its own individual character and design features. Use of private health spa, steam room and gymnasium.
The Derwent Lodge Traditional Inn and Restaurant with its open fires, in season, oak beams and real ales has been established for 10 years and is renowned for its excellent cuisine and friendly welcome.

Pets are welcome.
Tel. 017687 76606 or FREE PHONE 0800 092 3338
www.lakeland-timeshare.co.uk email. enquiries@derwentlodge.co.uk

---

KESWICK COTTAGES Kentmere, How Lane, Keswick CA12 5RS

Superb selection of cottages and apartments in and around Keswick. All of our properties are well maintained and thoroughly clean. From a one bedroom cottage to a four bedroom house we have something for everyone. Children and pets welcome. Contact us for a free colour brochure. **Tel: 017687 73895**
e-mail: info@keswickcottages.co.uk • website: www.keswickcottages.co.uk

Poets Corner

Luxurious Lakeland
Keswick ♙♙♙ Commended

Luxurious Flats and Cottages located in one of Keswick's most desirable areas, close to town centre, 200 yards from park and sports amenities. All are gas centrally heated - no meters; sleep 4/7 persons. Winter rates as low as £99.

SAE please for brochure and tariff:

John & Jean Mitchell, 35 Main Street, Keswick, Cumbria
Tel: 017687 72790; Home Tel. No: 016973 20220

THE SWAN HOTEL

A family-run 17th century former coaching inn set in idyllic surroundings twixt lake and mountains. For a true sense of beauty, history and relaxation, cossetted by polite friendly, staff catering for your every need. Enjoy an open fire, lake walks, imaginative home-cooking and real ales. Bed and Breakfast from £29 per person per night; Dinner, Bed and Breakfast from £45 per night. Three nights Dinner, Bed and Breakfast from £125 per person. Children and pets welcome. Open all year. Excellent restaurant and bar food. Winter Breaks November to March from £65 per person for 3 nights.

Please call Colin or Joy Harrison for a brochure. Website: www.swan-hotel-keswick.co.uk
The Swan Hotel, Thornthwaite, Keswick, Cumbria CA12 5SQ   Tel: 017687 78256
See also Colour Advertisement on page 12

ETC ◆◆◆◆

Personally run by Barrie and Sandra Littlefair. 17th century former Coaching Inn. Seven en-suite bedrooms are well-appointed two having four poster beds. Non-smoking. Excellent cuisine and fine wines. The convivial atmosphere assures guests of a memorable stay. Pets are welcome by arrangement. Golf bowls and tennis can be arranged locally. B & B from £27.00. D, B&B from £46.50.

Cottage in the Wood
Country House Hotel & Licensed Restaurant
Whinlatter Pass, Keswick CA12 5TW
Tel: 017687 78409 Fax: 017687 78064
E-mail: cottage@lake-district.net
cottage@whinlatter.fsnet.co.uk
Website: www.lake-district.net/cottage

Lakeside Studio Apartments, Derwentwater Marina
Portinscale, Keswick CA12 5RF Tel: 017687 72912

Three self catering apartments only yards from the water, with superb views over Derwentwater and the surrounding fells. Each apartment sleeps 2 with cot/folding bed available. Colour TV, heating and bed linen all included. From £140 to £240 pw. 20% off hire and tuition in sailing, canoeing and windsurfing for guests. Telephone for brochure.

PLEASE MENTION THIS GUIDE WHEN YOU WRITE

OR PHONE TO ENQUIRE ABOUT ACCOMMODATION

IF YOU ARE WRITING, A STAMPED, ADDRESSED

ENVELOPE IS ALWAYS APPRECIATED

KIRKWOOD
Prince's Road, Windermere
LA23 2DD
Tel: 015394 43907

KIRKWOOD occupies a quiet spot betwixt Windermere and Bowness, offering guests a warm and friendly atmopshere with an individual personal service. Rooms are large and all en suite with TV and tea/coffee making facilities; some have four-poster beds. Your hosts will be pleased to help plan tours or walks with maps provided. Three-night Special Breaks available. *B&B £24 - £30.* ◆◆◆◆

E-mail: neil.cox@kirkwood51.freeserve.co.uk   Website: www.kirkwood51.freeserve.co.uk

This beautiful late Georgian vicarage was built in 1803, but now has all the comforts of modern life. It is set in five acres of informal gardens and woodland, home to deer, red squirrels and an extraordinary variety of birds. The Old Vicarage is truly a place to unwind and forget, for a while, the stress of day-to-day life.

Witherslack, LA11 6RS
Tel: 015395 52381; Fax: 015395 52373;
E-mail: hotel@old-vic.demon.co.uk

Near to the Lakes, far from the crowds **The Old Vicarage**

DALES HOLIDAY COTTAGES offer a choice of around 100 superb, personally inspected holiday properties in beautiful rural and coastal locations, Wordsworth and Beatrix Potter country. Cosy cottages to country houses, many open all year. FREE brochure on request. DALES HOLIDAY COTTAGES, CARLETON BUSINESS PARK, SKIPTON, NORTH YORKSHIRE BD23 2AA (01756 799821 or 790919).
website: www.dales-holiday-cottages.com (online booking with secure server).

WELCOME COTTAGE HOLIDAYS. Quality Cottages in wonderful locations at welcoming low prices. Pets, linen and fuel mostly included. PHONE FOR FREE 2001 FULL COLOUR BROCHURE 01756 702208.

PUBLISHER'S NOTE

While every effort is made to ensure accuracy, we regret that FHG Publications cannot accept responsibility for errors, omissions or misrepresentations in our entries or any consequences thereof. Prices in particular should be checked because we go to press early. We will follow up complaints but cannot act as arbiters or agents for either party.

Allonby

Small coastal resort with sand and shingle beach, 5 miles from Maryport across Allonby Bay.

THE SHIP HOTEL, ALLONBY on the west Cumbrian coast offers comfortable accommodation for you and your pet. Real ales, good food and a warm welcome (Tel: 01900 881017). e-mail: allonbyship@ukonline.co.uk

Alston

Small market town 16 miles north-east of Penrith.

MRS CLARE LE MARIE, BROWNSIDE HOUSE, LEADGATE, ALSTON CA9 3EL (01434 382169 / 382100). A warm welcome awaits you in the unspoilt North Pennines. Country situation, superb views, large fenced garden for "walkies". Sitting room with log fire and TV. [🐾]

LOWBYER MANOR COUNTRY HOUSE HOTEL, ALSTON, CUMBRIA CA9 3JX (01434 381230). Set in the heart of England's Last Wilderness (Area of Outstanding Natural Beauty). 17th century Manor House. A la Carte menu (several vegetarian choices). Close to Hadrian's Wall, Lakes and Borders. Special Breaks available. AA/RAC ★★

Ambleside

Popular centre for exploring Lake District at northern end of Lake Windermere. Picturesque Stock Ghyll waterfall nearby, lovely walks. Associations with Wordsworth. Penrith 30 miles, Keswick 17, Windermere 5.

THE OLD VICARAGE, VICARAGE ROAD, AMBLESIDE LA22 9DH (015394 33364). "Rest awhile in style". Quality Bed and Breakfast set in tranquil wooded grounds in the heart of the village. Car park. All rooms en suite. Kettle, clock/radio, TV. Special breaks available. Friendly service where your pets are welcome. Telephone Ian or Helen Burt.

2 LOWFIELD, OLD LAKE ROAD, AMBLESIDE. Ground floor garden flat; sleeps 4/5. Linen supplied. Children and pets welcome. Ample private parking. Terms from £100 to £200 per week. Contact: MR P. F. QUARMBY, 3 LOWFIELD, OLD LAKE ROAD, AMBLESIDE LA22 0DH 015394 32326. [🐾]

IVY HOUSE, HAWKSHEAD, NEAR AMBLESIDE LA22 0HS (FREEPHONE 0800 0563533). Family-run listed Georgian hotel. 11 en suite bedrooms with colour TV and equipped with hot drinks trays. No charge for dogs. Children most welcome. Write or telephone David or Jane Vaughan for brochure. ETC ◆◆◆◆. [🐾]
website: www.ivyhousehotel.com

KIRKSTONE FOOT, KIRKSTONE PASS ROAD, AMBLESIDE LA22 9EH (015394 32232; Fax: 015394 32805). Country house with luxury self-catering Cottages and Apartments sleeping 2/7. Set in peaceful and secluded grounds. Adjoining lovely Lakeland fells, great for walking. Special winter breaks. **ETC ★★★★** [pw! Pets £3.00 per night.]
e-mail: kirkstone@breathemail.net

SKELWITH BRIDGE HOTEL NEAR AMBLESIDE, CUMBRIA LA22 9NJ (015394 32115 Fax: 015394 34254) Traditional seventeenth century Lakeland Inn. Well appointed en suite bedrooms with colour TV, radio, tea and coffee facilities, direct-dial telephone and hairdryer. Two private lounges, sun terrace and gardens. Children welcome. AA/RAC ★★. [Pets £3 per night, £21 per week]
e–mail: Skelwithbr@aol.com

FHG PUBLICATIONS

publish a large range of well-known accommodation guides. We will be happy to send you details or you can use the order form at the back of this book.

SMALLWOOD HOUSE HOTEL COMPSTON ROAD, AMBLESIDE LA22 9DJ (015394 32330) Dogs recommend us, they love the walks from here. Their owners love the rooms and the informality and enjoy their dinners. Car park. Residential licence. [🏕]
e–mail: enq@smallwoodhotel.co.uk
website: www.smallwoodhotel.co.uk

GREENHOWE CARAVAN PARK, GREAT LANGDALE, AMBLESIDE LA22 9JU (015394 37231; Fax: 015394 37464; Freephone: 0800 0688837). Permanent Caravan Park with Self Contained Holiday Accommodation. An ideal centre for Climbing, Fell Walking, Riding, Swimming, Water Skiing or just a lazy holiday. Winners of the Rose Award 1983-2000. Grading "Very Good". [Pets £3 per night, £15 per week]

NANNY BROW COUNTRY HOUSE HOTEL, CLAPPERSGATE, NEAR AMBLESIDE LA22 9NF (015394 32036; Fax: 015394 32450). Peacefully set in five acres of gardens and woodland. There are 17 bedrooms and suites. Outdoor activities, including golf, can be arranged through the hotel.
e-mail: reservations@nannybrowhotel.demon.co.uk
website: www.nannybrow.co.uk

WANSLEA GUEST HOUSE, LAKE ROAD, AMBLESIDE LA22 0DB (015394 33884). Spacious family-run guest house with walks beginning at the door. Comfortable rooms, mostly en suite. Licensed lounge. B&B from £17.50; Evening Meal available to party bookings. Non-Smoking. Pets welcome by arrangement. ETC ◆◆◆◆. [Pets £1 per night.]
e–mail: wanslea.guesthouse@virgin.net

Appleby

Pleasant touring centre on River Eden, between Pennines and Lake District. Castle and Moot Hall of historic interest. Trout fishing, swimming pool, tennis, bowls. Kendal 24 miles, Penrith 13.

APPLEBY MANOR COUNTRY HOUSE HOTEL, ROMAN ROAD, APPLEBY-IN-WESTMORLAND CA16 6JB (017683 51571; Fax: 017683 52888). Enjoy the comfort of Cumbria's award-winning Country House Hotel with superb meals, relaxing lounges, indoor leisure club and breathtaking scenery all around. Phone for a full colour brochure and interactive CD-ROM. [🏕 pw!]

THE GATE HOTEL, BONGATE, APPLEBY CA16 6LH (017683 52688). Family-run business, close to town centre shops, castle and swimming pool. Traditional log fire. Warm and friendly service all year round. En suite rooms. Enclosed garden and play area. Pets welcome by arrangement. Specialising in Thai food we also offer conventional English food. Licensed.
website: www.appleby/web.co.uk/gate.

JUBILEE COTTAGE, NORTH END, BOLTON, NEAR APPLEBY (017683 61868 or 01271 863769). Sleeps 6/7. Situated between North Lakes and Pennines. Fully equipped except linen. Two bedrooms, bathroom, lounge with colour TV and kitchen/diner with electric cooker, fridge, washing machine, iron, etc. Car essential, off road parking for two cars. Open Easter till October. Terms from £150 to £220. Well behaved pets welcome. Miss L. I. Basten.

Bassenthwaite

Village on Bassenthwaite Lake with traces of Norse and Roman settlements.

SKIDDAW VIEW HOLIDAY PARK, BOTHEL, NEAR BASSENTHWAITE CA5 2JG (Tel: 016973 20919; Mobile 07970 620044) Quality self-catering cottages and holiday caravans.Pets come free. Northern Lake District, near market towns of Cockermouth and Keswick. Full weeks from £89 to £325, Short breaks £99, prices include fuel (no meters).
website: www.20919.com

SYMBOLS

🏕   Indicates that pets are welcome free of charge.

£   Indicates that a charge is made for pets: nightly or weekly.

pw!   Shows some special provision for pets; exercise facility, feeding or accommodation arrangement.

⌂   Indicates separate pets accommodation.

Borrowdale

Scenic valley of River Derwent, splendid walking and climbing country.

MARY MOUNT HOTEL, BORROWDALE, NEAR KESWICK CA12 5UU (017687 77223). Set in 4½ acres of gardens and woodlands on the shores of Derwentwater. 2½ miles from Keswick in picturesque Borrowdale. Superb walking and touring. All rooms en suite with colour TV and tea/coffee making facilities. Licensed. Brochure on request. ★★. [🐾]

HILTON KESWICK LODORE HOTEL, BORROWDALE, NEAR KESWICK CA12 5UX (017687 77285; Fax: 017687 77343). Luxury Hotel with fabulous views overlooking Derwentwater and fells. Facilities include 71 bedrooms, restaurant and lounge, bar and leisure club. [Pets £2 per night, £14 per week.]

Brampton

Market town with cobbled streets. Octagonal Moat Hall with exterior staricases and iron stocks.

IRTHING VALE CARAVAN PARK, OLD CHURCH LANE, NRAMPTON, NEAR CARLISLE CA8 2AA (01697 73600). Cleanliness, peace and quiet, personal attention. 4½ acre site with pitches for 20 caravans plus space for camping. Modern amenities. Ideal for walking, fishing, touring and golf. AA 3 Pennants.
website: www.ukparks.com

Buttermere

Between lake of same name and Crummock Water. Magnificent scenery. Of special note is Sour Milk Ghyll waterfall and steep and impressive Honister Pass. Keswick 15 miles, Cockermouth 10.

BRIDGE HOTEL, BUTTERMERE, LAKE DISTRICT CA13 9UZ (017687 70252; Fax: 017687 70215). 21 bedrooms, all with private bathrooms; four-posters available. Daily freshly prepared menus, large selection wines; real ales. Superb walking and fishing. Dogs welcome. Self catering apartments available. [Pets £4 per night]
e-mail: enquires@bridge-hotel.com
website www.bridge-hotel.com

NEW HOUSE FARM, BUTTERMERE/LORTON VALLEY, COCKERMOUTH CA13 9UU (Tel & Fax: 01900 85404). New House Farm has 15 acres of fields, woods, streams and ponds which guests and dogs can wander around. Comfortable en suite accommodation and fine traditional food. Off season breaks. AA ◆◆◆◆◆. [🐾]
e-mail: hazel@newhouse-farm.co.uk
website: www.newhouse-farm.co.uk

Carlisle

Important Border city and former Roman station on River Eden. Castle is of historic interest, also Tullie House Museum and Art Gallery. Good sports facilities inc. football and racecourse. Kendal 45 miles, Dumfries 33, Penrith 18.

GRAHAM ARMS HOTEL, ENGLISH STREET, LONGTOWN, CARLISLE CA6 5SE (01228 791213; Fax: 01228 792830). 14 bedrooms, most en suite, including four-poster and family rooms, all with tea/coffee facilities, TV and radio. Secure courtyard locked overnight. Pets welcome with well-behaved owners. RAC ★★. [🐾]
website: www.cumbria.com/hotel

NEWPALLYARDS, HETHERSGILL, CARLISLE CA6 6HZ (01228 577308). Relax and see beautiful North Cumbria and the Borders. Self-catering accommodation in one Bungalow, 3/4 bedrooms; two lovely Cottages on farm. Also Bed and Breakfast or Half Board – en suite rooms. ETC ◆◆◆◆/★★★★[🐾]
e–mail: info@newpallyards.freeserve.co.uk
website: www.newpallyards.freeserve.co.uk

DALSTON HALL CARAVAN PARK, DALSTON HALL, DALSTON, NEAR CARLISLE CA5 7JX (01228 710165). Exit 42 off M6, follow signs for Dalston. Small family-run park set in peaceful surroundings. Electric hook-ups, shops, playground, launderette, fly-fishing, nine-hole golf course. ✓✓✓✓ [🐾 pw!]

Cockermouth

Market town and popular touring centre for Lake District and quiet Cumbrian coast. On Rivers Derwent and Cocker. Penrith 30 miles, Carlisle 26, Whitehaven 14, Keswick 12.

MRS B. WOODWARD, TODDELL FARM, BRANDLINGILL, COCKERMOUTH CA13 0RB (01900 828423). Unique family suite in barn conversion in 17th century farmhouse set in seven acres, en suite with own entrance. [Pets £2 per night]
website: www.lake-district.com

Coniston

Village 8 miles south-west of Ambleside, dominated by Old Man of Coniston (2635ft).

THE COPPERMINES AND CONISTON COTTAGES. Unique Lakeland cottages for 2 – 27 of quality and character in stunning mountain scenery. Log fires, exposed beams. Pets welcome! ETC ★★ - ★★★★(Tel: 015394 41765 (24hrs); Mobile: 07721 584488) [Pets £20 per week]
website: www.coppermines.co.uk

THE SUN HOTEL & 16TH CENTURY INN, CONISTON LA21 8HQ (015394 41248) Classic Lakeland real ale pub with pet-Friendly hotel attached. Comfortable en suite accommodation. Panoramic mountain views. Extensive menus. Good walks and large garden. [Pets £4 per night]

MRS ANNE HALL, DOW CRAG HOUSE, CONISTON LA21 8AT (015394 41558). Two chalet bungalows to let, sleeping two/six. Quiet location. Superb views across lake. Surrounded by gardens, farm fields. Well equipped. Owner maintained. [🐾]

Crosthwaite

Hamlet 4 miles west of Kendal

DAMSON DENE HOTEL, LYTH VALLEY, CROSTHWAITE, NEAR KENDAL LA8 8JE (015295 68676). Perfectly situated in the tranquil Lyth Valley. Best Lakes Breaks from £99 per person for 3 nights.
website: www.damsondene.co.uk

Elterwater

Village of green slate houses overlooked by stunning peaks of the Langdale Pikes.

**THE BRITANNIA INN, ELTERWATER, AMBLESIDE LA22 9HP (015394 37210; FAX: 015394 37311) The very picture of a traditional Inn, the Britannia overlooks the Green in the delightful village of Elterwater in the heart of the Lake District. Home cooked meals and real ales are served in cosy bars with oak beams and log fires. ETC ★.
e-mail: info@britinn.co.uk
website: www.britinn.co.uk**

Eskdale

Lakeless valley, noted for waterfalls and ascended by a light-gauge railway. Tremendous views. Roman fort. Keswick 35 miles, Broughton-in-Furness 10 miles.

THE BURNMOOR INN, BOOT, ESKDALE, CUMBRIA CA19 1TG (019467 23224 Fax: 019467 23337). Dogs welcome to lie by the fire in the bar. We do not make a charge for well behaved dogs. Special breaks available: Oct - Mar 3 for 2 B&B or DB&B. Call for a brochure. [🐾]

MRS J. P . HALL, FISHERGROUND FARM, ESKDALE CA19 1TF (01946 723319). Self-catering to suit everyone. Scandinavian pine lodges and cottages – on a delightful traditional farm. Adventure playground. Sports hall and games room. Pets' and children's paradise. Brochures available. ETC ★★★
E-mail: holidays@fisherground.co.uk
website: www.fisherground.co.uk[🏠]

Grange-Over-Sands

Quiet resort at the north of Morecambe Bay, convenient centre for Lake District. Fine gardens; golf, boating, fishing, tennis and bowls. Lancaster 25 miles, Windermere 16.

HAMPSFELL HOUSE HOTEL, HAMPSFELL ROAD, GRANGE-OVER-SANDS LA11 6BG (015395 32567). Peaceful country house hotel is set in two acres of mature woodland. The fell is ideal for walking dogs. All rooms en suite with colour TV and tea/coffee making facilities. Excellent food and wines. Ample safe parking. ETC/AA ★★. [🏠]

MR BILL LAMBERT, PROSPECT HOUSE, KENTS BANK ROAD, GRANGE-OVER-SANDS LA11 7DJ (015395 32116). A warm welcome awaits you at Prospect House. En suite rooms with TV, radio and tea/coffee making facilities. Residents' bar. Excellent food using fresh produce. B&B from £24.00; dinner £12.50. Our best advert is the many return visits we receive. [🏠]

Grasmere

Village famous for Wordsworth associations; the poet lived in Dove Cottage (preserved as it was), and is buried in the churchyard. Museum has manuscripts and relics.

ASH COTTAGE, RED LION SQUARE, GRASMERE LA22 9SP (015394 35224). **Centrally located guest house with comfortable en suite bedrooms. Licensed. residents' lounge. Quality British Cuisine served in an informal atmosphere with guests returning year after year. Pleasant award winning garden. Private car parking.**

MRS KING, LAKE VIEW COUNTRY HOUSE, LAKE VIEW DRIVE, GRASMERE LA22 9TD (015394 35384/35167). Excellent position near village centre. Quiet, secluded, with beautiful gardens and views. Ample parking. Private lakeshore access. B&B or self-catering accommodation, dinner by arrangement. Special breaks available. [Pets £2 per night, £10 per week]

GRASMERE HOTEL, GRASMERE LA22 9TA (015394 35277). **A family-run 12 bedroomed Country House Hotel. All rooms en suite. Quietly situated in picturesque village of Grasmere. Award winning restaurant overlooking large secluded garden, river and surrounding hills. Superb five course dinners and carefully chosen wine list. Special breaks throughout the year.**

Greystoke

Pretty village 6 miles from Penrith, 11 from Keswick. Famous for its fine old church, racehorses and heated outdoor swimming pool.

SMITHY COTTAGE, JOHNBY, NEAR GREYSTOKE, CUMBRIA CA11 0UU (017684 83564). Pretty cottage, warm, cosy and very well-equipped. One double, one twin and cot. Small garden with furniture. Open all year. Short Breaks available November – March. Dogs Welcome. [1st dog free, Extra dogs £2 per night each]

Hawkshead

Quaint village in Lake District between Coniston Water and Windermere. The 16th century Church and Grammar School, which Wordsworth attended, are of interest. Ambleside 5 miles.

KINGS ARMS HOTEL, HAWKSHEAD LA22 0NZ (015394 36372; Fax: 015394 36006). Traditional lakeland inn right in the heart of this conservation village. Cosy bedrooms all with CTV and tea/coffee facilities. Choice of freshly prepared food available in lounge bar and diningroom. Bed and Breakfast from £32 to £64. Three night Sunday to Thursday £75 pp. ETC ◆◆◆

BETTY FOLD COUNTRY HOUSE, HAWKSHEAD HILL, AMBLESIDE LA22 0PS (015394 36611). Self-catering cottage and apartment both sleeping four (reductions for reduced occupancy). Set in peaceful and spacious grounds, ideal for the walker and families with pets. Open all year. ETC ★★★ [Pets £2 per night.] See advertisement on page 138.
e-mail: holidays@bettyfold.freeserve.co.uk
website: www.bettyfold.freeserve.co.uk

Ireby

Quiet Cumbrian village between the fells and the sea. Good centre for the northern Lake District. Cockermouth 11 miles, Bassenthwaite 6.

WOODLANDS COUNTRY HOUSE AND COTTAGE, IREBY CA5 1EX (016973 71791). In private wooded grounds four miles from Bassenthwaite, ideal for Lakes and Borders. All bedrooms en suite with tea making facilities. Residential licence. B&B from £28.00. ETC ◆◆◆◆. [Pets £2 per night, £10 per week.]
e–mail:hj@woodlnd.u-net.com
website: www.woodlnd.u-net.com

Kendal

Market town and popular centre for touring the Lake District. Of historic interest is the Norman castle, birthplace of Catherine Parr. Penrith 25 miles, Lancaster 22, Ambleside 13.

ANNE TAYLOR, RUSSELL FARM, BURTON-IN-KENDAL, CARNFORTH, LANCS. LA6 1NN (01524 781334). Bed, Breakfast and Evening Meal offered. Ideal centre for touring Lakes and Yorkshire Dales. Good food, friendly atmosphere on working dairy farm. Modernised farmhouse. Guests' own lounge. [🐾]

MRS HELEN JONES, PRIMROSE COTTAGE, ORTON ROAD, TEBAY CA10 3TL (015396 24791). Excellent rural location for North Lakes and Yorkshire Dales. Superb facilities include jacuzzi bath and four-poster bed. One acre garden. Self-contained ground floor flat available. Pets welcome, very friendly. ETC ◆◆◆◆. [🐾]

Keswick

Famous Lake District resort at north end of Derwentwater with Pencil Museum and Cars of the Stars Motor Museum. Carlisle 30 miles, Ambleside 17, Cockermouth 12.

Warm, comfortable houses and cottages in Keswick and beautiful Borrowdale, welcoming your dog. Inspected and quality graded. LAKELAND COTTAGE HOLIDAYS, KESWICK CA12 5ES (017687 71071; Fax: 017687 75036).
e–mail: info@lakelandcottages.co.uk
website: www.lakelandcottages.co.uk

CHERRY TREES GUEST HOUSE, 16 ESKIN STREET, KESWICK CA12 4DQ (017687 71048). All bedrooms have colour TV, direct dial telephones, clock/radio alarms and tea/coffee facilities. Our double, twin and family rooms are all en suite. Tastefully furnished and fully centrally heated. B&B from £20. DB&B from £30. ETC ◆◆◆. [🐾]
e-mail: cherry.trees@virgin.net

PUBLISHER'S NOTE

While every effort is made to ensure accuracy, we regret that FHG Publications cannot accept responsibility for errors, omissions or misrepresentations in our entries or any consequences thereof. Prices in particular should be checked because we go to press early. We will follow up complaints but cannot act as arbiters or agents for either party.

SWINSIDE INN, NEWLANDS VALLEY, KESWICK CA12 5UE (Tel & Fax: 017687 78253). Beautiful views, walks galore, clean rooms, good beds, good food and good company. Open all year. Contact Tish or Tex for brochure and tariff. [🐾]

LUXURY LAKELAND HOLIDAY COTTAGES AND APARTMENTS. Tastefully appointed one or two bedroom self-catering apartments and cottages set amid tranquil surroundings on the fringe of a picturesque village. Full colour brochure on request. DERWENT MANOR, PORTINSCALE, KESWICK CA12 5RD (017687 72211).
e–mail: info@derwent-manor.com
website: www.derwent-manor.com

MRS J.M. ALMOND, IRTON HOUSE FARM, ISEL, COCKERMOUTH, NEAR KESWICK CA13 9ST (017687 76380). Farm location with superb views over lake and mountains. Sleeps 2/6. [Pets £15 per week]
Website: www.almondirtonhousefarm.com
e-mail: almond@farmersweekly.net

ROYAL OAK HOTEL, ROSTHWAITE, KESWICK CA12 5XB (017687 77214). Traditional Lakeland hotel with friendly atmosphere. Home cooking, cosy bar, comfortable lounge and some riverside rooms. Winter and Summer discount rates. Brochure and Tariff available. AA ★ Hotel. [🐾]
website: www.royaloakhotel.co.uk

CRAGSIDE GUEST HOUSE, 39 Blencathra Street, Keswick CA12 4HX (017687 73344). Quiet, comfortable guest house close to the centre of Keswick. All rooms tastefully decorated, centrally heated and have clock radio, colour TV and tea/coffee making facilities. En suite available. AA ◆◆◆. [🐾]

THORNTHWAITE HALL, THORNTHWAITE, NEAR KESWICK CA12 5SA (017687 78424; Fax 017687 78122). Traditional 17th century converted farmhouse, one acre of grounds and landscaped garden. Good home cooking, licensed. Ideally situated for walking and touring north lakes. Dogs welcome at no charge. Open February - November. ETC ◆◆◆◆. [🐾]
e-mail: thornthwaite@msn.com
website: www.cumbria-the-lake-district.co.uk

DERWENTWATER MARINA, PORTINSCALE, KESWICK CA12 5RF – Lakeside Studio Apartments. Self catering apartments sleep 2 plus child with superb views over the lake and fells. Includes colour TV, heating and bed linen. Tel: 017687 72912 for brochure. [🐾]

COTTAGE IN THE WOOD COUNTRY HOUSE HOTEL & LICENSED RESTAURANT, WHINLATTER PASS, BRAITHWAITE, KESWICK CA12 5TW (017687 78409 Fax: 017687 78064). 17th century former Coaching Inn. Seven en-suite bedrooms, two having four poster beds. Non-smoking. Excellent cuisine and fine wines. Pets are welcome by arrangement. Golf bowls and tennis available. ETC ◆◆◆◆.
e-mail: cottage@lakedistrict.net   or   cottage@whinlatter.fsnet.co.uk
website: www.lake-district.net/cottage

OVERWATER HALL, OVERWATER, NEAR IREBY, KESWICK CA7 1HH (017687 76566). Elegant Country House Hotel in spacious grounds. Dogs very welcome in your room. Any 4 nights from £180 per person, inclusive of Dinner, Room and Breakfast. Mini breaks also available all year. Award winning restaurant. [🐾]

VAL BRADLEY, RICKERBY GRANGE, PORTINSCALE, KESWICK CA12 5RH (017687 72344). Delightfully situated in quiet village. Licensed. Imaginative home-cooked food, attractively served. Open all year. AA/ETC ◆◆◆◆. RAC ◆◆◆◆ Sparkling Award. [Pets £2 per night, £10 per week].
e-mail: val@ricor.demon.co.uk
website: www.ricor.demon.co.uk

SYMBOLS

🐾   Indicates that pets are welcome free of charge.

£   Indicates that a charge is made for pets: nightly or weekly.

pw!   Shows some special provision for pets; exercise facility, feeding or accommodation arrangement.

⌂   Indicates separate pets accommodation.

THWAITE HOWE HOTEL, THORNTHWAITE, NEAR KESWICK CA12 5SA (017687 78281; Fax: 017687 78529). Small friendly country house hotel specialising in delicious home cooking and fine wines. Eight en suite bedrooms. Residents lounge and bar. Well behaved dogs welcome. Non-smoking rooms. ETC ★★ AA ★★. [Pets £3 per night per pet.]

KESWICK COTTAGES, KENTMERE, HOW LANE, KESWICK CA12 5RS (017687 73895). Cottages and apartments in and around Keswick. Properties are well maintained and clean. From a one bedroom cottage to a four bedroom house. Children and pets welcome. [Pets £10 per week]
e-mail: info@keswickcottages.co.uk
website: www.keswickcottages.co.uk

DERWENT LODGE LUXURY EXECUTIVE APARTMENTS, KESWICK (017687 76606; FREEPHONE: 0800 0923338) Situated in one of the Lake Districts most unspoilt locations. Originally a 17th century lakeland farm. Use of private health spa, steam room and gymnasium.
e-mail: enquiries@derwentlodge.co.uk
website: www.lakeland-timeshare.co.uk

LOW BRIERY RIVERSIDE HOLIDAY VILLAGE, KESWICK CA12 4RN (017687 72044). Cottages, flats, lodges and caravans; superb amenities and leisure facilities. On eastern outskirts of Keswick. [Pets £10 per week]
website: www.keswick.uk.com

ORCHARD HOUSE, APPLETHWAITE, NEAR KESWICK. A perfect place for dogs and children, with a secure paddock, quiet lanes and hundreds of walks, yet with the delights of Keswick and Lake Derwentwater just over a mile away. Sleeps up to 12. Booking and brochure telephone 01946 723319. ETC ★★★ [🐾]
e-mail: holidays@fisherground.co.uk
website: www.orchardhouseholidays.co.uk

JOHN & JEAN MITCHELL, 35 MAIN STREET, KESWICK (Tel & Fax: 017687 72790; Home Tel No: 016973 20220). Luxurious Lakeland flats and cottages located in one of Keswick's most desirable areas. All gas central heating. Some with two bathrooms (one en suite). From £99 weekly. [🐾]

COLIN AND JOY HARRISON, SWAN HOTEL, THORNTHWAITE, KESWICK CA12 5SQ (017687 78256). Family run 17th century former coaching inn. Excellent restaurant and bar food. Summer Prices, B&B £29; DBB £45; 3 nights DBB £125. Winter breaks, Nov-Mar from £65 per person for 3 nights. Pets welcome. [£1.75 per night]

Kirkby-in-Furness

Small coastal village (A595). 10 minutes to Ulverston, Lakes within easy reach. Ideal base for walking and touring.

MRS C. ENGLEFIELD, 1 FRIARS GROUND, KIRKBY-IN-FURNESS LA17 7YB (01229 889601). "Sunset Cottage." Self catering 17th century two-bedroom character cottage with garden. Panoramic views over sea/mountains; Coniston/Windermere 20 minutes. Terms from £115. Open all year. [🐾]

Kirkby Lonsdale

Georgian buildings and quaint cottages. Riverside walks from medieval Devil's Bridge.

MRS PAULINE BAINBRIDGE, TOSSBECK, MIDDLETON, KIRKBY LONSDALE LA6 2LZ (015242 76214). 17th century farmhouse, en suite and separate private facilities with television and drink making facilities. Bed and Breakfast from £17, Short Break offers. Non-smoking. Brochures available.

Kirkby Stephen (near Mallerstang)

5 miles south on B6259 Kirkby Stephen to Hawes road.

MRS S. CANNON, COLDBECK COTTAGE, RAVENSTONEDALE, KIRKBY STEPHEN, CUMBRIA CA17 4LW (Tel & Fax: 015396 23230). Accommodation for six, plus cot. Centrally heated. Ground floor bedroom suitable for wheelchair users, Accessible Grade 2. Two-acre garden. The country pub opposite provides inexpensive meals. [🐾]
e–mail: david.cannon@coldbeck.demon.co.uk

COCKLAKE HOUSE, MALLERSTANG CA17 4JT (017683 72080). Charming, High Pennine Country House B&B in unique position above Pendragon Castle in Upper Mallerstang Dale offering good food and exceptional comfort to a small number of guests. Two double rooms with large private bathrooms. Three acres riverside grounds. Dogs welcome.

Kirkoswald

Village in the Cumbrian hills, lying north west of the Lake District. Ideal for touring. Penrith 7 miles.

SECLUDED COTTAGES WITH PRIVATE FISHING, KIRKOSWALD CA10 1EU (24 hr brochure line 01768 898711 manned most Saturdays). Escape to quality cottages, clean, well equipped and well maintained. Centrally located for Lakes, Pennines, Hadrian's Wall, Borderland. Enjoy the Good Life in comfort. Pets' paradise. Bookings/enquiries 01768 896275. [pw! £2 per pet per night; £14 per week].

Little Langdale

Hamlet 2 miles west of Skelwith Bridge. To west is Little Langdale Tarn, a small lake.

HIGHFOLD COTTAGE, LITTLE LANGDALE. A very comfortable cottage, ideally situated for walking and touring. Superb mountain views. Sleeps 5. ETC ★★★. Personally maintained. Pets welcome. Weekly £180 - £310. MRS C.E. BLAIR, 8 THE GLEBE, CHAPEL STILE, AMBLESIDE LA22 9JT (015394 37686). [🐾]

Loweswater

Hamlet at end of Lake Loweswater (owned by National Trust). Beautiful hilly scenery.

LOWESWATER HOLIDAY COTTAGES, LOWESWATER, COCKERMOUTH CA13 9UX (01900 85232). Nestling among the magnificent Loweswater/Buttermere fells, our luxury cottages are available all year. They have open fires, colour TV, central heating, a four poster and gardens. Colour Brochure. ETC ★★★★/★★★★★. See also advert on p145. [Pets £15 per week].

Lowick

Delightful small village in Lake District National Park, 3 miles from Coniston Water and ideal for exploring the southern and western lakes.

MRS JENNY WICKENS, GARTH ROW, LOWICK GREEN, ULVERSTON LA12 8EB (01229 885633). Traditional cottage standing alone amidst farmland and common. Quality accommodation, good food, excellent walking, no smoking. Ideal for children and pets. B&B from £18.00. Brochure available. ◆◆◆. [🐾]

Milnthorpe

Village 7 miles south of Kendal

MR & MRS ELLIS, MILLNESS HILL HOLIDAY PARK, CROOKLANDS, NEAR MILNTHORPE LA7 7NU (015395 67306). Self-catering chalets and caravans for hire, touring park for caravans, motorhomes and tents. Ideal base for exploring the Lake District and Yorkshire Dales. Park adjacent to the picturesque Lancaster Canal.

Mungrisdale

Small village ideal for touring. keswick 8 miles.

NEAR HOWE FARM HOTEL AND COTTAGES, MUNGRISDALE, PENRITH CA11 0SH (Tel/Fax: 017687 79678). Quiet, away from-it-all. Within easy reach of Lakes, walking. Good food. Bar, log fire in cold weather. 5 Bedrooms en suite. B&B from £18, En suite £23. ETC ◆◆◆ [Pets – Hotel £1 per day. Cottages £10 per week.]

Near Sawrey

This beautiful village on the west side of Windermere has many old cottages set among trees and beautiful gardens with flowers. The world-famous writer Beattrix Potter lived at Hill Top Farm. A ferry travels across the lake to Hawkshead (2 miles). Far Sawrey ½ mile.

SAWREY HOUSE COUNTRY HOTEL & RESTAURANT, NEAR SAWREY, HAWKSHEAD LA22 0LF (015394 36387; Fax: 015394 36010). Elegant family-run hotel in three acres of peaceful gardens with magnificent views across Esthwaite Water. Excellent food, warm friendly atmosphere. Lounge, Bar. Children and pets welcome. AA 2 Rosettes for food. ETC/RAC/AA ◆◆◆◆. [Pets £3 per night.] website: www.sawrey-house.com

Newby Bridge

Village at southern end of Lake Windermere, 8 miles from Ulverston

NEWBY BRIDGE HOTEL, NEWBY BRIDGE LA12 8NA (015295 31222). Overlooking the southern shores of Lake Windermere. Best Lakes Breaks from £99 per person for 3 nights. website: www.newbybridgehotel.co.uk

Penrith

Market town and centre for touring Lake District. Of interest are 14th century castle, Gloucester Arms (1477) and Tudor House. Excellent sporting facilities. Windermere 27 miles, Keswick 18.

SECLUDED COTTAGES WITH PRIVATE FISHING, KIRKOSWALD CA10 1EU (24 hr brochure line 01768 898711, manned most Saturdays). Escape to quality cottages, clean, well equipped and well maintained. Centrally located for Lakes, Pennines, Hadrian's Wall, Borderland. Enjoy the Good Life in comfort. Pets' paradise. Bookings/enquiries 01768 898711. ETC ★★★ [pw! £2 per pet per night].

WESTMORLAND HOTEL, ORTON, PENRITH CA10 3SB (015396 24351; Fax: 015396 24354). Situated in the Lune Gorge with panoramic views of the Cumbrian Fells. 53 spacious en suite bedrooms. Impressive restaurant menu. First class service. AA ★★★ & Rosette, ETC/RAC ★★★. Pets welcome.
website: www.westmorland.com
e-mail: westmorlandhotel@aol.com

MRS MARY TEASDALE, LISCO FARM, TROUTBECK, PENRITH CA11 0SY (017687 79645). Comfortable accommodation offered in one double and two en suite family rooms, all with tea/coffee making facilities and washbasins. Outside accommodation available for dogs if required. A good base for touring Lakeland. [🐾]
e-mail: mary@liscofarm.co.uk
website: www.liscofarm.co.uk

MRS MARION BARRITT, LOW GARTH GUEST HOUSE, PENRUDDOCK, PENRITH CA11 0QU (017684 83492). Tastefully converted 18th century barn in peaceful surroundings with magnificent views, offering a warm welcome and Aga-cooked meals. En suite facilities. [🐾]

LYVENNET COTTAGES, THE MILL, KINGS MEABURN, PENRITH CA10 3BU (01931 714661/714226; Fax: 01931 714598) Four different cottages in and around the small farming village of Kings Meaburn in beautiful unspoilt 'Lyvennet Valley'. Ideal touring centre for the Lakes and Dales. ETC ♛♛♛/♛♛♛♛ *HIGHLY COMMENDED.*

BEST LAKES BREAKS, stunning offers from 3 hotels in lovely locations. Rates from £99 per person for 3 nights. For further information telephone 01539 568764.
website: www.bestlakesbreaks.co.uk

SYMBOLS
🐾   Indicates that pets are welcome free of charge.
£   Indicates that a charge is made for pets: nightly or weekly.
pw! Shows some special provision for pets; exercise facility, feeding or accommodation arrangement.
◻   Indicates separate pets accommodation.

Silloth

Solway Firth resort with harbour and fine sandy beach. Mountain views. Golf, fishing. Penrith 33 miles, Carlisle 23, Cockermouth 17.

MR AND MRS G.E. BOWMAN, TANGLEWOOD CARAVAN PARK, CAUSEWAY HEAD, SILLOTH CA5 4PE (016973 31253). Friendly country site, excellent toilet and laundry facilities. Tourers welcome or hire a luxury caravan. Telephone or send stamp for colour brochure. [🐾]

Thurstonfield

Village west of Carlisle. Ideal for visits to the Lake District or Southern Scotland.

THE TRANQUIL OTTER, LAKESHORE LODGES AND FLY FISHING, THURSTONFIELD CA5 6HB (01228 576661; Fax: 01228 576662). Peaceful, quiet and off-the-beaten-track beauty spot in North Cumbria. Six comfortable lakeside lodges, each with verandah and own boat. Set in 50 acres of private nature reserve. [Pets £20 per booking]
website: www.the-tranquil-otter.co.uk

Troutbeck

Village north of Lake Windermere. Church has east window by Burne-Jones.

HOLBECK GHYLL LODGE, TROUTBECK. Lakeland stone lodge. Two twin bedded bedrooms. Dining/livingroom with open fire and sofa bed. Secure covered way for bikes. Parking for three cars. Available Easter to end of October. Saturday change over. ETC ★★★★. MRS KAYE, HOLMDENE, STONEY BANK ROAD, HOLMFIRTH HD7 2SL (01484 684605; Fax: 01484 689051). [🐾]
e-mail: maggiekaye@hotmail.com

ROSE COTTAGE & BARN, MRS ANNE KELLY, 1 ROBIN LANE, TROUTBECK, WINDERMERE LA23 1PF (015394 32780). 18th century cottage and barn sleeps 2/6. Beautiful views and walks from the door. Warm and cosy. Two good food pubs nearby. [🐾]
e-mail: skelly99@hotmail.com
website: www.osakelly.homepage.com

Ullswater

Lake stretching for 7 miles with attractive Lakeside walks.

MR & MRS BURNETT, (FELL VIEW HOLIDAYS), FELL VIEW, GLENRIDDING, PENRITH CA11 0PJ (Tel & Fax: 017684 82342; Evenings 01768 867420) Sleep 2-6. Comfortable, well-equipped cottage/apartments in quiet, beautiful surroundings, all with lovely views. Use of gardens/grounds. Ideal walking base. Up to ᵞᵞᵞ Highly Commended. [🐾 pw!]

Ulverston

Old town and port with cobbled streets and market square. Laurel and Hardy Museum worth a visit.

LONSDALE HOUSE HOTEL, 11 DALTON GATE, ULVERSTON LA12 7BD (01229 58259). Conveniently located in a bustling market town. Best Lakes Breaks from £99 per person for 3 nights.
website: www.lonsdalehousehotel.co.uk

Windermere

Famous resort on lake of same name, the largest in England. Magnificent scenery. Car ferry from Bowness, one mile distant. Kendal 9 miles.

THE MORTAL MAN HOTEL, TROUTBECK WINDERMERE LA23 1PL (015394 33193; Fax: 015394 31261). Set in beautiful Troutbeck Valley, good food and wine, real ales and a pefect location for walkers of all abilities. B&B from £40 pppn.. Dogs go free. ETC ★★, Silver Award for Quality. [🐾]
e–mail: the-mortalman@btinternet.com

Many attractive self-catering holiday homes in a variety of good location, all well equipped and managed by our caring staff. pets welcome. Pets welcome. For brochure, contact: LAKELOVERS, THE NEW TOFFEE LOFT, KENDAL ROAD, WINDERMERE LA23 3RA (015394 88855; Fax: 015394 88857). [Pets £15.00 per week.]
e–mail: bookings@lakelovers.co.uk
website: www.lakelovers.co.uk

HOLBECK GYHLL HOTEL & SPA, HOLBECK LANE, WINDERMERE LA23 1LU (between Windermere and Ambleside). 19th century Hunting Lodge in 7 acres with breathtaking Lake views. Luxury accommodation and finest quality food combined with a warmth of hospitality for a relaxing stay. Rooms opening on to lawns and grounds. Tennis and Spa facilities. Direct access to mountains and fields for walking. Cumbria Tourist Board Hotel of the Year 1998 & 2000, AA 3 Rosettes and 3 Red Stars, RAC ★★★ and Blue Ribbon. Tel: 015394 32375 for colour brochure. [Pets £3 per night]

BURNSIDE HOTEL, KENDAL ROAD, BOWNESS ON WINDERMERE LA23 3EP (015394 42211; Fax: 015394 43824). Set in mature gardens with views of Lake Windermere. Choose either luxurious hotel or self-catering cottages and apartments. Full leisure facilities. Pets welcome. Freephone: 0800 220688 [🐾 (Hotel), at charge in self-catering properties]
E–mail: stay@burnsidehotel.com
Website: www.burnsidehotel.com

APPLETHWAITE HOUSE, 1 UPPER OAK STREET, WINDERMERE LA23 2LB (015394 44689). A warm welcome, clean, comfortable rooms and a hearty breakfast awaits you in our family run guest house. Quiet yet convenient location. All rooms have colour TV and complimentary hot drinks. Non-smoking. B&B from £16 per person. Pets stay free. [🐾]

LOW SPRINGWOOD HOTEL, THORNBARROW ROAD, WINDERMERE LA23 2DF (015394 46383). Twiggy, Millie and Lottie (Boxers) would like to welcome you to their peaceful Hotel in its own secluded gardens. Lovely views of the Lakes and Fells. All rooms en suite with colour TV etc. Some four-posters. Brochure available. [🐾 pw!]

WATERMILL INN, INGS, NEAR STAVELEY, KENDAL LA8 9PY (01539 821309; Fax: 01539 822309). Misty & Shelly (Dogs) welcome you to the award-winning inn. 16 real ales. Cosy fires en suite rooms, excellent bar meals. Doggie water and biscuits served in the bar. Good doorstep dog walking. ETC ◆◆◆. [Pets £2 per night].
E-mail: all@watermill-inn.demon.co.uk
Website: www.watermill-inn.demon.co.uk

HILLTHWAITE HOUSE HOTEL, THORNBARROW ROAD, WINDERMERE LA23 2DF (015394 43636; Fax: 015394 88660). Set in three acres of secluded gardens. All bedrooms en suite with satellite TV; some with personal jacuzzi. Superb leisure facilities including indoor pool. Pets welcome. [🐾]

DENE CREST GUEST HOUSE, WOODLAND ROAD, WINDERMERE LA23 2AE (015394 44979). Comfortable, tastefully furnished Guesthouse. All rooms en suite, colour TV, central heating, tea/coffee making. Open all year. Short Break terms available. Pets Welcome. [pw!, Pets £3 per stay]

KIRKWOOD, PRINCE'S ROAD, WINDERMERE LA23 2DD (015394 43907). A warm friendly atmosphere with individual personal service. En suite rooms with colour TV and tea/coffee making facilities. Hosts pleased to help plan tours and walks. ◆◆◆◆ [🐾]
e–mail: neil.cox@kirkwood51.freeserve.co.uk
website: www.kirkwood51.freeserve.co.uk

Witherslack

Hamlet 3 miles north of Lindale.

THE OLD VICARAGE, WITHERSLACK LA11 6RS (015395 52381; Fax: 015395 52373) Beautiful late Georgian vicarage set in five acres of informal gardens and woodland, home to deer, red squirrels and an extraordinary variety of birds. The Old Vicarage is truly a place to unwind and forget for a while the stress of day-to-day life [Pets £3 per night]
e-mail: hotel@old-vic-demon.co.uk

The Kings
—*at*—
Ivy House

Georgian Grade II Listed
Guest House with many original
features including log fires, flagstone
floors and listed barns.
Spectacular views.
All rooms en suite with baths.
Ideally situated in Peak Park.
Superb home-cooked evening meals.
Lovely relaxed atmosphere.
Non-smoking. Dogs Welcome.
B&B £29. Dinner £15. Open all year.
Winter Breaks available.

Mervyn & Debbie King,
The Kings at Ivy House,
Biggin-by-Hartington, Newhaven,
Buxton, Derbyshire SK17 0DT
Tel: 01298 84709
E-mail: kings.ivyhouse@lineone.net

English
Tourism
Council
◆◆◆◆ & Silver Award

Please mention *Pets Welcome*
when enquiring about accommodation featured in these pages.

Ashbourne

Market town on River Henmore, close to its junction with River Dove. Several interesting old buildings. Birmingham 42 miles, Nottingham 29, Derby 13.

Biggin

Situated 8 miles north of Ashbourne

Buxton

Well-known spa and centre for the Peak District. Beautiful scenery and good sporting amenities. Leeds 50 miles, Matlock 20, Macclesfield 12.

THE CHARLES COTTON HOTEL, HARTINGTON, NEAR BUXTON SK17 0AL (01298 84229; Fax: 01298 84301). Small hotel, AA & RAC star rated. Good home cooking and hospitality. In heart of Derbyshire Dales. Special diets catered for. Ideal for relaxing, walking, cycling, hang-gliding. [🐕] website: www.charlescotton.co.uk

NICK & FIONA CLOUGH, THE DEVONSHIRE ARMS, PEAK FOREST, NEAR BUXTON SK17 8EJ (01298 23875) Situated in a village location in the heart of the Peak District. All rooms en suite with tea/coffee and colour TV. Meals served every day. Excellent walking area. ◆◆◆ [🐕]

MRS PATRICIA GREEN, 21 THE PUNCH BOWL, MANCHESTER ROAD, BUXTON SK17 6TA. (01298 27565; Mobile; 07970 045794). Comfortably furnished with log fire, storage heaters, coal logs & bed linen provided. Several country pubs nearby. Garden with patio area. Children and pets welcome. £130 - £200. [🐕]

MANIFOLD VIEW, TOP FARM, LONGNOR, BUXTON SK17 0OR (01298 83271). Barn conversion adjacent to the original farmhouse. Rural position in the Peak National Park. Many walks and rides from the cottage door. Brochure available, dogs welcome, ample parking. e-mail: darryl.d@virgin.net

PRIORY LEA HOLIDAY FLATS. Close to Poole's Cavern Country Park. Fully equipped. Sleep 2/6. Cleanliness assured. Terms from £80 - £210. Open all year. Short Breaks available. 2-3 Keys Commended. MRS GILL TAYLOR, 50 WHITE KNOWLE ROAD, BUXTON SK17 9NH (01298 23737). [pw! Pets £1 per night.]

WHEELDON TREES FARM, EARL STERNDALE, BUXTON SK17 0AA (Tel and Fax: 01298 83219). Sleep 2-6. Eighteenth century barn conversion offers seven cosy self-catering holiday cottages. Laundry, payphone and games room. ♛♛♛♛ Commended. [🐕]

BUXTON VIEW, 74 CORBAR ROAD, BUXTON SK17 6RJ (01298 79222). Attractive house very near moors and 10 minutes from town centre. En suite rooms. Bed and Breakfast from £20pppn; Evening Meals available. Pets very welcome. ETC /AA ◆◆◆◆.

Matlock

Inland resort and spa in Derwent Valley. Chesterfield 9 miles.

TUCKERS GUEST HOUSE, 48 DALE ROAD, MATLOCK DE4 3NB (01629 583018). A welcoming, pet loving home where you can feel totally relaxed. Wonderful scenery and walks in the Peak District. Cliffs, rivers, hills and trails. No charge for dogs (or their breakfast)! Spacious rooms. B&B from £19 per person. Non-smokers please. [🐕].

MRS G. PARKINSON, DIMPLE HOUSE, DIMPLE ROAD, MATLOCK DE4 3JX (01629 583228). 19th Century house close to Matlock. Large garden. Ideal for visiting Chatsworth and Peak Park. TV and teamaking in all rooms. B&B from £20. No smoking. ETC ◆◆◆◆. [🐕]

Peak District National Park

A green and unspoilt area at the southern end of the Pennines, covering 555 square miles.

SHEFFIELD/HATHERSAGE. Sleeps 4. Well equipped converted barn, fenced garden, in open countryside, ideal for Peak Park and Sheffield. ETC ♛♛♛♛ Highly Commended. For brochure phone 0114 2301949.

BIGGIN HALL, PEAK PARK (01298 84451). Close Dove Dale. 17th century hall sympathetically restored. Baths en suite, log fires, C/H comfort, warmth and quiet. Fresh home cooking. Beautiful uncrowded footpaths. Brochure on request.

SEA BIRDS

Sea edge, pretty Georgian cottage facing directly out to the open sea. **Sea Birds** is a spacious cottage with large lounge, colour TV, dining room with french windows onto garden, modern fitted kitchen, 3 double bedrooms, bathroom, second WC downstairs. Lawned garden at back with garden furniture overlooking the sea. Sea views from most rooms and the garden are magnificent; views of the open sea, boats entering the estuary, sunset, sea birds, own parking. Appledore is still a fishing village; fishing trips from the quay, restaurants by the water. Area has good cliff and coastal walks, stately homes, riding, swimming, golf, surfing, excellent beaches. Off peak heating. Winter prices from £95 weekly. Other cottages available.

Ring 01237 473801 for prices and vacancies *only* or send SAE for brochure to
P.S. BARNES, 140 Bay View Road, Northam, Bideford, Devon EX39 1BJ

APPLEDORE   OTTER COTTAGE

Traditional fisherman's cottage with panoramic estuary views, 50 yards to slipway. Garden. Totally equipped – two TVs and VCR; microwave, autowasher, etc. Also unique harbourside apartments and modern bungalow. Brochure:

B.H. SMITH, 26 MARKET STREET, APPLEDORE, DEVON EX39 1PP
Tel: 01237 476154/478206 (or our Agent: 01271 378907)

Modernised granite cottages and converted coach house on 150-acre working family farm nestled in the picturesque valley of Widecombe, surrounded by unspoilt woodland moors and granite tors. Half a mile from village with post office, general stores, inn with dining room, church and National Trust Information Centre. Excellent centre for touring Devon with a variety of places to visit and exploring Dartmoor by foot or on horseback. Accommodation is clean and well-equipped with colour TV, central heating, laundry room. Children welcome. Large gardens and courtyard for easy parking. Open all year, so take advantage of off-season reduced rates. Short Breaks also available. Two properties suitable for disabled visitors. Brochure available.

ↂↂↂↂ *Commended.*

Mrs Angela Bell
Wooder Manor
Widecombe in the Moor
Near Ashburton TQ13 7TR
Tel & Fax: (01364) 621391

Parkers Farm Holiday Park

Come and stay on a real 400-acre farm in South Devon
FARM COTTAGES AND CARAVANS TO LET
All very clean. Discount for couples. Also LEVEL TOURING SITE in terraces with 2 fully tiled toilet/shower blocks (no meters). Electric hook-ups. We overlook Dartmoor, 12 miles Torquay; central for touring Devon and Cornwall.   Terms from £90 Low Season to £380 High Season.

PETS WELCOME

Small shop, family bar and restaurant main season. Games room, laundry, pay phone, etc.
How to find us from Exeter: Take A38 to Plymouth. When you see the sign "26 miles Plymouth",
take the second left at Alston Cross signposted to Woodland and Denbury.
British Farm Tourist Award, RAC Recommended, AA ✓✓✓, 1999 Gold Award for quality and Service,
Silver David Bellamy Conservation Award, Practical Caravan 1998 - Top 100 Parks, West Country Tourist Board ★★★
HIGHER MEAD FARM, ASHBURTON, NEWTON ABBOT, DEVON TQ13 7LJ
Tel: (01364 652598) Fax: (01364 654004) e-mail: parkersfarm@btconnect.com website: www.parkersfarm.co.uk

---

FHG PUBLICATIONS LIMITED publish a large range of well-known accommodation guides. We will be happy to send you details or you can use the order form at the back of this book.

The Church House Inn
Holne, Near Ashburton,
Devon TQ13 7SJ
Tel: 01364 631208
Fax: 01364 631525

14th century Inn within the Dartmoor National Park. Standard and en suite rooms available. Bars and restaurant with good fresh food, real ales and fine wines. Dogs welcome FREE OF CHARGE. Great walks!

A warm welcome to our Traditional English house standing on its own in a quiet countryside setting with panoramic views across the Taw valley. Pretty cottage garden. AA ◆◆◆◆◆ confirms we offer something special in the way of B&B accommodation.

Three en suite rooms furnished with care, with good quality beds, easy chairs, bath/shower rooms with powerful thermostatic showers. Plenty of hot water. Tea fac., C/H, col. TV. Fridge for your own use, fresh milk. Relaxing lounge. Perfect North Devon touring base, 20 mins coast. Near RHS Rosemoor, Clovelly, Woolacombe, Lynmouth, Exmoor. No-smoking. En suite B&B £18-£25. Dinner available. Open all year.

Phone 01769 560034. Springfield-Garden, Atherington, Umberleigh, N. Devon EX37 9JA.
www.broadgdn.eurobell.co.uk

Elaine Goodwin, Lodfin Farm, Morebath, Bampton EX16 9DD Tel & Fax 01398 331400.

The calming ambience of this beautiful 17th century Devon farmhouse offers everything to relax and unwind. Lodfin Farm is situated on the edge of Exmoor National Park, one mile north of the historic floral town of Bampton and nestles in a secluded valley, of which five acres is a natural woodland habitat, with a stream and lake, for our guests to enjoy. Accommodation is spacious, comfortable and inviting with log fires and interesting artefacts. Three pretty bedrooms, one en suite, with tea making facilities and television. Hearty Aga cooked breakfast served in the inglenook dining room. Children and pets welcome. Sorry, no smoking. Bed and Breakfast from £19.50 per person.   **ETC** ◆◆◆◆

e-mail: lodfin.farm@eclipse.co.uk • website: www.lodfinfarm.com

---

MRS V.M. CHUGG   **VALLEY VIEW**   TEL: 01271 343458
Guineaford, Marwood, Near Barnstaple, Devon EX1 4EA
Friendly Bed and Breakfast accommodation in bungalow situated on 300-acre farm. Near Marwood Hill Gardens and Arlington Court. Colour television and video. Children most welcome, free babysitting. Evening Meal available if required. Bedtime drink at no extra charge. Open all year round. Dogs by arrangement.
Terms from £15.

"Easily the best choice of cottages in Devon...
...and comfortably the best value."

Contact us now for a free colour guide and unbiased recommendation service to the 500 best value cottages around Exmoor and Devon's unspoilt National Trust Coast.

North Devon Holiday Homes
19 Cross Street, Barnstaple EX31 1BD
Tel:(01271) 376322 (24 hrs) Fax:(01271) 346544
E-mail: info@northdevonholidays.co.uk
Website: www.northdevonholidays.co.uk

See also Colour Advertisement on page 17

YOUR PET STAYS FREE

Sandy Cove Hotel stands in 20 acres of cliff, coast and garden. The Hotel Restaurant overlooks the sea and cliffs with spectacular views of the bay. You will probably wonder how we can do it for the price when we offer a FIVE-COURSE MEAL including seafood platters with lobster, smoked salmon and steak. Every Saturday a Swedish Smorgasbord and Carvery carved by the Chef, and followed by dancing till late. Live entertainment weekly from Whitsun until September. All bedrooms have colour TV, telephone, teamaking and are en suite. The cocktail bar overlooks the bay and you have the use of the hotel's 80° heated indoor pool and recreation centre with sauna, sunbed, gym equipment and whirlpool, ALL FREE OF CHARGE.

Please return this advertisement to qualify for "Pets Stay Free" offer. Bargain Breaks and weekly rates available all year. Includes 5-course Evening Meal and coffee. Children— free accommodation. Please send for free brochure pack. Children under 8 years completely free, including meals.

Sandy Cove Hotel
Combe Martin Bay, Devon, EX34 9SR
Tel: (01271) 882243 & 882888
E-mail: rg14003483@aol.com

Indoor pool heated to 80°F with roll-back sides to enjoy the sun

ETC ★★★

See also Colour Advertisement on page 21

MIDSHIPS, Instow, Bideford

A comfortable old cottage, less than 50yds from the sandy, estuary beach. 'Midships' sleeps up to six, with gas central heating, colour TV, washing machine, dryer and fridge/freezer and a small walled courtyard with flower tubs at the back. The Tarka trail runs through Instow and there is cycling, sailing and walking, plus boat trips to Lundy Island, all nearby. The village has several good restaurants and pubs for meals out, as well as a small Post Office and village shop. The market towns of Bideford and Barnstaple are within easy reach for cinema and leisure centre etc. Mrs M. Baxter, Panorama, Millards Hill, Instow, Bideford EX39 4JS.

Tel: 01271 861146

Jenny and Barry Jones offer a warm welcome and a peaceful, relaxing time at their home set in seven acres. Distant views from the grounds to Bideford and beyond to Lundy and Hartland Point. En suite rooms have colour TV and complimentary tea and coffee. Generous farmhouse style cooking, catering for all diets. Licensed. Children welcome. Wood-burning stove in lounge. Open all year. Bed and Breakfast from £33. Set meal £16. Weekly terms and weekend breaks in winter. Self-catering available.

Credit Cards • No Smoking
Telephone for brochure

e-mail:barry@thepinesateastleigh.co.uk

The Pines
at Eastleigh

Hotel & Cottages
Eastleigh, Near Bideford,
North Devon EX39 4PA
Tel: 01271 860561
Fax: 01271 861248
ETC ◆◆◆◆

SILVER AWARD

LITTLE SWINCOMBE FARM CHALLACOMBE, NEAR BARNSTAPLE EX31 4TU

Pretty, airy stone cottage within working farm. Two bedrooms, sleeps four plus two. Kitchen/diner, large living room. Central heating fired by wood burner. Private garden. Children most welcome. Dog, horse by arrangement. Lovely situation on moor. Sea 15 minutes.

Tel: 01598 763506 • e–mail: nash@lineone.net

SNAPDOWN FARM CARAVANS
Chittlehamholt, Umberleigh, North Devon EX37 9PF (01769) 540708

12 ONLY – 6 berth CARAVANS with all facilities in beautiful, peaceful, unspoilt country setting. Down quiet lane on farm, well away from busy roads. Each with outside seats and picnic table. Field and woodland walks, abundant wildlife, help feed and milk the goats. Easy reach sea and moors. Well behaved pets welcome.

£90 to £240 inc. gas and electricity in caravans. Illustrated brochure available. (Discount for couples early/late season.)

Northcott Barton Farm Cottage   ETC★★★

Beautifully equipped, spotlessly clean three bedroom cottage with large enclosed garden. A walker's and country lover's ideal: for a couple seeking peace and quiet or a family holiday. Very special rates for low season holidays, couples and short breaks. Near golf, riding, Tarka trail and R.H.S. Rosemoor. Character, comfort, beams, log fire, *"Perfick"*. Pets Welcome, no charge.

For availability please contact Sandra Gay, Northcott Barton, Ashreigney, Chulmleigh, Devon. Tel/Fax: 01769 520259

Manleigh Holiday Park

e-mail: info@manleighpark.co.uk

Graded
★★★★

Combe Martin Devon

Chalets and caravans on our quiet, private site set in beautiful countryside, near village, beaches, rocky coves and Exmoor. Also Bungalow available this year. No Club or Disco. Swimming Pool. Laundry.

SCENIC DOG WALK

Colour brochure: Mr M. J. Hughes
www.manleighpark.co.uk

(01271) 883353

COOMBE HOUSE COUNTRY HOTEL
Coleford, Crediton, Devon EX17 5BY   Tel: 01363 84487 Fax: 01363 84722

Peace and tranquillity pervade this elegant Georgian manor house nestling in 5 acres of a hidden valley at the rural heart of Devon, midway between Dartmoor and Exmoor, equidistant from North and South Coasts and yet only 15 minutes by car from the Cathedral city of Exeter.

AA★★★   RAC★★★
ETC★★★ *AA* 2 Rosettes

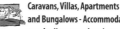

The Lodge, Ermington

Pretty detached thatched cottage. Country near village. Overlooking filelds. Area of
outstanding natural beauty. Three miles coast. Comfortably furnished.
Well equipped. Barbecue. Two bedrooms, sleeps four.

**Enquiries: Barters Old Farmhouse, North Whilborough, Newton Abbot TQ12 5LP Tel: 01803
873213; Fax: 01803 875096 E-mail: holcot@eclipse.co.uk**

The Lord Haldon Country House Hotel

Dunchideock, Nr Exeter, Devon EX6 7YF Tel: 01392 832483 Fax: 01392 833765
Extensive gardens amid miles of rolling Devon countryside.

★★★ AA/ETC   E-mail: lordhaldon@eclipse.co.uk

See also Colour Advertisement on page 20

TEIGN VALLEY FOREST

HALDON LODGE FARM, KENNFORD
NEAR EXETER, DEVON EX6 7YG Tel: 01392 832312

Delightful modern 34ft Caravan only five miles from Exeter and short distance
Dawlish, Teignmouth and Torbay, from £70 per week. Lounge (TV), two bedrooms,
kitchen, bathroom (H&C) and toilet. *Attractive private grounds in peaceful
surroundings. Famous village inns, two beautiful Coarse Fishing Lakes and farm
shop.* Small private camping site. Pony trekking available. Special welcome to less
experienced riders.

Pets Welcome ● Open all year ● Enquiries to D. L. Salter

Stag Hunters Hotel

Family-run village inn with frontage to the East Lyn river,
set in four acres of garden and paddock. Accommodation
available in 12 en suite bedrooms with central heating, TV
and tea/coffee making facilities. Meals are available in the
bar and restaurant using fresh local produce; vegetarian
dishes served. This cosy hotel features log fires, fine
wines and traditional ales. Fishing, shooting and riding
available; own stables. Ample car parking. Open all year.
Terms on request.

Brendon, Exmoor EX35 6PS

Tel: 01598 741222
Fax: 01598 741352

FHG

PLEASE MENTION THIS GUIDE WHEN YOU WRITE

OR PHONE TO ENQUIRE ABOUT ACCOMMODATION

IF YOU ARE WRITING, A STAMPED, ADDRESSED

ENVELOPE IS ALWAYS APPRECIATED

*PLEASE MENTION THIS GUIDE WHEN YOU WRITE
OR PHONE TO ENQUIRE ABOUT ACCOMMODATION.
IF YOU ARE WRITING, A STAMPED,
ADDRESSED ENVELOPE IS ALWAYS APPRECIATED.*

LONG CROSS HOUSE   Tel: 01409 231219

BLACK TORRINGTON NEAR HOLSWORTHY EX21 5QG

Situated at the edge of the delightfull village of Black Torrington, midway between the market towns of Holsworthy and Hatherleigh in rural North Devon. Rooms are en suite with central heating and have tea/coffee making facilities and TV. Children, dogs and horses welcome. Bed and Breakfast from £17.50 per person.

RaC SELECTED SITE

Hedley Wood Caravan & Camping Park

AA

Bridgerule (Near Bude), Holsworthy, Devon EX22 7ED Tel: 01288 381404 • Fax: 01288 381644

16 acre woodland family-run site with outstanding views, where you can enjoy a totally relaxing holiday with a laid-back atmosphere, sheltered and open camping areas. Just 10 minutes' drive from the beaches, golf courses, riding stables and shops. On site facilities include: Children's Adventure Areas, Bar, Clubroom, Shop, Laundry, Meals and all amenities. Free Hot Showers/Water. Clay pigeon shoot. Static caravans for hire. Caravan storage available. Nice dogs/pets are very welcome. Daily kennelling facility. Dog walks/nature trail.

Visit our website: www.hedleywood.co.uk or write or phone for comprehensive brochure

See also Colour Advertisement on page 16

LISTED SITE

THE CREST AA ◆◆◆ *Guest Accommodation*

A modern chalet style house nestling in the picturesque Umborne Valley; an area of outstanding natural beauty. The guest wing affords complete privacy with large modern en suite bedroom. Double glazed. Lying in two-and-a-half acres of garden. PETS WELCOME.

WILMINGTON, NEAR. HONITON. EX14 9JU - TELEPHONE: 01404 831 419
MOBILE: 07967 894670

The Belfry Country Hotel

Yarcombe, Near Honiton, Devon EX14 9BD

Victorian village school converted to a small luxury Hotel. All rooms en suite with lovely views. Licensed restaurant, fine wines and superb food. Ideal base for touring, walking, gardens, antiques.

Phone Brian & Jean Peirce 01404 861234 or Fax 01404 861579 for brochure and tariff. Non-Smoking Hotel.

MINOTEL
Great Britain

AA ★★ 76%

j

LOWER LUXTON FARM
Upottery, Honiton EX14 9PB
Tel & Fax: 01823 601269

If you are looking for a quiet, peaceful and relaxing holiday, come to Lower Luxton Farm, where a warm and friendly welcome awaits you. Situated in an Area of Outstanding Natural Beauty in the centre of the Blackdown Hills, overlooking the Otter Valley. Carp, tench and rudd fishing in our farm pond. Olde worlde farmhouse with inglenook and beams. Private or en suite rooms with tea/coffee making and TV. Good home cooking assured and plenty of it. Open all year. SAE or telephone Mrs Elizabeth Tucker for details.

Bed and Breakfast from £16 per night. Weekly Bed and Breakfast and six Evening Dinners from £130 per week.

FHG PUBLICATIONS LIMITED publish a large range of well-known accommodation guides. We will be happy to send you details or you can use the order form at the back of this book.

Gable Lodge
Lee Road, Lynton EX35 6BS   Tel: 01598 752367

We are sure you will enjoy your stay at our Victorian Grade II Listed building in England's "Little Switzerland". At Gable Lodge we offer a friendly and homely atmosphere with a good hearty breakfast to set you up for the day. An ideal spot for a relaxing holiday. Private car park and garden. Pets welcome. Non-smoking. Please ring for brochure.

THE CROWN Market Street, Lynton EX35 6AG Tel: 01598 752253 • Fax: 01598 753311

The Crown offers easy access to the dramatic Exmoor countryside and coastline, and is ideally placed for walking, driving, bird-watching, fishing, horse riding or just relaxing. Rooms are all en suite, with remote-control TV, tea/coffee making facilities, central heating and direct-dial telephones. Four-poster bedrooms and suites available. For relaxation, there is a billiard lounge and a library. The hotel diningroom offers a five-course table d'hôte menu; an à la carte menu is available in the Whip and Collar Bar. AA ★★   Website: www.thecrown-lynton.co.uk

See also Colour Advertisement on page 24

Brendon House Exmoor

ETC ◆◆◆

A charming 18th century Country House, steeped in history and character.

Formerly a farmhouse, Brendon House nestles in quiet hidden wooded valley beneath the rolling moors with a salmon river running at the foot of pretty gardens, a truly romantic setting. There are superb walks and scenery in every direction. Enjoy Devonshire home cooking, produce is fresh, many of the vegetables served are organically grown in the garden. Licensed with selection of fine wines from across the world. Packed lunches. Log fires. Non-smoking. All bedrooms have stunning Exmoor views, private bathrooms, TV and tea/coffee. Private parking. Perfectly situated for walking, fishing, horse riding or just unwind and enjoy Exmoor. Salmon and Trout permits sold. Pets welcome free of charge, by arrangement.

Non-smoking; Children over 12 years welcome
B & B per night from £22 – £26; Dinner per person from £15

Please ring David or Laura Hillier for our colour brochure
Brendon House, Brendon, Lynton EX35 6PS
Telephone: 01598 741206
Website: www.brendonvalley.co.uk/Brendon_House.htm

PLEASE MENTION THIS GUIDE WHEN YOU WRITE

OR PHONE TO ENQUIRE ABOUT ACCOMMODATION

IF YOU ARE WRITING, A STAMPED, ADDRESSED

ENVELOPE IS ALWAYS APPRECIATED

Please mention *Pets Welcome*
when enquiring about accommodation featured in these pages.

Seamark

Six 2/3 bedroom Cottages set in two acres of gardens. Indoor swimming pool. Sauna. Games room. Beach. Golf and Windsurfing close by

Brochure on request

Thurlestone Sands, Near Salcombe, Devon TQ7 3JY (01548) 561300

Sand Pebbles Hotel

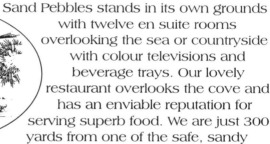

Sand Pebbles stands in its own grounds with twelve en suite rooms overlooking the sea or countryside with colour televisions and beverage trays. Our lovely restaurant overlooks the cove and has an enviable reputation for serving superb food. We are just 300 yards from one of the safe, sandy beaches that Hope Cove is renowned for, and the cliff top walks which give some of the most spectacular views in the south west. Hope Cove has a timeless quality all of its own and is one of England's most delightful places to retreat for a short break or a long holiday. There's nowhere else quiet like it. Please call June or Charles for a brochure.

Sand Pebbles Hotel & Restaurant, Hope Cove, Devon TQ7 3HF Tel: 01548 561673 Website: www.webmachine.co.uk/sandpebbles

See also Colour Advertisement on page 22

GRAFTON TOWERS HOTEL
Moult Road, Salcombe, South Devon TQ8 8LG
Tel: 01548 842882 / Fax: 01548 842857
Small luxury hotel with en suite rooms overlooking magnificent coastline. Convenient for ferry, town and spectacular walks. Home-cooked food a speciality.

FHG PUBLICATIONS
FHG publish a large range of well-known accommodation guides. We will be happy to send you details or you can use the order form at the back of this book.

See also Colour Advertisement on page 18

Please mention *Pets Welcome*
when enquiring about accommodation featured in these pages.

Sunnymeade Country Hotel

West Down, Near Woolacombe, North Devon EX34 8NT
01271 863668
website: www. sunnymeade.co.uk

Small, friendly, comfortable country hotel with our own large
enclosed garden set in beautiful countryside.

** A few minutes away from Ilfracombe, Exmoor and Woolacombe's Blue Flag
Beach, (where dogs are allowed).*
** Award winning home cooked traditional English food, using fresh local
produce.*
** Special diets can be accommodated, Vegetarian choice always available
Licenced Bar
** 8 en suite rooms 2 on the ground floor. Open all year including Christmas.
Pets Welcome-dogs are free*
* Lots of lovely walks accessible right from the door.

Pebbles Hotel and Restaurant

Family-run Hotel set in National Trust land overlooking the
sea and beaches. Glorious coastal walks direct from Hotel.
All 11 bedrooms en suite, with TV and tea/coffee making
facilities. Renowned for our cuisine, we offer table d'hôte
and full à la carte menus. £65.00 per person for Weekend
Breaks; £90.00 per person for 3-night Midweek Breaks,
Dinner, Bed and Breakfast. Write or phone for colour
brochure.

COMBESGATE BEACH, WOOLACOMBE   **Website: www.pebbleshotel.com**
NORTH DEVON EX34 7EA (01271) 870426   ETC ★

CROSSWAYS HOTEL

RAC ★ *Seafront, Woolacombe EX34 7DJ Tel/Fax: 01271 870395* AA ★

Homely, family-run, licensed Hotel surrounded by National Trust land

- Bathing and Surfing from Hotel
- Easily accessible to Exmoor
- Varied choice of bar snacks
- Centrally heated
- Free car parking

- Colour TV, tea/coffee-making facilities in rooms
- Well placed for Golf, Walks, Horse-Riding
- Menu choice for Breakfast, Evening Meal
- En suite facilities
- Children's menu

ETC ★   *CHILDREN HALF PRICE OR FREE*   *Silver* SILVER AWARD

A warm and friendly hotel where we do all we can to ensure a happy holiday

WEST COUNTRY COTTAGES (01626 333679). Hotels, Guesthouses, Bed and Breakfasts, Caravan and Camping. From Lands End to the New Forest. Free colour brochure. website: www.westcountrycottages.co.uk

RECOMMENDED COTTAGE HOLIDAYS. Selected cottages throught Devon, Southern England, Cotswolds and East Anglia. Low prices; pets welcome. For free brochure telephone 08700 718 718 website: www.recommended-cottages.co.uk

POWELLS COTTAGE HOLIDAYS, HIGH STREET, SAUNDERSFOOT, PEMBROKESHIRE SA69 9EJ. Many of our top quality holiday properties accept pets. Cottages in Devon, Cornwall, Cotswolds, Pembrokeshire and Heart of England. For colour brochure FREEPHONE 0800 378771 (24 hours).

HOLIDAY HOMES & COTTAGES S.W, 365A TORQUAY ROAD, PAIGNTON TQ3 2BT (01803 663650; Fax: 01803 664037). Hundreds of Self-Catering Holiday Cottages, Houses, Bungalows, Apartments, Chalets and Caravans in Devon and Cornwall. Please write or phone for free colour brochure. [Pets £15 per week]
e–mail: holcotts@aol.com
website: www.swcottages.co.uk

WELCOME COTTAGE HOLIDAYS. Quality Cottages in wonderful locations at welcoming low prices. Pets, linen and fuel mostly included. PHONE FOR FREE 2001 FULL COLOUR BROCHURE 01756 702203.

TOAD HALL COTTAGES. 100 outstanding waterside and rural properties in truly beautiful locations in Devon. Call for our highly acclaimed brochure. Video also available. Tel: 01548 853089.
website: www.toadhallcottages.com

A wonderful variety of over 450 cottages, houses and apartments all over the West Country, ideal for self catering holidays. Many accept pets. Free colour brochure from HELPFUL HOLIDAYS, COOMBE 49, CHAGFORD, DEVON TQ13 8DF (01647 433593 24hrs).

CLASSIC COTTAGES, HELSTON, CORNWALL TR13 8NA (01326 565555). Choose your cottage from 400 of the finest coastal and country cottages throughout the West Country. Many pets welcome.

SWEETCOMBE COTTAGE HOLIDAYS, ROSEMARY COTTAGE, WESTON, NEAR SIDMOUTH EX10 0PH (01395 512130; Fax: 01395 515680). Selection of Cottages, Farmhouses and Flats in Sidmouth and East Devon, all personally selected and very well-equipped. Gardens. Pets welcome. Please ask for our colour brochure. [🐴]
e–mail: enquiries@sweetcombe-ch.co.uk
website: www.sweetcombe-ch.co.uk

Appledore

Unspoilt resort and small port on estuaries of Taw and Torridge. Sandy beach, good bathing. Bideford 3 miles.

SEA BIRDS, pretty Georgian cottage facing directly out to the open sea. Spacious cottage with large lounge, colour TV, dining room, modern fitted kitchen and 3 double bedrooms, own parking. Other cottages available. SAE to P.S. BARNES, 140 BAY VIEW ROAD, NORTHAM, BIDEFORD EX39 1BJ (01237 473801). [pw] Dog £10 per week.]

OTTER COTTAGE. Traditional fisherman's cottage. Totally equipped – 2 TVs, VCR, microwave, autowasher etc. Also unique harbourside apartments and bungalow. Brochure from B.H. SMITH, 26 MARKET STREET, APPLEDORE EX39 1PR. Tel: 01237 476154/478206, (or our Agent: 01271 378907). [Pets £8 per week.]

SYMBOLS
🐴   Indicates that pets are welcome free of charge.
£   Indicates that a charge is made for pets: nightly or weekly.
pw!   Shows some special provision for pets; exercise facility, feeding or accommodation arrangement.
⌂   Indicates separate pets accommodation.

Ashburton

Delightful little town on southern fringe of Dartmoor. Centrally placed for touring and the Torbay resorts. Plymouth 24 miles, Exeter 20, Kingsbridge 20, Tavistock 20, Teignmouth 14, Torquay 14, Totnes 8, Newton Abbot 7.

MRS A. BELL, WOODER MANOR, WIDECOMBE IN THE MOOR, NEAR ASHBURTON TQ13 7TR (Tel & Fax: 01364 621391). Cottages on family farm. Surrounded by unspoilt woodland and moors. Clean and well equipped, colour TV, central heating, laundry room. Two properties suitable for disabled visitors. Colour brochure available. ♔♔♔♔ Commended. [pw! £15 per week for first dog; £10 per week for others. ◻]

PARKERS FARM HOLIDAY PARK, HIGHER MEAD FARM, ASHBURTON, NEWTON ABBOT TQ13 7LJ (01364 652598 Fax: 01364 654004). Farm Cottages and Caravans to let, also level touring site with two toilet/shower blocks and electric hook-ups. Central for touring; 12 miles Torquay. WCTB ★★★ [pw!]
e-mail: parkersfarm@btconnect.com
website: www.parkersfarm.co.uk

THE CHURCH HOUSE INN, HOLNE, NEAR ASHBURTON TQ13 7SJ (01364 631208). 14th Century inn within Dartmoor National Park. En suite rooms available. Bars and restaurant; real ales. Great walks. [🐾]

Atherington

Village 7 miles south of Barnstaple.

GILLIAN AND ROBERT SWANN, SPRINGFIELD GARDEN, ATHERINGTON, UMBERLEIGH, NORTH DEVON EX37 9JA (Tel & Fax: 560034). A substantial traditional English house on its own in a quiet countryside setting. Homely, clean, comfortable and friendly, en suite, B&B. Traditional English home cooking. B&B £18–£25 pppn.
e–mail: broadgdn@eurobell.co.uk
website: broadgdn.eurobell.co.uk

Bampton

Market town 6 miles north of Tiverton.

MRS E. GOODWIN, LODFIN FARM, MOREBATH, BAMPTON EX16 9DD (Tel & Fax: 01398 331400). Three pretty bedrooms, one en suite, with tea making facilities and TV. Hearty Aga cooked breakfast served in the inglenook dining room. Children and pets welcome. Sorry, no smoking. Bed and Breakfast from £19.50 per person. ETC ◆◆◆. [Pets £1.50 per night]
e-mail: lodfin.farm@eclipse.co.uk
website: www.lodfinfarm.com

Barnstaple

The largest town in Devon, once an important centre for the wool trade, now a lively shopping centre with thrice weekly market, modern leisure centre, etc.

MRS V.M. CHUGG, VALLEY VIEW, MARWOOD, BARNSTAPLE EX31 4EA (01271 343458). Bungalow on 300 acre farm. Bed and Breakfast accommodation. Near Marwood Hill Gardens and Arlington Court. Children most welcome, free baby-sitting. Dogs by arrangement. Terms from £15. [pw!]

NORTH DEVON HOLIDAY HOMES, 19 CROSS STREET, BARNSTAPLE EX31 1BD (01271 376322; Fax: 01271 346544). Free colour guide to the 500 best value cottages around Exmoor and Devon's National Trust Coast. [Pets £10 per week.]
e-mail: info@northdevonholidays.co.uk
website: www.northdevonholidays.co.uk

MR & MRS JOHN BLACKMORE, HILLCREST FARM, CENTERY LANE, BITTADON, BARSTAPLE, NORTH DEVON EX31 4HN (01271 863537). Comfortable, fully equipped two bedroom cottage-style accommodation. Situated on a quiet working farm. Sleeps 5/6. Close to both beach and Exmoor. Pets welcome. Open all year. Weekly tariff from £100 to £225.

Berrynarbor

This peaceful village overlooking the beautiful Sterridge valley has a 17th century pub and even older church, and is half-a-mile from the coast road between Combe Martin and Ilfracombe.

SANDY COVE HOTEL, BERRYNARBOR EX34 9SR (01271 882243 or 882888). Hotel set amidst acres of gardens and woods. Heated swimming pool. Children and pets welcome. A la carte restaurant. All rooms en suite with colour TV, tea-making. Free colour brochure on application. [🐾 One dog] e–mail: rg14003483@aol.com

Bideford

Neat port and resort on River Torridge. Attractive, many-arched stone bridge, wooded hills. Boat trips from quay. The sea is 3 miles distant at Westward Ho! Exeter 43 miles, Launceston 32, Bude 26, Ilfracombe 21, Barnstaple 9, Torrington 7.

MIDSHIPS, INSTOW, BIDEFORD (01271 861146). A comfortable old cottage, less than 50yds from the sandy, estuary beach. 'Midships' sleeps up to six, with gas central heating, colour tv, washing machine, dryer and fridge/freezer with a small walled courtyard. The market towns of Bideford and Barnstaple are within easy reach for cinema and leisure centre. Mrs M. Baxter, Panorama, Millards Hill, Instow, Bideford EX39 4JS.

JENNY AND BARRY JONES, THE PINES AT EASTLEIGH, NEAR BIDEFORD EX39 4PA (01271 860561; Fax: 01271 861248). A warm welcome and a peaceful relaxing time. En suite rooms. Generous farmhouse style cooking. Open all year. Licensed. Children welcome. B&B from £33. No smoking. ETC ◆◆◆◆ Silver Award. [Pets £2 per night, £10 per week] e–mail: barry@thepinesateastleigh.co.uk

Bigbury on Sea

A scattered village overlooking superb coastal scenery and wide expanses of sand.

PAT CHADWICK, "MARINERS", RINGMORE DRIVE, BIGBURY-ON-SEA, KINGSBRIDGE TQ7 4AU (01548 810454). Two large flats with extensive sea views. Sandy beaches within yards. Golf nearby. Dogs welcome free.[🐾]. e–mail: chad.29upper@virgin.net

MR SCARTERFIELD, HENLEY HOTEL, FOLLY HILL, BIGBURY-ON-SEA TQ7 4AR (01548 810240). Edwardian cottage-style hotel, spectacular sea views. Near good beach, dog walking. En suite rooms with telephone, tea making, TV etc. Home cooking. No smoking establishment. Licensed. ETC ★★ HOTEL and SILVER AWARD. AA ★★. [Pets £2.00 per night.]

MRS J. TUCKER, MOUNT FOLLY FARM, BIGBURY-ON-SEA, KINGSBRIDGE TQ7 4AR (01548 810267). Cliff top position, with outstanding views of Bigbury Bay. Spacious, self catering wing of farmhouse, attractively furnished. Farm adjoins golf course and River Avon. Lovely coastal walks, ideal centre for South Hams and Dartmoor. No smoking. Always a warm welcome, pets too!

Bovey Tracey

Little town nestling on southern fringe of Dartmoor. Fine scenery including Haytor Rocks (4 miles) and Becky Falls (3½ miles). Exeter 14 miles, Torquay 13, Newton Abbot 6, Chudleigh 4.

BLENHEIM COUNTRY HOUSE HOTEL, BOVEY TRACEY TQ13 9DH (01626 832422). Family Hotel on edge of Dartmoor National Park. RSPCA member. Open all year. All pets free. [🐾] [pw!]

Bradworthy

Village to the north of Holdsworthy. Well placed for North Devon and North Cornish coasts.

PETER & LESLEY LEWIN, LAKE HOUSE COTTAGES AND B&B (01409 241962). Three well equipped cottages sleeping two to six. Quiet rural position; one acre gardens and tennis court. Half-a-mile from village shops and pub. Spectacular coast eight miles. Also two lovely en suite B&B rooms, all facilities, from £20. ETC ★★★. [🐾] e–mail: lakevilla@bradworthy.co.uk

Bratton Fleming

Village 6 miles north-east of Barnstaple.

MRS A. DOUGLAS, FRIENDSHIP FARM, BRATTON FLEMING, BARNSTAPLE, EX31 4SQ (01598 763291 evenings). Bungalow (sleeps six plus cot) quietly situated in its own garden, surrounded by fields. 12 miles from Barnstaple and Ilfracombe, within easy reach of the beaches of Woolacombe and Combe Martin, with Exmoor literally on the doorstep. Linen supplied, lounge with TV, well equipped kitchen/dining room. Weekly terms, low season from £100, high season £250.

Brixham

Lively resort and fishing port, with quaint houses and narrow winding streets. Ample opportunities for fishing and boat trips.

ST. MARY'S BAY. A very special place! Award winning Holiday Park in an area of outstanding natural beauty. Close to Brixham on the English Riviera, overlooking its own superb, sandy beach. ◆◆◆◆. Telephone WESTSTAR HOLIDAY PARKS on 01392 447447 for further details.

DEVONCOURT HOLIDAY FLATS, BERRYHEAD ROAD, BRIXHAM TQ5 9AB (01803 853748 or 07050 338889 after office hours). 24 self-contained flats with private balcony, colour television, heating, private car park, all-electric kitchenette, separate bathroom and toilet. Open all year. [Pets £10 per week.]
e-mail: devoncourt@devoncoast.com

THE SMUGGLERS HAUNT HOTEL, CHURCH HILL, BRIXHAM TQ5 8HH (01803 853050; Fax: 01803 858738). Friendly 300-year-old hotel in the centre of old Brixham. Quality bar and à la carte menus. En suite rooms. Children and pets welcome. From £24 pppn B&B. AA ★. [🐾]
e-mail: enquiries@smugglershaunt-hotel-devon.co.uk
website: smugglershaunt-hotel-devon.co.uk

BRIXHAM HOLIDAY PARK, FISHCOMBE COVE, BRIXHAM (01803 853324). Situated on coastal path. Choice of one and two-bedroomed chalets. Indoor heated pool, free club membership, comfortable bar offering meals and takeaway service, launderette. 150 yards from beach with lovely walks through woods beyond. [Pets £25 per week]

Chagford

Unspoilt little town on the edge of Dartmoor in an area rich in prehistoric remains. Noted for 16th century bridge and Tudor and Georgian houses

I. SATOW, WEEK BROOK, CHAGFORD TQ13 8JQ (01647 433345). Away from the tumult of the world. One mile charming small Dartmoor town. Lovely ancient thatched house. Pets welcome. Bed and Breakfast £11.00 to £15.00.

Challacombe

Village west of Simonsbath on the edge of Exmoor.

MRS L. NASH, LITTLE SWINCOMBE FARM, CHALLACOMBE, NEAR BARNSTAPLE EX31 4TU (01598 763506). Exmoor – Pretty, airy stone cottage within working farm. Two bedrooms, sleeps four plus two. Kitchen/diner, large living room. Central Heating fired by wood burner. Private garden. Children most welcome. Dog, horse by arrangement. Lovely situation on moor. Sea 15 minutes.
e–mail: nash@lineone.net

PLEASE MENTION THIS GUIDE WHEN YOU WRITE
OR PHONE TO ENQUIRE ABOUT ACCOMMODATION.
IF YOU ARE WRITING, A STAMPED,
ADDRESSED ENVELOPE IS ALWAYS APPRECIATED.

Chittlehamholt

Standing in beautiful countryside in the Taw Valley and just off the B3227. Barstaple 9 miles, South Molton 5.

SNAPDOWN FARM CARAVANS, CHITTLEHAMHOLT, UMBERLEIGH, NORTH DEVON EX37 9PF (01769 540708). 12 only – 6 berth caravans with flush toilets, showers, colour TV, fridges, cookers and fires. Laundry room. Picnic tables. Unspoilt countryside. Field and woodland walks. Terms £90 to £240 inc. gas and electricity in caravans. [Pets £8.75 per week.]

Chulmleigh

Mid-Devon village set in lovely countryside, just off A377 Exeter to Barnstaple road. Exeter 23 miles, Tiverton 19, Barnstaple 18.

SANDRA GAY, NORTHCOTT BARTON FARM COTTAGE, NORTHCOTT BARTON, ASHREIGNEY, CHULMLEIGH EX18 7PR (Tel/Fax: 01769 520259). Three bedroom character cottage, large enclosed garden, log fire. Special rates low season, couples and short breaks. Near golf, riding, Tarka trail and R.H.S. Rosemoor. ETC ★★★ [🐕]

THE TOWERS HOTEL, CHAMBERCOMBE PARK, ILFRACOMBE EX34 9QN (Tel: 01271 862809; Fax: 01271 897442).Enjoy a relaxed stay with your dog at The Towers set in its own grounds with its own car park. Mostly en suite rooms, well-appointed, extras. Resident's lounge/bar. Non-smoking. ETC ◆◆◆.
e-mail: info@thetowers.co.uk

VIV & ALAN JONES, BANK HOUSE, FORE STREET, CHULMLEIGH EX18 7BR (Tel: 01769 580005; Fax: 01769 580977). B&B . Comfortable airy accommodation in traditional 17th century house. Walking, fishing, riding, golf. Twixt Exmoor and Dartmoor. Colour TV, coffee/tea, central heating, en suite private facilities. [🐕]
e-mail: vivyjones@hotmail.com

Combe Martin

Coastal village with harbour set in sandy bay. Good cliff and rock scenery. Of interest is the Church and "Pack of Cards" Inn. Barnstaple 14 miles, Lynton 12, Ilfracombe 6.

MR M. J. HUGHES, MANLEIGH HOLIDAY PARK, RECTORY ROAD, COMBE MARTIN EX34 0NS (01271 883353). Holiday Chalets, accommodate 4/6 persons. In 6 acres. Free use of swimming pool. Dogs welcome provided they are kept under control. Also 12 Caravans to let. Graded ★★★★. [Pets £16 per week. pw!]
e-mail: info@manleighpark.co.uk
website: www.manleighpark.co.uk

Crediton

Ancient small town. Chapter house with Cromwellian relics. Cidermaking. Cathedral-type church. 7 miles from Exeter.

COOMBE HOUSE COUNTRY HOTEL, COLEFORD, CREDITON EX17 5BY (01363 84487; Fax: 01363 84722). Peaceful and tranquil elegant Georgian manor house nestling in 5 acres of a hidden valley at the rural heart of Devon. AA 2 Rosettes, ETC/RAC/AA ★★★. [🐕]
e-mail: relax@coombehouse.com

Croyde Bay

Charming village nestling in a sheltered combe behind Croyde Bay.

MRS JENNIFER PENNY, CROYDE BAY HOUSE HOTEL, CROYDE BAY, NORTH DEVON EX33 1PA (01271 890270). Small hotel beside beach at Croyde Bay. All rooms en suite with tea/coffee making facilities. Good food and friendly atmosphere. AA ◆◆◆◆. [🐕]

Please mention *Pets Welcome*
when enquiring about accommodation featured in these pages.

Cullompton

Small market town off the main A38 Taunton - Exeter road. Good touring centre. Noted for apple orchards which supply the local cider industry. Taunton 19 miles, Exeter 13, Honiton 11, Tiverton 9.

FOREST GLADE HOLIDAY PARK (PW), KENTISBEARE, CULLOMPTON EX15 2DT (01404 841381; Fax: 01404 841593). Country estate with deluxe 2/4/6 berth caravans. All superbly equipped. Many amenities on site. Mother and Baby Room. Campers and tourers welcome. SAE for colour brochure. ETC ★★★★ [Pets 50p/£1 per night, pw!]
e–mail: forestglade@cwcom.net;
website: www.forestglade.mcmail.com

MRS B. HILL, SUNNYSIDE FARM, BUTTERLEIGH, NEAR CULLOMPTON, TIVERTON EX15 1PP (01884 855322). 130-acre mixed farm, central for touring Dartmoor and Exmoor. En suite bedrooms with tea/coffee facilities. Bed and Breakfast; Evening Meal optional. Children welcome. [🐾]

MRS M. CHUMBLEY, OBURNFORD FARM, CULLOMPTON EX15 1LZ (Tel & Fax: 01884 32292). Listed Georgian Farmhouse set in large gardens. Ideal National Trust, coasts, moors and M5 (J28). Bed and Breakfast with Evening meals with "Free Wine" £28 per night. Pets most welcome.

Dartmoor

365 square miles of National Park with spectacular unspoiled scenery, fringed by picturesque villages.

THE ROSEMONT GUEST HOUSE, GREENBANK TERRACE, YELVERTON PL20 6DR (01822 852175). Large Victorian house overlooking the green at Yelverton, just yards from lovely open moorland. All rooms en suite, all with TV and tea/coffee making facilities. B&B from £20.00. ETC ◆◆◆[🐾]
e–mail: b&b@rosemontgh.fsnet.co.uk

S. COURTNEY, POLTIMORE, RAMSLEY, SOUTH ZEAL EX20 2PD (01837 840209). Dartmoor National Park. Self catering/Bed & Breakfast accommodation consisting of summer chalet, granite barn conversion. Also pretty thatched guest house. All with direct access to the Moor. Write or phone for details. [1st dog free, others £7.50 per week]

MRS J. COLTON, PEEK HILL FARM, DOUSLAND, YELVERTON PL20 6PD (Tel/Fax: 01822 854808). Good breakfast and comfy beds; TV, kettle in rooms. Views from Dartmoor to Bodmin. Picnics can be provided. Good walking; cycle hire. Pleasant stay guaranteed. Open all year except Christmas. 2 Crowns Commended. [🐾]

SUE BOOTY, "ROGUES ROOST", POUNDSGATE, NEWTON ABBOT TQ13 7PS (01364 631223). Dartmoor National Park. Self-catering holiday accommodation, any number from 2 to 7. Excellent walking. Stunning Countryside. Off beaten track. [🐾]

PRINCE HALL HOTEL, TWO BRIDGES, DARTMOOR PL20 6SA (01822 890403; Fax: 01822 890676). Small, friendly, relaxed country house hotel with glorious views onto open moorland. Walks in all directions. Nine en suite bedrooms. Log fires. Gourmet cooking. Excellent wine list. Fishing, riding, golf nearby. Three Day Break from £205 per person. ETC ★★★. [🐾]
e-mail: bookings@princehall.co.uk

DARTMOOR COUNTRY HOLIDAYS, MAGPIE LEISURE PARK, DEPT PW, BEDFORD BRIDGE, HORRABRIDGE, YELVERTON PL20 7RY (01822 852651). Purpose-built pine lodges in peaceful woodland setting. Sleep 2-7. Furnished to very high standard (microwave, dishwasher etc.) Easy walk to village and shops. Launderette. Dogs permitted. (Pets £15.00 per week.) [🐾]

CHERRYBROOK HOTEL, TWO BRIDGES, YELVERTON PL20 6SP (01822 880260). Set in the heart of Dartmoor National Park. Seven comfortably furnished en suite bedrooms. Good quality home-cooked food with menu choice. Ideal for touring. AA QQQQ SELECTED. WCTB ◆◆◆◆. [🐾]

TWO BRIDGES HOTEL, TWO BRIDGES, DARTMOOR PL20 6SW (01822 890581; Fax: 01822 890575). Famous Olde World riverside Inn. Centre Dartmoor. Log fires, very comfortable, friendly, own brewed beer, excellent food. Ideal walking, touring, fishing, riding, golf. Warning – Addictive. ETC/AA/RAC ★★[🐾]

DEVONSHIRE INN, STICKLEPATH, OKEHAMPTON EX20 2NW (01837 840626). A real country pub! Out the back door past the water wheels, cross the river by ford or footbridge and up through the woods onto the north edge of Dartmoor proper. Dogs and horses always welcome, fed and watered. 1994 Winner National Beta Petfood Golden Bowl Competition for most dog-friendly pub!

EAST DART HOTEL, POSTBRIDGE, DARTMOOR PL20 6TJ (01822 880213; Fax: 01822 880313). Enjoy a break in the heart of beautiful Dartmoor from £24 pppn B&B, at a former coaching Inn, with wonderful walks all round. Enjoy fires, real ales, home cooked food. Riding, falconry, shooting and hunting available. Dogs very welcome.
website: www.dartmoorhotels.com

LYDGATE HOUSE, POSTBRIDGE, DARTMOOR PL20 6TJ (01822 880209; Fax: 01822 880202). Set in its own 36 acres in the heart of Dartmoor National Park. 7 en suite rooms. Idyllic location for walking, horse riding and fishing.
website: www.lydgate-house.fsnet.co.uk

Dartmouth

Historic port and resort on the estuary of the River Dart, with sandy coves and pleasure boat trips up the river. Car ferry to Kingswear.

RHODA WEST, LITTLE WEEKE HOUSE, WEEKE HILL, DARTMOUTH TQ6 0JT (01803 832380; Fax: 01803 832342). Enjoy a warm welcome at this luxurious Bed & Breakfast set in peaceful surroundings close to the south west coastal path and only one mile from the centre of Dartmouth. All bedrooms en suite. Private Parking. Dogs welcome.
e-mail: RJWesty@aol.com

PAM & GRAHAM SPITTLE, WATERMILL COTTAGES, HANSEL, DARTMOUTH TQ6 0LN (01803 770219). Comfortable, well equipped, old stone cottages in peaceful riverside setting. Wonderful walks in and around our idyllic valley near Slapton. 10 minutes from sea and dog friendly beach. Sleep 3-8. Open all year. Telephone for brochure. [Pets £15 per week]

MRS S.R. RIDALLS, THE OLD BAKEHOUSE, 7 BROADSTONE, DARTMOUTH TQ6 9NR (Tel & Fax: 01803 834585). Three cottages (one with four-poster bed). Sleep 2–6. Near river, shops, restaurant. Blackpool Sands 15 minutes' drive. TV, linen free, baby-sitting. Open all year. ETC ★★/★★★ Free Parking [🐾]

Dawlish

Bright resort with sandy beach and sandstone cliffs. lovely gardens with streams, waterfalls and famous black swans. Exeter 13 miles, Torquay 12.

MRS F. E. WINSTON, "STURWOOD", 1 OAK PARK VILLAS, DAWLISH EX7 0DE (01626 862660). Holiday flats. Comfortable, self-contained, accommodating 2-6. Own bathroom, 1/2 bedrooms. Colour television. Garden. Parking. Full Fire Certificate. Leisure centre and beach close by. Pets welcome. [🐾]

MRS P. KITSON, 3 CLEVELAND PLACE, DAWLISH EX7 9HZ (01626 865053). Town cottages – newly-built comfortable two/three bedrooms. Three minutes' walk beaches, etc. Parking. Patio garden. Terms from £95 to £350 per week inclusive. Reductions for couples. Also winter lets four to eight months. [🐾]

Dawlish Warren

A 500 acre nature reserve with a sandy spit at the mouth of the River Exe.

WELCOME FAMILY HOLIDAY PARK, DAWLISH WARREN, SOUTH DEVON EX7 0PH (Tel: 01626 862070). Activities include the Kaleidoscope Entertainment Centre, indoor heated four-pool complex, Children's Club with games arcade. Free electricity, linen. [Pets £25 per week.]
website: www.welcomefamily.co.uk

Dunsford

Attractive village in upper Teign valley with Dartmoor to the west. plymouth 35 miles, Okehampton 16, Newton Abbot 13, Crediton 9, Exeter 8.

ROYAL OAK INN, DUNSFORD, NEAR EXETER EX6 7DA (01647 252256). Welcome to our Victorian country inn with real ales and home-made food. All en suite rooms are in a 300-year-old converted barn. Well behaved children and dogs welcome. [ᕕ]

Eggesford (Chulmleigh)

Picturesque village, central for both north and south coasts, Exmoor and Dartmoor.

EGGESFORD COUNTRY HOTEL, EGGESFORD, CHULMLEIGH EX18 7JZ (01769 580345; Fax: 01769 580262). Family-run hotel in 10 acres of beautiful grounds with seven miles of fishing. Ideal centre for walking, touring and country pursuits. Open all year. Brochure. Pets welcome.

Ermington

Village on River Erme 2 miles south of Ivybridge.

THE LODGE, ERMINGTON. Pretty detached thatched cottage. Country near village. Overlooking fields. Area of Outstanding Natural Beauty. Three miles coast. Comfortably furnished. Well equipped. Barbecue. Two bedrooms, sleeps four. ENQUIRIES: BARTERS OLD FARMHOUSE, NORTH WHILBOROUGH, NEWTON ABBOT TQ12 5LP (01803 873213; Fax: 01803 875096). [Pets £8 per week]. e-mail: holcot@eclipse.co.uk

Exeter

Chief city of the South-West with a cathedral and university. Ample shopping, sports and leisure facilities.

THE LORD HALDON COUNTRY HOUSE HOTEL, DUNCHIDEOCK, NR EXETER, DEVON EX6 7YF (01392 832483, Fax: 01392 833765) Extensive gardens amid miles of rolling Devon countryside. AA/ETC ★★★. [ᕕ]

MRS D.L. SALTER, HALDON LODGE FARM, KENNFORD, NEAR EXETER EX6 7YG (01392 832312). Modern Holiday Caravan. Two bedrooms, kitchen, lounge, bathroom/toilet. TV. Farm shop, famous village Inns. Sea short distance. Private grounds near Teign Valley Forest with two Coarse Fishing lakes. Pets welcome. [pw! ᕕ]

MRS SALLY GLANVILL, RYDON FARM, WOODBURY, EXETER EX5 1LB (Tel and Fax: 01395 232341). 16th Century Devon Longhouse on working dairy farm. Bedrooms with private or en suite bathrooms, hairdryers, tea/coffee facilities. Romantic 4-poster. Open all year. ETC/AA ◆◆◆. From £24 to £27. [ᕕ]

Exmoor

265 square miles of unspoiled heather moorland with deep wooded valleys and rivers, ideal for a walking, pony trekking or fishing holiday.

THE STAG HUNTERS HOTEL, BRENDON, EXMOOR EX35 1PS (Tel: 01598 741222; Fax: 01598 741352). Family run village Inn set in four acres of garden and paddock. 12 en suite rooms with CH, TV and tea/coffee. Open all year. Shooting, fishing and riding. [ᕕ]

THE ROCKFORD INN, BRENDON, NEAR LYNTON EX35 6PT (01598 741214; Fax 01598 741265) Traditional Country Inn situated along the bank of the East Lyn River. Excellent location for fishing and exploring Exmoor National Park. Bed and Breakfast from £18 pppn.
e-mail: enquiries@therockfordinn.co.uk
website: www.therockfordinn.co.uk

JAYE JONES AND HELEN ASHER, TWITCHEN FARM, CHALLACOMBE, BARNSTAPLE EX31 4TT (01598 763568). Comfort for country lovers in Exmoor National Park. All rooms en suite with TV. Meals prepared with local and some organic produce. Stabling £35 per week. Dogs no charge. B&B £19–£26, DB&B £35–£42. [🐕]
e–mail: holidays@twitchen.co.uk
website: www.twitchen.co.uk

Exmouth

Holiday resort, popular since 18th century; long sandy shore. Working exhibits at The Country Life Museum.

MRS G. CLARKE, POUND HOUSE, POUND LANE, EXMOUTH EX8 4NP (01395 222684). Holiday house Exmoor centre. High standard; central heating; en suite bath/shower rooms. Acre secluded tranquil gardens. Pets and children welcome. Private car park. Details on request.[🐕]

Georgeham

Village 6 miles south-west of Ilfracombe.

MILTON COTTAGES, NORTH DEVON. Three/four bedroom character coastal holiday homes. Fully refurbished and equipped to a high standard. Rural views, gardens, parking. Short drive to sandy beaches. Colour brochure. MR AND MRS MILTON, FOURWINDS, DARRACOTT RISE, GEORGEHAM EX33 1JZ (01271 891078; Fax: 01271 342810).
e-mail: pjmilton@miltonpj.net

Harberton

Small picturesque village two miles from Totnes.

MIKE & JANET GRIFFITHS, "OLD HAZARD", HIGHER PLYMOUTH ROAD, HARBERTON, TOTNES TQ9 7LN (01803 862495). 3 miles Totnes. Attractive well-equipped cottage and spacious self-contained farmhouse flat. Convenient rural location. Open all year. Dogs welcome. Brochure on request. [Pets £7.00 per week].

Holsworthy

Town 9 miles east of Bude.

THE BARTON PANCRASWEEK, HOLSWORTHY, EX22 7JT (01288 381315). Family-run cattle farm in picturesque countryside. `three spacious double rooms, all en suite. TV lounge, dining room and large garden. Bed and Breakfast from £19, evening meal optional. No children aged under 5 years.

MRS S. PLUMMER, LONG CROSS HOUSE, BLACK TORRINGTON, NEAR HOLSWORTHY EX21 5QG (01409 231219). Long Cross House is situated at the edge of the delightfull village of Black Torrington, midway between the market towns of Holsworthy and Hatherleigh in rural North Devon. Rooms are en suite with central heating and have tea/coffee making facilities and TV. Children, dogs and horses welcome. Bed and Breakfast from £17.50 per person. Evening Meal by arrangement.

HEDLEY WOOD CARAVAN & CAMPING PARK, BRIDGERULE, (NR BUDE), HOLSWORTHY EX22 7ED (Tel: 01288 381404). 16 acre woodland family run site; childrens adventure areas, bar, clubroom, shop, laundry, meals & all amanities. Static caravans for hire, Caravan Storage available. [🐕, pw!, ⌂]
website: www.hedleywood .co.uk

Honiton

Busy South Devon town now happily by-passed. Noted for lace and pottery. Excellent touring centre. Newton Abbott 31 miles, Exmouth 18, Taunton 18, Exeter 17, Budleigh Salterton 16, Lyme Regis 15, Chard 13, Sidmouth 10.

MRS S. KIDWELL, THE CREST, WILMINGTON, NEAR. HONITON EX14 9JU (01404 831 419 Mobile: 07967 894670). A modern chalet style house nestling in the picturesque Umborne Valley. The guest wing affords complete privacy with large modern en suite bedroom. Double glazed. Lying in two-and-a-half acres of garden. Pets welcome. AA ◆◆◆ [🐾]

THE BELFRY COUNTRY HOTEL, YARCOMBE, NEAR HONITON, DEVON EX14 9BD (Tel: 01404 861234; Fax: 01404 861579). Small luxury Hotel in converted Victorian village school. All rooms en suite with lovely views. Licensed restaurant, fine wines and superb food. Ideal base for touring, walking, gardens, antiques. Non-smoking hotel.

LOWER LUXTON FARM, UPOTTERY, HONITON EX14 9PB (Tel & Fax: 01823 601269) Quiet, peaceful and relaxing in area of outstanding natural beauty in the centre of the Blackdown Hills. Fishing in our farm pond. Olde worlde farmhouse. Rooms en suite or private bathroom. Open all year. SAE or telephone Mrs Elizabeth Tucker for details.

Hope Cove

Attractive fishing village, flat sandy beach and safe bathing. Fine views towards Rame Head; cliffs. Kingsbridge 6 miles.

HOPE BARTON BARNS, HOPE COVE, NEAR SALCOMBE TQ7 3HT (01548 561393). 17 stone barns in two courtyards and three luxury apartments in farmhouse. Farmhouse meals. Free range children and well behaved dogs welcome. For full colour brochure please contact: Mike or Judy Tromans. ETC ★★★★ [pw! 🐾]

GRAYSTONE, HOPE BEACH HOUSE - Luxury apartment with sea views, 50 yards from safe beach and coastal footpaths, sleeps 6. Fully equipped washing machine/dryer, dishwasher, microwave, storage heating etc. Linen provided. Ideal location for children, boating. Available all year, . MR AND MRS HART, BANCHORY, OLD FARM ROAD, HAMPTON, MIDDLESEX TW12 3QT (Tel: 020 8979 5665) [Pets £12 per week]

Ilfracombe

This popular seaside resort clusters round a busy harbour. The surrounding area is ideal for coastal walks.

WESTWELL HALL HOTEL, TORRS PARK, ILFRACOMBE EX34 8AZ (Tel & Fax: 01271 862792). Elegant Victorian Licensed Hotel set in own grounds, adjacent to National Trust coastal walks. All spacious rooms en suite with colour TV and tea/coffee making facilities. AA/RAC/ETC ★. [🐾]

WATERMOUTH LODGES NEAR ILFRACOMBE, NORTH DEVON EX34 9SJ. Self-catering lodges in idyllic woodland setting with sea views, indoor/outdoor swimming pools, sauna, jacuzzi, bar/restaurant, ball, pool and games room. Call Sara on 01271 865361 for a brochure.

VARLEY HOUSE, CHAMBERCOMBE PARK, ILFRACOMBE EX34 9QW (Tel: 01271 863927; Fax: 01271 879299). Relax with your dog, fabulous walks nearby. Fully en suite non-smoking rooms with lots of thoughtful extras. Superb food, beautiful surroundings. Bar. Car Park. Children welcome over five years. ETC ◆◆◆◆ AA ◆◆◆◆ Selected Award. [🐾] WE WANT YOU TO WANT TO RETURN.
e–mail: info@varleyhouse.co.uk

ST BRANNOCKS HOUSE, ST BRANNOCKS ROAD, ILFRACOMBE EX34 8EQ (01271 863873). Good food and excellent accommodation guaranteed at this friendly Hotel. All rooms TV, tea making; en suite. Licensed bar. Parking. Children and pets welcome. RAC/ETC ◆◆◆ [🐾]

THE DARNLEY HOTEL, BELMONT ROAD, ILFRACOMBE, EX34 8DR (01271 863955). Elegant Victorian residence set in its own informal grounds. Exmoor National Park and the sandy beaches are only a short drive away. Pets sleep in your room with you. Phone for colour brochure. ETC ★★. website: www.northdevon.co.uk/darnley

THE TOWERS HOTEL, CHAMBERCOMBE PARK, ILFRACOMBE EX34 9QN (Tel: 01271 862809; Fax: 01271 897442). Enjoy a relaxed stay with your dog at The Towers set in its own grounds with its own car park. Mostly en suite rooms, with well-appointed extras. Resident's lounge/bar. Non-smoking. ETC ◆◆◆.
e-mail: info@thetowers.co.uk
website: www.thetowers.co.uk

Instow

On estuaries of Taw and Torridge, very popular with boating enthusiasts. Barnstaple 6 miles, Bideford 3.

BEACH HAVEN COTTAGE, INSTOW. Seafront cottage overlooking sandy beach. Extensive beach and sea views. Sleeps 5, own parking. Central heating, colour TV, coastal walks. Dog welcome. For colour brochure send SAE to 140 BAY VIEW ROAD, NORTHAM, BIDEFORD EX39 1BJ (01237 473801). [Dog £10 per week]

TIDES REACH COTTAGE, INSTOW. Seafront cottage overlooking sandy beach. Extensive beach and sea views. 3 bedrooms, own parking. Central heating, colour TV, coastal walks. Dog welcome. For colour brochure send SAE to Mrs P.T. BARNES, 140 BAY VIEW ROAD, NORTHAM, BIDEFORD EX39 1BJ (01237 473801). [Dog £10 per week]

Kingsbridge

Pleasant town at head of picturesque Kingsbridge estuary. Centre for South Hams disrict with its lush scenery and quiet coves.

GARA MILL. Self catering in comfortable detached lodges or flats in 16th century mill. TVs, laundry, play area, games room. Woodland walks. Ring or fax for brochure. ALLAN AND MARCIA GREEN, GARA MILL HOUSE, SLAPTON, KINGSBRIDGE TQ7 2RE (01803 770295). [Pets £12 per week.]

BEACHDOWN, CHALLABOROUGH BAY, KINGSBRIDGE TQ7 4JB (Tel & Fax: 01548 810089). Self catering holidays for families in pleasant cedarwood bungalows 200 yards from quiet, sandy beach. Children's playground. Local shopping. Pets welcome. Fully furnished and equipped. Approved Contact LIZ for details. [pw! £15 per week for first pet, £10 for second and subsequent.]

MRS B. KELLY, BLACKWELL PARK, LODDISWELL, KINGSBRIDGE TQ7 4EA (01548 821230). 17th century Farmhouse, 5 miles from Kingsbridge. Ideal centre for Dartmoor, Plymouth, Torbay, Dartmouth and many beaches. Some bedrooms en suite. Bed, Breakfast and Evening Meal or Bed and Breakfast. Pets welcome free of charge. ETC ◆◆. [pw!🐾]

RUTH AND JON SAUNDERS, DITTISCOMBE FARMHOUSE AND HOLIDAY COTTAGES, SLAPTON, KINGSBRIDGE TQ7 2QF (01548 521272; Fax: 01548 521425). Individual and comfortable self-catering cottages with gardens. Set in private 20 acre conservation valley with ponds and wildlife. Ideal area for dog-walking and bird-watching. [Pets £15 per week for first pet, £10 for each subse-quent pet]

THE SLOOP INN, BANTHAM, NEAR KINGSBRIDGE TQ7 3AJ. (01548 560489/560215; Fax: 01548 561940). Five en suite bedrooms, four luxury self-catering apartments. Pet friendly. Bed & Breakfast from £31 per person. Self-catering from £245 inclusive. Short breaks available. 2 Crowns Commended; ᵐᵐ Commended. AA QQQ Recommended.

LIPTON FARM, EAST ALLINGTON, NEAR TOTNES TQ9 7RN (01548 521252) Luxury 30 foot six berth caravan in quiet valley. Bed linen, microwave, colour TV, swimming pool. Kingsbridge 5 miles. Ideal for beautiful beaches and Dartmoor. From £150.00 per week. [Pets £5 per week.]

SYMBOLS

🐾	Indicates that pets are welcome free of charge.
£	Indicates that a charge is made for pets: nightly or weekly.
pw!	Shows some special provision for pets; exercise facility, feeding or accommodation arrangement.
◻	Indicates separate pets accommodation.

King's Nympton

3 miles north of Chulmleigh. Winner of CPRE Award for Devon Village of the year 1999.

Eight Country Cottages sleeping from 2 to 12 in rural area; lovely views, private patios and gardens. Well furnished and equipped. Heated pool, tennis court, BHS approved riding school. Laundry room. Open all year. APPLY: TERRY & JANE SHERAR, COLLACOTT FARM, KING'S NYMPTON, UMBER-LEIGH, NORTH DEVON EX37 9TP (01769 572491). [Pets £3 per night, £20 per week] website: http://members.aol.com/self.cater

Lapford

Village 5 miles south east of Chulmleigh.

MRS M. MILLS, RUDGE FARM, LAPFORD, CREDITON EX17 6NG (01363 83268). Set in beautiful grounds with pond, orchard and woods. Trout fishing and almost 200 acres to wander in. Much wildlife and perfect for watching buzzards and badgers. House very tastefully furnished and fully-equipped. Will sleep up to 8. No charge for dogs, linen or fuel. David and Marion Mills look forward to meeting you. Send for our brochure. [🐕]

Lynton/Lynmouth

Picturesque twin villages joined by a unique cliff railway (vertical height 500 ft). Lynmouth has a quaint harbour and Lynton enjoys superb views over the rugged coastline.

THE HEATHERVILLE HOTEL, TORS PARK, LYNMOUTH EX35 6NB (01598 752327). AA ◆◆◆. Country house hotel in peaceful setting with magnificent river and woodland views. Tea and coffee making in all rooms. All en suite rooms with colour TV. Traditional English cooking. Licensed. Four minutes' walk to village. Parking. Bargain Breaks. Pets very welcome free of charge.[🐕]

R.S. BINGHAM, NEW MILL FARM, BARBROOK, LYNTON EX35 6JR (01598 753341). Exmoor Valley. Two delightful genuine modernised XVII century cottages by stream on 100-acre farm with A.B.R.S. Approved riding stables. Free fishing. ETC 🏠🏠🏠 commended. SAE for brochure. [pw! Pets £15 per week.]

THE EXMOOR SANDPIPER INN, COUNTISBURY, NEAR LYNMOUTH EX35 6NE (01598 741263). This fine old coaching inn is in a beautiful setting with good food and hotel facilities for complete comfort. All 16 rooms are en suite with colour TV, and tea/coffee making facilities. [🐕 one dog] e–mail: exmoorsandpiper.demon.co.uk

GABLE LODGE, LEE ROAD, LYNTON EX35 6BS (01598 752367). Grade II Listed building. Friendly and homely atmosphere. En suite rooms with TV and beverage trays. Licensed. Good home cooking. Car park and garden. Non- smoking. [🐕]

THE CROWN, MARKET STREET, LYNTON, EX35 6AG (01598 752253; Fax: 01598 753311). The Crown offers easy access to the dramatic Exmoor countryside and coastline. Rooms are all en suite, with remote control TV, tea/coffee making facilities, central heating and direct-dial telephones. [🐕] website: www.thecrown-lynton.co.uk

MR AND MRS D. HILLIER, BRENDON HOUSE, BRENDON, LYNTON EX35 6PS (01598 741206). Charming country house in beautiful Lyn Valley. Licensed. Good Devon cooking. Fishing permits sold. Dogs welcome by arrangement. B&B from £22, DB &B from £37. [🐕] website: www.brendonvalley.co uk/Brendon_House.htm

MRS W. PRYOR, STATION HOUSE, LYNTON (01598 752275/752381 Fax: 01598 752475). Holiday Flat situated in the former narrow gauge railway station closed in 1935, overlooking the West Lyn Valley. Centrally placed for Doone Valley and Exmoor. Parking available. [🐕]

COUNTISBURY LODGE HOTEL, COUNTISBURY HILL, LYNMOUTH EX35 6NB (01598 752388). Former Victorian vicarage, peacefully secluded yet only 5 minutes to Lynmouth village. En suite rooms, central heating. Ideal for birdwatching and moors. Parking. Short Breaks. AA ◆◆◆◆ [🐕]

Morchard Bishop

An old traditional Devon village almost equal distances from both moors and both coasts.

MOLLY AND JEFF KINGABY, WEST AISH FARM, MORCHARD BISHOP, NEAR CREDITON EX17 6RX (Tel/Fax: 01363 877427). Two Self-Catering Cottages set in a former cobbled farmyard on a southerly slope overlooking Dartmoor. One cottage sleeps 5. Bungalow sleeps 4.£148 – £295. Short Breaks (3 nights) £110. If you have forgotten what peace and quietness is like, come and stay with us! [🐕 pw!]
e–mail: westaish@eclipse.co.uk
website: www. eclipse.co.uk/westaish

Mortehoe

Adjoining Woolacombe with cliffs and wide sands. Interesting rock scenery beyond Morte Point. Barnstaple 15 miles.

THE SMUGGLERS NORTH MORTE ROAD, MORTEHOE, EX34 7DR (TEL/FAX: 01271 870891). In the pretty village of Mortehoe The Smugglers offer luxury accommodation from twin rooms to family suites. En suite rooms, Satellite TV, Full English Breakfast, Licensed Bar, Beer Garden, Home-cooked Meals. Well trained pets welcome.

LUNDY HOUSE HOTEL, MORTEHOE, WOOLACOMBE EX34 7DZ (01271 870372). Quality en suite accommodation in small, friendly hotel. Superb food, licensed bar lounge, restaurant. TV & tea-making facilities in all rooms. Write or phone for full details.[🐕]

Newton Abbot

Known as the Gateway to Dartmoor and the coast, this lively market town has many fine buildings, parks and a racecourse.

ROSELANDS HOLIDAY CHALETS, TOTNES ROAD, IPPLEPEN, NEWTON ABBOT TQ12 5TD (01803 812701). Within easy reach of all South Devon attractions, detached, fully equipped chalets sleeping 2-5 persons; one suitable for wheelchairs. Sociable dogs have freedom of garden. Telephone for details. [pw! 1st pet free, extra pets £5 per week.]
e–mail: Roselands@FSBDial.co.uk
website: www.Roselands.net

MIKE & EMMA PALLETT, EAST BURNE FARM, BICKINGTON, NEWTON ABBOT TQ12 6PA (01626 821496; Fax: 01626 821105). East Burne is a 15th century medieval hall house. It is an ideal centre for exploring Dartmoor and numerous National Trust and other historic properties. Excellent golf, fishing and riding are availble locally. We can accommodate up to six guests for bed and break-fast in rooms with private facilities. AA Selected ◆◆◆◆.
e–mail: eastburnefarm@eastburnefarm.screaming.net

Okehampton

Market town on edge of Dartmoor.

MR I. HOWARD, OLDITCH FARM CARAVAN & CAMPING PARK, STICKLE PATH, NEAR OKEHAMP-TON EX20 2NT (01837 840734; Fax: 01837 840877). Small family-run site within Dartmoor National Park. Ideal base for touring Devon with easy access to both coasts. Small restaurant on site. Open March to November. Terms from £4.50 to £8.50 per night. We welcome well-behaved dogs. AA 3 Pennant. **ETC** ★★★.

Ottery St Mary

Pleasant little town in East Devon, within easy reach of the sea. Many interesting little buildings including 11th century parish church. Birthplace of the poet Coleridge.

MR AND MRS M. FORTH, FLUXTON FARM, OTTERY ST MARY EX11 1RJ (01404 812818). Charming 16th-Century farmhouse with large garden. Good food, log fires. Peace and quiet. Cat lovers' paradise. Licensed. AA Listed. [🐾 pw!]

Paignton

Popluar family resort on Torbay with long, safe sandy beaches and small harbour. Exeter 25 miles, Newton Abbott 9, Torquay 3.

J. AND E. BALL, DEPARTMENT P.W., HIGHER WELL FARM HOLIDAY PARK, STOKE GABRIEL, TOTNES TQ9 6RN (01803 782289). Within 4 miles Torbay beaches and 1 mile of River Dart. Central for touring. Dogs on leads. Tourist Board Graded park ★★. [Pets £12 per week in statics, free in tents and tourers.]

MR AND MRS BANKS, AMBER HOUSE HOTEL, 6 ROUNDHAM ROAD, PAIGNTON TQ4 6EZ (01803 558372). Family-run licensed hotel. En suite facilities and ground floor rooms. Good food. Highly recommended. A warm welcome assured to pets and their families. [🐾]

Plymouth

Historic port and resort, immpressively rebuilt after severe war damage. large naval docks at Devonport. Beach of pebble and sand.

CHURCHWOOD VALLEY, DEPT PW, WEMBURY BAY, NEAR PLYMOUTH PL9 0DZ (01752 862382). Relax in quality log cabins with own patio. In wooded valley leading to beach. Shop, launderette, riding stables. Two family pets welcome free of charge. [🐾]
e-mail: churchwoodvalley@btinternet.com

AVALON GUEST HOUSE, 167 CITADEL ROAD, THE HOE, PLYMOUTH PL1 2HU (01752 668127). Family run guest house, close to the sea front. All rooms have full central heating, colour TV and tea/coffee facilities. En suite available. Open all year round. [🐾]

CRANBOURNE HOTEL, 278/282 CITADEL ROAD, THE HOE, PLYMOUTH PL1 2PZ (01752 263858/661400/224646; Fax: 01752 263858). Convenient for Ferry Terminal and City Centre. All bedrooms with colour TV and tea/coffee. Licensed bar. Keys provided for access at all times. Under personal supervision. Pets by arrangement. ◆◆◆◆ [🐾]
e-mail: cran.hotel@virgin.net
website: www.cranbournehotel.co.uk

LAMPLIGHTER HOTEL, 103 CITADEL ROAD, THE HOE, PLYMOUTH PL1 2RN (Tel: 01752 663855; Tel/Fax: 01752 228139). Family-run hotel situated close to seafront, Barbican and city centre. All rooms with tea/coffee making facilites and TV/video. Car park. Pets by arrangement. Access and Visa accepted. AA ◆◆◆ Commended. [🐾]
e-mail: lamplighterhotel@ukonline.co.uk

Salcombe

Fishing and sailing centre in sheltered position. Fine beaches and coastal walks nearby.

SEAMARK, THURLESTONE SANDS, NEAR SALCOMBE TQ7 3JY (01548 561300). 6 lovely cottages adjoining coastal path. Beach close by, golf one mile. Indoor heated swimming pool, sauna and games room. Laundry room. Pay phone. Colour brochure. [🐾]

SYMBOLS

🐾   Indicates that pets are welcome free of charge.

£   Indicates that a charge is made for pets: nightly or weekly.

pw!   Shows some special provision for pets; exercise facility, feeding or accommodation arrangement.

⌂   Indicates separate pets accommodation.

SAND PEBBLES HOTEL, HOPE COVE, NEAR KINGSBRIDGE TQ7 3HF (01548 561673). In own grounds overlooking sea and countryside. Tastefully furnished bedrooms with bathroom or shower, TV, beverage facilities. Excellent restaurant. Golf, tennis, riding, within easy reach. website: www.webmachine.co.uk/sandpebbles

GRAFTON TOWERS HOTEL, MOULT ROAD, SALCOMBE TQ8 8LG (01548 842882; Fax: 01548 842857). Small luxury hotel, all en suite, overlooking magnificent coastline. Spectacular walks. [Pets £3.00 per night].

THE PORT LIGHT, BOLBERRY DOWN, MALBOROUGH, NEAR SALCOMBE TQ7 3DY (01548 561384 or 07970 859992). A totally unique location set amidst acres of National Trust coastline. Luxury en suite rooms. Superb home-cooked fare, specialising in local seafood. Licensed bar. Pets welcome throughout the hotel. Bargain Breaks throughout the year. [🐕]
e–mail: info@portlight-salcombe.co.uk
website: www.portlight-salcombe.co.uk

THE SALCOMBE BOAT COMPANY, WHITESTRAND, SALCOMBE TQ8 8ET (Tel: 01548 843730; Fax: 01548 844417). A holiday with a difference. Unwind with a houseboat holiday on Salcombe's tranquil estuary. Write or phone for brochure. [Pets £20 weekly.]

Seaton

Bright East Devon resort near Axe estuary. Shingle beach and chalk cliffs; good bathing, many lovely walks in vicinity. Exeter 23 miles, Sidmouth 11.

MILKBERE HOLIDAYS, MILKBERE HOUSE, 14 FORE STREET, SEATON EX12 2LA (01297 22925 – brochure/01297 20729 – bookings). Attractive self-catering Cottages, Bungalows, Apartments. Coast and Country on Devon/Dorset border. Free colour brochure. Pets welcome.

Shaldon

Delightful little resort facing Teignmouth across the Teign estuary. Sheltered by the lofty prominence of Shaldon Ness, beach side activities are largely concerned with boats and sailing; beaches are mainly of sand. Mini golf course. The attractions of Teignmouth are reached by a long road bridge or passenger ferry.

GLENSIDE HOUSE, RINGMORE ROAD, SHALDON, TQ14 0EP (01626 872448). Charming, waterside cottage. Level river walks to beach. En suite available. Self-catering available. Garden, car park. B&B from £20.00; DB&B from £35.00. Telephone for brochure. ETC/AA ◆◆◆. [Pets £2.50 daily, £10 weekly.]

Sidmouth

Sheltered resort, winner of many awards for its floral displays. Good sands at Jacob's Ladder beach.

OAKDOWN TOURING AND HOLIDAY HOME PARK, WESTON, SIDMOUTH EX10 0PH (Tel: 01297 680387; Fax: 01297 680541). Privately owned park set in East Devon Heritage Coast. Level, well drained and close mown. Luxury holiday homes to hire, pitches for touring units. Colour brochure. Calor Gas Best Park, BGHP ★★★★. [pw! from £1.00 per night.]
e-mail: oakdown@btinternet.com Website: www.bestcaravanpark.co.uk

ENID & BERT CARR, BARRINGTON VILLA GUEST HOUSE, SALCOMBE ROAD, SIDMOUTH EX10 8PU (01395 514252). A Regency Villa in beautiful gardens on the River Sid. Dog-walk riverside park nearby. Ample forecourt parking. Dogs with house trained owners most welcome.

LOWER KNAPP FARM, SIDBURY, SIDMOUTH EX10 0QN (Tel: 01404 871438; Fax: 01404 871597). Luxury self-catering cottages sleeping 2/9 set in 16 acres. Indoor heated pool, sauna, solarium. All cottages with fully fitted kitchens; colour TV etc. Linen supplied. Colour brochure on request. ETC ★★★★ [Pets £15 per week.]
e-mail: lowknapp@aol.com
website: www.knappfarm-holidays.co.uk

MRS B. SMITH, WILLOW BRIDGE HOTEL, MILLFORD ROAD, SIDMOUTH EX10 8DR (Tel & Fax: 01395 513599). The Willow Bridge has an enviable reputation for comfort and a happy, friendly atmosphere. Picturesque riverside setting overlooking Byes Park, yet only five minutes' walk from shops and esplanade. Bedrooms en suite with colour TV etc. Dining room, licensed bar. Private car park. non smoking. Full Fire certificate. ETC ◆◆◆◆. [🐕]

LEIGH FARM SELF-CATERING HOLIDAYS, WESTON, SIDMOUTH, DEVON EX10 0PH Cottage & Bungalows 150 yards from National Trust Valley leading to Coastal Path & Beach. Lovely cliff top walks and level walks around nearby Donkey Sanctuary fields. WCT ★★★ Contact: Geoff & Gill Davis Tel: 01395 516065 Fax: 01395 579582 . [Pets Welcome-£14 pw]
e-mail: leigh.farm@virgin.net
website: http://www.streets-ahead.com/leighfarm

BOSWELL FARM COTTAGES, SIDFORD, SIDMOUTH EX10 0PP (Tel & Fax: 01395 514162) 17th century farmhouse with seven individual cottages, lovingly converted from old farm buildings, each with its enclosed, delightful garden. Facilities available. Art studio, tennis court and trout pond. Idyllic walks in area of outstanding natural beauty, two miles from beach and heritage coastline. ETC ★★★★
e-mail: dillon@boswell-farm.co.uk
website: www.boswell-farm.co.uk

South Brent

Just off the busy A38 Plymouth to Exeter road, this is a good centre on the River Avon for Dartmoor and the South Devon resorts. plymouth 15 miles, Ashburton 8.

Enchanting, select site for those seeking a quiet restful holiday amidst beautiful surroundings, overlooking the Dartmoor Hills. Fully serviced luxury caravans, with colour TV, fridge, heater and shower. Separate low density site for tents/tourers. Several acres for carefree exercising. ✓✓✓.
APPLY – TREVOR AND JILL HORNE, WEBLAND FARM HOLIDAY PARK, AVONWICK, NEAR SOUTH BRENT TQ10 9EX (01364 73273). [pw! Pets £10 per week in caravans.]

South Molton

On the southern edge of Exmoor, 12 miles east of Barnstaple, this busy market town is noted for its antiques and elegant Georgian buildings.

WEST BOWDEN FARM, KNOWSTONE, SOUTH MOLTON EX36 4RP (01398 341224). Working farm with five en suite bedrooms and others with washbasins; all have tea/coffee making facilities. Real Devon hospitality. Terms from £155 per week for Bed, Breakfast and Evening Dinner.

MRS DIANA COLMAN, FISHERDOWN FARM, SOUTH MOLTON EX36 3QD (01769 572236). Bed and Breakfast, evening meal. Beef farm close to Exmoor and coastline. Superb for walking and touring. Good Devon cooking. Large garden. Home from home. [🐕]

NORTH LEE HOLIDAY COTTAGES, NORTH LEE FARM, SOUTH MOLTON EX36 3EH (Tel: 01598 740240/740675; Fax: 01598 740248) website: www.northleeholidaycottages.co.uk. Southern edge of Exmoor. Tastefully decorated barn conversions. Sleep 2-8. Working farm. Easy reach of Exmoor and Coast. Open all year. Weekend and short breaks available. ETC 🏠🏠🏠🏠 Self Catering [Pets £10 per week]
website: www.northleeholidaycottages.co.uk

Tavistock

Birthplace of Sir Francis Drake and site of a fine ruined Benedictine Abbey. On edge of Dartmoor, 13 miles north of Plymouth

MRS P.G.C. QUINTON, HIGHER QUITHER, MILTON ABBOT, TAVISTOCK PL19 0PZ (01822 860284). Modern self-contained barn conversion. Own private garden. Terms from £195 inc. linen, coal and logs. Electricity metered. [🐕]

Teign Valley

Picturesque area on edge of Dartmoor. The River Teign flows into the English Channel at Teignmouth.

S. & G. HARRISON-CRAWFORD, SILVER BIRCHES, TEIGN VALLEY, TRUSHAM, NEWTON ABBOT TQ13 0NJ (01626 852172). Comfortable riverside bungalow on the edge of Dartmoor. Good centre for bird-watching, forest walks, golf, riding; fishing. All rooms en suite. Two self-catering caravans in garden from £135 per week. B&B from £25.00 nightly. [🐾]

Teignmouth

Resort at mouth of River Teign. Bridge connects with Shaldon on south side of estuary.

LYME BAY HOUSE HOTEL, DEN PROMENADE, TEIGNMOUTH TQ14 8SZ (01626 772953). Near rail and coach stations and shops. En suite facilities available. Licensed. Lift – no steps. Bed and Breakfast. [🐾]

Tiverton

Market town on River Exe 12 miles north of Exeter, centrally located for touring both North and South coasts.

PALFREYS BARTON, COVE, TIVERTON EX16 7RZ (01398 331456). Four six-berth caravans on a 235 acre working dairy farm, beautifully sited adjacent to farmhouse, with marvellous views. All caravans fully equipped. Available March to October.

Torquay

Popular resort on the English Riviera with a wide range of attractions and entertainments. Yachting and watersports centre with 10 superb beaches and coves.

PARKFIELD LUXURY HOLIDAY APARTMENTS, JUNE & ROY LEWIS, CLADDON LANE, MAIDENCOMBE, TORQUAY TQ1 4TB (Tel & Fax: 01803 328952). We offer the warmest of welcomes to you, at the fairest of prices. Luxury 1, 2 and 3 bedroomed apartments with views overlooking Dartmoor in the distance. [Pets £10 per week]

MR AND MRS K. NOTON, CROSSWAYS AND SEA VIEW HOLIDAY APARTMENTS, MAIDEN-COMBE, TORQUAY TQ1 4TH (Tel and Fax: 01803 328369). Modern self-contained flats set in one-acre grounds. Sleep 2/5. Colour TV. Pets welcome – exercise area. Children's play area. [pw! £10 per week.]

CLEVEDON HOTEL, MEADFOOT SEA ROAD, TORQUAY TQ1 2LQ (01803 294260). Set in its own peaceful grounds 300 yards from beach and woods. En suite rooms with TV, radio/alarm and tea/coffee. Licensed bar. AA ♦♦♦ RAC Listed. [🐾]

RED HOUSE HOTEL AND MAXTON LODGE HOLIDAY APARTMENTS, ROUSDOWN ROAD, CHELSTON, TORQUAY TQ2 6PB (01803 607811; Fax: 01803 605357). Choose either the friendly service and facilities of a hotel or the privacy and freedom of self-catering apartments. The best of both worlds!, AA/ETC ★★ Hotel & ★★★ Self-catering. See our colour display advert on page 00 [🐾 in flats; £3 per night in hotel]
e-mail: stay@redhouse-hotel.co.uk
website: www.redhouse-hotel.co.uk

MR & MRS W. J. HANBURY AND FAMILY, FAIRLAWNS HALL, 27 ST MICHAELS ROAD, TORQUAY TQ1 4DD (01803 328904). Delightful self-catering holiday apartments and mews cottages. Pets welcome. Large woods nearby, gardens and parking. [Pets £15 per week]

PETITOR HOUSE, TORQUAY. Beautiful Victorian House. Panoramic sea views. Unique quiet idyllic clifftop position. House sleeps six in three bedrooms and is well-furnished and equipped. Pets welcome. Colour brochure from: LES & ANN SHAW, 52 PETITOR ROAD, TQ1 4QF (01803 327943) [🐾]

FAIRMOUNT HOUSE HOTEL, HERBERT ROAD, CHELSTON, TORQUAY TQ2 6RW (01803 605446). Somewhere special – a small licensed hotel with comfortable en suite bedrooms, cosy bar, delicious home cooking. Peaceful setting. One mile town centre. B&B from £25 per person. Bargain Breaks available. [Pets £2 per night.]

SOUTH SANDS APARTMENTS, TORBAY ROAD, LIVERMEAD, TORQUAY TQ2 6RG (01803 293521; Fax: 01803 293502). 18 superior self-contained ground and first floor Apartments for 1–5 persons. Central heating. Open all year. Parking. Beach 100 yards. Convenient Riviera Centre, theatre, marina. Short Breaks except Summer season. ETC ★★★ [pw! from £1 per night.] e–mail: southsands@easicom.com

MRS SUSAN MECHAN, THE STUMBLE INN, 31-33 MEADFOOT LANE, TORQUAY TQ12 2BW (01803 299996). Cosy country pub in the town, four minutes from harbour. Beams and log fire; good home-cooked food. B&B from £18 pppn. Dogs welcome throughout pub.

SILVERLANDS HOTEL, 27 NEWTON ROAD, TORQUAY TQ2 5DB (01803 292013). Situated on main route to town and beach. Superb family-run guest house. 12 superior rooms, mostly en suite. Satellite TV, tea and coffee making, full central heating. Ample car parking. Full English breakfast. Open all year. From £14 to £20 per person. ETC COMMENDED. AA QQQ.

LITTLECOURT HOLIDAY APARTMENTS, 458 BABBACOMBE ROAD, TORQUAY TQ1 1HW (01803 295654). Convenient for Torquay Harbour and town centre. Choice of nine self-contained apartments. Sleeps 2/6. Well furnished and fully equipped including bed linen with continental quilts, colour TV and own keys. Free car parking, private sun patios and free transport from railway or bus station. Reduced rates early/late season. Pets welcome

Torrington

Pleasant market town on River Torridge. Good centre for moors and sea. Exeter 36 miles, Okehampton 20, Barnstple 12, Bideford 7.

SALLY MILSOM, STOWFORD LODGE, LANGTREE, NEAR TORRINGTON EX38 8NU (01805 601540). Sleep 4/6. Away from the crowds. Four delightful cottages with heated indoor pool, and two secluded period farm cottages. Peaceful countryside, convenient North Devon coast and moors. Magnificent views and walks. Phone for brochure. ETC ★★★. [Pets £10 per week, pw!]

Totnes

Town at tidal estuary of River Dart, 7 miles west of Torquay

SEA TROUT INN, STAVERTON, NEAR TOTNES, DEVON TQ9 6PA (Tel: 01803 762274; Fax: 01803 762506) Hidden away in the tranquil Dart Valley but conveniently placed for Dartmoor, Torbay and the South Devon coast. Delightful cottage style bedrooms, two traditional English bars and elegant restaurant.

FLEAR FARM COTTAGES, EAST ALLINGTON, TOTNES, SOUTH DEVON TQ9 7RF (01548 521227; Fax 01548 521600). Superb cottages, indoor heated swimming pool, sauna, all weather tennis court, large indoor and outdoor play areas. Non-smokers only. Log fires and full central heating - perfect for off-season breaks. ETC ★★★★/★★★★★★ [Pets £15 per week].

Umberleigh

Quiet North Devon village on the River Taw, ideal for exploring Exmoor.

KINGFORD HILL HOLIDAY VILLAGE, HIGH BICKINGTON, UMBERLEIGH EX37 9BN (01769 560211). Glorious woodland country park. No lamp posts - no traffic, just 26 acres of trees! 21 detached self-catering chalets. Magnificent views. Shop, sauna and licensed restaurant and bar. [Pets £15 per week, maximum 2].

Westward Ho!

Charming village named after the novel by Charles Kingsley. Good sands; 2 mile long pebble ridge to the north west.

WEST PUSEHILL FARM COTTAGES. Set along the beautiful North Devon coast. Resident propri-etors are always available to ensure everyone enjoys their stay. Friendly country inn within grounds. Open all year. Brochure from: JOHN AND GILL VIOLET, WEST PUSEHILL FARM, WESTWARD HO! X39 5AH (01237 475638)
website: www.wpfcottages.co.uk

Woolacombe

Favorite resort with long, wide stretches of sand. Barnstaple 15 miles, Ilfracombe 6.

EUROPA PARK, STATION ROAD, WOOLACOMBE (01271 870159). Luxury bungalows, superb views. Touring caravans and tents. Full facilities. Pets welcome, 6-acre dog park. Indoor heated swimming pool. [pw! £5 per week.]

SUNNYMEADE COUNTRY HOTEL, WEST DOWN, NEAR WOOLACOMBE EX34 8NT (01271 863668). Small country hotel set in beautiful countryside. A few minutes away from Ilfracombe, Exmoor and Woolacombe's Blue Flag Beach. 8 en suite rooms 2 on the ground floor. Pets Welcome-dogs are free. [🐶, pw!]
website: www.sunnymeade.co.uk

MRS JOYCE BAGNALL, CHICHESTER HOUSE, THE ESPLANADE, WOOLACOMBE EX34 7DJ (01271 870761). Holiday apartments on sea front. Fully furnished, sea and coastal views. Watch the sun go down from your balcony. Open all year. SAE Resident Proprietor. [Pets £8 per week, pw!]

PEBBLES HOTEL, COMBESGATE BEACH, WOOLACOMBE EX34 7EA (01271 870426). Family-run Hotel overlooking sea and beaches. All rooms en suite, with colour TV, tea/coffee making etc. Special Short Break packages. Write or phone for colour brochure. [🐶]
website: www.pebbleshotel.com

CROSSWAYS HOTEL, SEAFRONT, WOOLACOMBE EX34 7DJ (Tel.& Fax: 01271 870395). Homely, family-run licensed Hotel surrounded by National Trust land. Silver Award Hotel ETC/AA/RAC ★ Children and pets welcome. [🐶]

Please mention *Pets Welcome*
when enquiring about accommodation featured in these pages.

CAIRNSMORE HOTEL

ETC
♦♦♦

Ideally situated, being next to the suspension footbridge spanning the pine-wooded glades of Alum Chine with several paths to explore. Only 4 minutes' walk to sandy beach on which dogs are allowed all year. We are renowned for our high standard of catering and cleanliness, e.g., fresh towels daily. Freshly prepared and home cooked meals. All bedrooms are en suite, have views of the wooded chine, colour TV and tea/coffee making facilities. Ground floor rooms. Parking.

* Licensed * Senior Citizens Special Rates *

Special Breaks of 2 or more days: October to April, Bed, Breakfast & Evening Dinner £27 per day. Weekly terms from £154. No charge for pets.

Please write or telephone for our colour brochure

**37 Beaulieu Road, Alum Chine, Bournemouth BH4 8HY
Tel: 01202 763705**

Alum Dene Hotel

2 Burnaby Road, Alum Chine,Bournemouth BH4 8JF Tel: 01202 764011
Renowned for good old fashioned hospitality and friendly service. Come and be spoilt at our licensed hotel. All rooms en suite, colour TV. Some have sea views. 200 metres sea. Parking. Christmas House party. No charge for pets.

DENEWOOD HOTEL

ETC ♦♦♦

Warm friendly hotel, near beach (500 yards away) and shops in excellent central location. Good parking. All rooms en suite. TV, tea, coffee and biscuits in rooms. Health and Spa on site. Open all year. Prices from £17 to £22 B&B. **www.denewood.co.uk** **40 Sea Road, Bournemouth BH5 1BQ** **Tel: 01202 309913** **Fax: 01202 391155**

Golden Sands Hotel

83 Alumhurst Road, Alum Chine, Bournemouth, Dorset BH4 8HR

Charming licensed hotel situated in a select area just a few minutes walk to the West Undercliff Promenade and the beach. Lounge and attractive sun lounge. Dining room with separate tables. All bedrooms are en suite with bath/shower, tea/coffee making facilities, colour television and clock radio. Full English breakfast. B&B £21 to £27 per night with weekly reductions. Evening meal available. Pets very welcome.

Tel & Fax 01202 763832   e-mail: goldensandshotel@btinternet.com

FHG PUBLICATION LIMITED publish a large range of well-known accommodation guides. We will be happy to send you details or you can use the order form at the back of this book.

Dolphins River Park

Small, very peaceful park set in beautiful landscaped grounds of mature trees, shrubs and lawns on the banks of the River Char.
Luxury fully self-contained 4 and 6 berth Caravans for hire and sale.
Facilities include laundry room, information room with payphone. Table tennis, Sandpit and Swing. Direct access to footpaths and fields.
One mile from the beach. *WELL CARED FOR PETS WELCOME*
Colour Brochure available from:
Dolphins, Berne Lane, Charmouth, Dorset DT6 6RD
FREEPHONE: 0800 0746375

NEW FOREST

BH & HPA Member

Country Holiday Chalet on small, quiet, secluded woodland park. Fenced private garden. Dogs welcome. Car parking. £100 to £295 per week. Write enclosing SAE or telephone:
Mrs L.M.Bowling, Owlpen, 148 Burley Road, Bransgore, Near Christchurch, Dorset BH23 8DB Tel: 01425 672875   Mobile: 0860 547391

The Old Post Office

Situated in the Winterbourne Valley, The Old Post Office is a stone and slate Georgian cottage used as the village post office until 1950. Five miles from coast and beach, an ideal walking and touring base. Pets and children welcome. Bed and Breakfast from £15 to £25.
Mrs Jane Rootham, The Old Post Office,
Martinstown, Dorchester DT2 9LF   Tel: 01305 889254

Grace Cottage
Waterside Lane,
Sydling St. Nicholas
Contact: Mrs Willis, Lamperts Cottage,
Sydling St. Nicholas DT2 9NU
Tel: 01300 341659 Fax: 01300 341699

Charming cottage with enclosed flint walled garden. Peaceful, secluded position in beautiful village situated in countryside made famous by Thomas Hardy. Large lounge/dining room with colour TV and video, study/bedroom, two bedrooms (double and twin), two bathrooms. Modern kitchen with cooker, microwave, fridge/freezer, washing machine, tumble dryer. Good touring centre, excellent walking country, beaches 12 miles. Guide books and maps available for guests' use. Pub nearby. Non-smokers only. Pets welcome.

ETC ◆◆◆ **CHURCHVIEW GUEST HOUSE** AA QQQ
Winterbourne Abbas, Dorchester, Dorset DT2 9LS   Tel/Fax: 01305 889296

Our 17th century Guest House, noted for warm hospitality, delicious breakfasts and evening meals, makes an ideal base for touring beautiful West Dorset. Our character bedrooms are all comfortable and well-appointed. Meals, served in our beautiful dining room, feature local produce, with relaxation provided by two attractive lounges and licensed bar. Your hosts, Jane and Michael Deller, are pleased to give every assistance, with local information to ensure a memorable stay. Non-smoking.
Terms: Bed and Breakfast: £22 – £32; Dinner, Bed and Breakfast: £36 – £44.
E-mail: stay@churchview.co.uk Website: www.churchview.co.uk

Please mention *Pets Welcome*
when enquiring about accommodation featured in these pages.

The Stables Hyde Crook, Frampton, Dorchester DT2 9NW Tel: 01300 320075

The Stables is a large equestrian property which sits in a small area of woodland off the A37 which provides easy travelling to Dorchester from a location which enjoys uninterrupted views of open Dorset countryside. We are a registered small holding of approximately 20 acres, with sheep, ducks and horses, and specialise in providing accommodation and livery for cross country riding. Well behaved dogs welcome and should provide their own beds. ETC/AA/RAC ◆◆◆

Situated in a secret spot, down a leafy lane, just a five minute walk from the sea. All 18 rooms en suite, with colour TV, tea and coffee making facilities and trouser press. Two of the rooms having four-poster beds. Restaurant with views over Lyme Bay. Smugglers Bar serving bar snacks lunchtimes and evenings with patio overlooking the sea. Enjoy the spectacular walks or just take in some of the many places of interest in the area. Don't just drive through Dorset, come and stay a while and experience the peace and tranquillity that still exists in this beautiful part of Dorset. Heidi our Dalmatian looks forward to meeting you and your Fido. Three day breaks available.

Eype's Mouth Country Hotel

Eype's Mouth Country Hotel, Eype, Bridport DT6 6AL
Tel: 01308 423300; Fax: 01308 420033
E-mail: eypehotel@aol.com

DORSET HOLIDAY COTTAGES.

Selection of quality cottages in stunning rural and coastal locations. Pets welcome in many homes. All furnished to the highest standards. Sleeping 1-20. Prices range from £100 - £1000 per week. Short Breaks Available.

Telephone: 01202 620490

e-mail: Dorsetcottageholidays@fsmail.net • website: www.cottageholidays.fsnet.co.uk

The Scott Arms Situated on the Isle of Purbeck, The Scott Arms is a traditional

18th century inn, with exposed oak beams, open fireplace, friendly atmosphere and a truly breathtaking view of Corfe castle from our beer garden. We offer a superb menu every lunchtime and evening, complemented by a selection of traditional ales, lagers, fine wines and spirits. Country inn accommodation is available, with all the amenities you would expect.
Kingston, Corfe Castle, Dorset BH20 5LW (Tel: 01929 480270 Fax: 01929 481570)

Mrs J Tedbury, Little Paddocks, Yawl Hill Lane, Lyme Regis DT7 3RW Tel: 01297 443085

A six-berth caravan on Devon/Dorset border in a well kept paddock overlooking Lyme Bay and surrounding countryside. Situated on a smallholding with animals, for perfect peace and quiet. Fully equipped except linen. Electric light, fridge, TV. Calor gas cooker and fire. Dogs welcome. Terms from £90. Also fully equipped chalet for two. (Terms from £75). SAE please.

WESTOVER FARM COTTAGES

In an area of outstanding beauty, Wootton Fitzpaine epitomizes picturesque West Dorset. Within walking distance of sea. 2 beautiful cottages sleep 6/7 with large secluded gardens. Car parking. Logs, Linen available, 3 bedrooms. £175-£520. Pets welcome.
Wootton Fitzpaine, Nr Lyme Regis, Dorset DT6 6N

Brochure: Debby Snook 01297 560451 *E-mail: wfcottages@aol.com* ETC★★★

Please mention *Pets Welcome*
when enquiring about accommodation featured in these pages.

THE
KNOLL HOUSE

STUDLAND BAY

A peaceful and relaxing holiday for all ages.
An independent country-house hotel, in an unrivalled position above
three miles of golden beach. Dogs are especially welcome and may
sleep in your room. Special diets arranged. Our 100 acre grounds offer
nice walks; squirrels and rabbits!

Good food and a sensible wine list.
Tennis courts; nine acre golf course and outdoor heated pool.
Health spa with Jacuzzi, Sauna, Turkish room, plunge pool and gym.
Many ground-floor and single rooms for older guests.

Family suites, of connecting rooms with bathroom,
separate young children's dining room.
Playrooms and fabulous SAFE adventure playground.

Daily full board terms: £90-£115. Children less, according to age.

Open Easter - end October

STUDLAND BAY
DORSET

BH19 3AW

For Colour Brochure
TEL 01929 · 450450   FAX 01929 · 450423
Email: enquiries@knollhouse.co.uk
Website: www.knollhouse.co.uk

See also Colour Advertisement on page 27

WELCOME COTTAGE HOLIDAYS. Quality Cottages in wonderful locations at welcoming low prices. Pets, linen and fuel mostly included. PHONE FOR FREE 2001 FULL COLOUR BROCHURE 01756 702204.

ISLAND COTTAGE HOLIDAYS. Charming individual cottages in lovely rural surroundings and close to the sea. Cottages situated on the Dorset coast. Attractive gardens and beautiful views in wonderful walking areas. All cottages equipped to a high standard and graded for quality by the Tourist Board. Brochure: HONOR VASS, THE OLD VICARAGE, KINGSTON, WAREHAM, DORSET BH20 5LH (01929 480080; Fax: 01929 481070)

Abbotsbury

Village of thatched cottages; Benedictine monks created the famous Abbotsbury Swannery.

MRS JOSEPHINE PEARSE, TAMARISK FARM, WEST BEXINGTON, DORCHESTER DT2 9DF (01308 897784). Self Catering properties sleep 4/6. Overlooking Chesil Beach: three large (one for disabled Cat 1) and two smaller Cottages (ETC 3/4 stars) and two secluded Chalets on mixed organic farm with arable, sheep, cattle, horses and market garden with vegetables on sale. Good centre for touring, sightseeing, walking. Pets and children welcome. Terms from £105 to £590. [🐾]

Blandford

Handsome Georgian town that rose from the ashes of 1731 fire; rebuilt with chequered brick and stone. Also known as Blandford Forum.

ANVIL HOTEL & RESTAURANT, PIMPERNE, BLANDFORD DT11 8UQ (01258 453431/480182). A typical Old English hostelry offering good old-fashioned English hospitality. Full à la carte menu with mouthwatering desserts in the charming restaurant with log fire, delicious desserts, bar meals, specials board. All bedrooms with private facilities. Ample parking. ETC ★★, Les Routiers. [Pets £2.50 per night]

Bournemouth

One of Britain's premier holiday resorts with miles of golden sand, excellent shopping and leisure facilities. Lively entertainments include Festival of Lights at the beginning of September.

BILL AND MARJORIE TITCHEN, WHITE TOPPS HOTEL, 45 CHURCH ROAD, SOUTHBOURNE, BOURNEMOUTH BH6 4BB (01202 428868). Situated in quiet position close to lovely walks and beach. Dogs essential. Free parking. Residential licence. [🐾 pw!]

ANNE & RICHARD REYNOLDS, THE VINE HOTEL, 22 SOUTHERN ROAD, SOUTHBOURNE, BOURNEMOUTH BH6 3SR (01202 428309). Small, family, Hotel only 3 minutes' walk from sea and shops. All rooms en suite. Residential licence. FHG Diploma 2000, STB ◆◆◆ [🐾]

MIKE AND LYN LAMBERT, AARON, 16 FLORENCE ROAD, BOURNEMOUTH BH5 1HF (01202 304925/01425 474007). Modern Holiday Apartments sleeping one to ten persons, close to sea and shops. Recently extensively renovated with new kitchens and bathrooms. Clean well-equipped flats. Car park and garages. Write or phone for colour brochure and terms. [Pets £14 weekly] website: www.bhfa.co.uk/aaron-lyttelton

Visit the **FHG** website

www.holidayguides.com

for details of the wide choice of accommodation featured in the full range of FHG titles

MRS LYNN WEETMAN, THE GOLDEN SOVEREIGN HOTEL, 97 ALUMHURST ROAD, ALUM CHINE, BOURNEMOUTH BH4 8HR (Tel & Fax: 01202 762088). Charming Victorian Hotel close to award winning beaches and wooded chine walks. Cosy bar, freshly cooked optional evening meals. En suite rooms, all with tea/coffee making facilities, television, clock/radio alarm and direct dial telephones with extra point for internet access. ETC ◆◆◆. [🐾]
e-mail: goldensov@aol.com
website: www.golden-sovereign.demon.co.uk

CAIRNSMORE PRIVATE HOTEL, 37 BEAULIEU ROAD, BOURNEMOUTH BH4 8HY (01202 763705). 4 minutes' walk through wooded glades to sea. Colour TV in all bedrooms, all en suite. Parking. BB&EM from £27 per person per day. Residential licence. Special diets catered for. No charge for pets. ETC ◆◆◆. [🐾 pw!]

ALUM DENE HOTEL, 2 BURNABY ROAD, ALUM CHINE, BOURNEMOUTH BH4 8JF (01202 764011) Renowned for good old fashioned hospitality and friendly service. Come and be spoilt at our licensed hotel. All rooms en suite, colour TV. Some have sea views. 200 metres sea. Parking. Christmas House party. No charge for pets. [🐾]

DENEWOOD HOTEL, 40 SEA ROAD, BOURNEMOUTH BH5 1BQ (01202 309913; Fax: 01202 391155). All rooms en suite. Residential and Residents' licence. Special weekly rates available. TV, tea, coffee and biscuits in rooms, Health and Beauty salon on site. Open all year. ETC ◆◆◆ [🐾]

ALUM GRANGE HOTEL, 1 BURNABY ROAD, ALUM CHINE, BOURNEMOUTH BH4 8JF (01202 761195). Pets and owners are assured of a warm welcome at this superbly furnished hotel, 250 yards from the beach. All rooms with colour TV and tea/coffee making. [🐾]

ROGER COATES-WALKER, GOLDEN SANDS HOTEL, 83 ALUMHURST ROAD, ALUM CHINE, BOURNEMOUTH BH4 8HR (Tel/Fax: 01202 763832). Charming licensed hotel; all bedrooms en suite with bath/shower, tea/coffee making facilities, colour television and clock radio. Full English breakfast, evening meal available.
e-mail: goldensandshotel@btinternet.com

HOLIDAY FLATS AND FLATLETS near sea and shops. Overlooking quiet, wooded Pleasure Gardens; superb for you and your dog. Both properties have good car parks; pay-phones, laundry, TV, fridges in all units. Clean and fully equipped. We like dogs. Apply: MRS INGLE, 14 MORLEY ROAD, BOURNEMOUTH BH5 2JJ or telephone 0208 4081576. [Pets £14 per dog, per week]

MRS SUE DOBSON, KIMBERLEY COURT HOTEL, 40 PINECLIFFE AVENUE, SOUTHBOURNE, BOURNEMOUTH BH6 3PZ (01202 427583). Small family run hotel open all year, especially Christmas. Excellent home-cooking, comfortable accommodation close to beach, shops and cliff top walks. Pets very welcome. [Pets £7 per week]

Three self-contained apartments in quiet avenue, one minute from clean, sandy beaches and five minutes from shops. Sleep 3/6. Fully equipped including linen. All have fridge, toilet and shower room, microwave, colour TV, central heating, electric meter. Parking. Terms from £75. Contact: MRS HAMMOND, STOURCLIFFE COURT, 56 STOURCLIFFE AVENUE, SOUTHBOURNE, BOURNEMOUTH BH6 3PX (01202 420698). [Pets £5 weekly]

Bridport

Market town of Saxon origin noted for rope and net making. Harbour at West Bay has sheer cliffs rising from the beach.

BRIDPORT ARMS HOTEL, WEST BAY, BRIDPORT DT6 4EN (01308 422994). Thatched Hotel on edge of beach in picturesque West Bay. Two character bars, real ale, wide range of bar meals. A la carte Restaurant featuring local fish. [🐾]

MRS CAROL MANSFIELD, LANCOMBES HOUSE, WEST MILTON, BRIDPORT DT6 3TN (01308 485375). Pretty cottages in converted barns. Panoramic views to sea four miles away. Set in 10 acres, some have fenced gardens. Many walks from our land. ETC ★★★

MR F. LOOSMORE, MANOR FARM HOLIDAY CENTRE, CHARMOUTH, BRIDPORT DT6 6QL (01297 560226). All units for four to six people. Ten minutes' level walk to beach, many fine local walks. Swimming pools, licensed bar with family room, shop, launderette. Sporting facilities nearby. Children and pets welcome. SAE for colour brochure. [Pets from £15 per week]

EYPE HOUSE CARAVAN & CAMPING PARK, EYPE, BRIDPORT DT6 6AL (01308 424903). Small, quiet family-run park lying on the Heritage Coastal Path 200 yards from the beach. Static vans for hire from £150 to £350, tent pitches (all terraced with sea views) £8 to £12 for four people. Sorry, no tourers. Children and dogs welcome.

MRS S. NORMAN, FROGMORE FARM, CHIDEOCK, BRIDPORT DT6 6HT (01308 456159). The choice is yours - Bed and Breakfast, optional Evening meal, in charming farmhouse, OR self-catering Cottage equipped for six, pets welcome. Brochure and terms free on request. [1st dog free, 2nd dog £3.00 per night, £15 per week]

Charmouth

Small resort on Lyme Bay, 3 miles Lyme Regis. Sandy beach backed by undulating cliffs where many fossils are found. Good walks.

DOLPHINS RIVER PARK, BERNE LANE, CHARMOUTH DT6 6RD (FREEPHONE 0800 0746375). Luxury 4 and 6 berth caravans on small, peaceful park. Coin-op laundry; children's play area. One mile from beach. Colour brochure available. [Pets £10 per week]

Christchurch

Residential town near coast. Yachting based on Christchurch harbour and Christchurch Bay.

COUNTRY HOLIDAY CHALET on small, quiet, secluded woodland park. Fenced private garden. Dogs welcome. Car parking. £100 to £295 per week. BH & HPA Member. Write enclosing SAE or telephone: MRS L. M. BOWLING, OWLPEN, 148 BURLEY ROAD, BRANSGORE, DORSET BH23 8DB (01425 672875; mobile 0860 547391). [🐾 pw!]

Dorchester

Busy market town steeped in history. Roman remains include Amphitheatre and villa.

MRS JANE ROOTHAM, THE OLD POST OFFICE, MARTINSTOWN, DORCHESTER DT2 9LF (01305 889254). Situated in the Winterbourne Valley, The Old Post Office is a stone and slate Georgian cottage used as the village post office until 1950. Five miles from coast and beach, an ideal walking and touring base. Pets and children welcome. Bed and Breakfast from £15 to £25. [🐾]

GRACE COTTAGE. Charming cottage with enclosed garden. Lounge/dining room, study/bedroom, two bedrooms, well equipped kitchen, two bathrooms. Pub nearby. Non smokers only Good touring centre. Apply: MRS WILLIS, LAMPERTS COTTAGE, SYDLING ST. NICHOLAS DT2 9NU (01300 341659; Fax: 01300 341699). [🐾]

CHURCHVIEW GUEST HOUSE, WINTERBOURNE ABBAS, DORCHESTER DT2 9LS (Tel & Fax: 01305 889296). Beautiful 17th Century Licensed Guest House set in the heart of West Dorset, character bedrooms, delightful period dining room, two lounges and bar. Non-smoking. B&B £22–£32 pp. B&BEM £36–£44. ETC ◆◆◆, AA QQQ. [🐾]
e-mail: stay@churchview.co.uk
website: www.churchview.co.uk

SYMBOLS

🐾   Indicates that pets are welcome free of charge.

£   Indicates that a charge is made for pets: nightly or weekly.

pw!   Shows some special provision for pets; exercise facility, feeding or accommodation arrangement.

◻   Indicates separate pets accommodation.

MRS JACOBINA LANGLEY, THE STABLES, HYDE CROOK (OFF A37), FRAMPTON, DORCHESTER DT2 9NW (01300 320075). A comfortable equestrian property in some 20 acres of grounds. Well situated for bridleways/footpaths. Guests' TV lounge, three bedrooms with en suite and private facilities. ETC/AA/RAC ◆◆◆. [pw! £1.50 per dog per night.]

Eype

Market town of Saxon origin noted for rope and net making. Harbour at West Bay has sheer cliffs rising from the beach.

EYPE'S MOUTH COUNTRY HOTEL, EYPE, BRIDPORT DT6 6AL (01308 423300; Fax: 01308 420033). Experience the tranquillity of Dorset. Situated in a secret spot, down a leafy lane, just a five minute walk from the sea. Restaurant with views over Lyme Bay. [Pets £2.00 per night]
e-mail: eypehotel@aol.com

Isle of Purbeck

Peninsula in south east Dorset bounded by English Channel, Poole Harbour and River Frome. Traversed by Purbeck Hills.

DORSET HOLIDAY COTTAGES (01202 620490).Selection of quality cottages in stunning rural and coastal locations. Pets welcome in many homes. All furnished to the highest standards. Sleeping 1-20. Prices range from £100 - £1000 per week. Short Breaks Available. [Pets £15 per week].
e-mail: Dorsetcottageholidays@fsmail.net
website: www.cottageholidays.fsnet.co.uk

Kingston

Village on Isle of Purbeck, 5 miles west of Swanage.

The Scott Arms, Kingston, Corfe Castle BH20 5LW (01929 480270; Fax: 01929 481570). Traditional 18th century inn. Accommodation at reasonable rates, which include en suite facilities, tea/coffee making, hairdryer, colour television, and of course a full English breakfast.

Kington Magna

Village lying to the south west of Gillingham.

MRS G. GOSNEY, KINGTON MANOR FARM, CHURCH HILL, KINGTON MAGNA NEAR GILLINGHAM SP8 5EG (01747 838371). Attractive farmhouse situated in a quiet, pretty village, with splendid views over the pastoral Blackmore Vale. Near the historic towns of Shaftesbury and Sherborne; Stourhead National Trust house and gardens and stately home of Longleat and Safari Park nearby. Bath 45 minutes' drive. Breakfast £22 per person per night. Reductions for children. Excellent pub food nearby. Outdoor swimming pool. ◆◆◆◆. [🐾]

Lyme Regis

Picturesque little resort with harbour, once the haunt of smugglers. Shingle beach with sand at low tide. Fishing, sailing and water ski-ing in Lyme Bay. Taunton 28 miles, Dorchester 24, Seaton 8.

MRS J TEDBURY, LITTLE PADDOCKS, YAWL HILL LANE, LYME REGIS DT7 3RW (01297 443085). A six-berth caravan on Devon/Dorset border overlooking Lyme Bay and surrounding countryside. Situated on a smallholding with animals. Fully equipped. Also fully equipped chalet for two. [🐾]

FHG PUBLICATIONS

publish a large range of well-known accommodation guides. We will be happy to send you details or you can use the order form at the back of this book.

WESTOVER FARM COTTAGES, WOOTTON FITZPAINE, NEAR LYME REGIS DT6 6NE (01297 560451). Within walking distance of the sea. Two beautiful cottages, sleep 6/7, with large secluded gardens. Car parking. Logs, Linen available. 3 bedrooms. Pets welcome. ETC ★★★ [Pets £10 per week.]
e-mail: wfcottages@aol.com

Piddletrenthide

Village 6 miles north of Dorchester.

THE POACHERS INN, PIDDLETRENTHIDE DT2 7QX (01300 348358; Fax: 01300 348153). On B3143 in lovely Piddle Valley, this delightful Inn offers en suite rooms with colour TV, tea/coffee making, phone. Swimming pool; residents' lounge. Restaurant or Bar meals available. Garden – good dog walks! B&B £30.00. ETC/AA ◆◆◆◆. [Pets £2 per night, £10 per week]

Poole

Popular resort, yachting and watersports centre with large harbour and many creeks. Sand and shingle beaches. Salisbury 30 miles, Dorchester 23, Blandford 14, Wareham 9, Burnemouth 5.

SANDFORD HOLIDAY PARK. A very special place! Situated in an area of outstanding natural beauty near the New Forest, Bournemouth and Poole. ★★★★. Phone WESTSTAR HOLIDAY PARKS on 01202 631600.

Ringwood

Town on east bank of River Avon, 10 miles north-east of Bournemouth.

OAKHILL FARM CARAVAN PARK, 234 RINGWOOD ROAD, ST. LEONARDS, RINGWOOD, HANTS BH24 2SB (01202 876968). Secluded, quiet 10 acre site within 40 acres of surrounding woodland. Dogs most welcome. Plenty of room for exercising off lead away from pitches. No club or amusements on site. Usual toilet, shower and laundry facilities. Electric hook-ups. Easter - October.

FOR THE MUTUAL GUIDANCE OF GUEST AND HOST

Every year literally thousands of holidays, short breaks and overnight stops are arranged through our guides, the vast majority without any problems at all. In a handful of cases, however, difficulties do arise about bookings, which often could have been prevented from the outset.

It is important to remember that when accommodation has been booked, both parties – guests and hosts – have entered into a form of contract. We hope that the following points will provide helpful guidance.

GUESTS: When enquiring about accommodation, be as precise as possible. Give exact dates, numbers in your party and the ages of any children. State the number and type of rooms wanted and also what catering you require – bed and breakfast, full board etc. Make sure that the position about evening meals is clear – and about pets, reductions for children or any other special points.

Read our reviews carefully to ensure that the proprietors you are going to contact can supply what you want. Ask for a letter confirming all arrangements, if possible.

If you have to cancel, do so as soon as possible. Proprietors do have the right to retain deposits and under certain circumstances to charge for cancelled holidays if adequate notice is not given and they cannot re-let the accommodation.

HOSTS: Give details about your facilities and about any special conditions. Explain your deposit system clearly and arrangements for cancellations, charges etc. and whether or not your terms include VAT.

If for any reason you are unable to fulfil an agreed booking without adequate notice, you may be under an obligation to arrange suitable alternative accommodation or to make some form of compensation.

While every effort is made to ensure accuracy, we regret that FHG Publications cannot accept responsibility for errors, omissions or misrepresentations in our entries or any consequences thereof.
Prices in particular should be checked because we go to press early. We will follow up complaints but cannot act as arbiters or agents for either party.

Sherborne

Town with abbey abd two castles, one of which was built by Sir Walter Raleigh with lakes and gardens by Capability Brown.

WHITE HORSE FARM, MIDDLEMARSH, SHERBORNE DT9 5QN. Toad Hall sleeps 4; Badger's sleeps 2; Ratty's sleeps 2/4; Moley's sleeps 2. Character self-catering holiday cottages in rural location. Well-equipped and comfortable. TV, video, free films. 3 acres of paddock, garden and duck pond. Inn 100 yards. ETC ★★★. DAVID, HAZEL, MARY AND GERRY WILDING (01963 210222)[🐕]
e-mail: enquiries@whitehorsefarm.co.uk
website: www.whitehorsefarm.co.uk

MRS S. STRETTON, BEECH FARM, SIGWELLS, CHARLTON HORETHORNE, NEAR SHERBORNE DT9 4LN (Tel & Fax: 01963 220524). Relaxed farmhouse accommodation on our 137 acre dairy farm. Centrally heated with double room en suite, a twin room and family room with guest bathroom. Evening Meals available locally, or by prior arrangement. £16 per person. Open all year. Pets and horses welcome. [🐕]

Studland Bay

Unspoilt seaside village at south western end of Poole Bay, 3 miles north of Swanage.

THE MANOR HOUSE, STUDLAND BAY BH19 3AU (01929 450288). An 18th Century Manor House, nestling in 20 acres of secluded grounds. All bedrooms en suite with central heating, colour TV, direct dial telephone, tea/coffee making facilities. STB ★★ [Pets £3.25 per night.]

KNOLL HOUSE HOTEL, STUDLAND BH19 3AW (01929 450450; Fax: 01929 450423). Country House Hotel within National Trust reserve. Golden beach. 100 acre grounds. Family suites, six lounges. Tennis, golf, swimming, games rooms, health spa. Full board terms £90-£115 daily. See our Full Page Advertisement under Studland Bay. [pw! £4 nightly]
e–mail: enquiries@knollhouse.co.uk
website: www.knollhouse.co.uk

Swanage

Traditional family holiday resort set in a sheltered bay ideal for water sports. Good base for a walking holiday.

LIMES HOTEL, 48 PARK ROAD, SWANAGE BH19 2AE (01929 422664; Fax: 0870 0548794). Small friendly Hotel. En suite rooms, tea/coffee making facilities. Licensed bar. Central heating. Children and pets welcome. Telephone or SAE for brochure. [🐕]
e–mail: info@limeshotel.demon.co.uk
website: www.limeshotel.demon.co.uk

MRS M. STOCKLEY, SWANAGE CARAVAN SITE, 17 MOOR ROAD, SWANAGE BH19 1RG (01929 424154). 4/5/6-berth Caravans. Pets welcome. Easter to October. Colour TV. Shop. Parking space. Rose Award Park ✓✓✓✓ [🐕]

Wareham

Picturesque riverside town almost surrounded by earthworks, considered pre-Roman. Nature reserves of great beauty nearby. Weymouth 19 miles, Bournemouth 14, Swanage 10, Poole 6.

CATRIONA AND ALISTAIR MILLER, CROMWELL HOUSE HOTEL LULWORTH COVE BH20 5RJ (01929 400253/400332; Fax: 01929 400566). Comfortable family-run hotel, set in secluded gardens with spectacular sea views. Heated swimming pool, 14 en suite bedrooms. Restaurant, bar wine list. ETC/AA/RAC ★★.

SYMBOLS

- 🐕 **Indicates that pets are welcome free of charge.**
- £ **Indicates that a charge is made for pets: nightly or weekly.**
- pw! **Shows some special provision for pets; exercise facility, feeding or accommodation arrangement.**
- ⌂ **Indicates separate pets accommodation.**

MRS L. S. BARNES, LUCKFORD WOOD HOUSE, EAST STOKE, WAREHAM BH20 6AW (01929 463098; Fax: 01929 405715). Spacious, peaceful surroundings. B&B luxurious farmhouse. Full English breakfast. Camping facilities include showers, toilets. Near Lulworth Cove, Studland Tank Museum and Monkey World. Open all year. From £18. LISTED. AA ◆◆◆. [Pets £5 per night]

West Bexington

Seaside village with pebble beach. Chesil beach stretches eastwards. Nearby is Abbotsbury with its Benedictine Abbey and famous Swannery. Dorchester 13 miles, Weymouth 13, Bridport 6.

GORSELANDS CARAVAN PARK, DEPT PW, WEST BEXINGTON-ON-SEA DT2 9DJ (01308 897232; Fax: 01308 897239). Holiday Park. Fully serviced and equipped 4/6 berth caravans. Shop and launderette on site. Glorious sea views. Good country and seaside walks. One mile to beach. Personal attention. Holiday apartments with sea views and private garden. Pets most welcome. Colour brochure on request. ETC ★★★★ [🐾]

Weymouth

Set in a beautiful bay with fine beaches and a picturesque 17th-century harbour, Weymouth has a wide range of entertainment and leisure amenities.

WEYMOUTH BAY HOLIDAY PARK, PRESTON. One 8-berth Caravan. Near sea. Dogs welcome. APPLY – MRS D. W. CANNON, 151 SANDSTONE ROAD, GROVE PARK, LONDON SE12 0UT (020 8857 7586) [🐾]

DURHAM

Castleside

A suburb 2 miles south-west of Consett.

LIZ LAWSON, BEE COTTAGE FARM, CASTLESIDE, CONSETT DH8 9HW (01207 508224). Working farm in lovely surroundings. You will be made most welcome. Ideal for Metro Centre, Durham Cathedral, Beamish Museum etc. Bed and Breakfast; Evening Meal available. ETC ◆◆◆. [🐾]

Waterhouses

6 miles west of Durham.

MRS P. A. BOOTH, IVESLEY EQUESTRIAN CENTRE, WATERHOUSES, DURHAM DH7 9HB (0191 373 4324; Fax: 0191 373 4757). Elegantly furnished comfortable country house set in 220 acres. Near Durham but quiet and rural. En suite bedrooms. Excellent food. Licensed. Equestrian facilities available. [Dogs £2 per day]

The **FHG**
GOLF GUIDE
Where to Play
Where to Stay
2001

Available from most bookshops, the 2001 edition of **THE GOLF GUIDE** covers details of every UK golf course – well over 2500 entries – for holiday or business golf. Hundreds of hotel entries offer convenient accommodation, accompanying details of the courses – the 'pro', par score, length etc.

In association with 'Golf Monthly' and including the Ryder Cup Report as well as Holiday Golf in Ireland, France, Portugal, Spain, The USA, South Africa and Thailand .

£9.99 from bookshops or £10.50 including postage (UK only) from FHG Publications, Abbey Mill Business Centre, Paisley PAI ITJ

Bourton-on-the-Water, Burford

ETC
★★★
Silver
Award
AA
★★★

CHARLTON
KINGS HOTEL
& RESTAURANT

LONDON ROAD,
CHELTENHAM,
GLOUCESTERSHIRE
GL52 6UU

RAC
★★★

The ideal venue for Cheltenham and the Cotswolds situated in an acre of garden in an area of outstanding natural beauty on the edge of town. Newly opened in 1991 after extensive refurbishment. Double en suite room from £45 per person for 1 night, £40 per person for 3 nights or £34 for 5 nights including full English breakfast. Most rooms (some reserved for non-smokers) have views of the Cotswold Hills, which are easily reached on foot – there is a footpath right alongside the hotel leading onto the famous Cotswold Way. There is plenty to do and see (our room information folder lists over 200 sights/activities), or simply watch the world go by from the conservatory. During your stay you will be tempted to try our cosy restaurant offering an imaginative and varied menu. Above all, we offer a standard of service only a small hotel can provide.

Tel: 01242 231061 / Fax: 01242 241900

See colour advertisement on page 28.

This charming 13th Century farmhouse Hotel in its own extensive grounds (14 acres) is ideal for dog walking. The Hotel is situated in the village of Clearwell bordering the Forest of Dean. 14 en suite bedrooms including Four-Posters and Cottage Suites. The award-winning restaurant serves a selection of traditional food and a comprehensive wine list. *B&B from £30.00pp. DB&B from £44.50pp. Please phone for brochure and information.* **WTB ★★★** *Hotel*

Tudor Farmhouse Hotel & Restaurant, Clearwell, Near Coleford, GL16 8JS (01594 833046) Email: reservations@tudorfarm.u-net.com

The
Bull Hotel

ETC ★★

AA
★★

The Market Place, Fairford, Gloucestershire GL7 4AA
Tel: 01285 712535/712217   Fax: 01285 713782

15th century family run coaching inn. Ideal for touring Cotswolds. A la carte restaurant situated in original stables. Ideal for conferences and weddings. 1½ miles private fishing on River Coln. The hotel has a choice of 22 fully equipped bedrooms with sloping roofs and oak beams. Four-poster beds available. There are good golf courses, squash and tennis courts, sailing facilities and fishing within easy reach of the hotel. Situated in the South Cotswolds.   Tariff: £47.50 - £89.50

FHG PUBLICATIONS LIMITED publish a large range of well-known accommodation guides. We will be happy to send you details or you can use the order form at the back of this book.

GUNN MILL HOUSE
Forest of Dean
Gloucestershire GL17 OEA

Silver
SILVER AWARD

GUEST
ACCOMMODATION

Tel & Fax: 01594 827577
E-mail: info@gunnmillhouse.co.uk Website: www.gunnmillhouse.co.uk

The Andersons invite you, and your owners, to stay in their Georgian home and 5 acre grounds right in the forest – walks galore! Antiques, a roaring log fire, old-fashioned luxury, with all en suite rooms and suites. First-class home cooked four-course dinners. Licensed. Non-smoking.

Bed & Breakfast– £50 - £75 per couple. Dog stay £5.

The Speech House
Coleford, Forest of Dean GL16 7EL
Tel: 01594 822607 Fax: 01594 823658

A friendly Hotel set in the heart of the Forest of Dean, perfect for walking dogs. Almost completely enveloped by trees, the Speech House is the perfect place to get away from it all. The hotel has 31 bedrooms, 25 of which are en suite, plus a newly opened Spa and Gym. The hotel has several four-poster beds and was built by King Charles II as a Hunting Lodge. Courtyard ground floor rooms are available. Pets are welcome.

AA/RAC ★★★

PARKEND HOUSE HOTEL
Parkend, Near Lydney, Gloucestershire GL15 4HL Tel: 01594 563666

Small Country House Hotel situated in the heart of the Royal Forest of Dean. All rooms en suite, TV etc. Ideal centre for touring Forest and Wye Valley. Horse-riding, Golf, Walking and Cycling.
Dinner, Bed and Breakfast from £36 pppn. Children and pets welcome.
Write or ring for brochure, sample menu and details of local places of interest.

The Laurels at Inchbrook

Mrs Lesley Williams-Allen, The Laurels at Inchbrook
Nailsworth GL5 5HA Tel & Fax: 01453 834021

A lovely rambling licensed house and cottage, where dogs and their owners are encouraged to relax and enjoy. All rooms are en suite and include family, twin and double rooms, each with colour TV and hospitality trays. There is wheelchair access and a ground floor room suitable for disabled guests. We have a ground floor panelled lounge full of interesting books and a piano, and on the top floor a games room.

Smoking is not allowed (except in the courtyard and garden). The secluded streamside garden with parking backs onto fields and offers a swimming pool and the opportunity to observe wildlife. We are ideally situated for touring all parts of the Cotswolds and West Country, surrounded by a wealth of beautiful countryside, first-class restaurants and pubs, and all kinds of activities. Children and pets welcome. Non-smoking. Bed and Breakfast from £21 per person. Dinner by arrangement. Brochure on request. RAC ◆◆◆

FHG

PLEASE MENTION THIS GUIDE WHEN YOU WRITE

OR PHONE TO ENQUIRE ABOUT ACCOMMODATION

IF YOU ARE WRITING, A STAMPED, ADDRESSED

ENVELOPE IS ALWAYS APPRECIATED

POWELLS COTTAGE HOLIDAYS, HIGH STREET, SAUNDERSFOOT, PEMBROKESHIRE SA69 9EJ. Many of our top quality holiday properties accept pets. Cottages in Devon, Cornwall, Cotswolds, Pembrokeshire and Heart of England. For colour brochure FREEPHONE 0800 378771 (24 hours). [Pets £15 per week].

RECOMMENDED COTTAGES. Selected cottages throughout Devon, Southern England, Cotswolds and East Anglia. Pets welcome. Low Prices. Free brochure 08700 718 718.
website: www.recommended-cottages.co.uk

WELCOME COTTAGE HOLIDAYS. Quality Cottages in wonderful locations at welcoming low prices. Pets, linen and fuel mostly included. PHONE FOR FREE 2001 FULL COLOUR BROCHURE 01756 702212.

Bourton-on-the-Water

Delightfully situated on the River Windrush which is crossed by minature stone bridges. Stow-on-the-Wold 4 miles.

CHESTER HOUSE HOTEL, VICTORIA STREET, BOURTON-ON-THE-WATER GL54 2BU (01451 820286; FREEPHONE 0800 0199577). Personally supervised by proprietor Mr Julian Davies. All rooms en suite, all with central heating, colour TV, radio, phone, tea/coffee making facilities. Ideal for touring Cotswolds. [🐾]
website: www.bizare.demon.co.uk/chester

Burford

Ancient wool town on River Windrush with a wealth of antique shops. Nearby Cotwold Wildlife Park has one of Englands foremost animal collections.

THE INN FOR ALL SEASONS, THE BARRINGTONS, NEAR BURFORD, OXFORDSHIRE OX18 4TN (01451 844324). Family run and owned Hotel based on traditional 16th century English Coaching Inn. Ideal base for touring, walking and garden visiting. From £56 pppn DB&B for a minimum of two nights.
e-mail: sharp@innforallseasons.com
website: www.innforallseasons.com

Cheltenham

Anglo-Saxon market town transformed into elegant Regency resort with the discovery of medicinal springs. 8 miles east of Gloucester.

CHARLTON KINGS HOTEL, CHELTENHAM GL52 6UU (01242 231061; Fax: 01242 241900). Ideal venue for Cheltenham and the Cotswolds. Double en suite room from £45 per person for 1 night, £40 per person for 3 nights or £34 for 5 nights including full English breakfast. Most rooms have views of the Cotswold Hills. We offer a standard of service only a small hotel can provide. ETC/AA/RAC ★★★, Silver Award. [🐾]

Coleford

Small town in Forest of Dean, 3 miles River Wye. Gloucester 19 miles, Chepstow 13, Monmouth 6.

TUDOR FARMHOUSE HOTEL & RESTAURANT, CLEARWELL, COLEFORD (01594 833046; Fax: 01594 837093). Extensive grounds (14 acres) ideal for dog walking. 14 bedrooms with bathrooms en suite, colour TV, tea/coffee facilities. Excellent traditional choice and a comprehensive wine list. e–mail:reservations@tudorfarm.u-net.com

Fairford

Small town 8 miles east of Cirencester.

THE BULL HOTEL, MARKET PLACE, FAIRFORD GL7 4AA (01285 712535/712217; Fax: 01285 713782). Ideal for holding conferences and wedding receptions. Restaurant offers à la carte menu and fine wines. The hotel has a choice of 22 fully equipped bedrooms with sloping roofs and oak beams. Four-poster beds available. ETC/AA ★★ [🅃]

Forest of Dean

Formerly a royal hunting ground, this scenic area lies between the rivers Severn aand Wye.

GUNN MILL HOUSE COUNTRY GUEST HOUSE, LOWER SPOUT LANE, MITCHELDEAN GL17 0EA (Tel & Fax: 01594 827577). Eight individually designed rooms including four-poster and suites with direct access to 5-acre garden and Forest of Dean. All en suite, TV. Fine dining. Licensed. [Pets £5 per stay]. SEE DISPLAY ADVERT.
e–mail: info@gunnmillhouse.co.uk
website: www.gunnmillhouse.co.uk

THE SPEECH HOUSE, COLEFORD, FOREST OF DEAN GL16 7EL (01594 822607; Fax: 01594 823658). A friendly Hotel set in the heart of the Forest of Dean. The perfect place to get away from it all. 25 en suite bedrooms. Lavish restaurant. Aqua spa and beauty suite. AA/RAC ★★★ [Pets £10 per stay]

DRYSLADE FARM, ENGLISH BICKNOR, COLEFORD (Tel & Fax: 01594 860259). Daphne and Phil warmly welcome you and your dogs at their 17th century farmhouse on family working farm, in Royal Forest of Dean, with its woodland walking. B&B with excellent breakfast, also spacious self-contained ground floor flat, recommended for disabled. ETC ◆◆◆◆ B&B, ETC ★★★ Self-catering. website: www.fweb.org.uk/dryslade

Lydney

Small town 8 miles north-east of Chepstow. Nearby Lydney Park has ruined 12th century castle and remains of Roman temple set amongst woodland, lakes, fine shrubs and trees.

PARKEND HOUSE HOTEL, PARKEND, NEAR LYDNEY GL15 4HL (01594 563666). Small Country Hotel surrounded by parkland. All rooms en suite. Good food and friendly service.Ideal for Cheltenham, Bath and Bristol. Pets and children welcome. [Pets £1.50 per night.]

Nailsworth

Hilly town 4 miles south of Stroud

LESLEY WILLIAMS-ALLEN, THE LAURELS, INCHBROOK, NAILSWORTH GL5 5HA (Tel/Fax: 01453 834021). A lovely rambling licensed house and cottage, where dogs and their owners are encouraged to relax and enjoy. Ideally situated for touring all parts of the Cotswolds and West Country. Brochure. B&B from £21. RAC ◆◆◆ [🅃]

SYMBOLS

🅃   Indicates that pets are welcome free of charge.

£   Indicates that a charge is made for pets: nightly or weekly.

pw!   Shows some special provision for pets; exercise facility, feeding or accommodation arrangement.

⌂   Indicates separate pets accommodation.

Painswick

Beautiful little Cotswold town with characteristic stone-built houses.

MISS E. COLLETT, HAMBUTTS MYND, EDGE ROAD, PAINSWICK GL6 6UP (01452 812352; Fax: 01452 813862). Bed and Breakfast in an old Converted Corn Mill. Very quiet with superb views. Three minutes to the centre of the village. Central heating. One double room, one twin, one single, all with TV. From £27 to £45 per night. ALL ROOMS EN SUITE. RAC/TBC ◆◆◆. [🐾]
e-mail: ewarland@aol.com

Stow-on-the-Wold

Charming Cotswold hill-top market town with several old inns and interesting buildings. Birmingham 45 miles, Gloucester 26, Stratford-upon-Avon 21, Cheltenham 18, Chipping Norton 9.

THE LIMES, EVESHAM ROAD, STOW-ON-THE-WOLD GL54 1EN (01451 830034/831056). Large Country House. Attractive garden, overlooking fields, 4 minutes town centre. Television lounge. Central heating. Car park. Bed and Breakfast from £20 to £25.00 pppn. Twin, double or family rooms, all en suite. Children and pets welcome. AA ◆◆◆, RAC Listed. [🐾]

Stroud

Cotswold town on River Frome below picturesque Stroudwater Hills, formerly renowned for cloth making. Bristol 32 mmiles, Bath 29, Chippenham 25, Cheltenham 14, Gloucester 9.

DOWNFIELD HOTEL, CAINSCROSS ROAD, STROUD GL5 4HN (01453 764496). Easy to find – just 5 miles from M5 – and easy to park. Ideal location for exploring Cotswolds. Comfortable lounges, home-cooked evening meal, cosy bar – all at sensible prices. Dogs and children most welcome. ETC ◆◆◆. [🐾]

COURT FARM, RANDWICK, STROUD GL6 6HH (01453 764210; Fax: 01453 766428). A 17th century beamed Farmhouse on working farm. Much of our food produced organically. Large garden. Abundant wildlife. Children and pets welcome. [🐾]
e-mail: johnetaylor@courfarm.freeserve.co.uk

TOM AND LESLEY WILLIAMS, ORCHARDENE, CASTLE ST, KINGS STANLEY, STONEHOUSE GL10 3JA (01453 822684; Fax: 01453 821554). Warm welcome at Cotswold Stone cottage. Seven minutes J13 M5. Ideal location to explore undiscovered Cotswold and Severn Vale. Glorious walks. B&B from £20. Evening Meal optional. Organic. [🐾]
e-mail: tokanda@talk21.com

Enchanting cottage nestling on wooded hillside above hidden valley. Exclusively for dog owners. Enclosed garden, swimming pool and hot tub. Breaks from £85. Colour brochure: MRS R SMITH, EDGECOMBE HOUSE, TOADSMOOR, STROUD GL5 2UE (01453 883147). [🐾 ⬜]

Symonds Yat

Popular beauty spot on River Wye, 4 miles north-east of Monmouth.

PAUL & CATHY KORN, SYMONDS YAT ROCK LODGE, HILLERSLAND, NEAR COLEFORD GL16 7NY (Tel & Fax: 01594 836191). Family-run Lodge in Royal Forest of Dean near Wye Valley. All rooms en suite, colour TV. 4 poster and family rooms. Licensed restaurant. Brochure available on request. Dogs welcome [🐾]

Westbury-on-Severn

Village 4 miles east of Cinderford. Nearby Westbury Court (NT) has a lovely formal water garden.

BAYS COURT, BOLLOW, WESTBURY-ON-SEVERN GL14 1QX (01452 750426). Listed Country Farmhouse in four acres of dog secure grounds. Large en suite rooms, TV, tea and coffee making facilities, guest lounge. Ideal for Forest of Dean and Cotswolds. B&B from £20 per night. See display for dog facilities. [🐾 pw!]

Please mention *Pets Welcome*
when enquiring about accommodation featured in these pages.

AA ◆◆◆◆ Ormonde House Hotel

NEW FOREST TOURISM

Southampton Road, Lyndhurst, Hampshire SO43 7BT

Telephone: 023 8028 2806 Fax: 023 8028 2004 Website: www.ormondehouse.co.uk

E-mail: info@ormondehouse.co.uk

Elegant luxury at affordable prices in England's historic New Forest. Set back from the road the hotel is situated opposite the open forest ideal for early morning strolls and offers 19 pretty en suite rooms all with Sky TV, phone and beverage making. Our super luxury rooms have whirlpool baths and super king sized beds. Dine with us — our two chefs have an excellent reputation amongst regular guests for their freshly prepared dishes, daily changing specials and wickedly tempting puddings. Close to Exbury Gardens and Beaulieu Motor Museum. Special 3 and 4 night breaks available. B&B from £23 pppn; DB&B from £34 per person per night.

See also Colour Advertisement on page 30

ST. URSULA ◆◆◆

30 Hobart Road, New Milton, Hants. BH25 6EG

Between sea and New Forest, comfortable family home. Excellent facilities & warm welcome for well behaved pets and owners. Ground floor suite suitable for disabled guests plus single and twin rooms.

Mrs Judith Pearce B&B from £20 Tel: 01425 613515

COTTAGE BED & BREAKFAST AT APPLEDORE

Holmsley Road, Wooton, New Milton, Hants, BH25 5TR

Tel: 01425 629506 • Mobile: 07773 527626

This graciously decorated New Forest Cottage is presented by myself, Mariette and my husband Trevor, whose home cooked breakfasts are a veritable joy, served in the conservatory overlooking the garden. Our Cottage is located in the heart of the New Forest where you can enjoy all the verdant tranquil beauty and step back in time as you traverse the leafy glades. Take care to observe the spectacular wildlife in their natural environment. There are many local pubs and restaurants which will happily welcome your pet. For pets and families alike we offer a warm and friendly welcome. All en-suite rooms, Tea/Coffee making facilities, TV, Towels and Toiletries.

NEW FOREST TOURISM

AA ◆◆◆◆

The Seacrest Hotel extends a very special welcome to all our four-legged friends (accompanied by their well-behaved two-legged companions). The best of 2 star accommodation with a superb location on Southsea seafront (beach and common across the road). All rooms en suite, satellite TV etc. Passenger lift. Licensed bar and Restaurant. Car Park. Brochure sent with pleasure - Antoinette Stretton.

SEACREST Hotel

12 South Parade, Southsea, Portsmouth PO5 2JB

Tel: 023 9273 3192 Fax: 023 9283 2523 *AA ★★ 72%*

See also Colour Advertisement on page 30

PUBLISHER'S NOTE

While every effort is made to ensure accuracy, we regret that FHG Publications cannot accept responsibility for errors, omissions or misrepresentations in our entries or any consequences thereof. Prices in particular should be checked because we go to press early. We will follow up complaints but cannot act as arbiters or agents for either party.

BURBUSH FARM

Pound Lane, Burley, New Forest, Near Ringwood BE24 4EF Tel: 01425 403238
Character cottages delightfully situated in the heart of the New Forest, offering seclusion and comfort yet close to Burley village. The cottages are equipped to the highest standard with dishwasher, washing machine/dryer, microwave, colour TV and central heating. Each cottage sleeps 5. Terms from £250 per week. ★★★★★

Brochure available Mr & Mrs D.C. Hayles   E-mail: burbush-farm@excite.com.uk • Web: www.burbush-farm.co.uk

Royal Hotel Winchester

Quality Hotel of character, quietly located in the heart of England's Ancient Capital. All rooms en suite with satellite TV, tea and coffee making facilities, direct-dial telephone, etc. Easy access to Hotel's large private walled garden. Two-Day Break, Half Board from £105.

Telephone anytime on 01962 840840   AA ★★★ and Rosette for Good Food

Ashurst

Three miles north-east of Lyndhurst.

WOODLANDS LODGE HOTEL, BARTLEY ROAD, ASHURST, WOODLANDS SO40 7GN (Tel: (023) 80 292257; Fax: (023) 80 293090). Luxury Hotel offering peace and tranquillity. 16 bedrooms, all en suite with whirlpool bath, with TV, hairdryer, telephone etc. AA Award Winning Restaurant. Excellent wine list. Stables available. ETC/AA ★★★.
e–mail: woodlands@nortels.ltd.uk
website: www.nortels.ltd.uk

Bramshaw

New Forest village surrounded by national Trust land. Southampton 10 miles, Lyndhurst 6.

BRAMBLE HILL HOTEL, BRAMSHAW, NEAR LYNDHURST SO43 7JG (023 8081 3165). Fully licensed country house hotel with own livery stables. Unique seclusion amidst glorious surroundings. Unlimited riding and walking territory. Dogs welcome. DIY livery for horses. [Pets £4 per night.]

Brockenhurst

Popular village surrounded by national Trust land. Southampton 10 miles, Lyndhurst 6.

WHITLEY RIDGE COUNTRY HOUSE HOTEL, BEAULIEU ROAD, BROCKENHURST SO42 7QL (01590 622354; Fax: 01590 622856). Georgian Hotel set in 5 acres of secluded grounds. 14 bedrooms, all en suite, cosy bar and splendid dining room. Superb cuisine, friendly and efficient service. Ideally located for the New Forest. ETC/AA ★★★ [Pets £4 per night, £25 per week]

Fareham

Old market town, 6 miles north-west of Portsmouth across the harbour.

ELLERSLIE TOURING CARAVAN & CAMPING PARK, DOWNEND ROAD, FAREHAM PO16 8TS (Tel/Fax: 01329 822248; Mobile 0411 446701). Small partly wooded site. Close to stables, health club, golf course, boating facilities, sites of historic interest. Car and caravan plus two persons £7 per night. Chemical emptying. Food preparation and wash room. Raised barbecues allowed. Free showers. Southern Tourist Board Graded, AA & RAC Listed

Lymington

Residential town and yachting centre 15 miles east of Bournemouth.

MRS R SQUE, HARTS LODGE, 242 EVERTON ROAD, LYMINGTON SO41 0HE (01590 645902). Bungalow (non smoking), set in three acres. Accommodation comprising double, twin and family en suite rooms, each with tea/coffee making facilities and colour TV. Horse riding, golf and fishing are nearby. Children and pets welcome. AA ◆◆◆◆. [Pets £1.50 per night, £7 per week].

MRS P. J. ELLIS, EFFORD COTTAGE, EVERTON, LYMINGTON SO41 0JD (Tel & Fax: 01590 642315; Fax: 01590 641030). Friendly, award winning Georgian cottage in an acre of garden. Excellent centre for New Forest and South Coat. All rooms en suite with luxury facilities. B&B from £25pp. No children RAC/AA/STB ◆◆◆◆◆.
e–mail: effcottage@aol.com

HONEYSUCKLE HOUSE, 24 CLINTON ROAD, LYMINGTON SO41 9EA (Tel & Fax: 01590 676635). Ground floor double room, en suite, non smoking. Woodland walk, park, quay and marinas nearby. B&B from £20 pppn. [🐕]
e-mail: skyblue@beeb.net

MRS J. FINCH, "DOLPHINS", 6 EMSWORTH ROAD, LYMINGTON SO41 9BL (Tel: 01590 676108/679545 Fax: 01590 688275). Single, twin, double and family rooms all with colour TV and tea/coffee making facilities; king-size or twin en suite available. Leisure facilities, beach chalet & mountain bikes. Doggy-bed provided if required. Park two minutes' walk.Please write or telephone for brochure. [🐕]

Lyndhurst

Good base for enjoying the fascinating New Forest as well as the Hampshire coastal resorts. Bournemouth 20 miles, Southampton 9.

THE CROWN HOTEL, LYNDHURST, NEW FOREST S043 7NF (023 8028 2922; Fax: 023 8028 2751). A mellow, listed building in the centre of the village, an ideal base for exploring the delights of the New Forest with your canine friend(s). Free parking, quiet garden, three star luxury and animal loving staff. [Pets £8.00 per night].
e–mail: crown@marstonhotels.co.uk

BEECHEN HOUSE, CLAYHILL, LYNDHURST SO43 7DN (023 8028 3584). Private Victorian home. English breakfast. Secure off road parking. Comfortable walking distance into New Forest. Non Smoking. Dogs welcome free. ETC ◆◆◆
website: www.newforest.demon.co.uk/beechen.htm

ORMONDE HOUSE HOTEL, SOUTHAMPTON ROAD, LYNDHURST SO43 7BT (023 8028 2806, Fax: 023 8028 2004). Opposite open forest, easy drive to Exbury Gardens and Bealieu. Pretty en suite rooms with Sky TV, phone and beverage making. Super lux rooms with whirlpool baths and king-size beds. Bar, lounge and delicious dinners available. Free room upgrade on 4 night midweek D, B&B bookings. AA ◆◆◆◆. [Pets £3 - £5 per night]
e-mail: info@ormondehouse.co.uk
website: www.ormondehouse.co.uk

New Forest

Area of heath and woodland of nearly 150 square miles, formerly Royal hunting grounds.

MRS J. PEARCE, ST. URSULA, 30 HOBART ROAD, NEW MILTON BH25 6EG (01425 613515). Excellent facilities and warm welcome for well behaved pets and owners! Ground floor suite suitable for disabled guests, plus single and twin rooms. Bed & Breakfast from £20. [🐕]

Luxury 2-bedroomed residential-type caravan. Sleeps 4/6. Maintained to high standard, full kitchen, bathroom, sitting/dining room, own garden. Idyllic setting in heart of New Forest. Non-smoking, ample parking. Children over 5 years. £185-£255 (May-Sept). Well behaved dogs welcome. MRS E. MATTHEWS, THE ACORNS, OGDENS, NEAR FORDINGBRIDGE SP6 2PY (01425 655552) [Pets £10 per week]
e-mail: e_mathews@talk21.com

THE WATERSPLASH HOTEL, THE RISE, BROCKENHURST SO42 7ZP. Prestigious New Forest family-run country house hotel set in large garden. Noted for fine personal service, accommodation and traditional English cuisine at its best. All rooms en suite. Luxury 4 poster with double spa bath. Swimming pool. RAC, AA ★★, Les Routiers, Ashley Courtenay. Colour brochure available (01590 622344).[🐕]

New Milton

Located 5 miles west of Lymington.

COTTAGE BED & BREAKFAST, APPLEDORE, HOLMSLEY ROAD, NEW MILTON BH25 5TR (01425 629506). Graciously decorated cottage in the heart of New Forest. Enjoy the spectacular wildlife. All rooms en suite with tea/coffee making facilities and TV. AA ◆◆◆◆

Portsmouth

Historic port and naval base, with Nelson's flagship HMS Victory in harbour.

The best of 2 star accommodation with a superb location on Southsea seafront. All rooms en suite, Satellite TV etc. Passenger lift, Licensed bar and Restaurant, Car Park. Brochure with pleasure. ANTOINETTE STRETTON, THE SEACREST HOTEL, 12 SOUTH PARADE, SOUTHSEA, PORTSMOUTH PO5 2JB (02392 733192; Fax: 02392 832523)

Ringwood

Busy market town, centre for trout fishing, trekking and rambling. Bournemouth 13 miles.

MR AND MRS D. C. HAYLES, BURBUSH FARM, POUND LANE, BURLEY, NEAR RINGWOOD BE24 4EF (01425 403238). Character cottages delightfully situated in the heart of the New Forest close to Burley village. Equipped to highest standard with central heating. Each sleeps five. From £250 per week. ★★★★★ [Pets £20 per week]
e-mail:burbush-farm@excite.com.uk
website: www.burbush-farm.co.uk

JENNY MONGER, LITTLE HORSESHOES, SOUTH GORLEY, RINGWOOD BH24 3NL (01425 479340). Cosy, superior modern bungalow, just for two, set in 3½ acres, with wild ponies grazing outside our gate. Wonderful walking and riding in the ancient New Forest. Horses and dogs welcome. ETC ⛫⛫⛫ Commended.
e–mail: jenny@littlehorseshoes.co.uk
website: www.littlehorseshoes.co.uk

Sway

Village in southern part of New Forest and within easy reach of sea. Lymington 4 miles south east.

MRS THELMA ROWE, 9 CRUSE CLOSE, SWAY SO41 6AY (Tel & Fax: 01590 683092). Ground floor and first floor suites. Both en suite with sitting room, teamaking facilities, fridge, TV and video. Quiet, very comfortable, friendly accommodation.
e-mail: ronrowe@talk21.com

Winchester

Site of an old Roman town. Ancient capital of Wessex and of England. Notable cathedral, famous boys' public school, a wealth of old and historic buildings.

ROYAL HOTEL, ST PETER STREET, WINCHESTER SO23 8BS (01962 840840; Fax: 01962 841582). Quality Hotel of character quietly located in the heart of England's Ancient Capital. All rooms en suite with satellite TV, tea and coffee making facilities and direct dial telephone. [Pets £8 per night]

SYMBOLS

🐾   Indicates that pets are welcome free of charge.

£   Indicates that a charge is made for pets: nightly or weekly.

pw!   Shows some special provision for pets; exercise facility, feeding or accommodation arrangement.

⌂   Indicates separate pets accommodation.

NICHOLSON FARM HOLIDAYS
BRIMSTONE COTTAGE, DOCKLOW, LEOMINSTER HR6 0SL
Mrs J. Brooke   Tel: 01568 760346

Self-catering properties on a working dairy farm. Beautiful views. Wide choice of restaurants and bar meals in the area. Supermarket 10 minutes. Excellent walking, golf, riding, carp fishing available on the farm, swimming and tennis 10 mins. Dogs are welcome but must not remain in during the owner's absence. Non- smoking.

FELTON HOUSE

ETC/AA   **Felton, Near Hereford HR1 3PH**
◆◆◆◆   **Tel/Fax: (01432) 820366**

Marjorie and Brian Roby offer guests, children and pets a very warm welcome to their home, a country house set in beautiful gardens. Relax with refreshments on arrival. Taste excellent evening meals at local inns. Sleep in an antique four poster or brass bed. Awake refreshed to enjoy breakfast from a wide choice of traditional and vegetarian dishes. **B&B £23 per person with en suite/private bathroom. AA/Tourist Board Silver Award Highly Recommended. Pets free.** Websites: www.smoothhound.co.uk/hotels/felton.html   www.herefordshirebandb.co.uk

See also Colour Advertisement on page 30

THE STEPPES
Ullingswick, Near Hereford HR1 3JG
Tel: 01432 820424
Fax: 01432 820042
Website:
www.steppeshotel.fs.business.co.uk
Resident Owners:
Henry and Tricia Howland

"The Steppes" is an award-winning hotel with an intimate atmosphere, abounding in antique furniture, inglenook fireplaces, oak beams and flag-stoned floors. The old dairy now houses a magnificent cobbled bar with Dickensian atmosphere. A restored timber-framed barn and converted stable accommodate six large luxury en suite bedrooms. Outstanding cordon bleu cuisine is served by candlelight, and highly praised breakfasts come with an imaginative selection.

Set in the tiny hamlet of Ullingswick in the Wye Valley, this is an excellent centre for visiting many areas of natural beauty and points of historic interest. It is ideal walking country being within easy reach of the Malvern Hills and Black Mountains.

Leisure breaks £59 per person per night to include breakfast, dinner and en suite bedroom. The Steppes is a non-smoking hotel.

ETC Silver Award   AA ★★,
Good Hotel Guide, "Which" County Hotel of the Year 1994,
Johansens Most Excellent Value Hotel 1996.

PLEASE MENTION THIS GUIDE WHEN YOU WRITE

OR PHONE TO ENQUIRE ABOUT ACCOMMODATION

IF YOU ARE WRITING, A STAMPED, ADDRESSED

ENVELOPE IS ALWAYS APPRECIATED

NEW PRIORY HOTEL
STRETTON SUGWAS, HEREFORD HR4 7AR.Tel: 01432 760264 Fax: 01432 761809

This friendly family-run Hotel is situated just a short distance from the Hereford city limits. Set in its own 3¹/₂ acres of beautiful Herefordshire with a large car park, lawned gardens and terraces. 10 Bedrooms, all with private bath or shower except for single rooms which have an adjacent shower. Two Four-poster beds. All rooms have central heating, TV and tea making facilities. Write or telephone for terms.

ETC ★★

Ridge View Cottage   Bradnor Green, Kington

Detached 17th century stone cottage beautifully located on Bradnor Hill, a mile above Kington. Outstanding views to the Brecon Beacons, superb walks, and golf course. Double and twin bedrooms, with a single room at the bottom of the stairs leading to a double room; ground floor bath/shower room. Sleeps 7. All electric, microwave and colour TVs. Terms from £130 - £240 per week. Pets welcome. **Apply:**
Mr and Mrs Thomas, 228 Mary Vale Road, Bournville, Birmingham B30 1PJ
(0121 628 0164) E-mail: keith@kect.freeserve.co.uk

Church Farm   Coddington, Ledbury HR8 1JJ   Tel: 01531 640271

Black and White listed farmhouse on working farm in quiet hamlet. Oak beamed accommodation in two double and one twin. Close to Malvern Hills. Ideal touring being equidistant Ross-on-Wye, Hereford, Worcester and Gloucester. Plenty of space and fields for walking dogs. Warm hospitality assured in quiet, relaxed atmosphere. Plenty of good English fare – evening meals if required. Log fires, TV. Excellent self catering unit also available.

Mocktree Barns Holiday Cottages

A small group of barns offering comfortable self-catering accommodation around sunny courtyard.• Well equipped, sleeping between two and six. • Friendly owners. • Open all year. • Short breaks available • Pets and children welcome. • Lovely views, excellent walks • Direct access to footpaths through farmland and woods. • Hereford, Cider Country, Shropshire Hills, Shrewsbury, Ironbridge and the splendid mid-Wales countryside all an easy drive away. • Beautiful Ludlow seven miles. • Guided Walks/tours arranged. • Golf, fishing, cycling nearby.

ETC ★★★

Colour brochure from Clive and Cynthia Prior,
Mocktree Barns, Leintwardine, Ludlow SY7 0LY (01547 540441)

See also Colour Advertisement on page 38

Cowarne Hall Cottages   UP TO ETC ★★★★

Project supported by the English Tourist Board

A splendid historic Gothic Hall with beams, open fireplaces, arched windows and doorways has been sensitively converted to provide luxurious cottage accommodation. Situated 'twixt the Malvern Hills and Wye Valley in a network of country lanes passing through rolling countryside. Convenient for the historic towns of Malvern, Bromyard, Ledbury, Hereford and Worcester. The cottages are centrally heated and have a patio, garden and parking. Details supplied of the area's attractions including working farms and vineyards, a Hop Trail, open gardens and National Trust walks. The lanes are ideal for dog walks. Free colour brochure.

Mr & Mrs R.M. Bradbury, Cowarne Hall Cottages, Much Cowarne,
Herefordshire HR7 4JQ Tel: 01432 820317; Fax: 01432 820093.
E-mail: rm@cowarnehall.freeserve.co.uk

FHG PUBLICATIONS LIMITED publish a large range of well-known accommodation guides. We will be happy to send you details or you can use the order form at the back of this book.

The Grove

Stone building, divided horizontally. Each flat has open plan lounge, fitted kitchen/dining area, bathroom and toilet. Electric storage heating, automatic washing machine, microwave, colour TV, radio, CD & cassette player. The Granary has a wood burner, the Dairy on the ground floor an open fireplace. All linen and towels included. Ideal base for touring beautiful Border country, black and white villages and for walking in some extremely peaceful surroundings. The farm is mixed arable and stock and there are lovely little woodland and riverside walks on the farm itself. Pets welcome under strict control. Friendly farm atmosphere. Sleeps 4. Terms from £140 per week.

Mrs N. Owens, Pembridge, Leominster HR6 9HP

ETC ★★★

Telephone 01544 388268

THE NEW INN

Owners Nigel and Jane Donovan have a fine reputation for supplying outstanding food and drink; the majority of dishes on the extensive menu being home-made and prepared from fresh local produce. Two well-appointed four-poster rooms, both with private bathroom. Children and pets welcome.

St Owen's Cross, Near Ross-on-Wye, Herefordshire HR2 8LQ 01989 730274

RAC Acclaimed   **W O O D L E A   H O T E L**

Symonds Yat West, Ross-on-Wye, Herefordshire HR9 6BL Tel and Fax: 01600 890206

Residential and restaurant licence; 7 bedrooms, all with private facilities; Pets most welcome.

Family-run hotel overlooking the famous Wye Rapids in peaceful and picturesque surroundings. Highest quality food and attentive service. Recommended for a quiet country holiday at any time of year, the hotel has splendidly equipped double, twin, single and family-size guest rooms, all with colour television; special 'bargain breaks' represent excellent value.

THE OLD COURT HOTEL

Symonds Yat West, Ross-on-Wye, Herefordshire
email: oldcourt@aol.com

John and Elizabeth Slade extend a warm welcome to dog owners and their pets who wish to explore the glorious Wye Valley and Forest of Dean. This 16th Century grade 2, star-listed hotel, includes character beamed bedrooms, bar and a restaurant in the former great hall and is complemented by superb cuisine supervised by our chef proprietor. The former home of the remarkable wife and companion of John Graves Simcoe, the founder of Canada. Only a short walk from riverside paths and the Wye Valley Way, it is ideal for an after dinner stroll to the idyllic St Dubricius church on the river bank. The perfect touring and walking base.

2 NTS DB&B FR £39.50 PPPN
RECEIVE 3RD NIGHT B&B FREE

Tel: 01600 890367
www.oldcourthotel.com

FHG

Visit the website

www.holidayguides.com

for details of the wide choice of accommodation
featured in the full range of FHG titles

Please mention *Pets Welcome*
when enquiring about accommodation featured in these pages.

Docklow

Village 4 miles east of Leominster.

NICHOLSON FARM HOLIDAYS, DOCKLOW, LEOMINSTER HR6 0SL (01568 760346) Self-catering properties on a working dairy farm. Beautiful views, ideal for walking, carp fishing available on the farm, swimming and tennis 10 mins. Dogs are welcome but must not remain in during the owner's absence. Non-smoking. [🐾]

Felton

Village on the A4103 north east of Hereford.

MARJORIE AND BRIAN ROBY, FELTON HOUSE, FELTON, NEAR HEREFORD HR1 3PH (Tel & Fax: 01432 820366). Period-furnished Country House in tranquil setting. Double, single, twin-bedded rooms. Bed and Breakfast £23.00. Vegetarian choice. Good local Inns for evening meals. Ideal locality for touring. Non-smoking. ETC/AA ◆◆◆◆. [🐾] websites:www.smoothhound.co.uk/hotels/felton.html   or   www.herefordshirebandb.co.uk

Great Malvern (Worcestershire)

Fashionable spa town in last century with echoes of that period.

KATE AND DENIS, WHITEWELLS FARM COTTAGES, RIDGEWAY CROSS, NEAR MALVERN WR13 5JS (Tel: 01886 880607; Fax: 01886 880360). Charming converted Cottages, sleep 2–6. Fully equipped with colour TV, microwave, barbecue, fridge, iron, etc. Linen, towels also supplied. One cottage suitable for disabled guests. Short breaks, long lets, large groups. ETC ★★★★ [Pets £10 per week. p.w!] Also see adverts under Great Malvern, Worcestershire. e–mail: Whitewells.Farm@btinternet.com

Hereford

Well-known touring centre on River Wye. Good sport and entertainment facilities including steeplechasing. Cheltenham 37 miles, Gloucester 28, Ross-on-Wye 15.

THE STEPPES, ULLINGSWICK, NEAR HEREFORD HR1 3JG (01432 820424; Fax: 01432 820042). Award-winning hotel with intimate atmosphere. Large luxury en suite bedrooms. Set in Wye Valley within easy reach of Malverns and Black Mountains. Non-smoking. WHICH? Hotel Guide, AA ★★, Good Hotel Guide, ETC Silver Award. [Pets £3 per night].

NEW PRIORY HOTEL, STRETTON SUGWAS, HEREFORD HR4 7AR (01432 760264; Fax: 01432 761809). The New Priory Hotel is situated just a short distance from the Hereford city limits in 3½ acre grounds. 10 bedrooms all with private bath or shower except for single rooms which have an adjacent shower. Two Four-poster beds. ETC ★★. [🐾]

The **FHG**
GOLF
GUIDE
Where to Play
Where to Stay
2001

Available from most bookshops, the 2001 edition of
THE GOLF GUIDE covers details of every UK golf course
– well over 2500 entries – for holiday or business golf. Hundreds
of hotel entries offer convenient accommodation, accompanying
details of the courses – the 'pro', par score, length etc.

*In association with 'Golf Monthly' and including the Ryder Cup
Report as well as Holiday Golf in Ireland, France, Portugal,
Spain, The USA, South Africa and Thailand .*

**£9.99 from bookshops or £10.50 including postage
(UK only) from FHG Publications,
Abbey Mill Business Centre, Paisley PAI ITJ**

DIANA SINCLAIR, HOLLY HOUSE FARM, ALLENSMORE, HEREFORD HR2 9BH (01432 277294; Fax: 01432 261285; Mobile: 0589 830 223). Escape with your horse or dog to our spacious luxury farmhouse. Bed and Breakfast from £20.
e-mail: hollyhousefarm@aol.com

Kington

Town on River Arrow, close to Welsh border, 12 miles north of Leominster.

RIDGE VIEW COTTAGE, BRADNOR GREEN, KINGTON. Detached 17th century cottage in beautiful location. Sleeps 7 plus cot. All electric, microwave and colour TVs. Terms from £130-£240 per week. Apply: MR AND MRS THOMAS, 228 MARY VALE ROAD, BOURNVILLE, BIRMINGHAM B30 1PJ (0121 628 0164). [🐾]
e-mail: keith@kect.freeserve.co.uk

MRS C. D. WILLIAMS, RADNOR'S END, HUNTINGTON, KINGTON HR5 3NZ (01544 370289). Sleeps 5. Detached cottage in lovely unspoiled Welsh border countryside, where rolling hills are home to Buzzard, Kestrel, Red Kite and a rich variety of other birds and wild flowers. Offa's Dyke footpath and Kilvert's Country nearby. Lawn. Ample parking. [🐾]

Ledbury

Pleasant town ideally situated for Cotswolds and Wye Valley. Good centre for bowls, dishing, riding and tennis. Monmouth 23 miles, Leominster 22, Gloucester 17, Tewkesbury 14, Malvern 8.

CHURCH FARM, CODDINGTON, LEDBURY HR8 IJJ (01531 640271). Black and white 16th-century Farmhouse on a working farm close to the Malvern Hills — ideal for touring and walking. Two double and one twin bedrooms. Excellent home cooking. Warm welcome assured. Open all year. [🐾]

Much Cowarne

Village 5 miles south west of Bromyard.

MR & MRS R.M. BRADBURY, COWARNE HALL COTTAGES, MUCH COWARNE HR7 4JQ (Tel: 01432 820317; Fax: 01432 820093). Luxurious holiday cottage accommodation, centrally heated, with patio, garden and parking. Within easy reach of Malvern, Bromyard, Hereford and Worcester. Ideal for dog walks. Up to ETC ★★★★ [pw! £12 per week per pet].
e–mail: rm@cowarnehall.freeserve.co.uk

Pembridge

Tiny medieval village surrounded by meadows and orchards.

MRS N. OWENS, THE GROVE, PEMBRIDGE, LEOMINSTER HR6 9HP (01544 388268). The farm is mixed arable and stock and there are lovely little woodland and riverside walks on the farm itself. Pets welcome under strict control. Friendly farm atmosphere. Sleeps 4. Terms from £140 per week. ETC ★★★. [Pets £5 per week, pw!]

Ross-on-Wye

An attractive town standing on a hill rising from the left bank on the Wye. Cardiff 47 miles, Gloucester 17.

THE NEW INN, ST OWEN'S CROSS, NEAR ROSS-ON-WYE HR2 8LQ (01989 730274). For a revivifying break away from so-called civilization come and visit us. Outstanding food mostly home-made with local produce. Two en suite four-poster bedrooms.

SYMBOLS

🐾   Indicates that pets are welcome free of charge.

£   Indicates that a charge is made for pets: nightly or weekly.

pw!   Shows some special provision for pets; exercise facility, feeding or accommodation arrangement.

◻   Indicates separate pets accommodation.

WOODLEA HOTEL SYMONDS YAT WEST, ROSS-ON-WYE HR9 6BL (Tel and Fax: 01600 890206). Family-run hotel in peaceful and picturesque surroundings. Highest quality food and attentive service. Double, twin, single and family-size guest rooms. Special 'bargain breaks' represent excellent value.

THE ARCHES, WALFORD ROAD, ROSS-ON-WYE HR9 5PT (01989 563348). Georgian-style House. Lovely rooms with all facilities; en suite available. Centrally heated. Pets welcome. Bed and Breakfast. Weekly reductions available. AA/ETC ◆◆◆◆, Les Routiers. [🐾]

**PANTRY COTTAGE, GOODRICH, NEAR ROSS-ON-WYE HR9 6JA (Tel & Fax: 01600 890502). Dogs simply adore the wonderful walks and scenery of the Wye Valley. Enjoy our comfortable well-equipped 18th century two bedroomed cottage (sleeps 5 plus cot). Featuring a cosy lounge with log fire, diningroom, kitchen, conservatory and enclosed garden. [🐾]
e-mail: pantry.cottage@talk21.com
website: www.oas.co.uk/ukcottages/pantrycottage**

THE OLD COURT HOTEL, SYMONDS YAT WEST, ROSS-ON-WYE (01600 890367) 16th Century grade 2, star-listed hotel, includes character beamed bedrooms, bar and restaurant. Short walk from riverside paths and the Wye Valley Way.
e-mail: oldcourt@aol.com
website: www.oldcourthotel.com

YE HOSTELRIE, GOODRICH, ROSS-ON-WYE HR9 6HX (01600 890241). Enjoy comfort and good food at this fully centrally heated 17th Century Inn. We have a reputation for quality food at a reasonable price. ETC/AA ★★ [🐾]

THE INN ON THE WYE, KERNE BRIDGE, GOODRICH, NEAR ROSS-ON-WYE HR9 5QT (01600 890872 Fax: 01600 890594). Beautifully restored 18th century coaching inn, near Goodrich Castle on the banks of the River Wye. All bedrooms en suite. Peaceful country walks, ideal base for touring.
e–mail: gkgardiner.attheinn@virgin.net
website: www.theinnonthewye.co.uk

THE KING'S HEAD HOTEL, 8 HIGH STREET, ROSS-ON-WYE HR9 5HL (FREEPHONE: 0800 801098). Small coaching inn dating back to the 14th century with all bedrooms offering en suite bathrooms and a full range of modern amenities. A la carte menu offers home-cooked food which is served in a warm and friendly atmosphere. Bargain breaks all year round. [🐾]
website: www.kingshead.co.uk

The Nodes Country Hotel
ISLE OF WIGHT

A lovely old Country House at the foot of the Tennyson Downs in grounds of 2½ acres with delightful views. Glorious walks, safe sandy beaches and facilities for horse riding, fishing, sailing and golf nearby. Full central heating, en suite rooms with tea/coffee making facilities. Enjoy good home-cooked food and relax in our cosy Courtyard Bar. Pets welcome.

AA, RAC Approved. "Pets Choice" Gold Award 96/97. UK Top 10 Establishments for Pets.

Alum Bay Road, Totland Bay PO39 0HZ Tel: 01983 752859

"A Peaceful Retreat in the tranquil walking/hiking countryside of West Wight"

The Country Garden Hotel
Church Hill, Totland Bay, Isle of Wight PO39 0ET

A five minute stroll to the Solent, surrounded by lovely walks and hikes, and a short drive to the bustling sailing port of Yarmouth this personable boutique hotel offers the best of all worlds. Ashley Courtenay sums it up: "a really superb hotel set in beautiful gardens - relish the superb cuisine" in one of the Isle's finest restaurants overlooking the gardens. **Garden & sea-views rooms available**, all en suite with TV, fridge, duvets and down pillows, phone, central heating, hairdryer, tea/coffee.

Ashley Courtenay   *ETC & RAC* ★★★
ANY DAY TO ANY DAY B&B, HALF BOARD

•*Doubles* • *Twins* • *Singles* • *Suite* • *Ground floor rooms*
FERRY INCLUSIVE RATES OCTOBER THRU APRIL
Prices from £39 pp/day and £320 pp/week

For brochure, tariff, sample menu and testimonials from recent guests:
Phone/Fax 01983 754 521   E-mail: countrygardeniow@cs.com

PUBLISHER'S NOTE

While every effort is made to ensure accuracy, we regret that FHG Publications cannot accept responsibility for errors, omissions or misrepresentations in our entries or any consequences thereof. Prices in particular should be checked because we go to press early. We will follow up complaints but cannot act as arbiters or agents for either party.

SENTRY MEAD HOTEL

MADEIRA ROAD · TOTLAND BAY
ISLE OF WIGHT PO39 0BJ
Tel/Fax: 01983 753212
email: pets@sentry-mead.co.uk
website: www.sentry-mead.co.uk

Sentry Mead is a tranquil retreat set in its own spacious gardens where well behaved dogs are welcome throughout the hotel (except in the dining room) and to sleep in guests' bedrooms; our own Labrador and Retriever always make our canine visitors feel at home as soon as they arrive. Personal care and attention to detail make this a very special 3 star hotel for both pets and people for either a short break or a longer stay.

AA ★★★   RAC ★★★   RAC AWARD FOR SERVICE, HOSPITALITY & COMFORT

See also Colour Advertisement on page 31

ACTUALLY ON THE BEACH

"The Waterfall", Shore Road, Bonchurch, Ventnor PO38 1RN
Completely self-contained flat. Sleeps up to 4. Fully equipped. Parking.
Sun verandah and Garden.
SAE for Brochure – **Mrs A. Evans**   **Tel: 01983 852246**

RAVENSCOURT HOLIDAY BUNGALOWS

2 Ocean View Road,
Ventnor,
Isle of Wight PO38 1AA

These self-catering holiday chalets are situated in the woodland grounds of an old private house, overlooking the picturesque town of Ventnor. There are some superb panoramic views over Ventnor and the sea from this small, quiet site and from some of the wonderful walks over the adjoining National Trust property, St Boniface Downs. Bungalows have two bedrooms plus sofa bed in the living room, bathroom, kitchenette and TV. Charges are from only £99 per bungalow (including your pet!).

Phone now (or SAE) for brochure: 01983 852555

Website: http://www.isleofwight.webjump.com/

See also Colour Advertisement on page 31

"TUCKAWAY"

Private, comfortable, self-catering Chalet, within a large secluded garden. Sleeps six (cot available). Colour TV, games room, swimming pool and laundry room. Ample parking. Large grassed exercise area available for dogs. Tourist Board Approved. Open all year. Apply for colour brochure or telephone:
**G & R.J. Bayldon, Furzebrake, Cranmore Avenue, Cranmore, Near Yarmouth,
Isle of Wight PO41 0XR Tel: (01983) 760082**

FHG PUBLICATIONS

publish a large range of well-known accommodation guides. We will be happy to send you details or you can use the order form at the back of this book.

ISLAND COTTAGE HOLIDAYS. Charming cottages in lovely rural surroundings and close to the sea. Some cottages on farms - some with swimming pools - some in walking distance of sandy beaches. All cottages equipped to a high standard and graded for quality by the Tourist Board. Brochure: HONOR VASS, THE OLD VICARAGE, KINGSTON, WAREHAM, DORSET BH20 5LH (Tel: 01929 480080; Fax: 01929 481070) [Pets £16 per week].
e-mail: enq@islandcottageholidays.com
website: www.islandcottageholidays.com

Alum Bay

On west if island, one mile from the Needles and lighthouse. Newport 13 miles, Yarmouth 5.

MARION SMITH, HEADON HALL, ALUM BAY PO39 0JD (01983 752123). Lovely two bedroom apartments, fully equipped for 4/6, including colour television. Breathtaking views. Dogs welcome. [🅷]

Bonchurch

One mile north-east of Ventnor

MR & MRS T.J. FOLEY, ASHCLIFF HOLIDAY APARTMENTS, BONCHURCH PO38 1NT(01983 853919). Four self-contained apartments within Victorian house. Large south facing gardens. Sea views. Large private car park. ETC ★★★★ [🅷]
e-mail: ashcliff.iow@virgin.net

Colwell Bay

Bay north of Totland extending from Warden Point to Cliff End.

CLIFTON HOUSE, COLWELL COMMON ROAD, COLWELL BAY PO39 0DD (01983 7532370). Family-run hotel. Home cooking. En suite bedrooms, licensed bar, private parking. Only four minutes' walk to the beach.

Cowes

Yachting centre with yearly regatta since 1814. Newport 4 miles.

SUNNYCOTT CARAVAN PARK, COWES PO31 8NN (01983 292859; Fax: 01983 295389). 20 Deluxe and Luxury 4 and 6 berth caravans on quiet country park in rural surroundings. Laundry room and shop on site. Bring your pets for a holiday too! ETC ★★★ [Pets £5 per week]

Niton Undercliffe

Delightful village near sea at the southernmost part of the island. Several secluded chines nearby, cliff walks. Ventnor 5 miles.

MR AND MRS D. A. HERON, WINDCLIFFE MANOR, SANDROCK ROAD, NITON UNDERCLIFFE PO38 2NG (Tel & Fax: 01983 730215). Bed, Breakfast and Evening Meal in a historic Manor House set in wooded gardens. Heated pool. Colour television. Games room. Children and dogs welcome. ETC ★★★. [pw!]

PLEASE MENTION THIS GUIDE WHEN YOU WRITE

OR PHONE TO ENQUIRE ABOUT ACCOMMODATION

IF YOU ARE WRITING, A STAMPED, ADDRESSED

ENVELOPE IS ALWAYS APPRECIATED

Ryde

Popular resort and yachting centre, fine sands, pier. Shanklin 9 miles, Newport 7, Sandown 6.

HILLGROVE PARK, FIELD LANE, ST HELENS, NEAR RYDE PO33 1UT (01983 872802). Family-run Caravan Park. Select site 10 minutes sea, 3 minutes bus stop. Self-service shop, heated swimming pool. Phone for brochure. Pets welcome. ETC ★★★★ Holiday Park. [Pets £15.00 per week]

Shanklin

Safe sandy beaches and traditional entertainments make this a family favourite. Cliff lift connects the beach and the cliff top.

ALAN AND LYN AYLOTT, HARROW LODGE HOTEL, EASTCLIFF PROMENADE, SHANKLIN PO37 8BD. (01983 862800; Fax: 01983 868889). Family-run Hotel, all rooms en suite with colour TV. Licensed bar, varied menu. Open March to October. ETC ★★ [Pets £3 per night, £10 per week] website: www.farringfordhotel.com

FARRINGFORD HOTEL, 19 HOPE ROAD, SHANKLIN PO37 6EA (01983 862176). Licensed hotel, close to beach and old village. TV, tea/coffee, hairdryer all rooms. All rooms en suite. Parking. B&B from £19. ETC ◆◆◆◆. [🐾]
e–mail: crrome@excite.com

Totland

Little resort with good sands, safe bathing and high cliffs. Newport 13 miles, Yarmouth3, Freshwater 2.

THE NODES COUNTRY HOTEL, ALUM BAY ROAD, TOTLAND BAY PO39 0HZ (01983 752859). Glorious walks, safe sandy beaches and facilities for horse riding, fishing, sailing and golf nearby. Full C/H, en suite rooms with tea/coffee making facilities. AA, RAC Approved. "Pets Choice Gold Award" 96/97. UK top ten establishments for pets. [🐾]

MRS J. SIMMONDS, NORTON LODGE, GRANVILLE ROAD, TOTLAND PO39 0AZ (01983 752772). Two purpose built holiday bungalows and one large caravan, all situated on a pleasant grassy site with beaches and breathtaking walks. Well behaved dogs most welcome. Prices from £125. [🐾]

COUNTRY GARDEN HOTEL, CHURCH HILL, TOTLAND BAY PO39 OET (Tel & Fax: 01983 754521). All en suite, garden and seaview rooms available; TV, phone, duvets, feather/down pillows, fridge, hairdryer etc. Special winter, spring, autumn rates. [pw!] pets £3 per day]
e-mail: countrygardeniow@cs.com

SENTRY MEAD HOTEL, MADEIRA ROAD, TOTLAND BAY PO39 OBJ (01983 753212). Get away from it all at this friendly and comfortable haven, just two minutes from a sandy beach and cliff walks. Bedrooms have en suite bath or shower, colour TV and radio. Delicious table d'hôte dinners; lunchtime bar menu. [Pets £3 per night]
e-mail: pets@sentry-mead.co.uk
website: www.sentry-mead.co.uk

Ventnor

Well-known resort with good sands, downs, popular as a winter holiday resort. Nearby is St Boniface Down, the highest point on the island. Ryde 13 miles, Newport 12, Sandown 7, Shanklin 4.

A. EVANS, "THE WATERFALL", SHORE ROAD, BONCHURCH, VENTNOR PO38 1RN (01983 852246). Spacious, self-contained Flat. Sleeps up to 4. Colour TV. Sun verandah and garden. The beach, the sea and the downs. [🐾]

SYMBOLS

🐾   **Indicates that pets are welcome free of charge.**

£   **Indicates that a charge is made for pets: nightly or weekly.**

pw!   **Shows some special provision for pets; exercise facility, feeding or accommodation arrangement.**

⌂   **Indicates separate pets accommodation.**

RAVENSCOURT HOLIDAY BUNGALOWS 2 OCEAN VIEW ROAD, VENTNOR PO38 1AA (01983 852555). Self-catering holiday chalets in woodland. Small, quiet site, wonderful walks. Two bedrooms plus sofa bed, bathroom, kitchenette and TV. £99 per bungalow (including your pet!). website: http://www.isleofwight.webjump.com/

Yarmouth

Coastal resort situated 9 miles west of Newport. Castle built by Henry VIII for coastal defence.

"TUCKAWAY" – Holiday Chalet in private, secluded position. Sleeps six. Swimming pool. Large grassed area. Tourist Board Approved. APPLY: G. BAYLDON, FURZEBRAKE, CRANMORE AVENUE, YARMOUTH PO41 OXR (01983 760082). Dogs welcome.[🐾]

THE ORCHARDS HOLIDAY CARAVAN & CAMPING PARK, NEWBRIDGE, YARMOUTH PO41 0TS (Dial-a-brochure 01983 531331; Fax: 01983 531666). Luxury holiday caravans, some with central heating. Excellent facilities including indoor pool with licensed cafe. Dog exercise areas. Coarse fishing; ideal walking, cycling and golf Open late February to New Year. e–mail: info@orchards-holiday-park.co.uk website: www.orchards-holiday-park.co.uk

FOR THE MUTUAL GUIDANCE OF GUEST AND HOST

Every year literally thousands of holidays, short breaks and overnight stops are arranged through our guides, the vast majority without any problems at all. In a handful of cases, however, difficulties do arise about bookings, which often could have been prevented from the outset.

It is important to remember that when accommodation has been booked, both parties – guests and hosts – have entered into a form of contract. We hope that the following points will provide helpful guidance.

GUESTS: When enquiring about accommodation, be as precise as possible. Give exact dates, numbers in your party and the ages of any children. State the number and type of rooms wanted and also what catering you require – bed and breakfast, full board etc. Make sure that the position about evening meals is clear – and about pets, reductions for children or any other special points.

Read our reviews carefully to ensure that the proprietors you are going to contact can supply what you want. Ask for a letter confirming all arrangements, if possible.

If you have to cancel, do so as soon as possible. Proprietors do have the right to retain deposits and under certain circumstances to charge for cancelled holidays if adequate notice is not given and they cannot re-let the accommodation.

HOSTS: Give details about your facilities and about any special conditions. Explain your deposit system clearly and arrangements for cancellations, charges etc. and whether or not your terms include VAT.

If for any reason you are unable to fulfil an agreed booking without adequate notice, you may be under an obligation to arrange suitable alternative accommodation or to make some form of compensation.

While every effort is made to ensure accuracy, we regret that FHG Publications cannot accept responsibility for errors, omissions or misrepresentations in our entries or any consequences thereof.

Prices in particular should be checked because we go to press early. We will follow up complaints but cannot act as arbiters or agents for either party.

THE CROFT HOUSE
Canterbury Road, Ashford, Kent TN25 4DU
Set in two acres of well-maintained gardens, the Croft Hotel is conveniently located on the A28 between Ashford and Canterbury. The M20 (Junction 9 the closest) and Ashford International Station, the gateway to Europe, are only minutes away. The Croft is family-owned and operated, and warmly welcomes pets to the Hotel and Grounds. It is surrounded by two footpaths that will lead you into the Kent countryside.

Tel: 01233 622140 Fax: 01233 635271 ETC/AA/RAC ◆◆◆

HANSON HOTEL (Lic.) **41 Belvedere Road, Broadstairs CT10 1PF Tel: (01843) 868936**
A small friendly Georgian hotel with relaxed atmosphere, centrally situated for beach, shops and transport. B/B only or renowned for excellent food, we offer a 5-course Evening Dinner with choice of menu prepared by Chef/Proprietor ★ Attractive Bar ★ Most en suite.
Children and pets welcome.

OPEN ALL YEAR   *S.A.E. or telephone for brochure to Trevor and Jean Webb*   SPRING AND WINTER BREAKS

The Tanner of Wingham

Tel/Fax: 01227 720532
Website: www.ttow.freeserve.co.uk

Family-run restaurant with bed and breakfast accommodation, situated in a building dating from 1440. Convenient for docks and Chunnel. Rooms are individually decorated with antique beds and furniture – some rooms heavily beamed. Families welcome, cot available. The many local attractions include historic houses and gardens, wildlife and bird parks. Bed and Breakfast from £39 double; Evening Meal £16.50.
Mrs D.J. Martin, The Tanner of Wingham, 44 High Street, Wingham, Canterbury CT3 1AB

STADE COURT
AA ★★★ RAC
DOGS WELCOME
★ Delightful location on seafront of historic Cinque Port of Hythe
★ Award Winning Restaurant ★ Terrace Bar
★ Single/Twin/Double/Split Level Rooms
★ Free access to Leisure Facilities 600 metres away at sister hotel

West Parade, Hythe, Kent CT21 6DT
Tel: 01303 268263, Fax: 01303 261803
Web Site http://www.marstonhotels.co.uk

"Give your dog a break
(and we'll provide the 'steak'!)"

PLEASE MENTION THIS GUIDE WHEN YOU WRITE

OR PHONE TO ENQUIRE ABOUT ACCOMMODATION

IF YOU ARE WRITING, A STAMPED, ADDRESSED

ENVELOPE IS ALWAYS APPRECIATED

Ashford

Market town on Great Stour River, 13 miles south-west of Canterbury.

MR & MRS CAMPONESCHI, THE CROFT HOTEL, ASHFORD TN25 4DU (01233 622140; Fax: 01233 635271). Family-owned Hotel set in two acres of gardens between Ashford and Canterbury. Pets warmly welcomed. ETC/AA/RAC ◆◆◆ [🐾]

Broadstairs

Quiet resort, once a favourite of Charles Dickens. Good sands and promenade.

HANSON HOTEL, 41 BELVEDERE ROAD, BROADSTAIRS (01843 868936). Small, friendly licensed Georgian Hotel. Home comforts; children and pets welcome. Attractive bar. SAE. [pw! Pets 50p p.n.]

Canterbury

Cathedral and university city on River Great Stour, 54 miles from London, Roman and medieval reamins including city walls.

THE TANNER OF WINGHAM, 44 HIGH STREET, WINGHAM, CANTERBURY CT3 1AB (Tel & Fax: 01227 720532) Family-run restaurant with bed and breakfast accommodation. Convenient for docks and Chunnel. Rooms are individually decorated with antique beds and furniture. [🐾] website: www.ttow.freeserve.co.uk

Hythe

Village on west bank of Southampton Water. Ferry connection for pedestrians.

STADE COURT, HYTHE CT21 6DT (01303 268263; Fax: 01303 261803). Situated on seafront close to beach and parks, the hotel has comfortable, well-equipped en suite bedrooms including colour TV and tea/coffee facilities. Free access to superb leisure and golf at sister hotel close by. Telephone for brochure and tariff. 'Doggie Dinner' [pw! £8.00 per night] website: www.marstonhotels.co.uk

St Margaret's Bay

4 miles north-east of Dover

DEREK AND JACQUI MITCHELL, REACH COURT FARM COTTAGES, REACH COURT FARM, ST MARGARET'S BAY, DOVER CT15 6AQ (01304 852159; TEL/FAX: 01304 853902). Situated in the heart of the Mitchell family farm, surrounded by open countryside, these five luxury self-contained cottages are very special. The cottages are set around the old farmyard, which has been attractively set to lawns and shrubs, with open views of the rural valley both front and back. ETC ★★★★

PUBLISHER'S NOTE

While every effort is made to ensure accuracy, we regret that FHG Publications cannot accept responsibility for errors, omissions or misrepresentations in our entries or any consequences thereof. Prices in particular should be checked because we go to press early. We will follow up complaints but cannot act as arbiters or agents for either party.

Blackpool, Pilling, Preston

SELECT HOLIDAY FLATLETS ADJOINING QUEENS PROMENADE
COTSWOLD HOLIDAY FLATLETS, 2A HADDON ROAD,
NORBRECK, BLACKPOOL FY2 9AH Tel:(01253) 352227
● Fully equipped including colour television and fridge ● Select area North Shore
● Cross road to beach and trams ● Short breaks early season and Illuminations
Can sleep up to six. Rates from £100 per week for two. Details from Mrs C. Moore
Open all year ● Phone or SAE for brochure ● Pets free.

Bell Farm Beryl and Peter welcome you to their 18th century farmhouse in the quiet village of Pilling. The area has many footpaths and is ideal for cycling. Easy access to Blackpool, Lancaster, the Forest of Bowland and the Lake District. One family room, one double and one twin with private bathroom. All rooms en suite. Tea and coffee making facilities. Lounge and dining room. Children and pets welcome. Open all year except Christmas and New Year. Bed and Breakfast from £20.00.
Beryl and Peter Richardson, Bell Farm, Bradshaw Lane, Scronkey, Pilling, Preston PR3 6SN. Tel: 01253 790324.

SIX ARCHES CARAVAN PARK SCORTON, GARSTANG NEAR PRESTON, LANCS PR3 1AL TEL: 01524 791683 FAX: 01524 792926	Situated on the banks of the River Wyre. Modern 6-berth caravans, fully equipped; touring pitches, some with electric hook-ups; large two-bedroom flats to sleep 6. Ideal for touring: Blackpool 14 miles, Lake District 30 miles. Facilities include licensed club with entertainment, heated pool, children's playground, fishing. Controlled dogs welcome. Write or phone for brochure. ETC ★★★

Blackburn

Idustrial town on River Darwen and on Leeds and Liverpool Canal

THE BROWN LEAVES COUNTRY HOTEL, LONGSIGHT ROAD, COPSTER GREEN, NEAR BLACKBURN BB1 9EU (01254 249523; Fax: 01254 245240). Situated on the A59 halfway between Preston and Clitheroe, five miles from Junction 31 on M6 in beautiful Ribble Valley. All rooms ground floor, en suite facilities, TV, tea-making and hairdryer. Guests' lounge and bar lounge. Car parking. Pets by arrangement. Member of Les Routiers, Winner of 1998 Casserole Award and 1998 Housekeeping Award. All credit cards welcome.

Blackpool

Famous resort with fine sands and many attractions and vast variety of entertainments. Blackpool Tower (500ft). Three piers. Manchester 47 miles, Lancaster 26, Preston 17, Fleetwood 8.

MRS C. MOORE, COTSWOLD HOLIDAY FLATLETS, 2A HADDON ROAD, NORBRECK, BLACKPOOL FY2 9AH (01253) 352227. Holiday Flatlets fully equipped. Cross road to beach and trams. Select area. Open all year. Short Breaks early season and Illuminations. Phone or SAE for brochure. [⌕]

THE BRAYTON HOTEL, 7-8 FINCHLEY ROAD, GYNN SQUARE, BLACKPOOL FY1 2LP. The small hotel with the BIG reputation. A family-run hotel overlooking Gynn gardens and the promenade offering quality food from a varied menu. Comfortable rooms and a licensed bar, easy parking. Open all year. For tariff and brochure ring 01253 351645. ETC ◆◆◆. [⌕]
e–mail: brayton@supanet.com

Clitheroe

Pleasant market town, with ruined Norman keep standing on limestone cliff above grey roofs. Pendle Hill 4 miles to the east, from where there are spectacular views of the Forest of Bowland.

MRS FRANCES OLIVER, WYTHA FARM, RIMINGTON, CLITHEROE BB7 4EQ (01200 445295). Farmhouse accommodation in heart of countryside. Panoramic views. Warm welcome. Accommodation comprises of en suite double and family rooms. Ideal touring centre. Bed and Breakfast from £15. Evening Meal £7. [pw! Pets £1 per day]

Mellor

Village 3 miles north-west of Blackburn

ROSE COTTAGE, LONGSIGHT ROAD, CLAYTON-LE-DALE BB1 9EX (01254 813223; Fax: 01254 813831). Picturesque 200-year-old cottage on A59 close to M6 and M65. Established by present owners 1984. Charming well-appointed rooms with private facilities. Weekend breaks available. Kennels/cattery nearby. Excellent one night stop travelling to and from Scotland. Credit Cards accepted. Stabling. [🐾]
e-mail: bbrose.cott@talk21.co.uk
website: www.SmoothHound.co.uk/hotels/rosecott.html

Morecambe

Popular family holiday resort 3 miles north-west of Lancaster

VENTURE CARAVAN PARK, LANGRIDGE WAY, WESTGATE, MORECAMBE LA4 4TQ (01524 412986; Fax: 01524 422029). Relaxing family park. Tourers and Tents welcome. Hire caravans including vans for disabled. Bar. Entertainment. Food. Shop. Off licence. Launderette. Indoor heated pool. Promenade ¾ mile. Pets on lead. AA/RAC.

Pilling

Small village 3 miles from Preesall, 12 miles from Blackpool

BERYL AND PETER RICHARDSON, BELL FARM, BRADSHAW LANE, SCRONKEY, PILLING, PRESTON PR3 6SN (01253 790324).18th century farmhouse with one family room, one double and one twin with private bathroom. All rooms en suite and centrally heated. Full English breakfast is served. Open all year except Christmas and New Year. B&B from £20.

Preston

Large town on River Ribble, 27 miles from Manchester.

SIX ARCHES CARAVAN PARK, SCORTON, GARSTANG, NEAR PRESTON PR3 1AL (01524 791683; Fax: 01524 792926). Modern 6-berth caravans, touring pitches; large two-bedroom flats to sleep 6. Blackpool 14 miles, Lake District 30 miles. Licensed club with entertainment. Controlled dogs welcome. ETC ★★★ [🐾]

St Annes

Very popular family resort with good sands. Good shopping centre. Preston 15 miles, Balckpool 5 miles.

MRS M. MACKOON, ORCHARD COURT, 50/52 ORCHARD ROAD, ST ANNES FY8 1PJ (01253 712653). Self-catering flats with en suite facilities and large gardens. 2 minutes to shops, cafes, beach. Linen provided. Open all year. Short Breaks. Car park. Brochure available. [🐾 pw!]

Southport

Elegant seaside resort with Victorian feel. Amusement park, zoo and Birkdale championship golf course.

THE GARDEN COURT HOTEL, 22 BANK SQUARE, SOUTHPORT PR9 0DG (Tel/Fax: 01704 530219). Recently renovated Victorian town house overlooking Floral Hall, Marine Lake and sea. All amenities and attractions within easy walking distance. Standard, en suite and four poster bedrooms with central heating, colour television etc. Licensed bar. Friendly, comfortable accommodation from £14.50 B&B pppn. [🐾]
e-mail: gardencourt@rapid.co.uk

SYMBOLS
🐾　Indicates that pets are welcome free of charge.
£　Indicates that a charge is made for pets: nightly or weekly.
pw!　Shows some special provision for pets; exercise facility, feeding or accommodation arrangement.
◻　Indicates separate pets accommodation.

Brook Meadow Holidays

* 3 self-catering chalets   ETC ★★★ to ★★★★
* Farmhouse Bed & Breakfast
* Camping & Caravan site (electric hookups)   * Carp fishing

Brochure- Mary Hart, Welford Road, Sibbertoft, Market Harborough, Leics LE16 9UJ Tel: 01858 880886 Fax: 01858 880485

e-mail: brookmeadow@farmline.com   web: www.brookmeadow.co.uk

---

SYSONBY KNOLL HOTEL
ASFORDBY ROAD
MELTON MOWBRAY
LEICESTERSHIRE LE13 0HP
Tel: **01664 563563**
Fax: **01664 410364**

Traditional Family-run Hotel on outskirts of market town. The bar, restaurant and conservatory overlook the gardens and paddock to the river. The à la carte, table d'hôte and bar menus are served until 9pm. All bedrooms, some ground floor, are en suite with TV and hospitality tray. Outdoor swimming pool.
Website: www.sysonby.knoll.btinternet.co.uk
ETC/AA ★★★

Market Harborough

Town on River Welland 14 miles south-east of Leicester

BROOK MEADOW HOLIDAYS. Three self-catering chalets, farmhouse Bed and Breakfast, Carp fishing, camping and caravan site with electric hookups. Phone for brochure. ETC ★★★ to ★★★★. MRS MARY HART, WELFORD ROAD, SIBBERTOFT, MARKET HARBOROUGH LE16 9UJ (01858 880886). [🛏 camping, £5 per night B&B, £10 Self-catering]
e-mail: brookmeadow@farmline.com
website: www.brookmeadow.co.uk

Melton Mowbray

Old market town, centre of hunting country. Large cattle market. Church and Anne of Cleves' House are of interest. Kettering 29 miles, Market Harborough 22, Nottingham 18, Leicester 15.

SYSONBY KNOLL HOTEL, ASFORDBY ROAD, MELTON MOWBRAY LE13 0HP (01664 563563; Fax: 01664 410364.). Traditional Family-run Hotel. All bedrooms (some ground floor) en suite with TV and hospitality tray. Outdoor swimming pool. Bar and restaurant. ETC/AA ★★★. [🛏]
website: www.sysonby.knoll.btinternet.co.uk

Cawthorpe Farm

Welcomes guests for bed & breakfast. Comfortable rooms full of character. Walking, cycling, birdwatching in nearby woods, Near Stamford, Peterborough and Lincoln. Stabling and grazing available for guests' horses. Pets welcome by arrangement. **Cawthorpe Farm, Cawthorpe, Bourne, Lincolnshire PE10 0AB**

Tel: 01778 426697   Fax:01778 421536

BELLE VIEW HOTEL

12 South Parade, Skegness PE25 3HW
Tel: 01754 765274

Please write or telephone for a brochure to: Geoff or Sue Dawson

	ALL ROOMS HAVE:	WE PROVIDE:
We have built up an excellent reputation for ensuring the comfort and well-being of our guests	Toilet, Free colour TV, Central Heating, Tea/coffee making facilities, Shaver points, Fitted carpets, Hair dryer, Radio, Access at all times, Most have shower/bath	A friendly atmosphere, Excellent service, Superb varied meals, Well stocked cosy bar, TV lounge, Bar snacks

Bourne

Town 10 miles west of Spalding.

CAWTHORPE FARM, CAWTHORPE, BOURNE, LINCOLNSHIRE PE10 0AB (Tel: 01778 426697 & Fax: 01778 421536) Comfortable rooms full of character. Walking, cycling and bird watching in nearby woods. Near Stamford, Peterborough and Lincoln. Stabling and grazing available. Pets welcome by arrangement.

Langton-by-Wragby

Village located south-east of Wragby.

MISS JESSIE SKELLERN, LEA HOLME, LANGTON-BY-WRAGBY, LINCOLN LN8 5PZ (01673 858339). Ground floor accommodation in chalet-type house. Central for Wolds, coast, fens, historic Lincoln. Market towns, Louth, Horncastle, Boston, Spilsby, Alford, Woodhall Spa. Two double bedrooms, washbasin; bathroom, toilet adjoining; lounge with colour TV, separate dining room. Drinks provided. Children welcome reduced rates. Car almost essential, parking. Numerous eating places nearby. B&B from £20 per person. Open all year. Tourist Board Listed [🛏]

Lincoln

County town and Cathedral City on River Witham, and on site of Roman Lindum.

SOUTH PARK GUEST HOUSE, 11 SOUTH PARK, LINCOLN LN5 8EW (01522 528243; Fax: 01522 524603). Warm welcome offered in restored Victorian detached house. All rooms en suite. Overlooking South Common. Short walk to shops, restaurants, pubs, city centre and tourist attractions. [🛏]

Mablethorpe

Coastal resort 11 miles from Louth.

MRS GRAVES, GRANGE FARM, MALTBY-LE-MARSH, ALFORD LN13 0JP (01507 450267; Fax: 01507 450180). Farmhouse B&B and country cottage set in six idyllic acres of Lincolnshire countryside. Peaceful base for leisure and sightseeing. Private fishing lake. Many farm animals. Brochure available. Pets welcome.

SYMBOLS

🛏 Indicates that pets are welcome free of charge.

£ Indicates that a charge is made for pets: nightly or weekly.

pw! Shows some special provision for pets; exercise facility, feeding or accommodation arrangement.

◻ Indicates separate pets accommodation.

Market Rasen

Market town and agricultural centre 14 miles north-east of Lincoln.

MR & MRS J. MATTHEWS, BEECHWOOD GUEST HOUSE, WILLINGHAM ROAD, MARKET RASEN LN8 3DX (01673 844043). Genuine hospitality at this period guest house on edge of Lincolnshire Wolds. Comfortable accommodation, home cooked meals, guest lounge and private parking. Brochure available. [🐕]

Skegness

Coastal resort 19 miles north-east of Boston.

BELLE VIEW HOTEL 12 SOUTH PARADE SKEGNESS PE25 3HW (01754 765274). Situated on the seafront, all rooms have toilet, colour TV, central heating, tea/coffee making facilities, shaver pionts, fitted carpets, hair dryer, and most have shower/bath.

RAVENNA CHALET PARK, ANDERBY CREEK, SKEGNESS, LINCOLNSHIRE PE24 5XP. A personal, friendly self-catering holiday. Quality accommodation, chalets, caravans, bungalows, cottage, house. Quiet location. Three minutes beach. Cleanliness assured. Personal supervision. Dogs welcome. JOY & BARRY WESTLEY (01754 872966).

LONDON

London

ST ATHANS HOTEL
20 Tavistock Place, Russell Square, LONDON WC1H 9RE
Tel: 020-7837 9140; Fax: 020-7833 8352
Bed and Breakfast, comfortable, ideal for families. Hotel situated near British Museum, convenient for shops, parks and theatres. Only 10 minutes from Euston and King's Cross. Pets welcome FREE.

London

Legislative capital of UK and major port. Theatres, shops, museums, places of historic interest. Airports at Heathrow and Gatwick.

ST ATHANS HOTEL, 20 TAVISTOCK PLACE, RUSSELL SQUARE, LONDON WC1H 9RE (Tel: 020-7837 9140; Fax: 020-7833 8352). Family Bed and Breakfast near British Museum, shops, parks and theatres. Russell Square two blocks away, Euston and King's Cross stations ten minutes. LTB LISTED. [🐕]

THE DRAGON HOUSE, 39 MARMORA ROAD, LONDON SE22 0RX (0208 693 4355; or 0956 645 894). Nearest thing to a farmhouse in London. Large freshly decorated rooms in peaceful cosseted atmosphere. Flowers, toiletries, television, magazines, tea/coffee, en suite. Evening meal available. Single £40, Double £50. Dogs' beds, walks, sitting services provided. Central London 10 minutes. Local pick up. Parking. London Tourist Board ◆◆◆◆.[🐕 pw!]

Visit the **FHG** website
www.holidayguides.com
for details of the wide choice of accommodation
featured in the full range of FHG titles

Please mention *Pets Welcome*
when enquiring about accommodation featured in these pages.

CASTAWAYS HOLIDAY PARK

BGHP ★★★★

Set in the Quiet, peaceful village of Bacton, with direct access to fine sandy beach, and ideal for touring Norfolk and The Broads. Modern Caravans, Lodges and Flats, with all amenities. Licensed Club, Entertainment, Amusement Arcade, Children's Play Area. PETS WELCOME.

Enquiries and Bookings to: Roger and Beccy Fitches, Castaways Holiday Park, Paston Road, Bacton-on-Sea, Norfolk NR12 0JB Tel: (01692) 650436 and 650418

Peacock House

Old farmhouse. Lovely countryside with good walks. 3¹/₂ miles from Dereham, close for Norwich, NT houses, Sandringham, beaches. All rooms en suite, tea/coffee facilities. TV's in all rooms. Own lounge, no smoking. Very warm welcome. B&B £20 to £25pp. Open all year. **Children and dogs welcome. ETC ◆◆◆ Gold Award.**
Mrs Jenny Bell, Peacock Lane, Old Beetley, Dereham, Norfolk NR20 4DG
Tel: 01362 860371 E-mail: Peackh@aol.com Web: www.SmoothHound.co.uk/hotels/peacockh.html

THE HOSTE ARMS

The Green, Burnham Market, Norfolk PE31 8HD

Award-winning 17th century Hotel in beautiful Georgian village. 28 elegantly furnished bedrooms, colour TV and telephone. Recently refurbished residents' conservatory lounge, and Gallery Restaurant. Excellent menu, varied cuisine and outstanding wine list. Local beaches provide wonderful dog walking.
E-mail: TheHosteArms@compuserve.com Website: www.hostearms.co.uk
🌼🌼🌼 *Highly Commended* **Tel: 01328 738257/738777 Fax: 01328 730103** *AA* ◎◎ Restaurant

See also Colour Advertisement on page 34

FHG

PLEASE MENTION THIS GUIDE WHEN YOU WRITE

OR PHONE TO ENQUIRE ABOUT ACCOMMODATION

IF YOU ARE WRITING, A STAMPED, ADDRESSED

ENVELOPE IS ALWAYS APPRECIATED

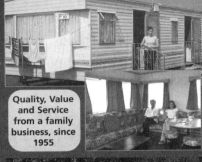

KING'S CHALET PARK (CROMER NR27 0AJ)

Families Welcome & Pets Free of Charge

Well equipped Chalets sleeping 2 to 6; shower/bathroom, microwave, TV. Tourist Board and NNH/GHA Approved. 1 Twin, 1 Double bedroom, bed sofa in lounge. Well-equipped kitchenette. Quiet site adjacent to woods, Golf Club and beach. Local shops nearby or pleasant 10 minutes walk into town.   ETC ♈♈

Telephone: 012623 511308

Pet welcome free of charge

Comfortable, well equipped chalets situated on beautiful, landscaped, quiet site. Ideally placed for walks to adjacent woods, cliffs and sandy beaches. 10 minutes' walk to town. Golf course and local shops nearby. 1 Twin, 1 Double Room, bed/sofa in lounge, bathroom, colour TV, microwave, well equipped kitchenette. Children welcome.

Short Breaks in Spring/Autumn 2 nights or more from £60
Spring/Autumn £90 – £165
June – September £165 – £225 per week.

DETAILS FROM: MRS I. SCOLTOCK, SHANGRI-LA, LITTLE CAMBRIDGE, DUTON HILL, DUNMOW, ESSEX (TEL: 01371 870482)

Kings Chalet Park, Cromer
Sleep 2 – 6
Open March to October

Scarning Dale

Dale Road, Scarning, East Dereham NR19 2QN
Tel: 01362 687269

A warm welcome awaits you. 16th Century house in 25 acres of landscaped gardens, paddocks and woodland. Excellent home cooking (à la carte and table d'hôte). Indoor heated swimming pool and full size snooker table. Good access Norfolk and Suffolk. Self-catering cottages also available. Tea shop. Art classes. Dogs welcome in self catering cottages. Grazing and Stables available.
Tariff: Single £50 – £60; Double £90 – £100.

BARTLES LODGE

Stay in the peaceful, tranquil heart of Norfolk's most beautiful countryside. All rooms tastefully decorated in country style, with full en suite facilities, TVs, tea/coffee making facilities, etc. Overlooking 12 acres of landscaped meadows with its own private fishing lakes. Bed and Breakfast from £20.
Recommended by "Which?" Good Bed & Breakfast Guide.
Bartles Lodge, Church Street, Elsing, Dereham NR20 3EA Tel: 01362 637177

Country Bed and Breakfast
STRENNETH
Airfield Road, Fersfield, Diss Norfolk IP22 2BP
Telephone: 01379 688182
Fax: 01379 688260
E-mail ken@strenneth.co.uk
Website: www.strenneth.co.uk

STRENNETH is a well-established, family-run business, situated in unspoiled countryside just a short drive from Bressingham Gardens and the picturesque market town of Diss. Offering first-class accommodation, the original 17th Century building has been carefully renovated to a high standard with a wealth of exposed oak beams and a newer single storey courtyard wing. There is ample off road parking and plenty of nice walks nearby. All seven bedrooms, including a Four Poster and an Executive, are tastefully arranged with period furniture

and distinctive beds. Each having remote colour television, hospitality trays, central heating and full en suite facilities. The establishment is smoke free and the guest lounge has a log fire on cold winter evenings. There is an extensive breakfast menu using local produce. Ideal touring base. Pets most welcome at no extra charge. Outside kennels with runs if required. Hair Salons. ETC ♦♦♦ Bed and Breakfast from £25.00

See also Colour Advertisement on page 32

FHG PUBLICATIONS LIMITED publish a large range of well-
known accommodation guides. We will be happy to send you
details or you can use the order form at the back of this book.

WELCOME COTTAGE HOLIDAYS. Quality Cottages in wonderful locations at welcoming low prices. Pets, linen and fuel mostly included. PHONE FOR FREE 2001 FULL COLOUR BROCHURE 01756 702205.

NORFOLK COUNTRY COTTAGES, MARKET PLACE, REEPHAM NR10 4JJ. Widest ever selection of cottages throughout Norfolk. Phone for brochure 01603 871872. [Pets £12 per week] website: www.norfolkcottages.co.uk

Acle

Small town 8 miles west of Great Yarmouth.

EAST NORWICH INN, OLD ROAD, ACLE, NORWICH NR13 3QN (01493 751112; Fax: 01493 751109). Midway between Norwich and Great Yarmouth, ideal for holiday attractions. All rooms en suite with colour TV and tea/coffee making. Pets welcome by arrangement. [🐾]

Bacton-on-Sea

Village on coast. 5 miles from North Walsham.

CASTAWAYS HOLIDAY PARK, PASTON ROAD, BACTON-ON-SEA, NORFOLK NR12 0JB (01692 650436 and 650418). In peaceful village with direct access to sandy beach. Modern caravans, Lodges and Flats, with all amenities. Licensed club, entertainment, children's play area. Ideal for touring Norfolk. [Pets £15 per week/£2.50 p.n.]

RED HOUSE CHALET AND CARAVAN PARK, PASTON ROAD, BACTON-ON-SEA NR12 0JB (01692 650815). Small family-run site, ideal for touring Broads. Chalets, caravans and flats all with showers, fridges and colour TV. Some with sea views. Licensed. Open March–January. [Pets £10 weekly.]

Beetley

Village 4 miles/6 km north of East Dereham, which is noteable for old buildings, including the parish church.

MRS JENNY BELL, PEACOCK HOUSE, PEACOCK LANE, OLD BEETLEY, DEREHAM NR20 4DG (01362 860371). Old farmhouse in lovely countryside. All rooms en suite, tea / coffee facilities. TV's in all rooms. Own lounge, B&B from £20 to £25 pp. Open all year. 4 diamonds Gold Award. Non-smoking. Children and dogs welcome. [pw! 🐾]
e-mail: peackh@aol.com
website: www.SmoothHound.co.uk/hotels.peacockh.html

Bradenham

Village 5 miles south-west of East Dereham.

MID NORFOLK - Charming cottage decorated and furnished to high standard. Sleeps two. Has well enclosed private garden. Situated in sleepy hamlet. Lovely walks. Pets welcome. MRS ROWNTREE, "FOXLEA", WEST END, BRADENHAM, NORFOLK IP25 7QZ (Tel: 01760 441733)

Burnham Market

Village 5 miles west of Wells-next-the-Sea

THE HOSTE ARMS, THE GREEN, BURNHAM MARKET PE31 8HD (Tel: 01328 738257/738777; Fax: 01328 730103). 17th century Hotel overlooking village green. 28 bedrooms, elegantly furnished, all en suite with colour TV and telephone. Bar and restaurant menus, AA 2 Rosettes. [🐾]
e–mail: TheHosteArms@compuserve.com
website: www.hostearms.co.uk

SYMBOLS

🐾   **Indicates that pets are welcome free of charge.**
£   **Indicates that a charge is made for pets: nightly or weekly.**
pw!   **Shows some special provision for pets; exercise facility, feeding or accommodation arrangement.**
◻   **Indicates separate pets accommodation.**

Caister-on-Sea

Historic site with Roman ruins and 15th century Caister Castle with 100 foot tower.

Go BLUE RIBAND for quality inexpensive self-catering holidays where your dog is welcome – choice of locations all in the borough of Great Yarmouth. Detached 3 bedroom bungalows, seafront bungalows, detached Sea-Dell chalets and modern sea front caravans. Free colour brochure: DON WITHERIDGE, BLUE RIBAND HOUSE, PARKLANDS, HEMSBY, GREAT YARMOUTH NR29 4HA (01493 730445). [pw! ✝].
website: www.blue-riband.com

Coltishall

Village to the north east of Norwich.

THE NORFOLK MEAD HOTEL, COLTISHALL, NORWICH, NORFOLK NR12 7DN (01603 737531 or 737521). Renowned restaurant offering superb cuisine and a comprehensive wine list. Well mannered dogs welcome. Johansen recommended. Best loved hotel. [Pets £5 per week]
e-mail: info@norfolkmead.co.uk
website: www.norfolkmead.co.uk

Cromer

Attractive resort built round old fishing village. Norwich 21 miles.

CHALET 49 ~ KINGS CHALET PARK,CROMER. Luxury, well equipped chalet , adjacent to beaches, woods, cliff-top walks and golf courses. Local shops. Two bedrooms, bathroom, fitted kitchen, microwave, colour TV, etc. Sleeps four to five. Cleaned and maintained by owner. Pets welcome. Open March to October. MRS M. WALKER, WHITE BARN, SANDY LANE, WEST RUNTON, NORFOLK NR27 9NB (01263 837494) [Pets £10]

All-electric two and three bedroom Holiday Cottages accommodating four to six persons in beautiful surroundings. Sandy beaches, sports facilities, Cinema and Pier (live shows). Parking. Children and pets welcome. Brochure: NORTHREPPS HOLIDAY PROPERTIES, CROMER, NORFOLK NR27 0JW (01263 513969 (answerphone after 1pm); Fax: 01263 515588). [Pets £12 weekly].
e-mail: estate.office@gurney.co.uk

CLIFTONVILLE HOTEL, SEAFRONT, CROMER NR27 9AS (01263 512543; Fax: 01263 515700). Ideally situated on the Norfolk coast. Beautifully restored Edwardian Hotel. 30 en suite bedrooms all with sea view. Executive suites. Seafood Bistro. à la carte Restaurant. [pw! pets £4 per night]

KINGS CHALET PARK, CROMER NR27 0AJ (01263 511308) . Well-equipped chalets sleeping 2 to 6; shower/bathroom, microwave and TV. 1 Twin, 1 Double bedroom, bed sofa in lounge, well-equipped kitchenette. Quiet site adjacent to woods, golf club and beaches. Local shops nearby. Pleasant 10 minutes' walk to town. Tourist Board and NNH/GHA Approved. Families welcome. ETC ඦ. [✝]

KINGS CHALET PARK, CROMER. Comfortable well-equipped chalets on quiet site; ideally placed for woodland and beach walks. 10 minutes' walk to town, shops nearby. Details from MRS I. SCOLTOCK, SHANGRI-LA, LITTLE CAMBRIDGE, DUTON HILL, DUNMOW, ESSEX (01371 870482). [✝]

PLEASE MENTION THIS GUIDE WHEN YOU WRITE
OR PHONE TO ENQUIRE ABOUT ACCOMMODATION

IF YOU ARE WRITING, A STAMPED, ADDRESSED

ENVELOPE IS ALWAYS APPRECIATED

Dereham

Situated 16 miles west of Norwich. St Nicholas Church has 16th century bell tower.

SCARNING DALE, SCARNING, EAST DEREHAM NR19 2QN (01362 687269). Self catering cottages (not commercialised) in grounds of owner's house. On-site indoor heated swimming pool and full-size snooker table. B&B for six also available in house. (sorry no pets in house). Grazing and Stables available.

BARTLES LODGE, CHURCH STREET, ELSING, DEREHAM NR20 3EA (01362 637177). Stay in the peaceful, tranquil heart of Norfolk's most beautiful countryside. All rooms en suite, TVs, tea/coffee making facilities, etc. Recommended by "Which?" Good Bed & Breakfast Guide. [pw! Pets £1 per night, £5 per week]

Diss

Twisting streets with Tudor, georgian and victorian architecture. 12th century St Mary's Church and 6 acre mere, haven for wildfowl.

BRENDA WEBB, STRENNETH, AIRFIELD ROAD, FERSFIELD, DISS IP22 2BP (01379 688182; Fax 01379 688260). Family run, fully renovated period property. All rooms en suite, colour TVs, hospitality trays. Ground floor rooms. Non smoking. Extensive breakfast menu. Licensed. Bed and Breakfast from £23.00. ETC ◆◆◆◆. [🅣]
e-mail ken@strenneth.co.uk
website: www.strenneth.co.uk

Downham Market

Market town and agricultural centre on the River Ouse, 10 miles south of King's Lynn.

CROSSKEYS RIVERSIDE HOTEL, BRIDGE STREET, HILGAY, NEAR DOWNHAM MARKET, NORFOLK PE38 0LD (01366 387777). A small country hotel beside the River Wissey. With free fishing from hotel frontage. All bedrooms (three four posters) have en suite bathrooms, colour TV, tea/coffee making facilities. Ground floor bedrooms available. Prices from £25. Reductions of 10% for long stays. Pets most welcome. Stabling available. [🅣]
website: www.crosskeys-hotel.fsbusiness.co.uk

Foxley

Village 6 miles east of East Dereham.

Self Catering Chalets (2/3 bedrooms) on working farm. All fully equipped, with central heating. 20 miles from coast, 15 from Broads. Mature woodland nearby. Ideal for walking. 🏠🏠🏠 Approved. MOOR FARM STABLE COTTAGES, FOXLEY NR20 4QN (01362 688523). [Pets £10 per week]

Gimingham

Village 4 miles north of North Walsham.

BRIDGE FARM STABLES, WINDMILL ROAD, GIMINGHAM, NEAR MUNDESLEY, NORFOLK NR11 8HL (01263 720028). Working stables situated on the outskirts of Gimingham village. Friendly atmosphere, good food, central heating and ideal for touring the Norfolk Broads. Fishing and golf nearby. Dogs welcome. Contact: Mr & Mrs J.A. Harris.

SYMBOLS

🅣   Indicates that pets are welcome free of charge.

£   Indicates that a charge is made for pets: nightly or weekly.

pw!   Shows some special provision for pets; exercise facility, feeding or accommodation arrangement.

⌂   Indicates separate pets accommodation.

Great Yarmouth

Traditional lively seaside resort with a wide range of amusements, including the Marina Centre and Sealife Centre.

CAREFREE HOLIDAYS, CHAPEL BRIERS, YARMOUTH ROAD, HEMSBY, GREAT YARMOUTH NR29 4NJ (01493 732176). A wide selection of superior chalets for live-as-you-please holidays near Great Yarmouth and Norfolk Broads. All amenities on site. Parking. Children and pets welcome. [Pets £10 per week, £5 on short breaks, 2nd pet free.]

MR AND MRS COLLIS, "ANCHOR", 21 NORTH DENES ROAD, GREAT YARMOUTH NR30 4LW (01493 844339/300050). Completely self-contained flats with own shower and toilet. Fully equipped at no extra cost. Reduced terms early and late season. Close by public amenities. Children and pets welcome. [🐾]

MRS J. S. COOPER, SILVERLEA, MILE ROAD, CARLETON RODE, NORWICH NR16 1NE (01953 789407). Modern holiday chalets at Winterton-on-Sea. Sleep six. Grassy site, with marvellous sea views close to beach . A pets' paradise! [Pets £10 per week.]

Superior brick built tiled roof cottages. Adjacent golf course. Lovely walks on dunes and coast. 2-4 night breaks early/late season, Christmas and New Year. Terms from £59 to £299. SAND DUNE COTTAGES, TAN LANE, CAISTER-ON-SEA, GREAT YARMOUTH NR30 5DT (01493 667786 / 03855 61363).

Holt

Small town 10 miles west of Cromer.

MARY ALEXANDER, THE MAP HOUSE, SMOKERS HOLE, SAXLINGHAM, HOLT, NR25 7JU (01263 741304) Historic gamekeeper's lodge set in peaceful countryside 4 miles from coast. B&B with 2 luxuriously totally private double suites (bedroom, bathroom and sitting room). Well behaved dogs welcome free. ETC ◆◆◆ Gold Award.[🐾]

Horning

Lovely riverside village ideally placed for exploring the Broads. Great Yarmouth 17 miles.

SILVER BIRCHES HOLIDAYS, GREBE ISLAND, LOWER STREET, HORNING NR12 8PF (01692 630858). Five individual houseboats, good size bungalows adoped for disabled use, and motor day launches. All the comforts of a caravan afloat! Surrounded by lawns, adjacent parking. Ideal for families, fishermen and their pets. [Pets £15 per stay] e-mail: cathy.saxelby@virgin.net

Hunstanton

Neat little resort which faces west across The Wash, Norwich 47 miles, Cromer 38.

MRS BROWN, MARINE HOTEL, HUNSTANTON PE36 5EH (01485 533310). Overlooking sea and green. Pets welcome, free of charge. Colour TV in all bedrooms. Open all year except Christmas period. SAE for terms and brochure. [🐾]

COBBLERS COTTAGE, 3 WODEHOUSE ROAD, OLD HUNSTANTON PE36 6JD (01485 534036). Near Royal Sandringham/Norfolk Lavender. All en suite twin/double rooms. Colour TV and tea-making facilities. Near the beach, golf, bird watching, pubs and restaurants. Sauna and jacuzzi. Also self catering annexe. ETC ◆◆◆, ♔♔♔ Commended. [🐾] e–mail: cobblerscottage@dial.pipex.com

King's Lynn

Ancient market town and port on the Wash with many beautiful medieval and Georgian buildings.

MRS J. E. FORD, LEZIATE DROVE, POTT ROW, KING'S LYNN PE32 1DE (01553 630356). Detached bungalow sleeps 4. In quiet village close to Sandringham and beaches. Facilities include colour TV, video, microwave, fridge/freezer, washing machine, off road parking, dog run. [🐾]

MRS G. DAVIDSON, HOLMDENE FARM, BEESTON, KING'S LYNN PE32 2NJ (01328 701284). 17th century farmhouse situated in central Norfolk within easy reach of the coast and Broads. Sporting activities available locally, village pub nearby. One double room, one twin and two singles. Pets welcome. Bed and Breakfast from £18 per person; Evening Meal from £12. Weekly terms available and child reductions. Two self-catering cottages. Sleeping 4/8. Terms on request. **ETC ★★★.**

MARANATHA/HAVANA GUEST HOUSE, 115/117 GAYWOOD ROAD, KING'S LYNN PE30 2PU (01553 774596/772331; Fax: 01553 763747). Detatched, friendly, family run with comfortable rooms. Evening meals, snacks available. Walking distance town centre. Close to Sandringham and coast. Pets free. Children special rates. Terms from £15. AA/EATB ◆◆◆/★★★. Welcome Host.

Mundesley-on-Sea

Small resort backed by low cliffs. Good sands and bathing. Norwich 20 miles, Cromer 7.

OVERCLIFF LODGE, CROMER ROAD, MUNDESLEY NR11 8DB (01263 720016).Comfortable 19th century Victorian house, a few minutes' walk from cliff tops and beach. Twin en suite downstairs room, TV, tea/coffee making facilities. Sorry no smoking. ETC ◆◆◆ graded. Well behaved dogs very welcome. (pets £3.50 per night, food not included).
e-mail: overclifflodge@btinternet.com

47 SEAWARD CREST, MUNDESLEY. West-facing brick built chalet on private site with lawns, flowers and parking. Large lounge/dining room, kitchenette, two bedrooms, bathroom. Beach and shops nearby. Weekly terms from £90. Pets most welcome. SAE please: MRS DOAR, 4 DENBURY ROAD, RAVENSHEAD, NOTTS, NG15 9FQ (01623 798032).

"WHINCLIFF", CROMER ROAD, MUNDESLEY NR11 8DU (01263 720961). Clifftop house, sea views and sandy beaches. Rooms with colour TV and tea-making. En suite family/twin room. Evening Meal optional, not Sundays. An abundance of coastal and woodland walks; many places of interest and local crafts. Well-behaved dogs welcome. Contact Mrs G. Faulkner. [🐕]

KILN CLIFFS CARAVAN PARK, CROMER ROAD, MUNDESLEY NR11 8DF (01263 720449). Peaceful family-run site situated around an historic brick kiln. Six-berth caravans for hire, standing on ten acres of grassy cliff top. All caravans fully equipped (except linen) and price includes all gas and electricity. [Pets £5 per week].

Narborough

Village 5 miles south-west of Swaffham.

Relax in our chalk Self-Catering cottage overlooking your horses field/stable. Enjoy the woodburner and four-poster bed. Village shop/pub. Dog welcome. Bridleways abundant. NICKY ST LAWRENCE, CHURCH FARM, NARBOROUGH, KINGS LYNN, NORFOLK PE32 1TE (Tel: 01760 337696 or 07801 641570; Fax: 01760 337858).[Pets £10 per week, horses £40 per week].
e-mail: nickytstlawrence@ouvip.com

Neatishead

Ideal for touring East Anglia. Close to Norwich. Aylsham 14 miles, Norwich 10, Wroxham 3.

ALAN AND SUE WRIGLEY, REGENCY GUEST HOUSE, THE STREET, NEATISHEAD, NORFOLK BROADS NR12 8AD (Tel & Fax: 01692 630233). 18th century five bedroomed guest house renowned for generous English breakfasts. Ideal East Anglian touring base. Accent on personal service. ETC/AA ◆◆◆◆. Dogs welcome. [Pets £4 per night.]

Please mention *Pets Welcome*
when enquiring about accommodation featured in these pages.

North Walsham

Market town 14 miles north of Norwich, traditional centre of the Norfolk reed thatching industry.

SCARBOROUGH HILL COUNTRY HOUSE HOTEL, OLD YARMOUTH ROAD, NORTH WALSHAM, NR28 9NA (01692 402151; FAX: 01692 406686). Elegant Regency country house hotel set in 9 acres of charming grounds. 9 en suite bedrooms with tea/coffee making facilities and telephone. Bed and Breakfast from £49.50 single, £75 double. Two/Three Night Weekend Breaks available. [Dogs from £5 per night (excludes food)].
e-mail: scarboroughhill@nascr.net
website: www.scarboroughhill.com

MRS V. O'HARA, GEOFFREY THE DYER'S HOUSE, CHURCH PLAIN, WORSTEAD, NORTH WALSHAM NR28 9AL (01692 536562). 17th century Listed weaver's house in centre of conservation village. Close to Broads, Coast, Norwich. Good walking and touring. All rooms en suite. Wholesome, well-cooked food. Dogs welcome. [🐕]
e–mail: oharafamily@freeserve.co.uk

Sheringham

Small, traditional resort built around a flint-built fishing village. Sandy beaches and amusements.

ACHIMOTA, 31 NORTH STREET, SHERINGHAM NR26 8LW (01263 822379). Award-winning small guest house in quiet part of Sheringham in "Area of Outstanding Natural Beauty", with Blue Flag beach and walks galore. All rooms have private facilities, easy chairs, TV, beverage tray and central heating. NO SMOKING. Brochure on request. ETC ◆◆◆. [🐕]
website: www.broadland.com/achimota.

Stalham

Village 7 miles south-east of North Walsham.

NORFOLK BROADS, NEAR WROXHAM. Quality spacious self-catering house in country, near beaches. Several dogs and well behaved owners welcome. Escape proof garden/orchard. Inclusive of bed linen, central heating, dof sofa covers etc. Also available B&B in owners bungalow. Own TV lounge, en suite whirlpool bath. Tea making facilities. Disabled facilities. (Tel: 01692 650901).
e-mail: dolphin@dial.pipex.com

Thetford

Town at confluence of Rivers Thet and Little Ouse, 12 miles north of Bury St Edmunds.

MRS DAY, BRUTON COTTAGE, LIME KILN LANE, FELTWELL BY THETFORD IP26 4BJ (01842 828368). Bed and Breakfast in 18th century cottage in farming village by Thetford Forest. Large garden. Pets welcome. B&B £15; evening meal by arrangement £20. Open all year. Log fire and central heating. [🐕]

Thornham

Village 4 miles east of Hunstanton. Site of Roman signal station.

THE LIFEBOAT INN, SHIP LANE, THORNHAM PE36 6LT (01485 512236 Fax: 01485512323) A welcome sight for the weary traveller for centuries. Dogs welcome. Restaurant (one AA rosette). Bird watching and walking along miles of open beaches. Please ring for brochure and tariff. [🐕]
website: www.lifeboatinn.co.uk

SYMBOLS
🐕 Indicates that pets are welcome free of charge.
£ Indicates that a charge is made for pets: nightly or weekly.
pw! Shows some special provision for pets; exercise facility, feeding or accommodation arrangement.
⌂ Indicates separate pets accommodation.

Thurne

Idyllic Broadland village. great Yarmouth 10 miles.

HEDERA HOUSE AND PLANTATION BUNGALOWS, THURNE NR29 3BU (01692 670242). Adjacent river, 7 bedroomed farmhouse, 10 competitively priced bungalows in lovely peaceful gardens. Outdoor heated pool. Enjoy boating, fishing, walking, touring, nearby golf, horseriding, sandy beaches and popular resorts.

Wells-next-the-Sea

Lovely little resort with interesting harbour, famous for its cockles, whelks and shrimps. A winding creek leads to a beach of fine sands with dunes. Norwich 31 miles, King's Lynn 27, Cromer 19.

MRS J. M. COURT, EASTDENE, NORTHFIELD LANE, WELLS-NEXT-THE-SEA NR23 1LH (01328 710381). Homely Guest House offers warm welcome. Bed and Breakfast from £19. Two double, one twin bedded rooms, all en suite; tea/coffee making facilities and colour TV. Private parking. [Pets £1 per night].

JEAN WHITAKER, OLD POLICE HOUSE, POLKA ROAD, WELLS-NEXT-THE-SEA NR23 1ED (01328 710630). Ground floor en suite rooms. Tea/coffee making facilities. Colour TV. Parking. Separate entrance. B&B from £22. ◆◆◆. [Dogs 50p per night]

Cosy, centrally heated cottage, sleeps 5-6. Quiet yet close to all facilities. Heat, power, linen all inclusive. Garage. Open all year. Short lets available winter. PETER & FIONA HARNETT, THE COTTAGE, CROSSBECK CLOSE, ILKNEY LS29 9JW (01943 601743) [🐾]
E-mail: fylfot@dialstart.net

Winterton-on-Sea

Good sands and bathing. Great Yarmouth 8 miles.

TIMBERS, WINTERTON-ON-SEA. Sleeps 5 plus cot. Self-contained ground floor of cottage in quiet seaside village. Broad sandy beach and pleasant walks. Close to Norfolk Broads. Secluded garden. Double, twin and single bedrooms. Bed linen provided. Fully equipped for self-catering family holiday. £200-£320 per week. Full details from MISS E. ISHERWOOD, 11 BIRNBECK COURT, 98 BELLS HILL, BARNET EN5 2TD (0208 441 3493). [Pets £5 per week]

WINTERTON VALLEY HOLIDAYS. A selection of modern superior fully appointed holiday chalets sleeping 2-6 persons. Duvets and colour TV in all chalets. Panoramic views of the sea from this quiet 35 acre estate. 5 minutes beach, 8 miles Great Yarmouth. Pets very welcome. For colour brochure; 15 KINGSTON AVENUE, CAISTER-ON-SEA NR30 5ET (01493 377175). [Pets £20 per week].

Wroxham

Village 7 miles north east of Norwich.

THE BROADS HOTEL, STATION ROAD, WROXHAM, NORWICH NR12 8UR (01603 782869; Fax: 01603 784066). Comfortable hotel owned and run by dog-loving family. Ideally situated for boating, fishing and exploring the beautiful Norfolk countryside and coastline. All rooms fully en suite. [🐾]

FHG PUBLICATIONS

publish a large range of well-known accommodation guides. We will be happy to send you details or you can use the order form at the back of this book.

𝕽𝖔𝖙𝖍𝖜𝖊𝖑𝖑 𝕳𝖔𝖚𝖘𝖊 𝕳𝖔𝖙𝖊𝖑

Bridge Street, Rothwell, Northamptonshire NN14 6JW

The Rothwell House, originally a Vicarage, has been extended to provide tasteful modernised Hotel facilities. The Hotel has 21 en-suite Bedrooms with remote control colour TV, tea/coffee making facilities and telephones. The Hotel also boasts an indoor swimming pool and fitness area. We also have conference facilities for up to 20 delegates. Rothwell is in the heart of rural England with plenty to do and see including Althorp House, Rockingham Castle, Wickstead Park and Silverstone all nearby.

Price Busters start at £19.50. Dinner, Bed and Breakfast at just £34.50 Telephone: 01536 713000 Fax: 01536 713888 for a Brochure.

Rothwell

Small town 4 miles north-west of Kettering.

ROTHWELL HOUSE HOTEL, BRIDGE STREET, ROTHWELL, NORTHAMPTONSHIRE NN14 6JW (01536 713000 Fax: 01536 7138888) 21 en suite bedrooms with remote control colour TV, tea/coffee making facilities and telephones. Indoor swimming pool and fitness area. Althorp House, Rockingham Castle, Wickstead Park and Silverstone all nearby.

FOR THE MUTUAL GUIDANCE
OF GUEST AND HOST

Every year literally thousands of holidays, short breaks and overnight stops are arranged through our guides, the vast majority without any problems at all. In a handful of cases, however, difficulties do arise about bookings, which often could have been prevented from the outset.

It is important to remember that when accommodation has been booked, both parties – guests and hosts – have entered into a form of contract. We hope that the following points will provide helpful guidance.

GUESTS: When enquiring about accommodation, be as precise as possible. Give exact dates, numbers in your party and the ages of any children. State the number and type of rooms wanted and also what catering you require – bed and breakfast, full board etc. Make sure that the position about evening meals is clear – and about pets, reductions for children or any other special points.

Read our reviews carefully to ensure that the proprietors you are going to contact can supply what you want. Ask for a letter confirming all arrangements, if possible.

If you have to cancel, do so as soon as possible. Proprietors do have the right to retain deposits and under certain circumstances to charge for cancelled holidays if adequate notice is not given and they cannot re-let the accommodation.

HOSTS: Give details about your facilities and about any special conditions. Explain your deposit system clearly and arrangements for cancellations, charges etc. and whether or not your terms include VAT.

If for any reason you are unable to fulfil an agreed booking without adequate notice, you may be under an obligation to arrange suitable alternative accommodation or to make some form of compensation.

While every effort is made to ensure accuracy, we regret that FHG Publications cannot accept responsibility for errors, omissions or misrepresentations in our entries or any consequences thereof. Prices in particular should be checked because we go to press early. We will follow up complaints but cannot act as arbiters or agents for either party.

Please mention *Pets Welcome*
when enquiring about accommodation featured in these pages.

NORTHUMBRIA COAST AND COUNTRY COTTAGES LTD. Selected self-catering Holiday Cottages. ETC Registered Agency. Discover beautiful, unspoilt, Northumberland in one of our personally selected properties – over 130 to choose from – pets welcome in many. Colour brochure available: 01665 830783/830902 (24hrs) [Pets £4.00 per week.] website: www.alnmarin.co.uk/nccc

DALES HOLIDAY COTTAGES offer a selection of superb, personally inspected holiday properties, in beautiful rural and coastal locations, including Cathering Cookson country and the Borders. Cosy cottages to country houses, many open all year. FREE brochure on request. Dales Holiday Cottages, Carleton Business Park, Skipton, North Yorkshire BD23 2AA (01756 799821 or 01756 790919). website: www.dales-holiday-cottages.com (online booking with secure server).

Alnmouth

Quiet little resort with wide sands. Alnwick with its impressive Norman Castle is 5 miles north west.

CAROL AND ALAN SWEET, THE HOPE & ANCHOR HOTEL, 44 NORTHUMBERLAND STREET, ALNMOUTH, ALNWICK NE66 2RA (01665 830363). "Sam" our cheeky Chihuahua says "Great for pets...sorry people as well!" Close to the beach yet on the edge of Northumberland's magnificent countryside. ETC ◆◆◆ [★]

JOHN AND CHRISTINA TANNEY, MARINE HOUSE PRIVATE HOTEL, 1 MARINE ROAD, ALNMOUTH NE66 2RW (01665 830349). Charming hotel in fine seafront location. Home cooking, cocktail bar, games room. Children over seven and pets very welcome. Canine Care Award. ETC ◆◆◆◆. [★]

Alnwick

Local attractions include the Norman castle. Dunstanburgh Castle and Warkworth Castle. Newcastle-upon-Tyne 34 miles, Berwick-upon-Tweed 30.

MRS A. STANTON, MOUNT PLEASANT FARM, ALNMOUTH, ALNWICK NE66 3BY (01665 830215). Situated at top of hill on outskirts of seaside village; convenient for castles and Holy Island. Self-contained annexe sleeps 2 adults; open-plan kitchen, shower room. Chalet and 6-berth caravan also available. [★]

VILLAGE FARM SELF CATERING, TOWN FOOT FARM, SHILBOTTLE, ALNWICK NE66 2HG (Tel/Fax: 01665 575591). Top quality accommodation with a choice of 17th century farmhouse or Scandinavian lodges and cottages. Indoor pool, fitness club, sauna, steamroom, beauty therapist, pony riding, fishing and award-winning beaches within 3 miles. Open all year. Short Breaks Autumn/Winter. Comprehensive brochure. [Pets £15 pw]. e–mail: crissy@villagefarm.demon.co.uk website: www.villagefarm.demon.co.uk

Bamburgh

Village on North Sea coast with magnificent castle. Grace Darling buried in churchyard.

MR P. LAVERACK, WAREN HOUSE HOTEL, WAREN MILL, BAMBURGH, NORTHUMBERLAND. NE70 7EE (01668 214581). Luxurious Country House Hotel. Excellent accommodation, superb food, moderately priced wine list. Rural setting. No children under 14 please. ★★★. e-mail: enquires@warenhousehotel.co.uk website: www.warenhousehotel.co.uk

THE MIZEN HEAD HOTEL, BAMBURGH NE69 7BS (Tel: 01668 214254; Fax: 01668 214104) A warm welcome awaits owners and pets alike at the Mizen Head. Close to the beautiful Northumbrian coastline and just a short drive from many lovely walks in the Ingram Valley. The hotel boasts log fires, good food and real ales. AA ★★

Beadnell

Fishing village and resort on North Sea coast.

MARILYN DAVIDSON, 7 BENTHALL, BEADNELL NE67 5BQ (Tel & Fax: 01665 720900). Pet-friendly, non-smoking B&B in 200 year old stone cottage; two luxury en suite bedrooms, sitting room with TV and teatray. Near picturesque harbour, glorious beaches. Surrounded by super opportunities for walkers, riders, golfers, divers, birdwatchers and artists. ETC ◆◆◆◆ [★]

Belford

Village 14 miles south-east of Berwick-upon-Tweed.

BLUEBELL FARM, WEST STREET, BELFORD, NORTHUMBERLAND NE70 7QE (Tel & Fax: 01668 213362) Sleeps 2/7 plus cot. Traditional self-contained stone cottages converted from original farm buildings. Ideal base for Heritage Coast, Holy Island (Lindisfarne), Farne Islands and Scottish Borders. Rates £140 to £200 - £260 to £380. Please contact for details : Howard Wells. e-mail: phyl.carruthers@virgin.net

ETIVE COTTAGE, WARENFORD, NEAR BELFORD. Originally a stable/blacksmith forge, tastefully converted into a two bedroomed cottage. Double glazed throughout with sweeping views to coast and Bamburgh Castle. Pets welcome, free of charge. ETC ϒϒϒ Contact THE COTT., WARENFORD, NEAR BELFORD, NORTHUMBERLAND NE70 7HZ (Tel/Fax: 01668 213233).[]

Belsay

Village 5 miles north west of Ponteland. Belsay Hall is a Neo-Classical building resembling a Greek temple.

MRS. KATH FEARNS, BOUNDER HOUSE, BELSAY, NEWCASTLE-UPON-TYNE NE20 0JR (01661 881267). Stone-built farmhouse situated in beautiful Northumbrian countryside. Two double rooms and a twin all with en suite facilities and a family room with private bathroom. All with colour TV and tea/coffee facilities. Pets welcome. Open all year.

Berwick-upon-Tweed

The most northerly town in England with elegant streets and 18th century town hall.

MRS M. J. MARTIN, FELKINGTON FARM, BERWICK-UPON-TWEED TD15 2NR (Tel & Fax: 01289 387220). Comfortable cottages – ideal base to explore the coast and Border country. Playground, games room, woodland walk. Children and pets welcome. ϒϒϒϒ Commended. Colour Brochure available.

Cornhill-on-Tweed

Village opposite Coldstream across the river and 12 miles south-west of Berwick-upon-Tweed.

TILLMOUTH PARK COUNTRY HOUSE HOTEL, CORNHILL-ON-TWEED TD12 4UU (01890 882255). Magnificent Country Mansion in 15 acres of secluded parkland near Scottish Border and River Tweed. Ideal location for peace and tranquillity. Country sports arranged. website: www.tillmouthpark.co.uk

Haltwhistle

Small town on north bank of River Tyne, 3 miles east of Hexham. nearby are remains of Roman military town of Corstopitum.

KATHRYN McNULTY, SAUGHY RIGG FARM, TWICE BREWED, HALTWHISTLE NE49 9PT (01434 344120). Close to the best parts of Hadrian's Wall. A warm welcome, real fires and good food. Parking. TV. Central heating. Children and pets welcome. Open January to Febuary. Prices from £15. ◆◆◆

Hexham

Market town on bank of River Tyne, with medieval priory church. racecourse 2 miles, Newcastle upon Tyne 20 miles.

MRS MAVIS OSTLER, TAYLOR BURN, NINEBANKS, HEXHAM NE47 8DE (01434 345343). Warm welcome and good food on quiet working hill farm. Large comfortable farmhouse with guests' bathroom, lounge and dining room. No smoking. Join in farm activities. [pw! Pets £1 per night, £5 per week]

RYE HILL FARM, SLALEY, NEAR HEXHAM NE47 0AH (01434 673259). Pleasant family atmosphere in cosy farmhouse. Bed and Breakfast and optional Evening Meal. Bedrooms with TV and tea/coffee making facilities. All en suite. Laundry facilities. Table licence. ◆◆◆◆. [Pets £1 per night, pw!]

MRS R. KEENLEYSIDE, STRUTHERS FARM, CATTON, ALLENDALE, HEXHAM NE47 9LP (01434 683580). Enjoy a break in the picturesque East Allen Valley. Ideal for walking and touring. Lakes, Hadrian's Wall, Metro Centre, Beamish, Newcastle and Hexham all within easy reach. Well appointed double en suite rooms. Excellent wholesome farmhouse fare. Ample safe parking. [🐕]

Warkworth

Village on River Coquet near North Sea coast north-west of Amble with several interesting historic remains.

WARKWORTH HOUSE HOTEL, BRIDGE STREET, WARKWORTH NE65 OXB (01665 711276; Fax: 01665 713323). Set in heart of small village, ideal for dog walking. Miles of open uncrowded beaches. Delicious evening meals. Phone for brochure. [🐕]
e-mail: welcome@warkworthhousehotel.co.uk
website: www.warkworthhousehotel.co.uk

Birling Vale is an attractive stone built detached house in secluded garden. Fully equipped, two double bedrooms, one twin, cot. Free central heating. Close to sandy beaches, trout and salmon rivers and many places of interest. Well-trained dogs welcome. Weekly rates from £125 Low Season, £250 Mid Season, £430 High Season. SAE to MRS J. BREWIS, WOODHOUSE FARM, SHILBOTTLE, NEAR ALNWICK NE66 2HR (01665 575222). [🐕]

NOTTINGHAMSHIRE

Blyth

Priory Farm Guest House ETC ◆◆◆
Hodsock Priory Estate, Blyth, Notts S81 0TY   Tel: 01909 591515
e-mail: vera@guesthse.force9.co.uk   website: http://www.guesthse.force9.co.uk

Located within five minutes of A1 and 10 miles of M1, giving easy access to North Yorkshire and Nottingham Borders. Country Walks. All four bedrooms have tea/coffee making facilities; two are en suite. Lounge with log fire and TV. Bed & Breakfast from £20. For details please contact Mrs Vera Hambleton.

Blyth

Village 6 miles from Retford.

MRS V. HAMBLETON, PRIORY FARM GUEST HOUSE, HODSOCK PRIORY ESTATE, BLYTH S81 0TY (01909 591515). Convenient for A1 and M1. All rooms with tea/coffee making facilities; two en suite. Lounge with log fire and TV. Bed & Breakfast from £20. Children and dogs welcome. [🐕]
e-mail: vera@guesthse.force9.co.uk
website: http://www.guesthse.force9.co.uk

Burton Joyce

Residential area 4 miles north-east of Nottingham.

MRS V. BAKER, WILLOW HOUSE, 12 WILLOW WONG, BURTON JOYCE, NOTTINGHAM NG14 5FD (0115 931 2070). Large Victorian house in quiet village location, two minutes walk River Trent, four miles city. Attractive accommodation in bright, clean rooms with tea/coffee making facilities, TV. Private parking. From £17.50 pppn. Reduced rates for children. Good local eating. Please phone first for directions.

Southwell

Beautiful Southwell Minster has splendid towers and spires dating from 1108.

THE OLD FORGE, BURGAGE LANE, SOUTHWELL NG25 0ER. Charming village house within a short walk of historic Minster, pubs and restaurants, shops and country walks. All rooms en suite, one ground floor. Private parking. B&B from £30 sharing. Reductions for longer stays. (01636 812809; Fax: 01636 816302). ETC ◆◆◆
website: http://www.southwell-online.co.uk/localpages/tholdforge.html

Easington House Hotel... RAC

Easington House dates back to 1575 when it was re built as a wedding present to Margaret Washington, the great, great aunt of George Washington, First President of America. During the last 16 years Malcolm and Gwynneth Hearne have transformed this beautiful property and gardens into an informal, relaxing atmospere. It offers old world charm with up-to-date facilities. All rooms en suite with IDD telephones. An ideal touring base for the Cotswolds. Pets welcome. All major credit cards welcome.

... The Only Country House in Banbury Town Centre

50 Oxford Road, Banbury, Oxon OX16 9AN
Tel: 01295 270181; Fax: 01295 269527
e-mail: easington@aol.com

See also Colour Advertisement on page 36

LITTLE ACRE
Charming country retreat with pretty landscaped gardens and waterfall. Quiet location but only two miles from J6 M40. Near Chilterns, Oxford, Cotswolds, Heathrow Airport. Comfy beds, hearty breakfasts, 'olde worlde' style dining room. Open all year with friendly, relaxed atmosphere. En suite rooms; ground floor bedrooms. Tea/coffee making and TV in rooms. Pets welcome. Highly recommended by previous guests. Bed and Breakfast from £18. Also available ♿ Self-Catering accommodation. **Tel: 01844 281423**

Gorselands Hall

Gorselands Hall, Boddington Lane,
North Leigh, Witney, Oxford OX8 6PU
Tel 01993 882292 • Fax 01993 883629
email: hamilton@gorselandshall.com
website: www.gorselandshall.com

Lovely old Cotswold stone farmhouse with oak beams and flagstone floors in delightful rural setting. Large secluded garden, grass tennis court and croquet lawn. Ideal for Blenheim Palace, the Cotswolds and Oxford. All rooms are en-suite, with colour television and tea/coffee making facilities. Non smoking. Lounge with snooker table for residents' use. A choice of excellent pubs within easy reach. B&B from £22.50. Winter discounts available.

See also Colour Advertisiment on page 37

**COTTAGE IN THE COUNTRY. Delightful holiday homes in central England - from London to Welsh Borders with extensive Cotswold choice. Comfort, quality and excellent value. Short breaks on late availablility. Small agency with personally known properties. Pets welcome at many. Regional Tourist Board Member. Tel:01993 831495/831743; Fax: 01993 813095.
e-mail: cottage@cottageinthecountry.co.uk
website: www.cottageinthecountry.co.uk**

Banbury

Market town and old coaching centre made famous by nursery rhyme.

EASINGTON HOUSE HOTEL, 50 OXFORD ROAD, BANBURY OX16 9AN (01295 270181; Fax 01295 269527). 400-year-old farmhouse hotel. Old world charm with up-to-date facilities. All rooms en suite. An ideal touring base for the Cotswolds. Pets welcome. [🐾].

Faringdon

Town on the A417 north east of Swindon.

FARINGDON HOTEL, 1 MARKET PLACE, FARINGDON SN7 7HL (01367 240536; Fax: 01367 243250). Delightful 17th century coaching Inn and authentic Thai restaurant. Located just south of the famous city of Oxford and close to the Cotswolds. For that quiet country break we provide traditional hospitality that allows you to relax in the beauty of the English countryside. AA/RAC ★★. [Pets £10 per night]

Tackley

Village 3 miles north-east of Woodstock.

JUNE AND GEORGE COLLIER, 55 NETHERCOTE ROAD, TACKLEY, KIDLINGTON, OXFORD OX5 3AT (01869 331255; Fax: 01869 331670). Bed and Breakfast in Tackley. An ideal base for touring, walking and riding. Central for Oxford, The Cotswolds, Stratford-on-Avon, Blenheim Palace. Woodstock four miles. There is a regular train and bus service with local Hostelries serving excellent food. [🐕]

Thame

Town on River Thame 9 miles south west of Aylesbury. Airport at Haddenham.

MS. JULIA TANNER, LITTLE ACRE, TETSWORTH, NEAR THAME OX9 7AT (01844 281423). A country house retreat offering every comfort, set in several private acres. Most rooms en suite. A perfect place to relax . . . your dog will love it. Three minutes Junction 6 M40. Also 🛏🛏 Self-catering accommodation. [🐕– Bring dog basket with you.]

Woodstock

Old town 8 miles north-west of Oxford. Home to Oxford City and County Museum.

GORSELANDS HALL, BODDINGTON LANE, NORTH LEIGH, WITNEY, OXFORD OX8 6PU (01993 882292; Fax: 01993 883629). Stone farmhouse with oak beams and flagstone floors. Large secluded garden, grass tennis court and croquet lawn. All rooms are en-suite, with colour television.[🐕]
e-mail: hamilton@gorselandshall.com
website: www.gorselandshall.com

FOR THE MUTUAL GUIDANCE
OF GUEST AND HOST

Every year literally thousands of holidays, short breaks and overnight stops are arranged through our guides, the vast majority without any problems at all. In a handful of cases, however, difficulties do arise about bookings, which often could have been prevented from the outset.

It is important to remember that when accommodation has been booked, both parties – guests and hosts – have entered into a form of contract. We hope that the following points will provide helpful guidance.

GUESTS: When enquiring about accommodation, be as precise as possible. Give exact dates, numbers in your party and the ages of any children. State the number and type of rooms wanted and also what catering you require – bed and breakfast, full board etc. Make sure that the position about evening meals is clear – and about pets, reductions for children or any other special points.

Read our reviews carefully to ensure that the proprietors you are going to contact can supply what you want. Ask for a letter confirming all arrangements, if possible.

If you have to cancel, do so as soon as possible. Proprietors do have the right to retain deposits and under certain circumstances to charge for cancelled holidays if adequate notice is not given and they cannot re-let the accommodation.

HOSTS: Give details about your facilities and about any special conditions. Explain your deposit system clearly and arrangements for cancellations, charges etc. and whether or not your terms include VAT.

If for any reason you are unable to fulfil an agreed booking without adequate notice, you may be under an obligation to arrange suitable alternative accommodation or to make some form of compensation.

While every effort is made to ensure accuracy, we regret that FHG Publications cannot accept responsibility for errors, omissions or misrepresentations in our entries or any consequences thereof.
Prices in particular should be checked because we go to press early. We will follow up complaints but cannot act as arbiters or agents for either party.

ROOMS WITH A VIEW

Bed and Breakfast accommodation situated in the beautiful Shropshire hills, one mile from Cardington village. Ideal walking and riding country. All rooms have wonderful views. Some good pubs nearby for eating out. Dogs and horses welcome. Non-smoking. Bed and full English breakfast from £18 per person

Mrs C. Brandon-Lodge, North Hill Farm, Cardington, Church Stretton SY6 7LL   Tel: 01694 771532

THE LONGMYND HOTEL

Tel: 01694 722244 Fax: 01694 722718
web-site: www.longmynd.co.uk

Church Stretton, Shropshire SY6 6AG

Perched high above the pleasant town of Church Stretton in grounds of ten acres, this fine hotel enjoys sweeping views over the beautiful Welsh border country. Luxury suites and bedrooms are fully equipped with the added luxury of an outdoor swimming pool, 9 hole pitch and putt course, sauna and solarium. There are also superb facilities for conferences and functions.   ★★★

See also Colour Advertisement on page 37

IDYLLIC RURAL HAMLET - SMALL HOTEL & RESTAURANT

Comfortable small family-run hotel and restaurant in quiet village. Fully en suite. Walks from the doorstep. Convenient for Ludlow, Shrewsbury, Ironbridge etc. Short Breaks available. Dogs free.

MYND HOUSE HOTEL, LITTLE STRETTON, CHURCH STRETTON, SHROPSHIRE SY6 6RB

Tel: 01694 722212   AA/ETC ★★   Fax: 01694 724180

AA ★★   **CLEOBURY MORTIMER, SHROPSHIRE DY14 8AA   RAC HOTEL ★★**

Tel: 01299 270395   e-mail jon@red-fern.demon.co.uk

A warm welcome awaits you and your pet at this hotel, with 11 en suite rooms, all with colour TV, tea/coffee making facilities, hair dryer and direct-dial telephone.

Fine fresh food is served in the award-winning Restaurant, complemented by an interesting wine list. AA Rosette.

Glorious walking in Shropshire countryside with the aid of our own book of local walks, or in the 6000 acre Forest of Wyre.

Bargain Breaks from £60.00 pppn DB&B

NO CHARGE FOR PETS TO PETS WELCOME! READERS

Please mention *Pets Welcome*
when enquiring about accommodation featured in these pages.

ETC **The Travellers Rest Inn**
◆◆◆ Upper Affcot, Church Stretton, SY6 6RL
Tel: 01694 781275 • Fax: 01694 781555
E-mail: reception@travellersrestinn.co.uk
Situated between Church Stretton and Craven Arms, and surrounded by The South Shropshire Hills. We, Fraser and Mauresia Allison, the owners assure you a warm welcome, good food, good beers, good accommodation, and good old fashioned service. For those wishing to stay overnight with us at The Travellers Rest we have 8 very nice en suite guest bedrooms: four of these being on the ground floor with easy access, and all have colour televisions and tea/coffee making facilities. The bedrooms are away from the main area of the Inn and have their own entrance to the car park and garden, ideal if you have brought your pet with you and a midnight walk is needed. Our well stocked Bar can satisfy most thirsts; cask ales, lagers, stouts, spirits, wines and minerals, throughout the day and the Kitchen takes care of your hunger; be it for a snack or a full satisfying meal, vegetarians no problem, food being served until 9pm in the evening.

Henwick House

Gravel Hill, Ludlow
Shropshire, SY8 1QU
Tel: 01584 873338
Mr & Mrs R. Cecil-Jones

Warm, comfortable Georgian coach house, friendly informal atmosphere, good traditional English Breakfast; delightful en-suite rooms. Easy walking distance from town centre and local inns. Lots of nice local walks. TV, tea /coffee making facilities in all rooms. One Double en suite, One twin en suite, One twin , private bathroom. Bed and Breakfast from £20pp

---

"WHICH? HOTEL"
RECOMMENDED

GOOD HOTEL GUIDE

ETC
★★★
(Silver Award)

★★★ 74%

Food Award

Pen-y-Dyffryn Country Hotel

RHYDYCROESAU, NEAR OSWESTRY, SHROPSHIRE SY10 7JD
This silver stone former Georgian Rectory, set almost a thousand feet up in the Shropshire hills, is in a dream situation for both pets and their owners. Informal atmosphere, no traffic, just buzzards, badgers and beautiful country walks, yet Shrewsbury, Chester, Llangollen and Lake Vyrnwy are all close by. The well-stocked bar and licensed restaurant are always welcoming at the end of another hard day's relaxing. All bedrooms en suite etc; two have their own private patios. Short breaks available from £57 pppd, dinner, b&b. Pets free.
TEL: 01691 653700 MILES AND AUDREY HUNTER
E-MAIL: stay@peny.co.uk WEBSITE: www.peny.co.uk

See also Colour Advertisement on page 37

FHG PUBLICATION LIMITED publish a large range of well-known accommodation guides. We will be happy to send you details or you can use the order form at the back of this book.

Pinfold Cottage

A picturesque country cottage surrounded by a garden full of rare and unusual plants, with a trout stream running by, children's play area and lovely views of open countryside. Five minutes from the A5 and A483 for easy access to Wales, Chester and Shrewsbury. Lovely local walks and an excellent base for exploring the area. Golf and riding nearby. A peaceful setting with a really friendly atmosphere, open fires, central heating and a sitting room with TV and games. One double room, one single room. Cot available. Bathroom and shower room. Delicious home-made dinners available on request from £10 per person. Vegetarian and special diets available. Children and pets welcome. Bed and Breakfast £17 per person. Reductions for children. *Contact: Mrs S.Barr*

Newbridge, Maesbury, Oswestry, SY10 8AY. Tel: 01691 661192

HEY YOU DOGS !!

BEATRICE and I would like you to stay with us in our lovely home and large garden, in a **very quiet and peaceful area**. We are Cocker Spaniels and the **big park by the river** is 6 minutes walk! Your "Mummy and Daddy" share **your room free!!**
See you soon. Love and licks, **JUDY.**

Tel: 01743 344 266
Mr David Collingwood

WEAVER HOUSE

26 Granville Street, Shrewsbury SY3 8NE
(formally of Talbot House Hotel)

★ CAREFULLY - Designed. Furnished, Equipped providing SUPERB Accommodation in YOUR comfortable, relaxing room.
★ CONTAINERS FULL of Chocolate, Coffee, Tea!
★ MINI-BAR, including PINT of fresh milk daily!
★ BREAKFASTS - served until 11am!
★ We only accommodate GUESTS WITH DOGS

DOUBLE/TWIN £30 per night (£15 each)
SINGLE £20 per night (in a double room)
MINIMUM STAY 2 NIGHTS

RYTON FARM HOLIDAY COTTAGES
Ryton, Dorrington, Shrewsbury SY5 7LY Tel: 01743 718449

Choose from a traditional country cottage sleeping six or a recently converted barn for either 2 or 4 persons. Some suitable for visitors with mobility difficulties. Ample parking, well-equipped kitchens, colour TV, fitted carpets. Pets especially welcome. Coarse fishing available. Quietly situated 6 miles south of Shrewsbury overlooking Shropshire Hills, convenient for Ironbridge, Ludlow and Shrewsbury.

Open all year **Weekly bookings or Short Breaks** **3 Keys Commended**

SANDFORD HOUSE HOTEL ETC/AA ◆◆◆

Warm, friendly Grade 2 listed Georgian townhouse. Car parking. Guest Lounge and dining room with usual facilities. Serves fine wines. En suite Bedrooms with tea/coffee, TV facilities. Rates £37.50 - £55.00

St. Julian's Friars, Shrewsbury, Shropshire SY1 1XL • Tel & Fax: 01743 343829
E-mail: sandfordhouse@lineone.net • Web: www.sandfordhouse.co.uk

---

BED & BREAKFAST   SELF CATERING
Central for Shrewsbury, Ironbridge, Ludlow

BED & BREAKFAST: from £20 per person. Enjoy a large country breakfast and a warm welcome. Four-poster en suite rooms, tea trays. Short Breaks available.

SELF-CATERING: three beautifully converted barn cottages, equipped and furnished to a high standard, Ground floor bedroom sleeps 2 to 8 people - wheelchair friendly.

Touring caravans and tents welcome.

Virginia Evans, Church Farm, Rowton, Near Wellington, Telford, Shropshire TF6 6QY

◆◆◆

Telephone and Fax: 01952 770381
E-mail: church.farm@bigfoot.com

Commended

THORPE HOUSE | *COALPORT, SHROPSHIRE TF8 7HP TELEPHONE 01952 586789*
Victorian House in Ironbridge Gorge World Heritage Site, beautiful views, peaceful. Breakfasts with free range meat and eggs. Teletext televisions, tea making facilities, magazines all rooms. Riverside/woodland walks, fishing, close Victorian Town and China Museum. ETC ◆◆◆. Also 18th century cottage in Ironbridge with beautiful views across the gorge, self-catering, sleeps 4, available weekly or for short breaks. ETC ★★★

Church Stretton

Delightful little town in lee of Shropshire Hills. Walking and riding country. Facilities for tennis, bowls, gliding and golf. Knighton 22 miles, Bridgnorth 19, Ludlow 15, Shrewsbury 12.

MRS C.F. BRANDON-LODGE, NORTH HILL FARM, CARDINGTON, CHURCH STRETTON SY6 7LL (01694 771532). Rooms with a view! B&B in beautiful Shropshire hills. TV in rooms, tea etc. Ideal walking country. From £18 per person. [🐾 ◻]

THE LONGMYND HOTEL, CHURCH STRETTON SY6 6AG (01694 722244; Fax: 01694 722718). Situated overlooking the beautiful Welsh border this hotel has a subtle mixture of superb modern and period rooms equipped with every refinement demanded by the discerning guest of today. ★★★. [pw! Pets £2 per night.]

MYND HOUSE HOTEL, LITTLE STRETTON SY6 6RB (01694 722212}. Comfortable small family-run hotel and restaurant in quiet village. Fully en suite. Walks from the doorstep. Convenient for Ludlow, Shrewsbury, Ironbridge etc. Short Breaks available. Dogs free. AA/ETC ★★

F. & M. ALLISON, TRAVELLERS REST INN, UPPER AFFCOT, NEAR CHURCH STRETTON SY6 6RL (01694 781275; Fax: 01694 781555). RAC Inn. Fully licensed inn on the main A49. Good base for touring. Ample parking space. Children and dogs welcome. SAE or phone for further details. ETC ◆◆◆ [pw! 🐾]

DON AND RITA ROGERS, BELVEDERE GUEST HOUSE, BURWAY ROAD, CHURCH STRETTON SY6 6DP (01694 722232). Pleasant, centrally heated family Guest House – attractive gardens. Parking. Hairdryers, shaver points, Teasmaids all rooms. Two lounges – TV. Packed lunches available. Bed and Breakfast from £24. Evening Meal £12. 10% reduction for weekly/party bookings. ETC ◆◆◆, AA & RAC APPROVED. [🐾]

Cleobury Mortimer

Charming little town of timbered and Georgian house. There is fishing on the River Rea, and walking in the Wyre Forest or on Clee Hill, which rises to over 1,600 ft. Ludlow 10 miles.

THE REDFERN HOTEL, CLEOBURY MORTIMER DY14 8AA (01299 270395). Eleven well-equipped bedrooms, all with private facilities and some on the ground floor. Award-winning restaurant noted for fine food. No charge for pets to PETS WELCOME! readers. AA/RAC ★★. [🐾]

Clun

Village 5 miles north of Knighton and 8 miles west of Craven Arms. Remains of 12th century Castle.

MRS ANGELA McHALE, SUN INN, 10 HIGH STREET, CLUN SY7 8JB (01588 640559). The XVth century Sun Inn serves excellent home-cooked food and real ales. Six en suite bedrooms. Private parking. Situated on the "Shropshire Way", ideal base for exploring Offa's Dyke, South Shropshire and the Welsh Marches. Ludlow, Montgomery and Shrewsbury all nearby. Listed in the Good Pub and Good Food Guides and Roger Protz, 'Britains Best 500 Pubs". ETC ◆◆◆

SYMBOLS

🐾   Indicates that pets are welcome free of charge.

£   Indicates that a charge is made for pets: nightly or weekly.

pw!   Shows some special provision for pets; exercise facility, feeding or accommodation arrangement.

◻   Indicates separate pets accommodation.

Craven Arms

Attractive little town with some interesting old half-timbered houses. Weekly cattle and sheep sales. Nearby is imposing Stokesay Castle (13th cent.). Bridgnorth 21 miles, Shrewsbury 20, Ludlow 8.

MRS J. WILLIAMS, HURST HILL FARM, CLUN, CRAVEN ARMS SY7 OJA (01588 640224). Comfortable riverside farmhouse. Woodlands. Riding pony. Convenient for Offa's Dyke, Stiperstones. Bed and Breakfast from £21, Dinner, Bed and Breakfast from £28. Winner "Great Farm Breakfast". AA ◆◆◆.

Ludlow

Lovely and historic town on Rivers Teme and Corve with numerous old half-timbered houses and inns. Impressive Norman castle; river and woodland walks. Golf, tennis, bowls, steeplechase course. Worcester 29 miles, Shrewsbury 27, Hereford 24, Bridgnorth 19, Church Stretton 16.

HENWICK HOUSE, GRAVEL HILL, LUDLOW SY8 1QU (01584 873338). Warm, comfortable Georgian coach house, good traditional English Breakfast. Easy walking distance from town centre and local inns. Lots of nice local walks. TV, tea/coffee making facilities. One double/ one twin en suite, one twin private bathroom. B&B from £20pp.

SALLY AND TIM LOFT, GOOSEFOOT BARN, PINSTONES, DIDDLEBURY, CRAVEN ARMS, SHROPSHIRE SY7 9LB (01584 861326). Converted in 2000 from stone and timbered barns, the three cottages are individually decorated to the highest standards. Each cottage has en suite facilities and private garden or seating area. Situated in a secluded valley. Ideally located for exploring south Shropshire. [🐾]
e-mail: sally@goosefoot.freeserve.co.uk

CLIVE & CYNTHIA PRIOR, MOCKTREE BARNS, LEINTWARDINE, LUDLOW SY7 0LY (01547 540441). Self-catering cottages around sunny courtyard. ETC ★★★. Sleep 2-6. Comfortable, well-equipped. Friendly owners nearby. Dogs & children welcome. Lovely country walks from door. Ludlow, seven miles. Brochure. [🐾] See also colour advertisement page 38.

Oswestry

Borderland Market town. Many old castles and fortifications including 13th century Chirk Castle, Whittington Castle, Oswestry's huge Iron Age hill fort, Offa's Dyke. Shrewsbury 16, Vyrnwy 18.

PEN-Y-DYFFRYN COUNTRY HOUSE HOTEL, NEAR RHYDYCROESAU, OSWESTRY SY10 7JD (01691 653700). Picturesque Georgian Rectory quietly set in Shropshire/ Welsh Hills. Ten en suite bedrooms, two with private patios. 5-acre grounds. No passing traffic. Johansens recommended. Dinner, Bed and Breakfast from £57.00 per person per day. AA/ETC ★★★. [🐾 pw!]
E-mail: stay@peny.co.uk
Website: www.peny.co.uk

PINFOLD COTTAGE, NEWBRIDGE, MAESBURY, OSWESTRY SY10 8AY (01691 661192) Picturesque country cottage, garden, trout stream, play area and lovely views of open countryside. Five minutes from the A5 and A483. Easy access to Wales, Chester and Shrewsbury. Golf and riding nearby. Friendly atmosphere, open fires, central heating. One double room, one single room. Cot available. Bathroom and shower room. Bed and Breakfast £17 per person. Reductions for children. Contact: MRS S. BARR. [🐾]

Shrewsbury

Fine Tudor Town with many beautiful black and white timber buildings, Abbey and Castle. Riverside walks, Quarry Park and Dingle flower garden. 39 miles north-west of Birmingham.

MR DAVID COLLINGWOOD, "WEAVER HOUSE", 26 GRANVILLE STREET, SHREWSBURY SY3 8NE (01743 344 266). Everything you could wish for: comfort, relaxation, freedom, extra facilities, with friendly, helpful host. Situated in a very quiet area, easy reach of riverside park and town centre. Only guests with dogs accommodated – only one booking taken at any one time and minimum stay is two nights. SEE DISPLAY ADVERT. [🐾]

RYTON FARM HOLIDAY COTTAGES, RYTON, DORRINGTON, SHREWSBURY SY5 7LY (01743 718449). Traditional country cottage sleeping 6 or converted barn for 2 or 4 persons. Well-equipped kitchens, colour TV, fitted carpets. Pets especially welcome. ♔♔♔ Commended. [Pets £22 per week].

MR C. RICHARDS, SANDFORD HOUSE HOTEL, ST. JULIANS FRIARS, SHREWSBURY SY1 1XL (Tel & Fax: 01743 343829). Warm, friendly Grade 2 listed Georgian townhouse. Car parking. Guest Lounge and dining room with usual facilities. Serves fine wines. En suite Bedrooms with tea/coffee, TV facilities. Rates £37.50 - £55.00. ETC/AA ◆◆◆ [🐕]
E-mail: E-mail: sandfordhouse@lineone.net
Website: www.sandfordhouse.co.uk

Telford

New town (1963). Ten miles east of Shrewsbury. Includes the south bank of the River Severn above and below Ironbridge, site of the world's first iron bridge (1777).

MRS RICHARDS, THORPE HOUSE, COALPORT, TELFORD TF8 7HP (01952 586789). Victorian House in Ironbridge Gorge World Heritage Site, beautiful views, peaceful. Breakfasts with free range meat and eggs. Teletext televisions, tea making facilities, magazines all rooms. Also Self-Catering cottage in Ironbridge, Sleeps 4. Dogs Welcome. [🐕]

B&B and self-catering in a quiet village yet equidistant from Shrewsbury and Ironbridge. Listed Grade II farmhouse; en suite rooms from £20pp. Self-catering barn conversion cottages sleeping 2-8 people. Ground floor bedroom from £160 per week. VIRGINIA AND ROBERT EVANS, CHURCH FARM, ROWTON, WELLINGTON, TELFORD TF6 6QY (01952 770381). [Pets £5 per week]
E-mail: church.farm@bigfoot.co.uk

SOMERSET

THE SHIP INN

Porlock TA24 8QT
(01643 862507)

The thatched 13th century Ship Inn is within walking distance of sea and moor. There is a genuine old bar with stone floors and roaring log fires in winter. There are 11 en suite bedrooms. Local produce supplements traditional English cooking in the candlelit diningroom, and bar snacks and real ales are served in the Smoke Room and Beer Garden.

EXMOOR

Winners of David Bellamy Gold Conservation Award

Six delightful Scandinavian style Cottages in three sheltered paddocks and comfortable wing of old Farmhouse. Campsite for tents by river.

Bracken, Molinia, Whortleberry & Ling Cottages are warm & cosy with woodburners and double-glazing. Suitable for disabled. Holly & Gorse are the popular, original log cottages. **E.T.C ★★ - ★★★★**

CHILDREN'S PARADISE

DOGS! Come to Westermill and take your owners on leads around the farm on the four waymarked walks.

A fascinating 500 acre farm in the centre of Exmoor National Park with over 2 miles of the upper reaches of the River Exe for fishing and bathing.

Free Brochure from: **EDWARDS FAMILY, Westermill Farm, Exford, Minehead, Somerset TA24 7NJ. Tel: 01643 831238; Fax: 01643 831660 E-mail: holidays@westermill-exmoor.co.uk Website: www.exmoorfarmholidays.co.uk**

Riscombe Farm Holiday Cottages – Exmoor National Park

Four charming self-catering stone cottages converted from barns surrounding an attractive courtyard with stables. Very comfortable, with log fires and equipped to a high standard, sleeping 2-7.
Peaceful, relaxing location beside the River Exe in the centre of Exmoor National Park.
Excellent walking and riding country in the valleys, across the moors or along the spectacular coast.
One and a half miles from Exford Village.
Dogs and horses welcome. Open all year.

Leone & Brian Martin, Riscombe Farm, Exford, Somerset TA24 7NH Tel & Fax: 01643 831480 www.riscombe.co.uk

ETC Rating: ★★★★

Please mention *Pets Welcome*
when enquiring about accommodation featured in these pages.

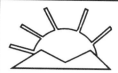

Bath

The best-preserved Georgian city in Britain, Bath has been famous since Roman times for its mineral springs. It is a noted centre for music and the arts, with a wide range of leisure facilities.

CHURCH FARM, WINSLEY, BRADFORD-ON-AVON, WILTS BA15 2JH (Tel/Fax: 01225 722246). Tastefully converted cottages. Working farm with sheep and horses. Countryside location. Bath 5 miles. Fully equipped, video, ample parking, enclosed garden. Short breaks when available. Colour brochure. [Pets £10 per week]

DAVID & JACKIE BISHOP, TOGHILL HOUSE FARM, FREEZING HILL, WICK, NEAR BATH BS30 5RT (01225 891261; Fax: 01225 892128). Luxury barn conversions on working farm 3 miles north of Bath. Each equipped to very high standard, bed linen provided. Also en suite B&B accommodation in 17th century farmhouse. [pw! Pets £2 per night, £8 per week]

THE OLD MALT HOUSE HOTEL, RADFORD, TIMSBURY, NEAR BATH BA3 1QF (01761 470106; Fax: 01761 472726). A relaxing, comfortable hotel, in beautiful surroundings between Bath and Wells. Gardens, lawns. All bedrooms en suite. Restaurant and bar meals. ETC/AA ★★. [Pets £3 per night.]
E–mail: hotel@oldmalthouse.co.uk
Website: www.oldmalthouse.co.uk

Brean

Coastal village with extensive sands. To north is the promontory of Brean Down. Weston super-Mare 9 miles.

WESTWARD RISE HOLIDAY PARK, SOUTH ROAD, BREAN, NEAR BURNHAM ON-SEA TA8 2RD (01278 751310). Highly Recommended Luxury 2/6 berth Chalet bungalows. 2 double bedrooms, shower, toilet, TV, fridge, cooker, duvets and linen. Open all year. Call for free brochure. [Pets £10 per week.]

BEACHSIDE HOLIDAY PARK FORMERLY EMBELLE HOLIDAY PARK, COAST ROAD, BREAN SANDS TA8 2QZ (Freephone 08000 190 322). Chalets and holiday homes on quiet park. Direct access to beach. Full facilities. Colour television. Pets welcome. Near entertainments. Club and restaurant. Free brochure. 4 Stars [Pets £15.00 per week].
website: www.beachsideholidaypark.co.uk

Bristol

Busy university city on River Avon, which is spanned by Brunel's famous suspension bridge. SS Great Britain, Brunel's iron ship, is moored in the old docks. Bath 13 miles.

MRS C. B. PERRY, CLEVE HILL FARM, UBLEY, NEAR BRISTOL BS18 6PG (01761 462410). Family-run dairy farm in beautiful countryside. Self-catering accommodation in "The Cider House". Fully equipped except towels and linen. £1 electricity meter. One double, one twin room, one double bed settee. Terms from £95 to £220 per week. Obedient pets welcome. [🐕]

Cheddar

Picturesque little town in the Mendips, famous for its Gorge and unique caves. Cheese-making is a speciality. Good touring centre. Bath 24 miles, Burnham-on-sea 13, Weston-super-Mare 11.

BROADWAY HOUSE HOLIDAY TOURING CARAVAN & CAMPING PARK, CHEDDAR BS27 3DB (01934 742610; Fax: 01934 744950). Holiday caravans for hire; premier touring and camping pitches. Heated pool, adventure playground, pub, shop. launderette. Superb range of activities. ★★★★

MRS CHRIS MARLOW, HOME FARM COTTAGES, BARTON, WINSCOMBE BS25 1DX (01934 842078). 15th Century Listed farmhouse. B&B available in detached Listed Bake House suite. A walkers paradise directly from cottages, yet near to Cheddar, Bristol, Wells and Bath. Whirlpool/spa available [Pets £2 per night, £14 per week. [pw!]
website: www.homefarmcottages.co.uk

SUNGATE HOLIDAY APARTMENTS, CHURCH STREET, CHEDDAR, SOMERSET BS27 3RA. Ideally situated for walking, cycling and touring the Mendips and the West Country. Competitively priced for short or longer holidays. For full details contact Mrs M. FIELDHOUSE. 01934 842273/742264; Fax: 01934 741411 [Small charge for pets].

MRS JENNIFER BUCKLAND, SPRING COTTAGES, VENNS GATE, CHEDDAR BS27 3LW (Tel/Fax: 01934 742493).Three single bedroom cottages sleeping 2/4 persons. The Gorge/Caves are within walking distance. An acre of paddock to exercise your pet. Non-smoking. Short breaks. ETC ★★★ SELF-CATERING. [Pets £3 per night, £20 per week].
E-mail: buckland@springcottages.co.uk
Web: www.springcottages.co.uk

Churchill

Village below the north slopes of the Mendip Hills.

WINSTON MANOR HOTEL, CHURCHILL BS25 5NL (01934 852348). Pets and well-trained owners most welcome! Secluded walled garden. Close to Wells, Glastonbury, Bath and Cheddar. Excellent walking country. Our guests tell us the food is excellent too! [🐾]

Dulverton

Attractively set between Exmoor and Brendon Hills. Good fishing. In vicinity, prehistoric Tarr Steps (A.M and N.T.). Exeter 27 miles, Taunton 26, Lynton 23, Minehead 19, Tiverton 13.

HIGHERCOMBE FARM, DULVERTON, EXMOOR TA22 9PT (01398 323616). A 450 acre farm on Exmoor and 100 acres of woodland in peaceful setting. Spectacular views. All rooms en suite. Bring your dog or horse and enjoy walking/riding directly onto moorland. Brochure available. Contact Abigail Humphrey. ETC ◆◆◆◆ and Silver Award. Self catering ETC ★★★ [Pets £2 per night].

Dunster

Pretty village with interesting features, including Yarn Market, imposing 14th century Castle. Priory Church and old houses and cottages. Minehead 3 miles.

THE YARN MARKET HOTEL, HIGH STREET, DUNSTER TA24 6SF (01643 821425; Fax: 01643 821475). An ideal location for walking and exploring Exmoor. Family-run hotel with a friendly, relaxed atmosphere, home cooking, en suite rooms with colour TV and tea making facilities. Non-smoking. When responding quote reference FHG01 to qualify for restaurant discount during your visit (cash only) - Pets Welcome [pw! 🐾, Please notify when booking.]
E–mail: yarnmarket.hotel@virgin.net

Exford

Fine touring centre for Exmoor and North Devon, on River Exe. Dulverton 10 miles.

BRYAN & JANE JACKSON, HUNTERS MOON, EXFORD, NEAR MINEHEAD TA24 7PP (01643 831695). Cosy bungalow smallholding in the heart of Exmoor. Good food (optional Evening Meal), glorious views, friendly atmosphere. Pets welcome free, stabling available. Open all year. ETC ◆◆◆ [pw! 🐾]

Exmoor

265 square miles of unspoiled heather moorland with deep wooded valleys and rivers, ideal for a walking, pony trekking or fishing holiday.

THE CROWN HOTEL, EXFORD TA24 7PP (01643 831554/5; Fax: 01643 831665). Situated in rural England. All bedrooms with bath, colour television, hairdryer. Excellent cuisine and fine wines. Bargain Breaks. Superb dog holiday country. [pw! 🏠]

Two cottages and two bungalows on 10 acre estate overlooking Barle Valley. Dogs and horses welcome. Shop and pub 300 metres. JULIA AND JERRY BEGGS, WESTERCLOSE HOUSE, WITHYPOOL TA24 7QR (01643 831302). [pw! Dogs £7 per week]
Website: www.westerclose.f9.co.uk

RALEGH'S CROSS INN, EXMOOR NATIONAL PARK, BRENDON HILL TA23 0LN (01984 640343) A warm friendly welcome in well-appointed Inn in the beautiful Brendon Hills. Superb walking country, fishing and riding nearby. Bar snacks and à la carte menu. "We're famous for our carvery". All rooms en-suite, hospitality trays, TVs, etc. [Pets £5 per night]

WOODCOMBE LODGES, BRATTON, NEAR MINEHEAD TA24 8SQ (Tel/Fax: 01643 702789). Four self-catering lodges in a tranquil rural setting on the edge of Exmoor National Park, standing in a beautiful 2¹/₂ acre garden with wonderful views. [🐾]
e–mail: nicola@woodcombelodge.co.uk
website: www.woodcombelodge.co.uk

MRS J. ROBINSON, THE SHIP INN, HIGH STREET, PORLOCK TA24 8QT (01643 862507). Thatched 13th cent inn within walking distance of sea and moor. There are 11 en suite bedrooms. Local produce supplements traditional English cooking in candlelit restaurant. [🐾⌂]

MRS P. EDWARDS, WESTERMILL FARM, EXFORD, MINEHEAD TA24 7NJ (01643 831238; Fax: 01643 831660). Six delightful Scandinavian pine log cottages and wing of old farmhouse. Campsite for Tents. A fascinating 500 acre farm, varied way-marked walks.[Pets 50p per night (camp), £9 per week in cottages].
E-mail: holidays@westermill-exmoor.co.uk
Website: www.exmoorfarmholidays.co.uk

LEONE & BRIAN MARTIN, RISCOMBE FARM HOLIDAY COTTAGES, EXFORD, MINEHEAD TA24 7NH (Tel & Fax: 01643 831480). Four self-catering stone cottages in the centre of Exmoor National Park. Excellent walking and riding country. Dogs and horses welcome. Open all year. ETC Rating: ★★★★ [Pets £1 per night, £7 per week.]
Website: www.riscombe.co.uk

STILEMOOR, EXFORD TA24 7NA. Charming cosy central heated detached bungalow with garden, superb views, walking, fishing, riding. Sleeps 6. JOAN ATKINS, 2 EDGCOTT COTTAGE, EXFORD, MINEHEAD TA24 7QG (01643 831564) [Pets £8 per week] WTB ★★★ COMMENDED
e-mail: j-atkins@altavista.com
website: http:\\homepage.altavista.com\stilemoor

THE EXMOOR WHITE HORSE INN, EXFORD TA24 7PY (01643 831229; Fax: 01643 831246). Family-run 16th century inn situated in charming Exmoor village. 26 bedrooms all en suite, with colour TV and tea making. Fully licensed. Restaurant with varied menu. [🐾] - one dog.
E–mail:exmoorwhitehorse.demon.co.uk

DUNKERY BEACON HOTEL, WOOTTON COURTENAY TA24 8RH (01643 841241). Country House Hotel with superb views. Fully en suite rooms, colour TV. Lots of lovely "walkies". Special Autumn and Spring breaks. Write or phone Kenneth or Daphne Midwood for details.[🐾] .
E-mail: dunkery.beacon@virgin.net
Website: www.homepage_virgin_net/dunkery_beacon

MRS C. B. PERRY, CLEVE HILL FARM, UBLEY, NEAR BRISTOL BS18 6PG (01761 462410). Family-run dairy farm in beautiful countryside. Self-catering accommodation in "The Cider House". Fully equipped except towels and linen. £1 electricity meter. One double, one twin room, one double bed settee. Terms from £95 to £220 per week. Obedient pets welcome. [🐾]

COMPREHENSIVE INTERNET DIRECTORY FOR THE EXMOOR VISITOR. LAST MINUTE COTTAGES, Pet-friendly accomodation. Hotels, Inns, B&B, Self-catering, Camping: Family, General Interest, Gardens, Walking, Riding, Outdoor and much more. Website: www.whatsonexmoor.com

JANE STYLES, WINTERSHEAD FARM, SIMONSBATH TA24 7LF (01643 831222; Fax: 01643 831628). Five tastefully furnished and well equipped cottages situated in the midst of beautiful Exmoor. Pets welcome, stables and grazing available. Colour brochure on request. [Dogs and horses £12 per week.]
Website: www.wintershead.co.uk

CUTTHORNE, LUCKWELL BRIDGE, WHEDDON CROSS TA24 7EW (01643 831255). Enjoy a touch of sheer luxury at our 14th century country house in glorious Exmoor. En suite facilities, log fires, candlelit dinners. ETC ◆◆◆ Gold award. ETC ★★★★★ Self Catering available [🐾 in B&B; Pets £11.75 per week S/C]
E–mail: durbin@cutthorne.co.uk
Website: www.cutthorne.co.uk

DRAYDON COTTAGES, EXMOOR. 7 attractive s/c barn conversion cottages situated 2 miles north-west of Dulverton. Well equipped and maintained with heating throughout. Excellent base for exploring Exmoor. KATHARINE HARRIS, 6 CRABB LANE, ALPHINGTON, EXETER, DEVON EX2 9JD (01392 433524).
E–mail: Kate@draydon.co.uk
Website: www.draydon.co.uk

CLEMENTS COTTAGE, TIVINGTON, NR MINEHEAD, SOMERSET TA24 8SU (01643 703970). 16th Century cross-passage house with spectacular views of the Bristol Channel and Dunkery Beacon. Central heating. Evening meals. Spring and summer bargain breaks. B&B from £18.50. Ring Una or Gordon for brochure. [Pets from £1.50 per night].

MRS JONES, HIGHER TOWN, DULVERTON, EXMOOR TA22 9RX (01398 341272). Bungalow set on its own, where visitors are welcome to walk over our beef and sheep farm. 80 acres set in National Parkland. Walkers paradise; half-a-mile walk from open moorland. Sleeps six, centrally heated, double glazed. Bed linen and electricity provided.

Hillfarrance

4 miles west of Taunton with its 12th century castle. Situated in valley of Taunton Deane, famed for its apples and cider.

ANCHOR COTTAGES, THE ANCHOR INN, HILLFARRANCE, TAUNTON TA4 1AW (01823 461334). Three self-catering cottages, each sleeps up to five. Full central heating, colour TV; tastefully furnished to high standard. Private gardens and ample parking. Anchor Inn renowned for good food. [🐾]

Langport

Market town on River Parrett, 7 miles north-west of Ilchester.

BOWDENS CREST, CARAVANS & CAMPING, BOWDENS, LANGPORT TA10 0DD (01458 250553). Tranquil Countryside Park. Caravans for sale and hire. Facilities include a Bar, Shop, Laundry, Hook-ups and woodland walks. [🐾]

AMBERLEY, LONG LOAD, LANGPORT TA10 9LD (01458 241 542). Quality B&B accommodation with warm, friendly welcome. On edge of Somerset Levels, far reaching views, good walking area. along footpaths and river. ETC ◆◆◆◆
e-mail: jeanatamberley@talk21.com

Minehead

Neat and stylish resort on Bristol Channel. Sandy bathing beach, attractive gardens, golf course and good facilities for tennis, bowls and horse riding. Within easy reach of the beauties of Exmoor.

MINEHEAD – SEA – EXMOOR –HOLIDAY FLATS. 30 yards to seafront, Level walk to town centre, Self contained, Fully furnished, Bath/shower, Colour TV, Large garden, Car park, Dogs welcomed SAE: MR T. STONE, TROYTES FARMSTEAD, TIVINGTON, MINEHEAD TA24 8SU (Tel: 01643 704531). [🐾]

MINEHEAD 16TH CENTURY THATCHED COTTAGES. Rose Ash - Sleeps 2, prettily furnished, all electric. Willow - Inglenook, oak panelling, electricity, gas, CH, Sleeps 6. Private car park. Enclosed gardens. Pets welcome. SAE: MR T. STONE, TROYTES FARMSTEAD, TIVINGTON, MINEHEAD TA24 8SU (Tel: 01643 704531). [🐾]

Porlock

Most attractive village beneath the tree-clad slopes of Exmoor. Picturesque cottages, old Ship Inn and interesting church). Good bathing from pebble beach at delightful Porlock Weir (2 miles).

MR & MRS A. D. HARDICK, PORLOCK CARAVAN PARK, HIGHBANKS, PORLOCK, NEAR MINEHEAD TA24 8NS (01643 862269; Fax: 01643 862239). Well-equipped Caravans for hire, with main drains and water, electric light, TV, launderette. Dogs welcome. Touring caravans, Dormobiles and tents welcome. Write or phone for a brochure. [Pets 50p per night]
E-mail: adhpcp@aol.com

CASTLE HOTEL, PORLOCK TA24 8PY (01643 862504). Fully licensed, family-run hotel in centre of lovely Exmoor village. 13 en suite bedrooms, all with colour TV. Pool, darts & skittles. Bar snacks and meals. Well-behaved children and pets welcome. [🐾]

MRS CHRISTINE FITZGERALD, "SEAPOINT", UPWAY, PORLOCK TA24 8QE (Tel/Fax:01643 862289). Spacious Edwardian house overlooking Porlock Bay. Open log fires. Coastal/moorland walks. Excellent traditional or vegetarian food. All bedrooms en suite with tea/coffee facilities. ETC ◆◆◆◆. [🐾]

Taunton

County town, rich in historical associations. Good touring centre. Many sporting attractions. Bristol 43 miles, Exeter 32, Weston-super-Mare 29.

STEPHEN & HILARY MURPHY, HATCH BEAUCHAMP, TAUNTON TA3 6SG (01823 480664; Fax: 01823 481118). Nine bedroomed Country house hotel in 3 acres with seperate detached cottage, Log fires, chef proprietor, picturesque village, 30 minutes to south or west coast or Cotswolds. Pets welcome. [🐾]
Website: www.farthingshotel.com

Watchet

Small port and resort with rocks and sands. Good centre for Exmoor and the Quantocks. Bathing, boating, fishing, rambling. Tiverton 24 miles, Bridgwater 19, Taunton 17, Dunster 6.

WEST BAY CARAVAN PARK, WATCHET TA23 0BJ (01984 631261). Small, quiet park with panoramic sea views. Ideal for relaxing and touring Exmoor and Quantock Hills. Open March-October. ETC ★★★★★ Rose Award. Pets welcome. [Pets £12 weekly.]

LORNA DOONE CARAVAN PARK, WATCHET TA23 0BJ (01984 631206). Small quiet 5 star holiday park with beautiful views of the coastline and Quantock Hills. Luxury, fully-equipped Rose Award caravans. [Pets £2 per night]
Website: www.lornadoone.co.uk

SUNNY BANK HOLIDAY CARAVANS, DONIFORD, WATCHET TA23 0UD (01984 632237). Small picturesque family park overlooking sea. All caravans with mains services. Colour TV. Showers. Heated swimming pool. Shop. Launderette. Tourist Board ★★★★★. Also caravans for sale. Brochure. [Pets £2 per night, £14 per week.]
Website: www.sunnybankcp.co.uk

MR D. ALBUTT, CROFT HOLIDAY COTTAGES, THE CROFT, ANCHOR STREET, WATCHET TA23 0AZ. (Tel & Fax: 01984 631121). Cottages and Bungalow. Private parking, central heating, TV, washing machine, fridge, microwave. Use of lawned area and heated indoor swimming pool. Each unit has barbecue. Five self-contained units; sleeping 2-8. £100 to £470 per unit per week. ETC up to ★★★★ [🐾]

Wells

England's smallest city. West front of Cathedral built around 1230, shows superb collection of statuary.

INFIELD HOUSE, 36 PORTWAY, WELLS BA5 2BN (01749 670989). Richard and Heather invite you and your pet to visit England's smallest city. Wonderful walks on Mendip Hills No smoking. Bountiful breakfasts, dinners by arrangement. AA ◆◆◆◆.

Weston-Super-Mare

Popular resort on the Bristol Channel with a wide range of entertainments and leisure facilities. An ideal base for touring the West Country.

CAROLINE AND NOEL TROTT, L'ARRIVEE, 75-77 LOCKING ROAD, WESTON-SUPER-MARE, AVON BS23 3DW (0934 625328) The L'arrivee is near all local places of entertainment. Comfortable residents' lounge, Full English breakfast. En-suite rooms. Free car parking. Evening meals available. ETC/RAC ◆◆◆

MR AND MRS C. G. THOMAS, ARDNAVE HOLIDAY PARK, KEWSTOKE, WESTON-SUPER-MARE BS22 9XJ (01934 622319). Caravans - De luxe. 2-3 bedrooms, shower, toilet, colour TV's, duvets and covers included. Parking. Dogs welcome. Graded ★★★. [🐾 pw!]

BRAESIDE HOTEL, 2 VICTORIA PARK, WESTON-SUPER-MARE BS23 2HZ (Tel/Fax: 01934 626642). Delightful, Family-run Hotel, close to shops and sea front. All rooms en suite, colour TV, tea/coffee making. November to April THIRD NIGHT FREE. See display advertisement. ETC/AA ◆◆◆◆ [🐾] E–mail: braeside@tesco.net

STAFFORDSHIRE

Leek

Village 10 miles from Stoke-on-Trent

ROSEWOOD HOLIDAY FLATS, LOWER BERKHAMSYTCH FARM, BOTTOM HOUSE, NEAR LEEK ST13 7QP (Tel & Fax: 01538 308213). 2 cosy flats each with private entrance. Ground floor flat sleeps 6. First floor flat sleeps 7. Colour TV, microwave, and shower rooms in both flats. Play area and patio sitting area. Terms from £120 to £235 per week, includes electricity and linen. Well behaved pets welcome. ☖☖☖ Commended.

SUFFOLK

Aldeburgh, Chelsworth, Dunwich, Kessingland, Lowestoft

WENTWORTH ROAD, ALDEBURGH, SUFFOLK IP15 5BD

WENTWORTH HOTEL

The Wentworth Hotel, privately run since 1920, offers a perfect and welcome retreat. 37 comfortable, elegantly furnished bedrooms, most en suite, have colour television, radio and direct dial telephone. Fresh local produce such as fish, crab and lobster is extensively used in the relaxed atmosphere of the restaurant.

For a reservation, please Telephone 01728 452312 or Fax: 01728 454343   AA ★★★ 72%
E–mail: wentworth.hoteL@anglianet.co.uk

See also Colour Advertisement on page 42

Peacock Inn
37 The street
Chelsworth, Near Lavenham
Suffolk IP7 7HU
Tel: 01449 740758

The welcoming 'Peacock Inn' dates from 1870 and is full of character. Cask conditioned ales and excellent wines make the perfect complement for fine food served every lunchtime and evening. Only a few miles from the picturesque wool town of Lavenham with its Tudor, timber and plaster houses, this is a recommended port of call with genuine oak beams, an impressive inglenook fireplace and beer garden for warmer weather. A most rewarding place to stay.

MIDDLEGATE COTTAGE MIDDLEGATE BARN, DUNWICH IP17 3DW
Situated in a quiet, private road 200 yards from the sea. Furnished and equipped to a high standard. Centrally heated; available all year.

Tel: 01728 648741

KNIGHTS HOLIDAY HOMES • KESSINGLAND
Quality **SEASIDE BUNGALOWS**. Open all year, central heating, colour TV, parking, bed linen, heating and lighting included. 2/8 persons. Direct access to award-winning beach. Pets very welcome.
KNIGHTS HOLIDAY HOMES, 198 CHURCH ROAD, KESSINGLAND, SUFFOLK NR33 7SF

Freephone: 0800 269067

Aldeburgh

Coastal town 6 miles south-east of Saxmundham. Annual music festival at Snape Maltings.

WENTWORTH HOTEL, ALDEBURGH IP15 5BD (01728 452312). Country House Hotel overlooking the sea. Immediate access to the beach and walks. Two comfortable lounges with log fires and antique furniture. Refurbished bedrooms with all facilities and many with sea views. Restaurant specialises in fresh produce and sea food. [Pets £2 per day]

Bury St Edmunds

This prosperous market town on the River Lark lies 28 miles east of Cambridge.

RAVENWOOD HALL COUNTRY HOUSE HOTEL AND RESTAURANT, ROUGHAM, BURY ST EDMUNDS IP30 9JA (01359 270345; Fax: 01359 270788). 16th century heavily beamed Tudor Hall set in seven acres of perfect dog walks. Beautifully furnished en suite bedrooms; renowned restaurant; relaxing inglenook fires. AA ★★★. [🐾 pw!] website: www.ravenwoodhall.co.uk

Chelsworth

Village 4 miles north west of Hadleigh.

PEACOCK INN, 31 THE STREET, CHELSWORTH, NEAR LAVENHAM IP7 7HU (Tel: 01449 740758). A welcoming traditional inn; 3 comfortable bedrooms full of beams, nooks and crannies. Cask conditionaed ales and excellent wine served with fine food every lunchtime and evening.

Dunwich

Small village on coast, 4 miles south west of Southwold.

MRS ELIZABETH COLE, MIDDLEGATE COTTAGE, MIDDLEGATE BARN, DUNWICH IP17 3DW (01728 648741). Situated in a quiet, private road 200 yards from the sea. Furnished and equipped to a high standard. Centrally heated; available all year. [🐾]

Hadleigh

Historic town on River Brett with several old buildings of interest including unusual 14th century church. Bury St Edmunds 20 miles, Harwich 20, Colchester 14, Sudbury 11, Ipswich 10.

EDGEHALL HOTEL, 2 HIGH STREET, HADLEIGH IP7 5AP (01473 822458; Fax: 01473 827751). 16th-century property offering a warm welcome. Comfortable accommodation and good home-cooked food. Licensed. SAE or telephone for details. Pets welcome. ETC ◆◆◆◆. [🐾]

Kessingland

Little seaside place with expansive sandy beach, safe bathing, wildlife park, lake fishing. To the south is Benacre Broad, a beauty spot. Norwich 26 miles, Aldeburgh 23, Lowestoft 5.

Quality seaside Bungalows, open all year, central heating. Colour TV, parking, bed-linen, heat and light included. 2/8 people. Direct access to award winning beach. Pets very welcome. APPLY– KNIGHTS HOLIDAY HOMES, 198 CHURCH ROAD, KESSINGLAND, SUFFOLK NR33 7SF (FREEPHONE 0800 269067).

Comfortable well-equipped bungalow on lawned site overlooking beach, next to Heritage Coast. Panoramic sea views. Easy beach access. Unspoiled walking area. ETC 🏡 Commended. MR AND MRS J. SAUNDERS, 22 WANSTEAD PARK AVENUE, LONDON E12 5EN (020 8989 5636). [Pets £10 per week].

Long Melford

Small town 3 miles north of Sudbury. Melford Hall and Kentwell Hall of interest.

BLACK LION HOTEL & RESTAURANT, THE GREEN, LONG MELFORD CO10 9DN (01787 312356; Fax: 01787 374557). 17th Century hotel opposite The Green. Leave your car and walk the dog. Contemporary restaurant, bar meals. Stylish en suite bedrooms, cosy lounge. Short breaks available. [🐾 pw!]

Lowestoft

Holiday resort and fishing port. Britains most easterly point. Maritime museum traces seafaring history.

IVY HOUSE FARM HOTEL, IVY LANE, OULTON BROAD, LOWESTOFT, NORFOLK NR33 8HY (01502 501353/588144; Fax: 01502 501539). A relaxing, tranquil location with walks from your bedroom door. 'Oulton Broad's hidden oasis'. See our full colour advert under Norfolk.

Sudbury

Birthplace of Thomas Gainsborough, with a museum illustrating his career. Colchester 13 miles.

Situated in small, picturesque village within 15 miles of Sudbury, Newmarket Racecourse and historic Bury St Edmunds. Bungalow well equipped to accommodate 4 people. All facilities. Car essential, parking. Children and pets welcome. Terms from £56 to £115 per week. For further details send SAE to MRS M. WINCH, PLOUGH HOUSE, STANSFIELD, SUDBURY CO10 8LT (01284 789253).

Wenhaston

Village 3 miles south-east of Halesworth.

THE COMPASSES INN, WENHASTON IP19 9EF (01502 478319). B&B in cosy country inn run by dog lovers. Real ale, log fires and evening bistro. Many walks, commons and river. Garden. Car park. Stairlift. No children. [pw! 🐾]

Woodbridge

Town on River Deben, 8 miles east of Ipswich.

THE CROWN AND CASTLE, ORFORD, WOODBRIDGE, SUFFOLK IP12 2LJ (01394 450205 Fax: 01394 450176). Comfortable and very dog-friendly hotel situated close to 12th century castle in historic and unspoilt village of Orford. Honest good food served in award-winning Trinity Restaurant.[🐾]
E-mail: info@crownandcastlehotel.co.uk
Website: crownandcastlehotel.co.uk

Kingston-upon-Thames

Market town, Royal borough, and administrative centre of Surrey, Kingston is ideally placed for London and environs.

CHASE LODGE HOTEL, 10 PARK ROAD, HAMPTON WICK, KINGSTON-UPON-THAMES KT1 4AS (020 8943 1862; Fax: 020 8943 9363). Award-winning hotel offering quality en suite bedrooms. Easy access to town centre and major transport links. à la carte menu, licensed bar. ETC AA ★★★, RAC Highly Acclaimed. [⊀]

EAST SUSSEX

Arlington, Battle, Burgess Hill

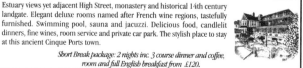

JEAKE'S HOUSE

Mermaid Street, Rye, East Sussex TN31 7ET
Telephone: 01797 222828 Fax: 01797 222623
E-mail: jeakeshouse@btinternet.com • Web:
www.jeakeshouse.com

Dating from 1689, this beautiful Listed Building stands in one of England's most famous streets. Oak-beamed and panelled bedrooms overlook the marsh to the sea. Brass, mahogany or four-poster beds with linen sheets and lace; honeymoon suite. En suite facilities, TV, radio, telephone. Residential licence. Traditional and vegetarian breakfast served. £28.50-£48.50pp. Private car park. Access, Visa and Mastercard accepted.

AA PREMIER	**RƏC** SPARKLING DIAMOND	**Good Hotel Guide**
♦♦♦♦♦ SELECTED	♦♦♦♦♦ & WARM WELCOME AWARD	César Award

See colour advertisement on page 44

BEACH COTTAGES, CLAREMONT ROAD, SEAFORD BN25 2QQ
Well-equipped, three-bedroomed terraced cottage on seafront. CH, open fire and woodburner. South-facing patio overlooking sea. Downland walks (wonderful for dogs), fishing, golf, wind-surfing, etc. *Details from*
Julia Lewis, 47 Wandle Bank, London SW19 1DW Tel: 0208 542 5073

Arlington

Village in valley of River Cuckmere below the South Downs. Hailsham 3 miles.

MRS P. BONIFACE, LAKESIDE FARM, ARLINGTON, POLEGATE BN26 6SB (01323 870111). Situated on the edge of Arlington Reservoir. Eastbourne within 15 miles. Accommodation sleeps 4–6 with two double rooms, lounge, dining area, kitchen, bathroom. Open April to October. Weekly from £175. [🐾]

Battle

Site of the famous victory of William the Conqueror; remains of an abbey mark the spot where Harold fell.

LITTLE HEMINGFOLD HOTEL, TELHAM, BATTLE TN33 0TT (01424 774338). In the heart of 1066 Country, 40 acres of bliss for you and your pets. Farmhouse hotel, all facilities. Fishing, boating, swimming, tennis. Special Breaks all year. Discounts for children. FREE accommodation for pets. [🐾]

Brighton

Famous resort with shingle beach and sand at low tide. Varied entertainment and nightlife; excellent shops and restaurants. Portsmouth 48 miles, Hastings 37, Newhaven 9.

BEST OF BRIGHTON & SUSSEX COTTAGES has available a very good selection of houses, flats, apartments and cottages in Brighton and Hove as well as East and West Sussex from Eastbourne to Chichester. Town centre/seaside and countryside locations – many taking pets. (01273 308779; Fax: 01273 300266). [Pets £15/£20 per week.]

ST BENEDICT'S, 1 MANOR ROAD, BRIGHTON BN2 5EA (01273 674140). Convent Guest House. Comfortable rooms, mostly en suite. TV. Also self-catering flat sleeps 6. Hermitage sleeps 1. Near sea, on bus route. Daily mass available. Pets welcome. Apply to Sister Superior. [🐾]

KEMPTON HOUSE HOTEL, 33/34 MARINE PARADE, BRIGHTON BN2 1TR (01273 570248). Private seafront hotel, relaxed and friendly atmosphere, overlooking beach and pier. En suite rooms available, all modern facilities. Satellite TV. Choice of breakfasts. B&B from £25 to £39. Pets and children always welcome. AA ♦♦♦[🐾]
website: www.s-h-systems.co.uk/hotels/kemptonh.html

Burgess Hill

Town 9 miles north of Brighton

DANCY'S, THEOBALDS ROAD, BURGESS HILL RH15 0SU (01273 683491/01444 232436). Centrally heated mobile home deep in the Sussex countryside. Kennels for 10-12 dogs. Lovely walks, no passing traffic, easy reach of Brighton (10 miles), Gatwick (13 miles). Open all year. [🏠]

Chiddingly

Charming village, 4 miles north-west of Hailsham. Off the A22 London-Eastbourne road.

Adorable, small, well-equipped cottage in grounds of Tudor Manor. Two bedrooms. Full central heating. Colour TV. Fridge/freezer, laundry facilities. Large safe garden. Use indoor heated swimming pool, sauna/jacuzzi and tennis. From £350 to £625 per week inclusive. ETC ★★★. Contact: EVA MORRIS, "PEKES", 124 ELM PARK MANSIONS, PARK WALK, LONDON SW10 0AR (020 7352 8088; Fax: 020 7352 8125). [2 dogs free, extra dog £5 (max. 4) pw!] e–mail: pekes.afa@virgin.net

Fairlight

Village 3 miles east of Hastings.

JANET & RAY ADAMS, FAIRLIGHT COTTAGE, WARREN ROAD, FAIRLIGHT TN35 4AG (01424 812545). Country house in idyllic location with clifftop walks. Tasteful en suite rooms, comfortable guest lounge. Dinner by arrangement, bring your own drinks. No smoking, . Dogs stay with owners. ETC ◆◆◆◆ [🐾]

Hastings

Seaside resort with a famous past — the ruins of William the Conqueror's castle lie above the Old Town. Many places of historic interest in the area, plus entertainments for all the family.

BEAUPORT PARK HOTEL, BATTLE ROAD, HASTINGS TN38 8EA (01424 851222). Georgian country mansion in 33 acres. All rooms private bath, colour television, trouser press, hairdryer, telephone. Country house breaks available all year. [pw!]

Herstmonceaux

Small village four miles north-east of Hailsham. Royal Observatory at Herstmonceux Castle.

CLEAVERS LYNG 16th-CENTURY COUNTRY HOTEL, CHURCH ROAD, HERSTMONCEUX BN27 1QJ (01323 833131; Fax: 01323 833617). Privately owned country hotel in heart of rural East Sussex. Bedrooms en suite with tea making, direct dial telephones. Oak-beamed non-smoking restaurant, bar, lounge bar, residents' lounge. Tariff from £30.00 per person sharing a double or twin room. Pets welcome. [🐾]

Polegate

Quiet position, 5 miles from the popular seaside resort of Eastbourne. London 58 miles, Lewes 12

MRS P. FIELD, 20 ST JOHN'S ROAD, POLEGATE BN26 5BP (01323 482691). Homely private house. Quiet location; large enclosed garden. Parking space. Ideally situated for walking on South Downs and Forestry Commission land. All rooms, washbasins and tea/coffee making facilities. Bed and Breakfast. Pets very welcome. [pw!]

Rye

Picturesque hill town with steep cobbled streets. Many fine buildings of historic interest. Hastings 12 miles, Tunbridge Wells 28.

RYE LODGE HOTEL, HILDER'S CLIFF, RYE TN31 7LD (01797 223838; Fax: 01797 223585). Elegant deluxe rooms named after French wine regions, tastefully furnished. Swimming pool, sauna and jacuzzi. Delicious food, candlelit dinners, fine wines, room service and private car park. The stylish place to stay at this ancient Cinque Ports town. [Pets £3 per night] website: www.ryelodge.co.uk

CADBOROUGH FARM, UDIMORE ROAD, RYE, EAST SUSSEX TN31 6AA (01797 225426 Fax: 01797 224097) Five newly converted individual cottages. Each sleeps two, some with own courtyards. Double and Twin available. Pets welcome. [Pets £2 per night].
e-mail: cadfarm@marcomm.co.uk
website: www.marcomm.co.uk/cadborough

JEAKE'S HOUSE, MERMAID STREET, RYE TN31 7ET (01797 222828; Fax: 01797 222623). Dating from 1689, this Listed Building has oak-beamed and panelled bedrooms overlooking the marsh. En suite facilities, TV, radio, telephone. £28.50-£48.50 per person. AA 5 Diamond Premier Selected. [Pets £5 per night]
e-mail: jeakeshouse@btinternet.com
website: www.jeakeshouse.com

FLACKLEY ASH HOTEL, PEASMARSH, RYE TN31 6YH (01797 230651; Fax: 01797 230510). Georgian Country House Hotel in beautiful grounds. Indoor swimming pool and Leisure Centre. Inner Sanctuary Beauty Treatments. Visit Rye and the castles and gardens of East Sussex and Kent. AA/RAC ★★★ [Pets £7.50 per night.]

Seaford

On the coast midway between Newhaven and Beachy head.

BEACH COTTAGES, CLAREMONT ROAD, SEAFORD. Well-equipped, three-bedroomed terraced cottage on seafront. CH, open fire and woodburner. South-facing patio overlooking sea. Downland walks (wonderful for dogs), fishing, golf, wind-surfing, etc. Details from JULIA LEWIS, 47 WANDLE BANK, LONDON SW19 1DW (0208 542 5073). [🐾]

WEST SUSSEX

Barnham, Chichester

THE **Lillies** TEL & FAX: 01243 552081

A *quiet secluded site offering touring pitches and holiday homes for hire. Open all year S.A.E. for brochure.*

THE LILLIES NURSERY & CARAVAN PARK, YAPTON ROAD, BARNHAM, BOGNOR REGIS, WEST SUSSEX PO22 0AY

THE MILLSTREAM
HOTEL AND RESTAURANT
BOSHAM

Ideal setting in a tranquil quayside village with beautiful shoreline walks – 4 miles west of Chichester. Dogs very welcome – £2 per day (inc blanket and dinner of fresh meat and vegetables).

• *RAC/AA ★★★ and Rosette Award for Food Excellence*
• *'Johansens', 'Which? Hotel' and 'Good Hotel' guides recommended*
• *English Tourism Council Silver Award*

Bosham, Chichester PO18 8HL 01243 573234

See also Colour Advertisement on page 45

MOSELEYS BARN Hardham, Near Pulborough RH20 1LB Tel & Fax: 01798 872912

Converted 17th century barn with galleried beamed hall and panoramic views of South Downs. Conveniently placed for RSPB Reserve, South Down Way, and also Arundel, Petworth, Chichester, Goodwood and coast. Accommodation consists of 2 double en suite rooms and a twin bedroom all with TV and tea/coffee making facilities. Also available one bedroomed stone cottage on a B&B or self catering basis. No smoking. ETC ◆◆◆ Silver Award

ST ANDREWS LODGE Chichester Road, Selsey PO20 0LX

Family-run hotel with reputation for an excellent farmhouse breakfast. Situated on Manhood peninsula south of Chichester, close to unspoilt beaches and countryside. 10 bedrooms (single, double, twin and family), all en suite, with direct dial telephones and modem point, some on ground floor. Spacious lounges with log fire; friendly bar for residents only. Excellent Grade 1 (ETC Accessible Scheme) wheelchair access. Large car park. Evening meals by prior arrangement. ETC/AA ◆◆◆◆.

Bed and breakfast from £27.50pppn. **Tel: 01243 606899 Fax: 01243 607826**

See also Colour Advertisement on page 45

Selsey Bill, Near Chichester – spectacular sea views from seafront cottages.

Delightful detached self-catering cottages and one railway carriage. Sleep 2–6, 6–12 plus cot. All fully equipped and centrally heated. One cottage suitable for disabled. Secluded gardens. Sandy beach at low tide. Superb walks. Close to Pagham Harbour Nature Reserve, ideal for touring South Downs and Chichester. Children and pets welcome. For colour brochure contact: **MRS SUE GRAVES,**
28 WISE LANE, MILL HILL, LONDON NW7 2RE (TEL/FAX: 0208 959 2848)
e-mail: sue@suegraves.demon.co.uk   Website: www.shortlet.dircon.co.uk

Cavendish Hotel
115 Marine Parade
Worthing BN11 3QG
Tel: 01903 236767
Fax: 01903 823840

The prime sea front location provides an ideal base for touring Sussex villages and the rolling South Downs. Dogs allowed on the beach 1st October until 30th April and on the beach half a mile away all year.
Nearby are Arundel, Chichester and Goodwood House; to the east is Brighton and the Royal Pavilion and the historic town of Lewes.
All rooms at the Cavendish are en suite, have satellite television, direct-dial telephone and tea/coffee making facilities. The friendly bar is a popular rendezvous with the locals and offers real ale with a wide range of beers, lagers, wines and spirits.

£80 per person for any two nights Dinner, Bed & Breakfast.
E-mail: thecavendish@mistral.co.uk   **Website:** www3.mistral.co.uk/thecavendish/
No charge for dogs belonging to readers of Pets Welcome!

Barnham

Village 4 miles north east of Bognor Regis.

THE LILLIES NURSERY & CARAVAN PARK, YAPTON ROAD, BARNHAM, BOGNOR REGIS PO22 0AY (Tel & Fax: 01243 552081). A quiet secluded site offering touring pitches and holiday homes for hire. Open all year S.A.E. for brochure. [pets £1.00 per night]

Chichester

County town dating from Roman times. Festival Theatre holds annual summer season.

THE MILLSTREAM HOTEL AND RESTAURANT, BOSHAM, CHICHESTER PO18 8HL (01243 573234). Ideal setting in a tranquil quayside village with beautiful shoreline walks. Dogs very welcome – £2 per day (inc blanket and dinner of fresh meat and vegetables). [pw!]

Pulborough

Popular fishing centre on the River Arun. South Downs Way nearb; Arundel 8 miles.

MOSELEYS BARN, HARDHAM, NEAR PULBOROUGH RH20 1LB (Tel & Fax: 01798 872912). Converted 17th century barn with galleried beamed hall and panoramic views of South Downs. 2 double en suite rooms and a twin bedroom all with TV and tea/coffee making facilities. ETC ◆◆◆ Silver Award [🐾]

BEACON LODGE, LONDON ROAD, WATERSFIELD, PULBOROUGH RH20 1NH (Tel/Fax: 01798 831026). Charming self-contained annexe. B&B accommodation, en suite, TV, coffee/tea making facilities. Wonderful countryside views. B&B from £24pppn. No charge for your pets!. Telephone for more details. [🐕]
e-mail: beaconlodge@beaconlodge.co.uk
website: www.beaconlodge.co.uk

Selsey

Seaside resort 8 miles south of Chichester. Selsey Bill is headland extending into English Channel.

ST ANDREWS LODGE HOTEL, CHICHESTER ROAD, SELSEY PO20 0LX (01243 606899; Fax: 01243 607826). 10 bedrooms, all en suite, with direct dial telephones and modem point, some on ground floor. Spacious lounges with log fire; friendly bar for residents only. Excellent Grade 1 wheelchair access. Evening meals by prior arrangement. ETC/AA ◆◆◆◆.

SELSEY BILL, NEAR CHICHESTER. Delightful detached self-catering cottages one suitable for disabled and one railway carriage, sleep 2/6, 6/12 plus cot. Superb walks; ideal for touring. Chidren and pets welcome. Colour brochure: MRS SUE GRAVES, 28 WISE LANE, MILL HILL, LONDON NW7 2RE (Tel & Fax: 0208 959 2848).
e–mail: sue@suegraves.demon.co.uk
website: www.shortlet.dircon.co.uk

Worthing

Residential town and seaside resort with 5-mile seafront. Situated 10 miles west of Brighton.

CAVENDISH HOTEL, 115 MARINE PARADE, WORTHING BN11 3QG (01903 236767; Fax: 01903 823840). Ideal base for touring Sussex villages and the rolling South Downs. All rooms are en suite, have TV, direct-dial telephone and tea/coffee facilities. No charge for dogs belonging to readers of Pets Welcome!. [🐕]
e–mail: thecavendish@mistral.co.uk
website: www3.mistral.co.uk/thecavendish/

WARWICKSHIRE

Stratford-upon-Avon

RAYFORD CARAVAN PARK
RIVERSIDE, TIDDINGTON ROAD,
STRATFORD-UPON-AVON CV37 7BE
Tel: (01789) 293964
PETS WELCOME. A HAPPY AND INTERESTING HOLIDAY FOR ALL

Holiday & Home Parks

River Launch Service to Stratford

Situated within the town of Stratford-upon-Avon, on the banks of the river, Rayford Park is ideally placed for visiting all Shakespearean attractions and the beautiful Cotswolds. In Stratford itself there is everything you could wish for: shops, pubs, restaurants, swimming pool, sports centre, the Royal Shakespeare Theatre, and a generous helping of history and the Bard! The luxury 12ft wide Caravan Holiday Homes accommodate up to 6 persons in comfort. All have kitchen with full-size cooker, fridge; bathroom with shower/washbasin/WC; two bedrooms, one double-bedded and one with two single beds (cot available);double dinette/two single settees in lounge; gas fires, colour TV, carpeted throughout. Also available: TWO COTTAGES, "Sleepy Hollow" and "Kingfisher Cottage", all modern facilities, set on riverside. Private fishing. BROCHURE ON REQUEST.

Woodside Guest House
Langley Road, Claverdon, Warwick CV35 8PJ
Tel: 01926 842446; Fax: 01926 843697
A peaceful family guest house in 22 acres of own gardens and woodland. Lovely views, walks, log fires. Happy to welcome four-legged guests. ETC ◆◆◆. Brochure available. Special Autumn Breaks.

THE CROFT
Haseley Knob, Warwick CV35 7NL
Tel and Fax: 01926 484447
This four-acre smallholding has a friendly, family atmosphere and is situated in picturesque rural surroundings. Very comfortable accommodation. Bedrooms, most en suite, with colour TV, tea/coffee making facilities. Ground floor en suite bedrooms available. Bed and Full English Breakfast from £34 single or from £23 per person sharing a double/twin room. Pets welcome.

Stratford-Upon-Avon

Historic town famous as Shakespeare's birthplace and home. Birmingham 24, Warwick 8.

DEREK & SUSAN LEARMOUNT, GREEN HAVEN, 217 EVESHAM ROAD, STRATFORD-UPON-AVON CV37 9AS (01789 297874). Cosy, pretty, refurbished guest house. Central heating, colour TV's courtesy trays. All en suite. Private parking. payphone. Easily accessible to Cotswolds and Warwick. ETC ◆◆◆◆
e-mail: susanlearmount@green-haven.co.uk or information@green-haven.co.uk
website: www.green-haven.co.uk

MRS H. J. MELLOR, ARRANDALE, 208 EVESHAM ROAD, STRATFORD-UPON-AVON CV37 9AS (01789 267112). Guest House situated near River Avon, theatre, Shakespeare properties. Washbasins, tea making, TV, central heating, en suite available. Children, pets welcome. Parking. Bed and Breakfast £15.50-£18.00. Weekly terms £105-£120. Evening Meal £6.50. [🐾]

RAYFORD CARAVAN PARK, TIDDINGTON ROAD, STRATFORD-UPON-AVON CV37 7BE (01789 293964). Luxury Caravans, sleep 6. Fully equipped kitchens, bathroom/ shower/WC. Also two riverside Cottages, all modern facilities to first-class standards. Private fishing. On banks of River Avon. [Pets £12 weekly.]

Warwick

Town on the River Avon, 9 miles south-west of Coventry, with medieval castle and many fine old buildings.

THE OLD RECTORY, VICARAGE LANE, SHERBOURNE, WARWICK CV35 8AB (01926 624562; Fax: 01926 624995). Grade II Listed Georgian country house with 14 elegantly appointed en suite bedrooms, some antique brass beds. Four-posters and spa baths available. À la carte restaurant. Beautiful surroundings. Ideal for Stratford, Cotswolds and many National Trust properties. Half-mile M40 Junction 15. RAC ◆◆◆. [🛏]

WOODSIDE GUEST HOUSE, CLAVERDON, NEAR WARWICK CV35 8PJ (01926 842446; Fax: 01926 843697). A peaceful family guest house in 22 acres of own gardens and woodland. Lovely views, walks, log fires. Happy to welcome four-legged guests. ETC ◆◆◆. Brochure available. Special Autumn Breaks.[Pets £2 per night, £12 per week].

MR & MRS D. CLAPP, THE CROFT, HASELEY KNOB, WARWICK CV35 7NL (Tel & Fax: 01926 484447). Smallholding with a friendly, family atmosphere and situated in picturesque rural surroundings. Very comfortable accommodation. Bedrooms, most en suite, with colour TV, tea/coffee making facilities. Ground floor en suite bedrooms available. Bed and Full English Breakfast from £34 single or from £23 per person sharing a double/twin room. Pets welcome. [Pets £2 per night].

WEST MIDLANDS

Birmingham

The secong-largest city in Britain, with Art Galleries to rival London. The Bull Ring has been modernised and includes an impressive shopping centre, but there is still plenty of the old town to see; the town hall, the concert hall and the Cathedral Church of St Philip.

ANGELA AND IAN KERR, THE AWENTSBURY HOTEL, 21 SERPENTINE ROAD, SELLY PARK, BIRMINGHAM B29 7HU (0121-472 1258). Victorian Country House. Large gardens. All rooms have colour TV, telephones and tea/coffee making facilities. Some rooms en suite, some with showers. All rooms central heating, wash-basins. Near BBC Pebble Mill, transport, University, city centre. Bed and Breakfast from £33 Single Room, from £48 Twin Room, inclusive of VAT.

Malmesbury, Salisbury

Dairy Farm on the Wiltshire/Gloucestershire borders. Malmesbury 3 miles, 15 minutes M4 (junction 16 or 17). **SELF CATERING:** The Bull Pen and Cow Byre each sleep 2/3 plus cot. Double bedded room, bathroom, kitchen, lounge. 3 KEYS COMMENDED . **B&B** in 15th century farmhouse – three comfortable rooms, one en suite. ◆◆◆◆

John & Edna Edwards, Stonehill Farm, Charlton, Malmesbury SN16 9DY Tel: 01666 823310

Swaynes Firs Farm   ETC ◆◆◆

Mr A. Shering, Grimsdyke, Coombe Bissett, Salisbury, Wiltshire SP5 5RF
Small working farm with horses, cattle, poultry, geese and duck ponds. Spacious rooms, all en suite with colour TV and country views. Ideal for visiting the many historic sites in the area. Rates: Adults £22 per night B/B. Children £11 sharing adults' room. Dogs– Free.
Tel: 01725 519240 Web: http://freespace.virgin.net/swaynes.firs/index.htm E-mail: swaynes.firs@virgin.net

the lamb at hindon Hindon, Near Salisbury, Wilts SP3 6DP

Tel: 01747 820573 Fax: 01747 820605

| RAC/AA ★★ |
| Courtesy & Care Award |

Charmingly furnished single, double and four-poster bedrooms provide overnight guests with cosy country-style accommodation. Good quality meals served in the bar and restaurant. Real ales can be enjoyed in the friendly bar, where crackling log fires bestow charm and atmosphere as well as warmth.

Chippenham

Town on River Avon 12 miles north-east of Bath.

ROWARD FARM, DRAYCOT CERNE, CHIPPENHAM SN15 4SG (01249 758147). Three self-catering cottages (♔♔♔♔ Highly Commended) in peaceful Wiltshire countryside, overlooking open fields. Convenient for Cotswolds and Bath. Sleep two to four people in fully-equipped accommodation. Non-smoking. Well behaved pets welcome. Call or write for brochure.

Malmesbury

Country town on River Avon with a late medieval market cross. Remains of medieval abbey.

MRS A. HILLIER, LOWER FARM, SHERSTON, MALMESBURY SN16 0PS (01666 840391). Self-contained wing of old farmhouse. Sleeps 3/5. Working farm. Large lawn. Fishing. Half mile to shops and pubs. Wiltshire/Gloucestershire Borders. Available until August only. £95-£160 per week. Electricity £1 meter. [Pets £5 each per week.]

JOHN AND EDNA EDWARDS, STONEHILL FARM, CHARLTON, MALMESBURY SN16 9DY (01666 823310). Family-run dairy farm, ideal for touring. 3 comfortable rooms, one en suite. Also 2 fully equipped bungalow-style barns, each sleeps 2/3 plus cot, self catering.

Salisbury

13th century cathedral city, with England's highest spire at 404ft. Many fine buildings.

MR A. SHERING, SWAYNES FIRS FARM, GRIMSDYKE, COOMBE BISSETT, SALISBURY SP5 5RF (01725 519240). Small working farm with horses, poultry, geese and duck ponds. Spacious rooms, all en suite with colour TV. Ideal for visiting the many historic sites in the area. ETC ◆◆◆ [🐾]
E-mail: swaynes.firs@virgin.net
Website: http://freespace.virgin.net/swaynes.firs/index.htm

THE LAMB AT HINDON, HINDON, NEAR SALISBURY SP3 6DP (01747 820573; Fax: 01747 820605). Charmingly furnished single, double and four-poster bedrooms provide overnight guests with cosy country-style accommodation. Good quality meals served in the bar and restaurant. Real ales can be enjoyed in the friendly bar, where crackling log fires bestow charm and atmosphere as well as warmth. AA/RAC ★★ Courtesy & Care Award.

Broadway

Small town below escarpment of Cotswold Hills, 5 miles south-east of Evesham.

DORMY HOUSE, Willersey Hill, Broadway WR12 7LF (01386 852711; Fax: 01386 858636). The 17th-century Dormy House Hotel is set high in the rolling Cotswold countryside. Adjacent to Broadway Golf Course, it is a really lovely place in which to relax with your dog(s) and enjoy a one night stay, Champagne Weekend or Carefree Midweek Break. Telephone: 01386 852711 for brochure/booking. AA/RAC ★★★

Great Malvern

Fashionable spa town in last century with echoes of that period.

ANN AND BRIAN PORTER, CROFT GUEST HOUSE, BRANSFORD, WORCESTER WR6 5JD (01886 832227; Fax: 01886 830037). 16th-18th century country house. 10 minutes from Worcester, Malvern and M5. En suite rooms, tea coffee trays, central heating, TV in all bedrooms. Dinners available; residential licence. Sauna and family jacuzzi. Children and dogs welcome. Cot and baby listening service; family room. AA ◆◆◆. [🐾]

KATE AND DENIS, WHITEWELLS FARM COTTAGES, RIDGEWAY CROSS, NEAR MALVERN WR13 5JS (01886 880607; Fax: 01886 880360). Charming converted Cottages, sleep 2–6. Fully equipped with colour TV, microwave, barbecue, fridge, iron, etc. Linen, towels also supplied. One cottage suitable for disabled guests. Short breaks, long lets, large groups. ETC ★★★★ [Pets £10 per week. p.w!]
E–mail: Whitewells.Farm@btinternet.com

THE COTTAGE IN THE WOOD (01684 575859) High on Malvern hills. Accommodation over three buildings. 2 AA Restaurants, Rosettes, over 600 wines. "Best view in England" - The Daily Mail. Call for brochure. ★★★ [🐾]
website: www.cottageinthewood.co.uk

MALVERN HILLS HOTEL, WYNDS POINT, MALVERN WR13 6DW (01684 540690). Enchanting family owned and run hotel nestling high in the hills. Direct access to superb walking with magnificent views.Oak-panelled lounge, log fire, real ales, fine food and friendly staff. Great animal lovers. ETC/AA/RAC ★★. [🐾]

PLEASE MENTION THIS GUIDE WHEN YOU WRITE

OR PHONE TO ENQUIRE ABOUT ACCOMMODATION

IF YOU ARE WRITING, A STAMPED, ADDRESSED

ENVELOPE IS ALWAYS APPRECIATED

PUBLISHER'S NOTE

While every effort is made to ensure accuracy, we regret that FHG Publications cannot accept responsibility for errors, omissions or misrepresentations in our entries or any consequences thereof. Prices in particular should be checked because we go to press early. We will follow up complaints but cannot act as arbiters or agents for either party.

WELCOME COTTAGE HOLIDAYS. Quality Cottages in wonderful locations at welcoming low prices. Pets, linen and fuel mostly included. PHONE FOR FREE 2001 FULL COLOUR BROCHURE 01756 702209.

Bridlington

Traditional family holiday resort with picturesque harbour and a wide range of entertainments and leisure facilities. Ideal for exploring the Heritage coastline and the Wolds.

THE TENNYSON HOTEL, 19 TENNYSON AVENUE, BRIDLINGTON YO15 2EU (Tel & Fax: 01262 604382). 1994 Golden Bowl Award Winner for the Most Pet-Friendly Hotel in Yorkshire. Offering fine cuisine in attractive surroundings. Close to beach and cliff walks. ETC ◆◆◆. [🛏 pw!]

Great Driffield

Town 11 miles south west of Bridlington

MRS TIFFY HOPPER, KELLEYTHORPE FARM, GREAT DRIFFIELD YO25 9DW (01377 252297). Friendly atmosphere, antique furniture, pretty chintzes, new bathrooms, one en-suite. Children welcome. Large garden with swings and playcastle. Bed and Breakfast from £17; optional Evening Meal from £10 by prior arrangement. 10% discount for seven nights or more. Reductions for children under 12 years.[🛏]

Kilnwick Percy

LOcated 2 miles east of Pocklington

PAWS-A-WHILE, KILNWICK PERCY, POCKLINGTON, YO42 1UF (01759 301168; Mobile: 07711 866869). Small family B & B set in forty acres of parkland twixt York and Beverley. Fishing, golf, sauna, walking, riding. Pets and horses most welcome. Brochure available.[pw! 🛏]
e-mail: paws.a.while@lineone.net
website: www.pawsawhile.net

North Dalton

On the Yorkshire Wolds between Great Driffield and Pocklington.

THE STAR INN, WARTER ROAD, NORTH DALTON, EAST RIDING OF YORKSHIRE YO25 9UX (01377 217688; Fax: 01377 217791). Delightful 18th Century Coaching Inn. Excellent à la carte Restaurant, Bar meals and pulled beers. Seven en-suite bedrooms. Ideal for walking, rambling and touring. For more details contact Keith or Jo.
Website: www.inonthepond.com

NORTH YORKSHIRE

Askrigg

The Queens Arms Inn   Litton, Skipton BD23 5QJ

Traditional 17th century country inn. The cheerful welcome you receive from Neil and Tanya Thompson is mirrored in the blazing open fire and oaken beams. The wholesome country fare fit not only for Yorkshire folk but enjoyed by an international clientele is well matched by the Real Ale served from the pumps on the wooden bar. Comfortable en suite accommodation with views over beautiful Littondale. The Queens Arms is renowned for its good food and extensive menu at lunchtimes and evenings.

Tel: 01756 770208 • website: www.yorkshiredales.net/stayat/queens

---

HOLIDAY COTTAGES IN THE YORKSHIRE DALES, YORK, MOORS, COAST, PEAK AND THE LAKE DISTRICT

Over 200 super Self-catering Cottages. For our fully illustrated brochure apply:

Holiday Cottages (Yorkshire) Ltd, Water Street, Skipton (18), North Yorkshire BD23 1PB

Tel: (01756) 700872 E-mail: p@holidaycotts.co.uk

Golden Fleece

Market Square, Thirsk,
North Yorkshire YO7 1LL
Tel: 01845 523108
Fax: 01845 523996

This Characterful old Coaching Inn offers good food and up to date facilities. All rooms have new bathrooms, satellite TV, phone, trouser press, hairdryer. On site parking. Perfect for Dales and Moors touring and walking or shopping in York or Harrogate.

ETC ★★ Silver Award   AA ★★ 69%

Foxhills Hideaways, Felixkirk, Thirsk YO7 2DS

Quiet, no hassle holidays in cosy Scandinavian log cabins. Secluded garden setting. Central for the Moors, Dales, York and the coast. Village pub round the corner. Fully inclusive prices. Open all year. Please write or phone for a brochure

TELEPHONE 01845 537575

Long Ashes Inn Threshfield, Near Grassington, North Yorkshire BD23 5PN

En suite accommodation • Home-cooked food
Hand-pulled ales • Heated indoor pool
Perfect for exploring the Dales

AA & ETC ◆◆◆   Visit our website for photographs

Ask for our colour brochure
Tel: 01756 752434 Fax: 01756 752937
e-mail: info@longashesinn.co.uk
www.longashesinn.co.uk

PLEASE MENTION THIS GUIDE WHEN YOU WRITE OR PHONE TO ENQUIRE ABOUT ACCOMMODATION.

IF YOU ARE WRITING, A STAMPED, ADDRESSED ENVELOPE IS ALWAYS APPRECIATED.

Panoramic views, waterfalls, wild birds and tranquillity

Stone farmhouse with panoramic views, high in the Yorkshire Dales National Park (Herriot family's house in 'All Creatures Great and Small' on TV). Three bedrooms (sleeps 6-7), dining and sittingrooms with traditional fireplaces, kitchen, bathroom with electric storage heating and views! Equipment includes electric cooker, microwave, fridge, colour TV, telephone (charge cards). Garden, stables, barn. Access from lane, private parking, no through traffic. Near Wensleydale, excellent walking from front door. Pets welcome. Self-catering from £300 per week.

**Westclose House (Allaker), West Scrafton,
Near Leyburn DL8 4RM
For bookings telephone 020 8567 4862
e-mail: caveconsult@compuserve.com**

See also Colour Advertisement on page 47

The Ship Inn

Arrive as guests and leave as friends.

DOGS MADE VERY WELCOME
A traditional family run pub set in a small seaside hamlet, with a choice of Cask conditioned ales and good home cooked meals. Bed and traditional Breakfast accommodation in two double/family rooms and two singles.
From £16.50pppn.
Bob & Kay Hartley, The Ship, Port Mulgrave, Hinderwell, Near Whitby TS13 5JZ
Tel: 01947 840303 E-mail: kayhartley@lineone.net

See also Colour Advertisement on page 47

The Seacliffe Hotel 12 North Promenade, West Cliff, Whitby YO21 3JX

Friendly family run hotel overlooking the sea. Licensed à la carte restaurant specialising in fresh local seafoods, steaks and vegetarian dishes. Open all year. RAC Highly Acclaimed. AA Selected. Les Routiers
Freephone 08000 191747   www.seacliffe.co.uk   ETC/AA ◆◆◆

KIRKLANDS PRIVATE HOTEL   Bed, Breakfast and Evening Meal.

John & Jo Halton,   Family-run hotel, good home cooking.
17 Abbey Terrace,
West Cliff,   Licensed. All en suite or private bathroom;
Whitby YO21 3HQ   all have tea/coffee making facilities and colour TV.
Tel: 01947 603868   * Pets welcome. **Pets charged at £3 per day.** *

Sneaton Hall

This stone built Georgian House is at the heart of a small North Yorkshire country village, three miles south of Whitby. All eight bedrooms en suite; tea making facilities, TV. Our candlelit Restaurant offers distinguished foods with a fine selection of wines. Hotel Pleasant gardens. Panoramic sea views. Private car parking. Well stocked lounge bar with a good selection of bar meals. Children and pets most welcome. Non-smoking.
Sneaton, Whitby YO22 5HP   Tel: 01947 605929; Fax: 01947 820177

PARTRIDGE NEST FARM

Eskdaleside, Sleights, Whitby YO22 5ES Tel: 01947 810450
Six caravans on secluded site, five miles from Whitby and sea. Ideal touring centre. All have mains electricity, colour TV, fridge, gas cooker.

FAIRHAVEN COUNTRY HOTEL

The Common, Goathland, North Yorkshire, YO22 5AN
Tel: 01947 896361 • Fax: 01947 896099
E-mail: royellis@thefairhavenhotel.co.uk
Website: www.thefairhavenhotel.co.uk

An Edwardian Country House Hotel in the centre of the village of Goathland, with a log fire and glorious moorland views. Warm hospitality, home cooked food, fine wines and a relaxed atmosphere. An ideal base for exploring the Moors and the coast. The NYM Steam Railway is nearby. The hotel has 9 bedrooms with a mix of en suite and standard. It is a non smoking hotel and people with special dietary requirements are catered for with prior arrangement.

WEIR CARAVAN PARK

With its picturesque setting on the banks of the River Derwent, is the ideal location for you to enjoy a Yorkshire holiday that can be as active or as relaxed as you want it to be!

TWO *GREAT* YORKSHIRE PARKS

ALLERTON CARAVAN PARK

Situated in the heart of beautiful Yorkshire. A perfect base to discover a variety of attractive historic towns and villages, the moor, dales and Yorkshire coast.

**Stamford Bridge
North Yorkshire
Tel: 01759 371377**

www.yorkshireholidayparks.co.uk

**Allerton,
Nr Knaresborough
North Yorkshire
Tel: 01423 330569**

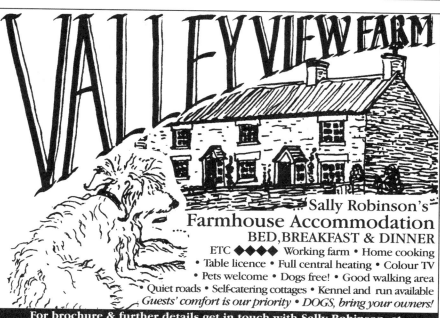

VALLEY VIEW FARM

Sally Robinson's Farmhouse Accommodation

BED, BREAKFAST & DINNER

ETC ◆◆◆◆ Working farm • Home cooking • Table licence • Full central heating • Colour TV • Pets welcome • Dogs free! • Good walking area • Quiet roads • Self-catering cottages • Kennel and run available *Guests' comfort is our priority • DOGS, bring your owners!*

For brochure & further details get in touch with Sally Robinson, at Valley View Farm, Old Byland, Helmsley, York YO6 5LG Tel: 01439 798221 E-mail: sally@valleyviewfarm.com Website: www.valleyviewfarm.com

Askrigg

TV series based on popular "Vet" stories by James Herriot filmed here. St. Oswald's Church, "Cathedral of Wensleydale", dates from late 15th and early 16th centuries.

KATE EMPSALL, WHITFIELD, HELM, ASKRIGG, NEAR LEYBURN DL8 3JF (Tel & Fax: 01969 650565). Relax at 950 feet in peaceful surroundings. All rooms en suite with spectacular views over Wensleydale and nearby waterfall walks. Non smoking. From £22 pppn. AA ◆◆◆. Cosy cottages in Askrigg and Hawes, sleep up to six. Non-smoking. Terms £150 to £400 per week. ETC ⚥⚥⚥ up to Highly Commended. [🐾]
e-mail: empsall@askrigg.yorks.net
website: www.wensleydale.org

Bentham

Quiet village amidst the fells. Good centre for rambling and fishing. Ingleton 5 miles N.E.

MRS L. J. STORY, HOLMES FARM, LOW BENTHAM, LANCASTER LA2 7DE (015242 61198). Cottage conversion in easy reach of Dales, Lake District and coast. Central heating, fridge, TV, washer, games room. ★★★★. [🐾]

Bedale

Small town 7 miles south-west of Northallerton.

MS B. BAVER, BOBBIES XVII CENTURY COTTAGE, AISKEW, BEDALE DL8 1DD (01677 423385). Half-a-mile from A1. Ideal stop over for dog shows. Twixt Dales/Moors. Bobbie keeps several 'shelties' herself. Off-road gated parking. Ideal dog walking nearby.

Clapham

Attractive village with caves and pot-holes in vicinity, including Gaping Ghyll. Nearby lofty peaks include Ingleborough (2,373ft.) to the north. Kendal 24 miles, Settle 6.

DAVID & JACKIE KINGSLEY, ARBUTUS GUEST HOUSE, RIVERSIDE, CLAPHAM, NEAR SETTLE LA2 8DS (015242 51240). Restored Georgian vicarage in a delightful setting. All rooms en suite, or private facilities. TV, tea/coffee. Central heating. Delicious home cooking. Open all year round. ETC/AA ◆◆◆◆ Pets welcome. [🐾]
E-mail: info@arbutus.co.uk
Website: www.arbutus.co.uk

Coverdale

Small village set in Yorkshire Dales, in heart of Herriot Country.

MRS JULIE CLARKE, MIDDLE FARM, WOODALE, COVERDALE, LEYBURN DL8 4TY (01969 640271). Peacefully situated farmhouse away from the madding crowd. B&B with optional Evening Meal. Home cooking. Pets sleep where you prefer. Ideally positioned for exploring the beautiful Yorkshire Dales. [🐾 pw!]
e-mail(text only): middlefarm@talk21.com

Danby

Village on River Esk 12 miles west of Whitby.

THE FOX & HOUNDS INN, AINTHORPE, DANBY YO21 2LD (01287 660218; Fax: 01287 660030). Residential 16th Century Coaching Inn. Comfortable en suite bedrooms available. Enjoy our real ales or quality wines. Special mid-week breaks available Oct - May. Open all year. [🐾]

THE DUKE OF WELLINGTON INN, WEST LANE, DANBY, NEAR WHITBY YO21 2LY (01287 660351) Ivy-clad 18th century traditional inn located in the heart of the North York Moors, convenient for Whitby & the coast. Real ales, interesting wines and home cooked food. Eight en-suite rooms equipped with television & tea/coffee making facilities. Dogs are very welcome. ETC ◆◆◆ [🐾]
e-mail: landlord@dukeofwellington.freeserve.co.uk
website: www.dukeofwellington.co.uk

Easingwold

Small market town with cobbled streets where weathered red brick dwellings are grouped around a large green. 12 miles north-west of York.

MRS R. RITCHIE, THE OLD RECTORY, THORMANBY, EASINGWOLD, YORK YO61 4NN (01845 501417). Ideal for touring Herriot Country, Moors, Dales. TWO SELF-CONTAINED COTTAGES sleeping four to six. Also Bed and Breakfast. Three spacious bedrooms, two en suite. SAE or phone for brochure. [🐾]

GARBUTTS GHYLL, THORNTON HILL, NEAR EASINGWOLD YO6 3PZ (01347 868644). Georgian working farm which is peaceful, friendly and homely and is located off the beaten track. Furnished in olde worlde style with en-suite facilities and open sitting room. Home organic cooking. Excellent facilities for children and animals. Open March - November.

Filey

Well-known resort with sandy beach. Off-shore is Filey Brig. Hull 40 miles, Bridlington 11, Scarborough 7.

DAVID & ANN TINDALL, THE BEACH HOLIDAY FLATS, 9/10 THE BEACH, FILEY YO14 9LA (01723 513178). Only 30 yards from the sea with magnificent views of Filey Bay. Ideal for Rambling, Golf, Fishing and Sightseeing. ETC ⛫ /⛫⛫⛫ COMMENDED. [🐾]

Goathland

Centre for moorland and woodland walks and waterfalls. Village of 19th century houses scattered over several heaths.

WHITFIELD HOUSE HOTEL, DARNHOLM, GOATHLAND, NORTH YORKSHIRE YO22 5LA (01947 896215) A former 17th Century farmhouse in the beautiful North York Moors National Park, Whitfield House Hotel offers a relaxed and friendly atmosphere with superb cuisine, fully equipped bedrooms, a lounge and lounge bar. ETC ★★ GuestAccom Good Room Award. [Pets £1.50 per night, £7 per week]

Grassington

Wharfedale village in attractive moorland setting. Ripon 22 miles, Skipton 9.

FORESTERS ARMS, MAIN STREET, GRASSINGTON, SKIPTON BD23 5AA (01756 752349; Fax: 01756 753633). The Foresters Arms is situated in the heart of the Yorkshire Dales and provides an ideal centre for walking or touring. Within easy reach of York and Harrogate. ETC ◆◆◆ [🐾]

JERRY AND BEN'S HOLIDAY COTTAGES. Seven comfortable properties on private estate near Grassington in Yorkshire Dales National Park. Wooded mountain becks, waterfalls, rocky crags and accessible hill and footpath walking. Brochure from: MRS J. M.JOY, JERRY AND BEN'S HOLIDAY COTTAGES, HEBDEN, SKIPTON BD23 5DL (01756 752369; Fax: 01756 753370). [pw! one pet free, subsequent pets £5 per week] [🐾]

GRASSINGTON HOUSE HOTEL, THE SQUARE, GRASSINGTON BD23 5AQ (01756 752406; Fax: 01756 752135). A small hotel with a big reputation. All rooms en suite, colour TV, tea making. Parking. Ideal for walking or touring. AA Rosette for Food. ETC ★★. [🐾]

Harrogate

Charming and elegant spa town set amid some of Britain's most scenic countryside. Ideal for exploring Herriot Country and the moors and dales. York 22 miles, Bradford 19, Leeds 16.

ROSEMARY HELME, OLD SPRING WOOD LODGES & COTTAGES, HELME PASTURE, HARTWITH BANK, SUMMERBRIDGE, HARROGATE HG3 4DR (01423 780279, Fax: 01423 780994). Country accommodation for dogs and numerous walks in unspoilt Nidderdale. Central for Harrogate, York, Herriot and Bronte country. National Trust area. 4 stars/keys Highly Commended. [pw! Pets £3 per night, £15 per week.]
E-mail: info@oldspringwoodlodges.co.uk
Website: oldspringwoodlodges.co.uk

RUDDING HOLIDAY PARK, FOLLIFOOT, HARROGATE HG3 1JH (01423 870439; Fax: 01423 870859). Luxury cottages and lodges sleeping two to ten people. All equipped to a high standard. Pool, licensed bar, golf and children's playground on estate. Illustrated brochure available. ETC ★★★. [🐾]

SCOTIA HOUSE HOTEL, 66 KINGS ROAD, HARROGATE HG1 5JR (01423 504361; Fax: 01423 526578). Award winning licensed Hotel five minutes' walk town centre. En suite bedrooms with colour TV, hospitality tray, telephone. Central heating throughout. On site parking. Pets and owners welcome. ETC ◆◆◆, AA/RAC ★. [🐾]
e-mail: info@scotiahotel.harrogate.net
website: www.scotiahotel.harrogate.net

Harwood Dale

Village 7 miles north-west of Scarborough.

ROSALIE'S, ROSALIE & HOWARD RICHARDSON, CHAPEL FARM, HARWOOD DALE, SCARBOROUGH YO13 0LB (01723 870288) Two very well equipped self-contained cottages sleeping 2-6. Reduction for 2 people in either cottage. (Excluding Bank Holidays & School Holidays). En suite Bed and Breakfast also available. All set in 30 acres of gardens and open countryside including wood and stream. Many excellent walks from your back door for you and your pet. [First 2 pets free, then £2 per night for others].

Hawes

Small town in Wensleydale. Situated 14 miles south-east of Kirkby Stephen.

COUNTRY COTTAGE HOLIDAYS, DRYDEN HOUSE, MARKET PLACE, HAWES DL8 3RA (01969 667654). 100 cottages in the lovely Yorkshire Dales. Colour TV, central heating, open fires. Gardens, private parking. Many allow pets. Rents £135 – £495 per week. Sleeep 1-10.

SIMONSTONE HALL, HAWES, WENSLEYDALE DL8 3LY (01969 667255; Fax: 01969 667741). Facing south across picturesque Wensleydale. All rooms en suite with colour TV. Fine cuisine. Extensive wine list. Friendly personal attention. A relaxing break away from it all. AA ★★ [🐾 ⌂]
E - m a i l : information@simonstonehall.demon.co.uk
Website: www.simonstonehall.co.uk

STONE HOUSE HOTEL, SEDBUSK, HAWES DL8 3PT (01969 667571; Fax: 01969 667720). This fine Edwardian country house has spectacular views and serves delicious Yorkshire cooking with fine wines. Comfortable en suite bedrooms, some ground floor. Phone for details. [🐾]

Hawes near (Mallerstang)

12 miles north west on the Hawes to Kirkby Stephen road.

COCKLAKE HOUSE, MALLERSTANG CA17 4JT (017683 72080). Charming, High Pennine Country House B&B in unique position above Pendragon Castle in Upper Mallerstang Dale, offering good food and exceptional comfort to a small number of guests. Two double rooms with large private bathrooms. Three acres riverside grounds. Dogs welcome.

Helmsley

A delightful stone-built town on River Rye with a large cobbled square. Thirsk 12 miles.

Scandinavian Pine Lodges, each sleeping up to five persons. Fully centrally heated and double glazed. Set in 60 acres, surrounded by pine forests. Open all year. CRIEF LODGE HOLIDAY HOMES, WASS, YORK YO61 4AY (01347 868207 or Fax: 01347 868202) [🐾]

CROWN HOTEL, MARKET SQUARE, HELMSLEY YO62 5BJ (01439 770297). Fully residential old coaching inn. Bedrooms are very well appointed, all have tea and coffee-making facilities, colour TV, radio and telephones. Traditional country cooking. ETC/AA/RAC ★★. [🐾]

Huby

Small village 9 miles north of York. Ideal as base for exploring Dales, Moors and coast

THE NEW INN MOTEL, MAIN STREET, HUBY, YORK YO61 1HQ (01347 810219). Ideal base for Yorkshire attractions. Ground floor rooms, en suite, colour TVs etc. Bed and Breakfast from £25 pppn (Evening Meal available). Pets welcome. Special 3 & 4 day breaks. Telephone for brochure. AA ◆◆◆. Pets welcome. [🐕].

Kilburn

Village to south of Hambleton Hills. Near White Horse carved into hillside. Helmsley 9 miles, Thirsk 6.

CHAPEL BARN. Converted barn, one bedroom, in excellent area for touring Moors, Dales and coast. Range of sports facilities and restaurants in area. No children please. CLAIRE STRAFFORD, CHAPEL COTTAGE, KILBURN, YORK YO61 4AH (01347 868383). ALL PETS VERY WELCOME. [pw! 🐕]

Kirkbymoorside

Small town below North Yorkshire Moors, 7 miles west of Pickering. Traces of a medieval castle.

MRS F. WILES, SINNINGTON COMMON FARM, KIRKBYMOORSIDE, YORK YO62 6NX (Tel & Fax: 01751 431719). Newly converted cottages, tastefully furnished and well equipped, on working family farm. Sleep 2/8 from £115 per week including linen and heating. Also spacious ground floor accommodation (teamakers, colour TV, fridge, radio). Disabled facilities, separate outside entrances. B&B from £18.00. ETC ◆◆◆◆ (B&B), ★★★/★★★★ (SC) [🐕 pw!]
e-mail: felicity@scfarm.demon.co.uk
website: www.scfarm.demon.co.uk

Leeming Bar

Small, pretty village two miles north-east of Bedale.

THE WHITE ROSE HOTEL, LEEMING BAR, NORTHALLERTON DL7 9AY (01677 422707/424941, Fax: 01677 425123). Ideally situated for touring the spectacular scenery of two National Parks, Yorkshire Dales, coastal resorts, Herriot & Heartbeat Country. 18 rooms, all private bathroom, Colour TV/Radio, Tea & Coffee, hair dryer, trouser press and telephone. B&B from £24 per person. AA/RAC ★★ [🐕]
e-mail: royston@whiterosehotel.co.uk
website: www.whiterosehotel.co.uk

Leyburn

Small market town, 8 miles south-west of Richmond, standing above the River Ure in Wensleydale.

BARBARA & BARRIE MARTIN, THE OLD STAR, WEST WITTON, LEYBURN DL8 4LU (01969 622949). Former 17th century Coaching Inn now run as a guest house. Oak beams, log fire, home cooking. En suite from £19. ETC ◆◆◆. [🐕]

Malham

In picturesque Craven District with spectacular Malham Cove (300ft.) and Gordale Scar with waterfalls. Malham Tarn (N T.) is 4 miles north, Skipton 12 miles.

MRS C. SHARP, MIRESFIELD FARM, MALHAM, SKIPTON BD23 4DA (01729 830414). In beautiful gardens bordering village green and stream. Excellent food. 11 bedrooms, all with private facilities. Full central heating. Two well-furnished lounges and conservatory. ETC◆◆◆ B&B from £24pppn. [🐕 pw!]

Oldstead

Hamlet 7 miles east of Thirsk in beautiful North Yorkshire Moors.

THE BLACK SWAN INN, OLDSTEAD, COXWOLD, YORK YO61 4BL (01347 868387). 18th-century Country Freehouse offers Chalet-style accommodation, en suite, colour TV, central heating, tea/coffee facilities. Real ale. A la Carte Restaurant. Fine wines. Brochure available. [Pets £1 per night]

Pately Bridge

Small town in the heart of beautiful Nidderdale, bordering the Dales National Park. Excellent walking country and a good centre for touring the Dales, Moors, Herriot Country etc.

RIVULET COURT, PATELEY BRIDGE. Spacious 18th century cottage. Comfortable for six, plus children. Owner managed. Private gated garden. Convenient village amenities. Central heating, dishwasher, fridge freezer, laundry. Rates £230-£450. No extras. ♔♔♔♔ Highly Commended (ETC). For colour brochure contact: ANNE RACK, BLAZEFIELD, BEWERLEY, HARROGATE HG 23 5BS (01423 711001).

Pickering

Pleasant market town on southern fringe of North Yorkshire Moors National Park with moated Castle (Norm.). Bridlington 31 miles, Whitby 20, Scarborough 16, Helmsley 13, Malton 3.

MRS ELLA BOWES, BANAVIE, ROXBY ROAD, THORNTON-LE-DALE, PICKERING YO18 7SX (01751 474616). Large stone-built semi-detached house set in Thornton-le-Dale. Ideal for touring. One family bedroom and two double bedrooms, all en suite. All with TV, shaver points, central heating and tea-making facilities. Open all year. Car park, cycle shed. B&B from £18. Welcome Host and Hygiene Certificate held. ETC ◆◆◆◆. [⌂]

VIVERS MILL, MILL LANE, PICKERING YO18 8DJ (01751 473640). Bed and Breakfast in Ancient Watermill in peaceful surroundings. Comfortable TV lounge and en suite rooms with beamed ceilings. Tea making facilities. Ideal for Moors, Historic Railway, Coastline, and York. Bed and Breakfast from £24 [⌂]
e-mail: viversmill@talk21.com
website: www.viversmill.com

THE WHITE SWAN AT PICKERING, YORKSHIRE HOTEL OF THE YEAR 2000. One of only a handful of inns with thr Silver Quality award. Tel: 01751 472288 or www.white-swan.co.uk for brochure. Dog friendly with excellent: service, rooms, food and wine. "...consistently brilliant.." [Pets £7.50 per visit]

MRS S. M. PICKERING, 'NABGATE', WILTON ROAD, THORTON-LE-DALE, PICKERING YO18 7QP (Tel: 01751 474279; Mobile: 0403 804859). All rooms en suite. TV, courtesy trays, central heating. Good food and a very warm welcome for pets and owners. Central for coast, steam railway, moors. Nearby walks for dogs. Own keys. Car park. Hygiene and Welcome Host Certificates. Open all year. Bed and Breakfast from £18.00. ETC ◆◆◆◆ [⌂]

Port Mulgrave

Located 1km north of Hinderwell.

NORTH YORK MOORS NATIONAL PARK. Stone cottage sleeps 4 in North York Moors National Park. Seaview near Cleveland coastal footpath. Log fire, non-smoking. Whitby 9 miles. Brochure available (Tel & Fax: 01642 613888) [⌂]
e-mail: JHiley1679@aol.com

Rathmell

Village 2 miles north-west of Long Preston.

FIELD HOUSE, RATHMELL, SETTLE (01729 840234; Fax: 01729 840775). Sleep 2-10. Working sheep farm. Cottages with lovely views of countryside. Open fires, cobbled courtyards and attractive garden. 4 miles from Settle. Prices from £190 to £570. Colour brochure available. Pets welcome. ETC ♔♔♔♔ Highly Commended
E-mail: rosehyslop@easynet.co.uk

Rosedale Abbey

Village 6 miles north of Kirkbymoorside, with remains of 12th century priory.

THE WHITE HORSE FARM HOTEL, ROSEDALE ABBEY, NORTH YORKSHIRE YO18 8SE (01751 417239; Fax: 01751 417781). A charming Georgian Country Inn with panoramic views over the Moors. Ideal for walkers. All rooms en suite. BB / DBB. Mid-week breaks available. [⌂]

Scalby Nabs

Hamlet close to Scarborough, yet still in the beautiful North York Moors National Park.

EAST FARM COUNTRY COTTAGES, SCALBY NABS, SCALBY, SCARBOROUGH (01723 506406). Single-storey two-bedroom stone cottages (no steps/stairs) set in the area's prettiest location. Ideal base for walking or touring. £155 - £410 per week. ETC ★★★-★★★★[🐾] website: www.eastfarmcottages.co.uk

Scarborough

Very popular family resort with good sands. York 41 miles, Whitby 20, Bridlington 17, Filey 7.

THE PREMIER HOTEL, ESPLANADE, SOUTH CLIFF, SCARBOROUGH YO11 2UZ (01723 501062) (Fax:01723 501112) The Premier Hotel is situated on the Esplanade. All rooms have private bath/shower and toilet en suite, colour TV, clock-radio, tea/coffee making facilities and full central heating. [Pets £3 per night] E–mail: mike@thepremier.co.uk

SUE AND TONY HEWITT, HARMONY COUNTRY LODGE, LIMESTONE ROAD, BURNISTON, SCARBOROUGH YO13 0DG (0800 2985840). A peaceful retreat set in two acres of private grounds with 360° panoramic views of the National Park and sea. An ideal centre for walking or touring. En suite centrally heated rooms with superb views. Fragrant massage available. B&B from £20.50 to £30. Non smoking, licensed, private parking facilities. ◆◆◆. [🐾 pw!] website: www.spiderweb.co.uk/Harmony

FORGE VALLEY COTTAGES. Three superb stone-built cottages (sleeping 1-5) in delightful village on River Derwent, Gateway to the North Yorks Moors and coast, yet only 10 minutes from Scarborough. Highly equipped, cosy and comfortable — the perfect holiday base. 🏆🏆🏆🏆 Highly Commended. For colour brochure: DAVID OR JANE BEELEY, BARN HOUSE, WESTGATE, OLD MALTON YO17 7HE (01653 698251). [🐾]

ANCHOR GUEST HOUSE, NORTHSTEAD MANOR DRIVE, SCARBOROUGH YO12 6AF (01723 364518). Pets are welcome at this detached hotel overlooking Peasholm Park. Close to beach and swimming pools. All rooms en suite, TV, tea making facilities. Car parking. B&B from £15. [🐾]

KERRY LEE (100% NON SMOKING) HOTEL, 60 TRAFALGAR SQUARE, SCARBOROUGH YO12 7PY (01723 363845). Small North Bay hotel. Open all year. B&B from £12. Also cottage near castle. Log fire, sea view, microwave etc. Sleeps 4 – 6. Non smokers only. [🐾]

HARMONY GUEST HOUSE, PRINCESS ROYAL TERRACE, SCARBOROUGH YO11 2RP (01723 373562). Friendly licensed guest house, near South Bay attractions. We offer quality en suite and four-poster rooms. Excellent food. Bar. Brochure on request. Five bedrooms B&B £20, DB&B £26 [Pets £2 per night].

Skipton

Airedale market town, centre for picturesque Craven district. Fine Castle (14th cent). York 43 miles, Manchester 42, Leeds 26, Harrogate 22, Settle 16.

THE QUEENS ARMS INN, LITTON, SKIPTON BD23 5QJ (01756 770208). The cheerful welcome you receive from Neil and Tanya Thompson is mirrored in the blazing open fire and oaken beams. Comfortable en suite accommodation with views over beautiful Littondale. website: www.yorkshiredales.net/stayat/queens

Over 200 super self-catering Cottages, Houses and Flats throughout the Yorkshire Dales, York, Moors, Coast, Peak and Lake District. For our fully illustrated brochure apply: HOLIDAY COTTAGES (YORKSHIRE) LTD, WATER STREET, SKIPTON (18). BD23 1PB (01756 700872). E-mail:p@holidaycotts.co.uk [🐾]

Thirsk

Market town with attractive square. Excellent touring area. Northallerton 3 miles.

GOLDEN FLEECE HOTEL, MARKET SQUARE, THIRSK YO7 1LL (01845 523108; Fax: 01845 523996). Characterful Coaching Inn offering good food and up to date facilities. All rooms have new bathrooms, satellite TV, phone, trouser press, hairdryer. AA ★★. [🐾]

FOXHILLS HIDEAWAYS, FELIXKIRK, THIRSK YO7 2DS (01845 537575). Scandinavian, heated throughout, linen provided. A supremely relaxed atmosphere on the edge of the North Yorkshire Moors National Park. Open all year. Village pub round the corner. [🐾]

Thresfield

Village 1 mile west of Grassington.

LONG ASHES INN THRESHFIELD, NEAR GRASSINGTON BD23 5PN (01756 752434; Fax: 01756 752937). En suite accommodation, home-cooked food, hand-pulled ales, heated indoor pool, perfect for exploring the Dales. AA & ETC ◆◆◆◆. [🐾] bring own bedding and food bowls. e-mail:info@longashesinn.co.uk
website: www.longashesinn.co.uk

Wensleydale

Possibly the most picturesque of all the Dales, ideal for touring some of the most beautiful parts of Yorkshire and nearby Herriot Country. Kendal 25 miles, Kirkby Stephen 15.

MRS PAT COOPER, MOORCOTE FARM, ELLINGSTRING, MASHAM HG4 4PL (01677 460315). Three delightful cottages around a sunny courtyard, sleeping 4-6. All equipped to very high standard. Children and pets welcome. Open all year round. [Pets £10 per week.]

THE WENSLEYDALE HEIFER INN, WEST WITTON, WENSLEYDALE DL8 4LS (01969 622322; Fax: 01969 624183). A 17th Century Inn of character and style offering eleven en suite bedrooms and 3 Four Posters. Real Ales with Bistro and Bar Food. Home cooking specialising in Fish and Seafood. ETC ★★. [Pets £3 per night, £15 per week]
E–mail: heifer@daelnet.co.uk

MRS SUE COOPER, ST. EDMUNDS, CRAKEHALL, BEDALE DL8 1HP (01677 423584). Set in Swaledale and Wensleydale, these recently renovated cottages are fully equipped and are an ideal base for exploring the Dales and Moors. Sleep 2–7 plus cot. Up to ೯೯೯೯ Commended. Brochure available. [🐾]

West Scrafton

Village 3 miles south of Wensley

ADRIAN CAVE, WESTCLOSE HOUSE (ALLAKER), WEST SCRAFTON, NEAR LEYBURN DL8 4RM (020 8567 4862 for bookings). Traditional stone farmhouse. Three bedrooms sleeping six/seven. Storage heating, microwave, fridge, electric cooker, colour TV. Large barn/playroom and garden. Pets welcome. Ideal for families/walkers. Self-catering from £300 per week. [pw 🐾]

Whitby

Charming resort with harbour and sands. Of note is the 13th-century ruined Abbey. Stockton-on-Tees 34 miles, Scarborough 20, Saltburn-by-the-Sea 19.

THE SHIP, PORT MULGRAVE, HINDERWELL, NEAR WHITBY TS13 5JZ (01947 840303) Traditional family run pub with a choice of Cask conditioned ales and good home cooked meals. B&B in two double/family rooms and two singles. From £16.50pppn. Dogs made very welcome. E-mail: kayhartley@lineone.net

JULIE A. WILSON, THE SEACLIFFE HOTEL, WEST CLIFF, WHITBY Y021 3JX (Tel & Fax: 01947 603139). Friendly family run hotel overlooking the sea. Licensed à la carte restaurant specialising in fresh local seafoods, steaks and vegetarian dishes. ETC/AA four diamonds. Freephone 0800 191747. [🐾]

JOHN & JO HALTON, KIRKLANDS PRIVATE HOTEL, 17 ABBEY TERRACE, WEST CLIFF, WHITBY YO21 3HQ (01947 603868). Bed, Breakfast and Evening Meal. Family-run hotel, good home cooking. Licensed. Some rooms en suite; all have tea/coffee making facilities and colour TV. Pets welcome. [Pets £3 per day]

SNEATON HALL HOTEL, SNEATON, WHITBY YO22 5HP (01947 605929; Fax: 01947 820177). Small, friendly. Three miles south of Whitby. All rooms en suite; tea making facilities, TV. Good food, pleasant gardens. Panoramic sea views. Fully licensed; open to non-residents. Pets most welcome. [Pets £2 to £6 per night]

PARTRIDGE NEST FARM, ESKDALESIDE, SLEIGHTS, WHITBY YO22 5ES (01947 810450). Six caravans on secluded site, five miles from Whitby and sea. Ideal touring centre. All have mains electricity, colour TV, fridge, gas cooker. [Dogs £1 per day per dog]

FAIRHAVEN COUNTRY HOTEL THE COMMON GOATHLAND YO22 5AN (01947 896361; Fax 01947 896099). Edwardian Country House Hotel in the centre of Goathland with glorious moorland views. Home cooked food and fine wines. Ideal base for exploring the Moors. 9 bedrooms, some en suite. Non smoking.
e-mail: royellis@thefairhavenhotel.co.uk
website: www.thefairhavenhotel.co.uk

WHITE ROSE HOLIDAY COTTAGES, NEAR WHITBY. Superior centrally heated village cottages and bungalows. Available all year. Ideal for coast and country. Up to ★★★★. APPLY: MRS J. ROBERTS (PW), 5 BROOK PARK, SLEIGHTS, NEAR WHITBY YO21 1RT (01947 810763) [£5 per week, pw!] website: www.whiterosecottages.com

MR T.R. NOBLE, SUMMERFIELD FARM, HAWSKER, WHITBY YO22 4LA (01947 602677). Six-berth caravan with all modern conveniences, on secluded private farm site. Safe for children and pets. It is two miles from Whitby and 17 miles from Scarborough, near Robin Hood's Bay. Beautiful coast, sandy beach one mile. Many local attractions. Dogs welcome. SAE for details.

MRS JILL McNEIL, SWALLOW HOLIDAY COTTAGES, THE FARM, STAINSACRE, WHITBY YO22 4NT (01947 603790). Discover historic Whitby, pretty fishing villages, countryside with way-marked walks, etc. Four cottages. One or two bedrooms, plus a three bedroom detached house. Private parking. Children and dogs welcome. Non-smoking accommodation available. Weekly rates from £120 to £450. Please phone or write for a brochure. ETC ♙♙♙

York

Historic cathedral city and former Roman Station on River Ouse. Magnificent Minster and 3 miles of ancient walls. Facilities for a wide range of sports and entertainments. Horse-racing on Knavesmire. Bridlington 41 miles, Filey 41, Leeds 24, Harrogate 22.

WEIR CARAVAN PARK, STAMFORD BRIDGE; ALLERTON CARAVAN PARK, NEAR KNARESBOROUGH. Weir Caravan Park is set on the banks of the River Derwent and is the ideal location a holiday that can be as active or relaxed as you want. (01759 371377). Allerton Caravan Park is situated in the heart of Yorkshire. A perfect base to discover a variety of historic towns and villages.(01423 330569). website: www.yorkshireholidayparks.co.uk

MRS SALLY ROBINSON, VALLEY VIEW FARM, OLD BYLAND, HELMSLEY, YORK YO6 5LG (01439 798221). ETC ◆◆◆◆. B&B £30. BB&D £43.50 Working farm, home cooking, table licence, private parking, full central heating, colour TV. Self catering cottages. Kennel and run available. Pets Welcome. [♙pw!]
E–mail: sally@valleyviewfarm.com
Website: www.valleyviewfarm.com

HIGH BELTHORPE, BISHOP WILTON, YORK YO4 1SB (01759 368238; Mobile: 07720 651500). Set on an ancient moated site at the foot of the Yorkshire Wolds, this spacious Victorian farmhouse offers huge breakfasts, open fires, private fishing and fabulous walks. Dogs and owners will love it! Open all year. Prices from £15.00 + VAT. [pw! ♙]

YORK LAKESIDE LODGES, MOOR LANE, YORK YO24 2QU (01904 702346; Fax: 01904 701631). Self-catering pine lodges. Mature parkland setting. Large fishing lake. Nearby superstore with coach to centre every 10 mins. ETC 4-5 Star Self-catering. [pw! Pets £15 per week]
Website: www.yorklakesidelodges.co.uk

3 attractive self-catering choices. 12 miles from York. WOODLEA detached house sleeping 5–6, with kitchen, dining area, large lounge and colour TV, bathroom, cloakroom, 3 bedrooms. BUNGALOW adjacent to farmhouse sleeps 2–4. Kitchen, bathroom, lounge/dining room with colour TV and double bed-settee. Twin room with cot. STUDIO adjacent to farmhouse, sleeping 2. Kitchen, lounge/dining-room with colour TV, twin bedroom, bathroom/toilet. SAE for details: MRS M. S. A. WOODLIFFE, MILL FARM, YAPHAM, POCKLINGTON, YORK YO4 2PH (01759 302172).

MONK FRYSTON HALL HOTEL, MONK FRYSTON, NR YORK & LEEDS LS25 5DU (Tel:01977 682369; Fax: 01977 683544). A perfect retreat for business or pleasure; simply relax in a secluded 30 acre oasis. Enjoy antiques, log fires, fresh flowers, good food, fine wines and cheerful staff! 30 bedrooms. Monk Fryston Hall Restaurant: Superb quality English cuisine. Johansen's Recommended. AA/RAC ★★★. [pw! £5 per night] See entry on page 338
E-mail: reception@monkfryston-hotel.com
Website: www.monkfryston-hotel.com

CLIFTON VIEW GUEST HOUSE, 118/120 CLIFTON, YORK YO3 6BQ (01904 625047). Victorian family-run guest house 12 minutes' walk from City Centre. All rooms have colour TV, tea coffee facilities; most have shower. Private car park. B&B from £13 to £18 p.p.p.n. ETC ◆◆◆ [🛏]

MR G. JACKSON, VICTORIA VILLA GUEST HOUSE, 72 HESLINGTON ROAD, YORK YO10 5AU (01904 631647). Ten minutes' walk from city centre. Comfortable double, twin, single and family bedrooms, all with TV. Open all year. B&B from £13 to £20 per person. Children and pets welcome. [🛏 pw!]

ST. GEORGE'S HOUSE HOTEL, 6 ST. GEORGE'S PLACE, YORK YO24 1DR (01904 625056). Family-run Hotel in quiet cul-de-sac near racecourse. All rooms en suite with colour TV, tea/coffee making facilities. Private parking. Pets welcome. ETC/RAC/AA ◆◆◆. [🛏]
e–mail: sixstgeorg@aol.com
website: www.members.aol.com/sixstgeorg/

WEST YORKSHIRE

Haworth

woof! woof! woof!
Hi, my name is Domino, my mum and dad have a fabulous country cottage in the village of Haworth, Yorkshire. Great for long rambling walks and fabulous scenery. Our cottage is well equipped and is ideal for dogs who want to bring along up to four of their human friends too. I have left you my tried and tested guide to some of my favourite walks in Brontë country!

Full colour literature available on request
Telephone:
01943 434333 (Day)
01535 643280 (Eve/Weekends)
www.bronte-cottage.co.uk

Bingley

Town on River Aire five miles north-west of Bradford.

MRS P. OXLEY, FIVE RISE LOCKS HOTEL, BECK LANE, BINGLEY BD16 4DD (01274 565296; Fax: 01274 568828). Charming Victorian Mill owner's house in mature terraced gardens, minutes walk from the famous Five Rise Locks. Individually designed and furnished en suite bedrooms with panoramic views of the Aire Valley. Relaxed atmosphere complemented by interesting menus and wine list. ETC SILVER AWARD , RAC DINING AWARD, ETC/RAC/AA ◆◆◆◆ [🛏].
e-mail: info@five-rise-locks.co.uk
website: www.five-rise-locks.co.uk

Calderdale

Administrative District of West Yorkshire, industrial museum in town.

ASHENHURST COTTAGE, TODMORDEN, IN CALDERDALE, WEST YORKSHIRE. Our warm stone cottage is quiet and comfortable with everything provided. Convienient for town and direct access to the country from the door. Ideal for touring/walking in Lancashire and Yorkshire. Non-smoking. Open May - October. Sleeps 2/4. Prices £157 - £192 for two. Brochure available from MRS HEATHER GRIEVE, ASHENHURST HOUSE, TODMORDEN OL14 8DS (01706 812086) ★★ Self-Catering. ♔♔♔ Commended [pets £5]

Haworth

Above the River Worth Valley. The one-time home of the Brontë Family, now a museum.

BRONTË COTTAGE, QUEEN STREET, HAWORTH BD22 8QB (01535 643280). Dogs very, very welcome. Domino (Dalmatian) welcomes you to our fabulous country cottage in a beautiful village with superb moorland. Full colour literature on request.[pw! 🐕] website: www.bronte-cottage.co.uk

CHANNEL ISLANDS

Jersey

• JERSEY •

HOLIDAY Three bungalows a few metres direct access to beach. Reasonable *BUNGALOWS* rates.Electric cooking and heating. Near golf course, shops and bus. Family accommodation with cot. Open most of the year with reduced rates out of season. Well equipped. Jersey is a beautiful place to visit all year round. Plenty to see and do on the island. Excellent restaurants, shops (no VAT) and entertainment. Easy access to the other Channel Islands and France for day trips. Access by air and boat from Poole and Weymouth (both take cars). Please phone **(01534) 853333** early evening, or write to: **Mrs. P. Johnson, 'Mon Repos', Coast Road, Grouville, Jersey C.I. JE3 9FG PETS MOST WELCOME (FREE)**

MRS. P. JOHNSON, 'MON REPOS', COAST ROAD, GROUVILLE, JERSEY JE3 9FG (01534 853333). Three well-equipped bungalows. Direct access to beach, Near golf course, shops and bus. Reasonable rates. Electric cooking and heating. Family accommodation with cot. [🐕]

FHG PUBLICATIONS

publish a large range of well-known accommodation guides. We will be happy to send you details or you can use the order form at the back of this book.

INNFINITE HOSPITALITY. (01292 284883 or Mobile: 0780 800 2543) Small Scottish Hotels and Inns offering a very personal touch. Enjoy a range of outdoor activities including golf, fishing, cycling and hill walking. Unwind in the relaxing atmosphere of your hotel and enjoy good food from "Scotland's Larder", fine ales and an excellent selection of whiskies.

ABERDEEN, BANFF & MORAY

Banchory, Crathie, Turriff

Raemoir House Hotel and Self-Catering Apartments

STB ★★★★ Self-Catering

Raemoir House Hotel is part of an idyllic 3,500 acre estate, situated on Royal Deeside and within easy reach of Aberdeen. Within the grounds of the hotel the original coach house and stable buildings have been converted into four de luxe self-catering cottages with one, two or three bedrooms, sleeping up to 8 people. Full details available on request. Pets always welcome

Raemoir House Hotel, Raemoir, Banchory, Kincardineshire AB31 4ED
Tel: 01330 824884   Fax: 01330 822171   See colour advertisement on page 48.

Inver Hotel *Crathie, Aberdeenshire AB35 5UL. Tel: (013397 42345)*
Family run Hotel located in the village of Crathie, close to Balmoral Castle, situated on Deeside Road (A93) amidst stunning scenery with Grampian and Cairngorm mountains as a spectacular backdrop. All 9 bedrooms are en-suite with bath and shower along with TV and tea/coffee making facilities. Full Scottish breakfast served. Friendly lounge bar with large selection of malt whiskies. Main area of Hotel has original open hearth fire. Residents' lounge for quiet relaxation. Lovely beer garden and good food served all day. Leisure pursuits include: Fishing, Deerstalking, Mountaineering, Mountain-Biking and Ski-ing. Highland Games held every week all throughout Summer with the Royal Family attending the Braemar Games.

HOLIDAY COTTAGES

The Estate lies along the beautiful Deveron River and our traditional stone cottages nestle in individual seclusion. The sea is only nine miles away, and the market town of Turriff only two miles.
Terms: from £145 weekly. Special Winter lets. 10 cottages sleeping 6-9. Children and reasonable dogs welcome. STB Inspected.
For a brochure contact: Mrs P. Bates, HOLIDAY COTTAGES, Forglen Estate, Turriff, Aberdeenshire AB53 4JP   Tel: 01888 562918/562518; Fax: 01888 562252

See also Colour Advertisement on page 48

FHG

Visit the 🖼 website

www.holidayguides.com

for details of the wide choice of accommodation featured in the full range of FHG titles

Banchory

Small town on River Dee 11 miles north-west of Stonehaven.

WELLHEAD COTTAGE, UPPER ARBEADIE ROAD, BANCHORY AB31 4EP. Very private, well equipped cottage. Half-a-mile from Banchory. Situated on two acres with play area, garden and woodland. Terms from £190 to £295. APPLY: MS JUNE MITCHELL, 'KE-LYN', PANTOCH, BANCHORY AB31 5PY (Tel & Fax: 01330 824325).

RAEMOIR HOUSE HOTEL, RAEMOIR, BANCHORY, KINCARDINSHIRE, AB31 4ED (01330 824884; Fax: 01330 822171). Original coach house and stable buildings have been converted into four de luxe self-catering cottages with one, two or three bedrooms, sleeping up to 8 people. Full details available on request. STB ★★★★.

Crathie

Village on River Dee, with famous church used by Royalty when in residence at nearby Balmoral Castle.

INVER HOTEL, CRAITHIE, BY BRAEMAR, ABERDEENSHIRE AB35 5YR. (013397 42345)Family run Hotel located in the village of Crathie, close to Balmoral Castle. All 9 bedrooms are en-suite with bath and shower along with TV and tea/coffee making facilities. Lounge bar, residents' lounge and beer garden. Ideal for fishing, deerstalking, mountaineering and ski-ing. Highland Games held throughout the summer. Contact Fraser Mathieson.

Ellon

Small town 15 miles north of Aberdeen.

MRS CHRISTINE STAFF, SUNNYBRAE FARM, GIGHT, METHLICK, ELLON AB41 7JA (01651 806456). Comfortable accommodation on a working farm situated in a quiet, peaceful location with superb views. Centrally situated for many places of interest. Double and twin rooms, all en suite. Open all year. Bed and Breakfast from £18. STB ★★. [🛏]

Grantown-On-Spey

Market town 19 miles south of Forres.

MR AND MRS J. R. TAYLOR, MILTON OF CROMDALE, GRANTOWN-ON-SPEY PH26 3PH (01479 872415). Fully modernised Cottage with large garden and views of River Spey and Cromdale Hills. Golf, tennis and trekking within easy reach. Fully equipped except linen. Two double bedrooms. Shower, refrigerator, electric cooker, colour television. Car desirable. Open March to October. £100 per week. Children and pets welcome. [🛏]

Turriff

Small town in agricultural area, 9 miles south of Banff.

MRS P E. BATES, HOLIDAY COTTAGES, FORGLEN ESTATE, TURRIFF AB53 4JP (01888 562918/562518). Estate on the beautiful Deveron River. Sea only nine miles away, Turriff two miles. 10 cottages sleeping 6–9. From £145 weekly. Special Winter lets. Children and reasonable dogs welcome. [🛏]

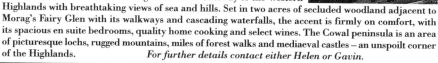

See also Colour Advertisement on page 50

Please mention *Pets Welcome*
when enquiring about accommodation featured in these pages.

Appin

Mountainous area bounded by Loch Linnhe, Glan Creran and Glen Coe.

MRS J PERY, ARDTUR, APPIN PA38 4DD (Tel: 01631 730223 or 0162 834172)
Two adjacent cottages in secluded surroundings. Ideal for hill walking, climbing, pony trekking, boating and fly fishing. Shop one mile; sea 200 yards; car essential; pets allowed.
e-mail: pery@eurobell.co.uk

Ballachulish

Impressively placed village at entrance to Glencoe and on Loch Leven. Magnificent mountain scenery including Sgorr Dhearg (3362 ft). Good centre for boating, climbing and sailing. Glasgow 89 miles, Oban 38, Fort William 14, Kinlochleven 9.

Cottages and Chalets in Natural Woodland sleeping two to six people. The Glencoe area is lovely for walking and perfect for nature lovers too. Regret no smokers. No VAT. Brochure available.
APPLY: HOUSE IN THE WOOD HOLIDAYS, GLENACHULISH, BALLACHULISH PA49 4JZ (01855 811379). Pets welcome. [🐾]

Dalmally

Small town in Glen Orchy. To the south-west is Loch Awe with romantic Kilchurn Castle (14th century) Edinburgh 98 miles, Glasgow 69, Ardrishaig 42, Oban 25, Inveraray 16.

ARDBRECKNISH HOUSE, SOUTH LOCHAWESIDE, BY DALMALLY, ARGYLL PA33 1BH (01866 833223/833242). Self-catering apartments and holiday cottages set in 20 acres of garden woodland on the south shore of Loch Awe. Breathtaking panoramic views over loch, mountain and glen. [Pets £15 per week]
E–mail: ardbreck01@aol.com
Website: www.ardbrecknish.com

ROCKHILL WATERSIDE COUNTRY HOUSE, ARDBRECKNISH, BY DALMALLY PA33 1BH (01866 833218). 17th Century guest house on waterside with spectacular views over Loch Awe. Five delightful rooms with all modern facilities. First class home cooking with much home grown produce.

Dunoon

Lively resort reached by car ferry from Gourock. Cowal Highland Gathering held at end of August.

ABBOT'S BRAE HOTEL, WEST BAY, DUNOON PA23 7QJ (01369 705021; Fax: 01369 701191). Small welcoming hotel at the gateway to the Western Highlands with breathtaking views. Comfortable, spacious, en suite bedrooms, quality home cooking and select wines. [🐾].
e–mail: enquiry@abbotsbrae.co.uk
website: www.abbotsbrae.co.uk

ENMORE HOTEL, MARINE PARADE, DUNOON PA23 8HH (01369 702230; Fax: 01369 702148). Small luxury Hotel with well-tended garden, situated overlooking the beautiful Firth of Clyde. Own shingle beach. Promenade and superb walking in the hills and forests within five minutes' drive. Owners have two young labrador cross dogs. STB ★★★★ HOTEL. AA ★★. AA Rosette. [Pets £3.50 per night, pw!]
e–mail: enmorehotel@btinternet.com
website: www.enmorehotel.co.uk

Duror of Appin

River running west into Cuil Bay on the east shore of Loch Linnhe.

MRS ELSPETH MALCOLM, ACHADH NAN SGIATH, CUIL BAY, DUROR OF APPIN PA38 4DA (01631 740259). Sleeps 4 adults; 2 children. Spacious flat. Own entrance. Uninterrupted views of Loch Linnhe. One double and two twin-bedded rooms, sittingroom, bathroom/ toilet; kitchen/breakfast room – all electric. Linen provided, small charge. Three hotels near; village shop one mile, sea 500 yards. Weekly terms from £80 to £230 according to season. Open all year.

Loch Goil

Peaceful loch running from Lochgoilhead to Loch Long.

Five self-catering Chalets on the shores of Loch Goil in the heart of Argyll Forest Park. Fully equipped except linen. Colour TV, fitted kitchen, carpeted. Pets very welcome. Open all year. DARROCH MHOR, CARRICK CASTLE, LOCH GOIL PA24 8AF (01301 703249/703432). [🐾]

Lochgoilhead

Village at head of Loch Goil in Argyll

MRS ROSEMARY DOLAN, THE SHOREHOUSE INN, LOCHGOILHEAD PA24 8AJ (01301 703340). Small friendly informal Inn with panoramic views down Loch Goil. Seven letting rooms, Bar and Restaurant. Local amenities include swimming pool, golf course, tennis, bowls, water sports, fishing. Good area for walking. Rates from £16 pp B&B, en suite £20 pp. Well-trained dogs welcome. [🐾]

Oban

Popular Highland resort and port, yachting centre, ferry services to Inner and Outer Hebrides. Sandy bathing beach at Ganavan Bay. McCaig's Tower above town is Colosseum replica built in 1890s.

WILLOWBURN HOTEL, CLACHAN SEIL, BY OBAN PA34 4TJ (01852 300276). Peaceful, relaxing, informal and addictive. Superb setting overlooking the Sound of Seil. Walk, fish, birdwatch or simply just laze. Tempted? Bring your owners too! [🐾]

TRALEE BAY HOLIDAYS, BENDERLOCH BY OBAN, PA37 1QR (01631 720255/217). Overlooking Ardmucknish Bay. The wooded surroundings and sandy beaches make Tralee the ideal destination for a self catering lodge or caravan holiday anytime of the year. STB ★★★★.
e-mail: tralee@easynet.co.uk
website: www.tralee.com
FREE Classified listing:

ELSPETH CAMPBELL, ASKNISH COTTAGE, ARDUAINE, BY OBAN PA34 4XQ (01852 200247). Superb views overlooking islands. Ideal base for touring, activities or relaxation; walking, boattrips, diving, horse riding. Wild garden, tame owner. Double/twin, prices from £17.00. Pets welcome. [Pets £1 per night, £3 per week.]

Well equipped Scandinavian chalets in breathtaking scenery near Oban. Chalets sleep 4–7, are widely spaced and close to Loch Tralaig. Car parking. From £205 per week per chalet. Available March to January. STB ★★ Self Catering. APPLY – ANNE & ROBIN GREY, ELERAIG HIGHLAND CHALETS, KILNINVER, BY OBAN PA34 4UX (01852 200225) [🐾]
Website: www.scotland2000.com/eleraig

MELFORT PIER AND HARBOUR, KILMELFORD, BY OBAN PA34 4XD (01852 200333; Fax: 01852 200329). Superb lochside houses each with sauna, spa, satellite TV, telephone, on the shores of Loch Melfort. Excellent base for touring Argyll and the Isles. From £60 to £185 per house/night. Minimum stay of two consecutive nights. Boats and pets very welcome. STB ★★★★★ Self Catering. [Pets £10 per stay]
E–mail: melharbour@aol.com.
Website: www.scotland2000.com/melfort

LAGNAKEIL HIGHLAND LODGES, LERAGS, OBAN, ARGYLL PA34 4SE (01631 562746; Fax: 01631 570225). Our Timber Lodges are nestled in 7 acres of scenic wooded glen overlooking Loch Feochan, only 3.5 miles from the picturesque harbour town of Oban: "Gateway to the Isles". Fully equipped Lodges to a high standard, including linen and towels, country pub a short walk. O.A.P. discount. Free loch fishing. Special Breaks from £38 per lodge per night, weekly from £170. Our colour brochure will tell lots more. [Pets £10 per week].
E–mail:lagnakeil@aol.com
Website: www.lagnakeil.co.uk

MRS LINDA BATTISON, COLOGIN FARM HOLIDAY CHALETS, LERAGS GLEN, BY OBAN PA34 4SE (01631 564501; Fax: 01631 566925). Cosy timber chalets, sleep two to six, all conveniences. Situated on farm, wildlife abundant. Games room, Launderette, licensed bar serving home-cooked food. Free fishing. Playpark. Live entertainment. [pw! Pets £1.50 per night, £10.50 per week.]

Roseneath

Village on west side of Gare Loch 2 miles north east of Kilcreggan.

ROSNEATH CASTLE CARAVAN PARK, ROSNEATH, NEAR HELENSBURGH G84 0YS (01436 831208). Holiday Park with licensed bistro and shop, Fun Club, outdoor play area for children and state of the art touring block. Space for 28 touring caravans.

Strontian

Beautifully situated at head of Loch Sunart which stretches 20 miles to the sea..

SEAVIEW GRAZINGS HOLIDAYS, STRONTIAN PH36 4HZ (01967 402191). Quality self catering in Scandinavian log houses overlooking Loch Sunart. Sleep up to eight. TV, washer/dryer etc. Pubs/hotels five minutes. Pets welcome. Ideal touring centre. Send for colour brochure. [🐾]
e-mail: seaviewgrazings@amserve.net
website: www.ardnamurchan.com

Tarbert

Fishing port on isthmus connecting Kintyre to the mainland.

AMANDA MINSHALL, TARBERT, DUNMORE COURT, WEST LOCH, PA29 6XZ, (01880 820 654). Four cottages on 1000 acre estate with three miles of shore on West Loch Tarbert. Bird-watching, sailing, sea fishing, unrestricted walking, Terms from £165 - £425. ASSC member. STB ★★★/★★★★ SELF CATERING [Pets £15 per week].
e-mail: dunmorecourtsc@cs.com

WEST LOCH HOTEL, BY TARBERT, LOCH FYNE PA29 6YF (01880 820283). Attractive traditional coaching inn on the shore of West Loch. Bright, comfortable accommodation, cosy atmosphere, superb food and wines. Open all year. [🐾]

MISS V. BARKER, BARFAD FARMLANDS, TARBERT PA29 6YH (Tel & Fax: 01880 820549). 3 Stone cottages set in 80 acres of woodland with beaches and beautiful scenery. All cottages include colour TV, laundry room (shared), parking, electricity by £1 card meter, electric heating, linen and towels. Pets welcome. [🐾]

Peaceful, unspoilt West Highland estate. Traditional Cottages, well equipped including TV, dinghy in summer and open fires. Sleep 4–10. Pets welcome. Walks, pony trekking, golf nearby. APPLY SOPHIE JAMES, SKIPNESS CASTLE, BY TARBERT PA29 6XU (01880 760207; Fax: 01880 760208). [🐾]

Ayr, Ballantrae, Catacol, Lamlash, Monkton

HORIZON HOTEL Esplanade, Ayr KA7 1DT

A welcome guest. *In all my years of experience of this business, I have never received a complaint about a dog slamming bedroom doors late at night, talking loudly in the corridors or driving away noisily from the car park when other guests are trying to sleep. Never has a dog made cigarette burns on the carpets, furniture or in the bath. No dog has ever stolen my towels, sheets or ashtrays. No cheque written by a dog has ever bounced and no dog has ever tried to pay with a stolen credit card. Never has a dog insulted my waitress or complained about food or wine. Neither have we ever had a dog who was drunk. In short you are welcome whenever you wish to come to this hotel and if you can vouch for your master, you are welcome to bring him along too!!*

Ayr's only seafront hotel, just five minutes' walk from town centre. Lunches, high teas, dinners and bar suppers served. Phone for colour brochure.

Under the personal supervision of Mr & Mrs J. Meikle and Mr & Mrs A.H. Meikle.

Tel: 01292 264384   Fax: 01292 264011

E-mail: mail@horizonhotel.com   Web-site: www.horizonhotel.com

LAGGAN HOUSE LEISURE PARK

Roger & Marilyn Bourne

Tel: 01465 831229
Fax: 01465 831511

STB ★★★★

Peaceful parkland setting in the grounds of an old country house overlooking secluded countryside and the sea. Luxury caravans and chalets for hire, with heated indoor pool, sauna, solarium, bar and children's playground. Pets are welcome. The park provides a superb base from which to explore the magnificent coastline, the inland hills and Galloway Forest. Local activities include fishing, golf, cycling, walking or just doing nothing. Short Breaks available.

Catacol Bay hotel

Catacol, Isle of Arran KA27 8HN
Tel: 01770 830231 Fax: 01770 830350

Escape from the pressures of mainland life. Stay awhile by clear shining seas, rocky coast, breathtaking hills and mountains. Comfortable, friendly, small country house hotel where good cooking is our speciality. Extensive bar menu, meals are served from noon until 10pm. Centrally heated. Open all year. Details of Special Breaks and brochure on request. Les Routiers. Children and pets welcome.

Find us on the web at www.catacol.co.uk   E-mail: davecatbay@lineone.net

LILYBANK Lamlash, Isle of Arran KA27 8LS

Beautifully situated on the shores of Lamlash Bay, overlooking the Holy Isle. Comfortable en suite bedrooms. Delicious Breakfasts using local produce. Restricted smoking areas. Private Parking and gardens. Well-behaved dogs welcome. **For your brochure Tel/Fax: 01770 600230**   STB ★★★★ *GUESTHOUSE*

e-mail: colin369.richardson@virgin.net • website: www.SmoothHound.co.uk/hotels/lilybank

Muirhouse Guest House   Tel: 01292 475726

Muirhouse, Kilmarnock Road, Monkton, by Prestwick KA9 2RJ

A warm, helpful welcome awaits all in this small family-owned guesthouse in quiet location, within easy reach of Airport and station. Ideal for golf, bowling, yachting and touring. All rooms have central heating, colour TV and tea making facilities. En suite rooms available. Comfortable lounge and Dining Room.

Ayr

Popular family holiday resort with sandy beaches. Excellent shopping; theatre; racecourse.

HORIZON HOTEL, ESPLANADE, AYR KA7 1DT (01292 264383; Fax: 01292 264011). Highly recommended for golf breaks; special midweek rates. Coach parties welcome. Lunches, high teas, dinners and bar suppers served. Phone for colour brochure. [🅣]
E–mail: mail@horizonhotel.com
Web-site: www.horizonhotel.com

Ballantrae

Small fishing port 12 miles south-west of Girvan.

ROGER AND MARILYN BOURNE, LAGGAN HOUSE LEISURE PARK, BALLANTRAE KA26 0LL (Tel: 01465 831229; Fax: 01465 831511). Luxury caravans and chalets for hire. Overlooking secluded countryside and sea. Heated indoor pool, sauna, solarium, bar, children's playground. Short Breaks available. [Pets £1 per night].

Brodick (Isle of Arran)

Small port and resort on east coast of Arran. Brodick Castle (NTS) 2 km north.

MR GILMORE, ORMIDALE HOTEL, BRODICK, ISLE OF ARRAN KA27 8BY (01770 302 293; Fax: 01770 302 098). Family owned inn, very convenient for both hill-walking anf golfing. Excellent bar meals, malt whiskies and CAMRA recommended ales. Three twin rooms, three double rooms, one family room, one single room. All rooms with colour television and tea making facilities. B&B £28.00 en suite, £23.00 standard.
E-mail: reception@ormidale-hotel.co.uk
Website: www.ormidale-hotel.co.uk

Catacol (Isle of Arran)

Location on north side of Catacol Bay on north-west coast of Arran.

CATACOL BAY HOTEL, CATACOL, LOCHRANZA KA27 8HN (01770 830231; Fax: 01770 830350). Comfortable, friendly, small country house hotel where good cooking is our speciality. Extensive bar menu, meals are served from noon until 10pm. Centrally heated. Open all year. Details of Special Breaks and brochure on request. Les Routiers. Children and pets welcome.[🐾]
E-mail: davecatbay@lineone.net
Website: www.catacol.co.uk

Girvan

Fishing town and resort at mouth of Water of Girvan, 17 miles south-west of Ayr.

MRS ISOBEL KYLE, HAWKHILL FARM, OLD DAILLY, GIRVAN KA26 9RD (Tel: 01465 871232). Comfortable old farmhouse, former coaching inn, spacious rooms with private facilities. Two double, one twin. Tranquil spot. Home-baking etc., walking, gardens, pony trekking, golf, Culzean castle, Burns country. STB ★★★★ B&B [🐾]
e-mail: hawkhill@infinnet.co.uk
website: www.sujo.com/cte/hawkhill.htm

Lamlash (Isle of Arran)

Small port on the east coast of Arran.

LILYBANK, LAMLASH, ISLE OF ARRAN KA27 8LS. Situated on the shores of Lamlash Bay, over-looking Holy Isle. Comfortable en suite bedrooms. Delicious breakfasts using local produce. Restricted smoking areas. Private parking and gardens. Well-behaved dogs welcome. STB ★★★★ Guest House. Tel & Fax: 01770 600230 for your brochure. [🐾
e-mail: colin369.richardson@virgin.net
website: www.SmoothHound.co.uk/hotels/lilybank

Monkton

Small village near Prestwick Airport, 4 miles north of Ayr.

MUIRHOUSE GUEST HOUSE, MUIRHOUSE, KILMARNOCK ROAD, MONKTON, BY PRESTWICK KA9 2RJ (01292 475726). Small, family owned guest house in quiet location, within easy reach of airport and station. All rooms with central heating, colour TV and tea making facilities. En suite available.

Bonchester Bridge

Village on Rule Water, 6 miles east of Hawick. To east is Bonchester Hill surmounted by ancient earthworks.

WAUCHOPE COTTAGES, BONCHESTER BRIDGE, HAWICK TD9 9TG (01450 860630). Sleeps 2-4. Three detatched cottages each with kennel in enclosed garden. Quiet location with stunning scenery near Wauchope Forest. Ideal for walking. STB ★★★ SELF CATERING. [🐾]

Jedburgh

Small town on Jed Water, 10 miles north east of Hawick. Ruins of abbey founded in 1138.

ALAN & CHRISTINE SWANSTON, FERNIEHIRST MILL LODGE & RIDING CENTRE, JEDBURGH TD8 6PQ (Tel & Fax: 01835 863279). A chalet style guest house set in grounds of 25 acres. All rooms en suite with tea/coffee making facilities. Licensed for residents. Well behaved pets (including horses) welcome by arrangement. STB, AA, RAC, ABRS, TRSS Approved. [🐾]

Innerleithen

Small town at confluence of Leithen Water and River Tweed, 6 miles south east of Peebles.

MRS J. A. CAIRD, THE SCHOOL HOUSE, TRAQUAIR, INNERLEITHEN EH44 6PS(Tel & Fax: 01896 830425). Comfortable house at edge of picturesque Traquair on the S.U.W. Spectacular views up Tweed Valley. Within three miles of golf, fishing. Historical house. Open garden.

Kelso

Market town 18 miles north west of Hawick and 20 miles south west of Berwick-upon-Tweed.

WESTWOOD HOUSE, OVERLOOKING SCOTLAND'S FAMOUS RIVER TWEED. (07788 134 832 Fax: 01263 712128) Enclosed and secluded riverside cottage with walled gardens and own private island. Sleep 2-8 persons plus child, from £250 per week. 2 person discounts. STB ★★★ For brochure contact: DEBBIE CRAWFORD, PIPPIN HEATH FARM, HOLT, NORFOLK NR25 6SS [🐾] E-mail: westwood.house@lineone.net

Peebles

On the River Tweed, famous for tweeds and knitwear.

MS S. BELL, THE CROOK INN, TWEEDSMUIR, PEBBLES ML12 6QN (01899 880272; Fax: 01899 880294). All rooms en-suite. Full breakfast included in charge. Bar meals always available as well as dining-room menu in evenings. Children & Pets welcome. E-mail: thecrookinn@btinternet.com Website: www.crookinn.co.uk

West Linton

Village on east side of Pentland Hills, 7 miles south-west of Penicuik. Edinburgh 18 miles.

MRS C. M. KILPATRICK, SLIPPERFIELD HOUSE, WEST LINTON EH46 7AA (Tel & Fax: 01968 660401). Two excellently equipped converted cottages set in 100 acres of lochs and woodlands. America Cottage sleeps 6, STB ★★★★. Loch Cottage sleeps 4, STB ★★★ Available all year - Central Heating. Car essential. Self Catering. [🐾]
E-mail: cottages@slipperfield.com
Website: www.slipperfield.com

DUMFRIES & GALLOWAY

Annan,

Annan

Victorian red brick town overlooking River Annan, famous for trout and salmon.

Auchencairn

Spectacular cliffs, and sandy beaches lie near this whitewashed village.

Borgue

Village south west of Kircudbright, setting for Robert Louis Stevenson's "Master of Ballantrae".

FOUR QUALITY CARAVAN PARKS IN BEAUTIFUL S.W. SCOTLAND. Touring caravans, lodges and holiday caravans to rent or buy. Family camping. For details: MR D. GILLESPIE, BRIGHOUSE BAY, BORGUE, KIRKCUDBRIGHTSHIRE, DUMFRIES & GALLOWAY DG6 4TS (01557 870267). E-mail: fhg@gillespie.leisure.co.uk

Castle Douglas

Old market town at the northern end of Carlingwalk Loch, good touring centre for Galloway.

MR P. W. BALL, BARNCROSH FARM, CASTLE DOUGLAS DG7 1TX (Tel: 01556 680216; Fax: 01556 680442). Self catering. Comfortable Cottages and flats. Fully equipped, including linen. Colour TV. Children and dogs welcome. Beautiful rural surroundings. Brochure on request. STB ★/★★★ [Pets £20 weekly]
E-mail: enq@barncros.demon.co.uk
Website: www.aboutscotland.com/south/barncros.html

MRS CELIA PICKUP, "CRAIGADAM", CASTLE DOUGLAS DG7 3HU (Tel & Fax: 01556 650233). Family-run 18th century famhouse. All bedrooms en suite. Billiard room. Lovely oak-panelled dining room offering Cordon Bleu cooking using local produce such as venison, pheasant and salmon. Trout fishing, walking and golfing available. STB ★★★★ Farmhouse, RAC ◆◆◆◆, AA ◆◆◆◆ . [🛏]

URR VALLEY HOTEL, ERNESPIE RD, CASTLE DOUGLAS, DUMFRIES & GALOWAY DG7 3JG. (01556 502188; Fax: 01556 504055) Hotel within easy walking distance of Castle Douglas and Galloway. Sandy beaches, grouse moors, harbour villages and forest walks. Log fires, Sportsman's bar, 17 en suite rooms, colour TV, tea/coffee making facilities, and direct dial telephones. AA ★★ [🛏]

Dalbeattie

Small granite town on Kirkgunzeon Lane (or Burn), 13 miles south-west of Dumfries.

CLONYARD HOUSE HOTEL COLVEND DALBEATTIE DG5 4QW (01556 630372; Fax 01556 630422) AA/STB ★★. Situated in 6 acres of wooded grounds within the Colvend National Scenic area, close to the Solway Coast. Family run hotel. All bedrooms en suite, good selection of wines and malt whiskies, freshly prepared cuisine.
e-mail: nickthompson@clara.net

Dumfries

County town of Dumfriesshire and a former seaport, Dumfries contains many interesting buildings including an 18th century windmill containing a camera obscura. Robert Burns lived in the town before his death in 1796

BAREND HOLIDAY VILLAGE, DALBEATTIE (01387 780663; Fax: 01387 780283). Escape to the quiet and comfort of our centrally heated, well equipped Scandinavian style log chalets overlooking loch and golf course. Bar, restaurant, indoor heated pool and sauna on site, beach nearby. Brochure on request. [Pets £20 per week]
Website: www.barendholidayvillage.co.uk

DAVID & GILL STEWART, GUBHILL FARM, AE, NEAR DUMFRIES DG1 1RL (01387 860648). Listed farm steading flats in peaceful pastoral valley surrounded by wooded hills and forest lanes. Nature-friendly management. Lower flat wheelchair compatible. Riding, fishing, mountain biking and hillwalking all nearby.
E–mail: stewart@creaturefeature.freeserve.co.uk

Gatehouse of Fleet

Small town near mouth of Water of Fleet, 6 miles north-west of Kirkcudbright.

RUSKO HOLIDAYS, RUSKO, GATEHOUSE OF FLEET, CASTLE DOUGLAS. DG7 2BS (01557 814215; Fax: 01557 814679). Spacious farmhouse and cosy, comfortable cottages near beaches, hills and golf course. Walking, fishing, tennis, pets, including horses, welcome. Rates £150-£600. ★★ to ★★★ Self Catering..

Glenluce

Village 9 miles east of Stranraer.

KELVIN HOUSE HOTEL, GLENLUCE, NEWTON STEWART DG8 0PP (Tel/Fax: 01581 300303). Situated in picturesque village of Glenluce. Long renowned for its good food, good cheer and cosy bedrooms. STB ★★★ AA★★
E-mail: kelvinbridge@lineone.net
Website: www.kelvin-house.co.uk

Kirkcudbright

Small town on River Dee estuary 10 miles south of Castle Douglas.

BAY COTTAGE, ROSS BAY, KIRKCUDBRIGHT DG6 4TR. Traditional waterside farm cottage. Level access. Mooring available; suitable for sailing and fishing. Quiet peaceful location with abundance of wildlife. Well behaved pets welcome. MR & MRS B. FINLAY, MANOR COTTAGE, BORGUE DG6 4TR (01557 870381). [1 dog free, 2 dogs £10, 3 dogs £20]

Lockerbie

Market town 11 miles east of Dumfries.

LOCKERBIE MANOR COUNTRY HOTEL, LOCKERBIE DG11 2RG (01576 202610/ 203939). Splendid Georgian mansion house set in 78 acres of beautiful grounds. Ideal base for exploring countryside. Single, twin, double and family rooms, all en suite, and equipped with colour TV, tea-making etc. [pw! ♥]

Moffat

At head of lovely Annandale, grand mountain scenery. Good centre for rambling, climbing, angling and golf. The 'Devil's Beef Tub' is 5 miles, Edinburgh 52 miles, Peebles 33, Dumfries 21.

BUCCLEUCH ARMS HOTEL, HIGH STREET, MOFFAT DG10 9ET (01683 220003; Fax: 01683 221291). Ideally situated for exploring the unspoilt South West of Scotland. Single, double/twin and family rooms, all with private bathroom. Open all year. B&B from £40 single, £32.50 double/twin. [♥]

ANNANDALE ARMS HOTEL, HIGH STREET, MOFFAT DG1O 9HF (01683 220013 Fax: 01683 221395). A warm welcome is offered at the Annandale Arms to dogs with well-mannered and house-trained owners. Excellent restaurant and a relaxing panelled bar. Large private parking area. £64.00 per room for two; £45.00 per room for one. [♥]

MORLICH LICENSED GUEST HOUSE, BALLPLAY ROAD, MOFFAT DG10 9JU (01683 220589; Fax: 01683 221032). Set in beautiful 'Burns Country' Morlich House is a superb Victorian country house. Rooms are en suite with TV, radio alarm, tea/coffee and telephone, four-poster available. Private car park. B&B from £20pp, 3 course evening meal from £9.50. Weekly terms. Open Feb/Nov. STB ★★. [♥]

BARNHILL SPRINGS COUNTRY GUEST HOUSE, MOFFAT DG10 9QS (01683 220580). Early Victorian country house overlooking some of the finest views of Upper Annandale. Comfortable accommodation, residents' lounge with open fire. Situated on the Southern Upland Way half-a-mile from A74/M74 Moffat Junction. Pets free of charge. Bed & Breakfast from £20; Evening Meal (optional) from £14. STB ★★ Guest House. AA ◆◆◆. [♥]

New Galloway

Small town on west side of Water of Ken valley, 17 miles north of Kirkcudbright.

LEAMINGTON HOTEL, HIGH STREET, NEW GALLOWAY DG7 3RN (01644 420350). Unspoiled scenic beauty. Ideally situated for excursions, golf, fishing, sailing, walking, cycling or bird watching. Evening meals. Private parking. Cats, dogs and other animals welcome. [♥]
Website: www.leamington-hotel.com

DUNBARTONSHIRE

Loch Lomond

Largest stretch of inland water in Britain. Extends from Ardlui in the north to Balloch in the south.

MRS SALLY MACDONELL, MARDELLA FARMHOUSE, OLD SCHOOL ROAD, GARTOCHARN, LOCH LOMOND G83 8SD (01389 830428). Set on a quiet country lane, surrounded by fields. Friendly and comfortable, where the kettle's always boiling. AA QQQQ, RAC Listed, AA "Landlady of the Year" 1995 Finalist; Winner AA Scotland B&B of the Year 1995. [🐾]

DUNDEE & ANGUS

Broughty Ferry

KINGENNIE LODGES STB ★★★★ SELF-CATERING

Kingennie, Broughty Ferry, By Dundee. DD5 3RD

TEL: 01382 350777
FAX: 01382 350400

All lodges furnished to the highest standards and are open plan and centrally heated. Each has a double and twin bedrrom as well as folding sofa bed in the lounge; bathroom with shower over bath; fully-equipped kitchen with dishwasher, microwave and washer/dryer. Our "Clova" Lodge has full disabled facilities. Bed linen and towels provided, cot and highchair available upon request. Pets welcome. Lodge terms weekly from £205. Further details contact: Neil Anderson.
E-mail: kingennie@easynet.co.uk   Website: www.kingennie-fishings.com

Broughty Ferry

On the outskirts of Dundee with restored 15th century castle housing a museum of Tayside's natural history and whaling industry.

KINGENNIE FISHINGS & WOODLAND LODGES, KINGENNIE, BROUGHTY FERRY, DUNDEE DD5 3RD (01382 350777; Fax: 01382 350400). Each has a double and twin bedroom as well as folding sofa bed in the lounge; bathroom with shower over bath; fully-equipped kitchen with dishwasher, microwave and washer/dryer. Our "Clova" Lodge has full disabled facilities. Pets welcome. Further details contact: NEIL ANDERSON. [Pets £15 per week] e-mail: kingennie@easynet.co.uk website: www.kingennie-fishings.com

EDINBURGH & LOTHIANS

Haddington

THE MONKS' MUIR   STB ★★★★★

Haddington EH41 3SB
Tel: 01620 860340; Fax: 01620 861770
E-mail: d@monksmuir.com Website: www.monksmuir.co.uk
A secluded, friendly, green, sheltered place, but with direct access to the main A1 road. One of the oldest and best-loved caravan and camping parks in Scotland, only 15 minutes from the fringes of famous Edinburgh, in an area of great beauty, with glorious beaches, rich farmland, a plethora of golf courses and fascinating villages. Excellent facilities include the best park shop and cafe/bistro in the business! Appointed by every motoring and caravanning organisation, with the Scottish Tourist Board's "Thistle" Award for Accomodation Excellence,'Green Apple' Environmental Award, David Bellamy Gold Award. 1999 Finalist Calor 'Best Park in Scotland'. Tourers, campervans and tents all welcome. Luxury four/six berth caravans to rent. Open all year. Brochure with pleasure from Deirdre.

Hunter Holiday Cottages	Thornton Farm, Rosewell, Edinburgh, EH24 9EF Contact Duncan Hunter Tel: 0131 448 0888 Fax: 0131 440 2082 E-mail: hunter@holidaycottages.demon.co.uk Website: www.holidaycottages.demon.co.uk

Hunter Holiday Cottages offer a range of cottages in beautiful countryside only eight miles from Edinburgh City Centre. These superior cottages are recently renovated, have all modern facilities and sleep six to eight plus. They provide the ideal base for the perfect Scottish holiday from their location in Midlothian's historic countryside. There is easy access to Scotland's capital and the major routes to the rest of Scotland. For more information visit our website. Also B&B, £20-£25 per night.

See also Colour Advertisement on page 52

Edinburgh

Scotland's capital with magnificent castle overlooking "The Athens of the North".

MRS GARVIE, THE JOPPA ROCKS GUEST HOUSE, 99 JOPPA ROAD, EDINBURGH EH15 2HB (0131 669 8695). Joppa Rocks Guest House is a small family-run guest house, ideally situated to visit Edinburgh and surrounding countryside. Situated toward the east of the city, accessed by road from the A1 and the city bypass. Excellent bus service to the city.

Haddington

Historic town on River Tyne 16 miles east of Edinburgh. Birthplace of John Knox, 1505. Renovated Church of St Mary, 14c-15c; St Martin's Church, AM.

THE MONKS' MUIR, HADDINGTON EH41 3SB (01620 860340; Fax: 01620 861770). Secluded and tranquil amidst beautiful countryside, only 15 minutes from Edinburgh. Tourers, tents and luxury hire caravans. Multi-award winning. Lovely facilities, totally 'green' and very friendly. EXCELLENT. STB ★★★★★ . [🐾]
E-mail: d@monksmuir.com
Website: www.monksmuir.co.uk

Musselburgh

Town to the east of Edinburgh famous for golf.

MRS GARVIE, ARDEN HOUSE, 26 LINKFIELD ROAD, MUSSELBURGH EH21 (Tel & Fax: 0131 665 0663). AA ★★★★. Family run guest house five miles from Edinburgh, opposite race track. [Pets £2 per night.]

Rosewell

Village four miles south west of Dalkeith, to the south east of Edinburgh

HUNTER HOLIDAY COTTAGES, DUNCAN HUNTER (0131 448 0888 Fax: 0131 440 2082). Superior cottages, recently renovated with modern facilities, sleeping six to eight plus, in beautiful countryside only eight miles from Edinburgh. The ideal base for the perfect Scottish holiday. Also B&B, £20-£25 per night. [🐾]
E-mail: hunter@holidaycottages.demon.co.uk
Website: www.holidaycottages.demon.co.uk

St Andrews

Home of golf – British Golf Museum has memorabilia dating back to the origins of the game. Remains of castle and cathedral. Sealife Centre and beach Leisure Centre. Excellent sands. Ideal base for exploring the picturesque East Neuk of Fife.

HIGHLANDS

Applecross, Aultbea

Choose from three renowned Hotels in the West Highlands

Enjoy the freedom to select the Hotel which sets the right atmosphere for your break -whichever you choose you are assured of a pet-friendly welcome at the foot of dramatic Glencoe.

LUXURY BREAKS
£99 per person for 3 nights B&B -
Dinner only £16 per night
subject to availability

Discover a *sense of history* at the baronial **Ballachulish Hotel**. Seek out *seclusion and serenity* in the elegant surroundings of The Lodge on the Loch. Enjoy the *family atmosphere* of **The Isles of Glencoe Hotel & Leisure Centre** - a friendly place to go!

Call Now 01855 821582
www.freedomglen.co.uk

The Freedom of the Glen Family of Hotels, Onich, Near Fort William, The Scottish Highlands, PH33 6RY
fax: 01855 821463   e-mail: reservations@freedomglen.co.uk

CAIRNGORM HIGHLAND BUNGALOWS

Glen Einich, 29 Grampian View,
Aviemore, Inverness-shire PH22 1TF

Tel: *01479 810653* Fax: *01479 810262*

e-mail: linda.murray@virgin.net

website: www.cairngorm-bungalows.co.uk

Beautifully furnished and well-equipped bungalows ranging from one to four bedrooms. All have colour TV, video, microwave, cooker, washer-dryer, fridge and patio furniture. Some have log fires. Leisure facilities nearby include golf, fishing on the River Spey, swimming, sauna, jacuzzi, tennis, skating and skiing. Within walking distance of Aviemore. Ideal touring base. Children and pets welcome. Phone for colour brochure. Open all year.

For the best in Highland Holidays

PINE BANK CHALETS

See also Colour Advertisement on page 53

Enjoy the stunning beauty of the Highlands and the **Cairngorm Mountains** from our choice of cosy log cabins & 9 quality chalets.
◆ Great location – close to **River Spey** ◆ Video, **Sky TV**, BBQ, Mountain Bikes
◆ **Leisure pool** and restaurants nearby ◆ Pets Welcome ◆ Mini Breaks
◆ Large choice of style and price ◆ Free Brochure

Dalfaber Road, Aviemore PH22 1PX   Tel: (0)1479 810000 Fax: (0)1479 811469
e-mail: pinebank@enterprise.net   http://www.scotland2000.com/pinebank

---

KERROW HOUSE

STB: ★★★ *SELF CATERING* ★★★ *B&B*

Country House accommodation and 5 self-catering cottages in 12 acres of wooded grounds, with 3 $1/2$ miles of private trout fishing FREE to guests. Spectacular walking in Glens Affric, Cannich and Strathfarrar. Enjoy B&B in traditional surroundings and a relaxed atmosphere.

A haven for animal lovers !!

**Contact: Gill Kirkpatrick, Kerrow House, Cannich, By Beauly, Inverness-shire IV4 7NA
Tel: 01456 415243 • Fax: 01456 415425 •
E-mail: Gill@kerrow-house.demon.co.uk • Web: www.kerrow-house.demon.co.uk**

---

xOur views are breathtaking – from both the hotel and the numerous miles of wonderful walks around us. "Hamish", our lovable labrador (together with owners, Ann and Martyn), looks forward to welcoming you and your dog(s) to their lovely home. You'll enjoy good "Taste of Scotland" food, log fires and a well-equipped bedroom in which you are as welcome as your dog!

Coul House Hotel

**Contin, By Strathpeffer, Ross-shire IV14 9EY
Tel: 01997 421487; Fax: 01997 421945**

STB ★★★★ Hotel

FHG PUBLICATION LIMITED publish a large range of well-known accommodation guides. We will be happy to send you details or you can use the order form at the back of this book.

TORGUISH HOLIDAY HOMES
Daviot, Inverness IV2 5XQ Tel: 01463 772208 • Fax: 01463 772308
e-mail: torguish@torguish.com　　website: www.torguish.com

Set in the grounds of Torguish House, former childhood home of the late Alistair MacLean, author of novels such as *The Guns of Navarone* and *Where Eagles Dare*. Four self-catering cottages converted from the Old Steading into compact, high quality accommodation, fully furnished to a high standard.

• *Laundry room facilities* • *Play area in garden with putting green, sand pit, swings and tree house* • *Pets welcome at no extra charge.*

Inverness (4 miles) has many amenities including theatre, cinema, 10-pin bowling, leisure complex, shopping. Aviemore and the Lecht within easy reach for ski-ing. Many golf courses in the area including Nairn and Royal Dornoch. Loch Ness close by, plus many famous historic sites. Open all year. Terms £120-£310 per week

TORGUISH HOUSE
Daviot, Inverness IV2 5XQ

Torguish House, former childhood home of the late Alistair MacLean, author of novels such as *The Guns of Navarone* and *Where Eagles Dare*, is the perfect base for exploring the many attractions of Inverness and the Highlands.

Now converted into a comfortable Guest House, it offers Bed & Breakfast in comfortable en suite rooms, all with TV and tea/coffee-making facilties. Ample parking. Outdoor play area for children. Pets welcome. B&B from £19 to £25.

Inverness (4 miles) has many amenities including theatre, cinema, 10-pin bowling, leisure complex, shopping. Aviemore and the Lecht within easy reach for ski-ing. Many golf courses in the area including Nairn and Royal Dornoch. Loch Ness close by, plus many famous historic sites. Open all year.

Tel: 01463 772208 • Fax: 01463 772308 • e-mail: torguish@torguish.com • website: www.torguish.com

---

GLENURQUHART
LODGES

Situated between Loch Ness and Glen Affric in a spectacular setting ideal for walking, touring or just relaxing in this tranquil location. Four spacious chalets all fully equipped for six people, set in wooded grounds. Owners hotel adjacent where guests are most welcome in the restaurant and bar.

NEAR DRUMNADROCHIT, INVERNESS IV3 6TJ
Tel: 01456 476234
Fax: 01456 476286

Nether Lochaber Hotel
Onich, Fort William, Inverness-shire PH33 6SE
Tel: 01855 821235; Fax: 01855 821545

An ideal centre from which to explore Lochaber, the Ardnamurchan Peninsula and Glencoe. Traditional home cooking goes hand in hand with homely service, comfortable accommodation and private facilities. The inn stands on the shores of beautiful Loch Linnhe at Corran Ferry, 8 miles south of Fort William.

Terms from £20-£35 per person Bed and Breakfast. Children and Pets Welcome!

Please mention *Pets Welcome*
when enquiring about accommodation featured in these pages.

LOCH NESS　SELF CATERING

Newlands Cottage, South Loch Ness, is a former croft situated half a mile north of Errogie and 16 miles south of Inverness.
Secluded and private, yet not isolated, it has views east to the Monadliath mountains and south across Loch Farraline towards Fort Augustus. Its central location makes it an ideal base for touring the Highlands.

The shores of Loch Farraline are but 5 minutes' walk from the cottage and a 10 minute drive takes you through the beautiful Pass of Inverfarigaig that winds down through the forest and precipitous cliffs following the burn to the Great Glen and the mysterious waters of Loch Ness. Comfortable lounge with quality soft furnishings, Digital TV and open fireplace. Separate dining room. Spacious fitted kitchen with cooker, microwave, fridge/freezer, dishwasher, washing machine and coffee maker. Utility with ironing facilities and clothes dryer. Three bedrooms, two with double beds, and one with twin beds. Duvets and bed linen provided. Hairdryer. Cot and highchair available on request. Oil fired central heating. Oil and electricity are free. Coal and logs free. Payphone. Large parking area and garage. Pets welcome.

Other cottages in the area, up to STB 4 Stars

Tariffs: from £190 to £475.

For a colour brochure contact:
**Andy and Rosemary Holt
Island Cottage, Inverfarigaig,
Inverness IV2 6XR
Tel/Fax: 01456 486631
E-mail: rosemary@wildernesscottages.com
Website: www.wildernesscottages.com**

South Loch Ness • WILDSIDE HIGHLAND LODGES

Set on the banks of a rocky river deep in the countryside, amidst spectacular scenery, with a choice of accommodation.
• Cosy studio units built for two. • Well appointed stone and cedar lodges for up to six. • Spacious grounds and private lawns.
• Large picture windows to enjoy the scenery. • Country pub nearby and a choice of places to eat out. • Open all year round, with free central heating.
• Mini breaks available and pets welcome. • See our colour brochure or visit our web site.

**Wildside, Whitebridge, Inverness IV2 6UN　　Tel: 01456 486 373　　E-mail: info@wildsidelodges.com
Website: www.wildsidelodges.com　　STB ★★★ to ★★★★ SELF CATERING**

See also Colour Advertisement on page 53

Springbank Guest House　　　　　STB ★ GUEST HOUSE.

Overlooking the harbour and the Sound of Sleat to Skye. Five minutes' walk from railway station at the end of the world-famous West Highland Line, and from the ferry terminal to Skye, the "Small Isles" and Knoydart. The house is fully centrally heated and double glazed. Bed and Breakfast from £16 to £18 per night. Evening meal by arrangement. Children and pets welcome. Phone for brochure.

Jill and Tom Smith, Springbank Guest House, East Bay, Mallaig PH41 4QF　Tel & Fax: 01687 462459

---

*E-mail: enquiry@crubenbeg.com
Website: www.crubenbeg.com*

CRUBENBEG FARM STEADING
Newtonmore, Inverness-shire PH20 1BE
Tel: 01540 673566 Fax: 01540 673509

Surrounded by hills, woodlands and beside the River Truim is this small complex of 4 star Holiday cottages which sleep 2-5 guests. Children & Pets welcome. For more information and brochure please telephone Jennifer Graham.

FHG PUBLICATION LIMITED publish a large range of well-known accommodation guides. We will be happy to send you details or you can use the order form at the back of this book.

Mansfield House Hotel *Scotsburn Road, Tain, Ross-shire IV19 1PR*

Heather and Beth are two Golden Retrievers/Head Receptionists and look forward to welcoming you and your pets to their lovely Scottish Mansion. The hotel is rated STB 4 Stars following independent Lab. tests. Its pedigree includes Merit Awards for Hospitality, Comfort and Cuisine, and the Restaurant is accredited by Taste of Scotland (i.e Top Eaters recommend it) and has 2 AA Rosettes. All well-trained pets and owners welcome. **Telephone 01862 892052 www.mansfield-house.co.uk   AA ★★★ RAC**

BORGIE LODGE HOTEL Skerray, Tongue, Sutherland KW14 7TH

Set in a secluded highland glen by one of Scotlands most beautiful beaches lies Borgie Lodge. Billie Maclean tunes his bagpipes while tales of massive salmon and red deer stags mingle with peaty malt whisky. Your hosts

"The MacGregors" will ensure you are very well looked after, Peter taking guests fishing and shooting and Jacqui preparing local venison, salmon, lobster and lamb served with her own organic vegetables. Try pony trekking along the sands, cycling, swimming or hillwalking - we have it all.

Tel: 0164 521 332
e-mail: info@borgielodgehotel.co.uk
website: www.borgielodgehotel.co.uk
Jake and Sandy, Borgie Lodge pets, would like to make new friends.

STB ★★★★

ISLANDS & HIGHLANDS COTTAGES. Awesome scenery, breathtaking sunsets, miraculous dawns and an abundance of wildlife to be found within the islands and highlands of Scotland. We have holiday properties to suit all tastes and pockets. Please send for our brochure. Islands & Highlands Cottages, The Isle of Skye Estate Agency, Bridge Road, Portree, Isle of Skye IV51 9ER (01478 612123).
website: www.ihc.ndirect.co.uk

Applecross

Village at south end of Applecross bay on west coast of Ross and Cromarty District.

APPLECROSS HOTEL, APPLECROSS, WESTER ROSS, ROSS-SHIRE IV54 8LR (01529 744262 FAX: 01520 744400) Magnificent views overlooking the Inner Sound, island of Raasay and the Cullin Hills of Skye. Naturalist's paradise. Restaurant serving local produce. AA, Good pub guide, "Which?" Guide, Egon Ronay. Children and pets welcome. [🐾]

Aultbea

Village on east shore of Loch Ewe, 5 miles north of Poolewe.

COVE VIEW, 36 MELLON CHARLES, AULTBEA IV22 2JL (01445 731351). Wester Ross is ideal for hill walking or a quiet restful holiday. Detached chalet with two small bedrooms, sitting room, bathroom and mini kitchen. From £150 to £200 per week. A warm welcome awaits you and your pet. [🐾]

Aviemore

Scotland's leading ski resort in Spey valley with superb sport and entertainment facilities. All-weather holiday centre with accommodation to suit all pockets. Excellent fishing. Centre for exploring Cairngorms. Edinburgh 129 miles, Grantown-on-Spey 14, Kingussie 12, Carr-Bridge 7.

CAIRNGORM HIGHLAND BUNGALOW'S, GLEN EINICH, 29 GRAMPIAN VIEW, AVIEMORE (01479 810653; Fax: 01479 810262). Bungalows ranging from one to four bedrooms. All have colour TV, microwave, cooker, washer-dryer, fridge and patio furniture. Children and pets welcome. [🐾]
e-mail: linda.murray@virgin.net
website: www.cairngorm-bungalow's.co.uk

PINE BANK CHALETS, DALFABER ROAD, AVIEMORE PH22 1PX (01479 810000; Fax: 01479 811469). Cosy Log Cabins and 9 Quality Chalets, situated in a secluded area near the River Spey. Superb Family/Activity Holidays by mountains. Ideal skiing, walking, fishing and golf. Sky TV, mountain bikes. Short breaks available. Pets welcome. Open all year. ASSC Member. Brochure. [Pets £10 per week.]

Ballachulish

Locality on south shore of Loch Leven in Lochaber district.

ISLES OF GLENCOE HOTEL AND LEISURE CENTRE, BALLACHULISH, NEAR FORT WILLIAM PH49 4HL (01855 821582; Fax: 01855 821463). Almost afloat, this stylish, modern Hotel nestles on the lochside. Spacious bedrooms offer a commanding panorama of sky, mountain and loch. Delicious cuisine in Conservatory Restaurant. Heated pool & Leisure Centre. [pw! £3.50 per night] E–mail: reservations@freedomglen.co.uk
Website: www.freedomglen.co.uk

Boat of Garten

Village on Speyside 5 miles from Aviemore.

CONIFER COTTAGES - Two adjacent, well-equipped cottages. Sleep 5/6. Large secure garden. Surrounding woodlands and walks, bird reserve (Ospreys), golf, Speyside walk and steam railway nearby. J. WEIR, GLENLORA COTTAGE, LOCHWINNOCH PA12 4DN (01505 842062). STB ★ [🐾]
e-mail: jbdevweir@ukonline.co.uk

Cannich

Village known as Gateway to Glen Affric, 25 miles west of Inverness..

GILL KIRKPATRICK, KERROW HOUSE, CANNICH, BY BEAULY, INVERVESS-SHIRE, IV4 7NA (01456 415243; Fax: 01456 415425). Country house B & B accommodation and five self-catering cottages in the grounds with 3½ miles private trout fishing free to all guests. Excellent walking & Wildlife. [Pets £10 per week]
E–mail: Gill@kerrow-house.demon.co.uk
Website: www.kerrow-house.demon.co.uk

Carrbridge

Village on River Dulnain, 7 miles north of Aviemore. Landmark Visitor Centre has exhibition explaining history of local environment.

LYNN & DAVE BENGE, THE PINES COUNTRY HOUSE, DUTHIL, CARRBRIDGE PH23 3ND (01479 841220). Relax and enjoy our Highland hospitality, woodland setting; all rooms en suite. Traditional or vegetarian home cooking. B&B from £19 daily; DB&B from £183 weekly. Children and pets welcome. STB ★★ Guest House. [🐾]
website: www.dbenge.freeserve.co.uk

Contin

Village in Ross and Cromarty district two miles south-west of Strathpeffer.

COUL HOUSE HOTEL, CONTIN, BY STRATHPEFFER IV14 9EY (01997 421487; Fax: 01997 421945). Hamish, our lovable labrador looks forward to welcoming you. "Taste of Scotland" food, log fires, well-equipped bedrooms. Miles of wonderful walks. STB ★★★★ Hotel. [🐾 pw!]

Daviot

Village 5 miles south-east of Inverness, the Highland "capital".

TORGUISH HOUSE, DAVIOT, INVERNESS IV2 5XQ (01463 772208; Fax: 01463 772308). Comfortable B&B; all rooms en suite with TV and tea/coffee making facilities. Outdoor play area for children. Inverness 4 miles. Pets welcome. 🐾]
E–mail: torguish@torguish.com
Website: www.torguish.com

TORGUISH HOLIDAY HOMES, DAVIOT, INVERNESS IV2 5XQ (01463 772208; Fax: 01463 772308).
Four high quality self-catering cottages, fully furnished to high standard. Laundry room; outdoor
play area for children; all pets welcome. Ideal for exploring Highlands.[🐾]
E–mail: torguish@torguish.com
Website: www.torguish.com

Drumnadrochit

Village on the shores of Loch Ness with monster visitors centre. Sonar scanning cruises.

CAROL HUGHES, GLENURQUHART LODGES, BY DRUMNADROCHIT, INVERNESS-SHIRE IV3 6TJ
(01456 476234; Fax: 01456 476286). Situated between Loch Ness and Glen Affric in a spectacular
setting ideal for walking, touring or just relaxing in this tranquil location. Four spacious chalets all
fully equipped for six people, set in wooded grounds. Owners hotel adjacent where guests are most
welcome in the restaurant and bar. [Pets £10 per week.]

Fort William

Small town at foot of Ben Nevis, ideal base for climbers and hillwalkers.

NETHER LOCHABER HOTEL, ONICH, FORT WILLIAM PH33 6SE (01855 821235; 01855 821545).
Traditional home cooking goes hand in hand with homely service, comfortable accommodation and
private facilities on the shores of beautiful Loch Linnhe. B&B from £20-£35 per person. [🐾]

MRS M. MATHESON, THISTLE COTTAGE, TORLUNDY, FORT WILLIAM (01397 702428). Central for
touring the Highlands - 3½ miles from Fort William. Double and family rooms with TV, tea/coffee
making facilities. En suite available. Ample parking. B&B from £13 per night. STB ★★ B&B [🐾]

LINNHE LOCHSIDE HOLIDAYS, DEPT PW, CORPACH, FORT WILLIAM PH33 7NL (01397 772376).
Almost a botanical garden Linnhe is stunning. "Best Park in Scotland Award 1999". Deluxe chalets
and holiday caravans for hire. Touring pitches. Private beach, free fishing. Prices from £180/week.
[pw! £2/night, £15/week].
E-mail: holidays@linnhe.demon.co.uk
Website: www.linnhe-lochside-holidays.co.uk

THE CLAN MACDUFF HOTEL, ACHINTORE, FORT WILLIAM PH33 6RW (01397 702341; Fax: 01397
706174). This family-run hotel overlooks Loch Linnhe, two miles south of Fort William, excellent for
touring the rugged mountains of the West Highlands. All rooms have TV, hair dryer and hospitality
tray; all with private facilities. Three nights DB&B from £89 pppn. STB ★★ Hotel. Phone or write for
colour brochure and tariff. [🐾]

ACHINTEE FARM, GLEN NEVIS, FORT WILLIAM PH33 6TE (01397 702240; Fax: 01397 705899).
Achintee Farm sits quietly beside the river in Glen Nevis - at the start of the Ben Nevis Footpath.
B&B from £20. Self-catering from £40 per night. [🐾]

MRS MARY MACDONALD, AONACH-MOR HOUSE, TORLUNDY, FORT WILLIAM PH33 6SW (01397
704525). Bungalow overlooking Ben Nevis set in quiet location on edge of forest. Ideal for doggie
walking. 3 miles north of Fort William. 2 family/1 double room, en suite. TV, teamakers, Scottish
breakfast. From £14 p.p.p.n., reductions for children.

**THE BALLACHULISH HOTEL, BALLACHULISH, NEAR FORT WILLIAM PH49 4JY (Tel: 01855
821582; Fax: 01855 821463) Glide through the dramatic pass of Glencoe and the mountains divide
to reveal this breathtaking lochside setting. Fulfill your dream of the perfect historic Highland Hotel
by staying here amongst the turrets. STB ★★★★.
e-mail: reservations@freedomglen.co.uk
website: www.freedomglen.co.uk**

Garve

Locality in Ross and Cromarty District, 10 miles west of Dingwall.

INCHBAE LODGE HOTEL, BY GARVE IV23 2PH (01997 455269; Fax: 01997 455207). In outstanding
mountain scenery between Inverness and Ullapool. Family-run Victorian hunting lodge in riverside
eight acres. Good Scottish food. Real ale. Ideal centre for all outdoor activities. . Bargain breaks eg:
four nights DB&B £149 per dog, owner free. STB ★★★. [pw! 🐾]

Invergarry

Village south of Fort Augustus on the shore of Loch Oich

INVERGARRY HOTEL, INVERGARRY, INVERNESS-SHIRE PH35 4HJ (01809 501206 Fax: 01809 501400). Fine Scottish produce and a well-stocked bar in a distinctive Victorian building, amidst the beautiful scenery of the Scottish Highlands. Ten comfortable en suite rooms. STB ★★★ Hotel.[🐕]
E–mail: hotel@invergarry.net
Website: www.invergarry.net/hotel

Inverness

Capital of the Highlands. Lively tourist centre and good base for visiting local attractions.

HAZEL AND GEORGE STUART, HAZELDEAN HOUSE, 125 LOCHALSH ROAD, INVERNESS IV3 5QS (01463 241338; Fax: 01463 236387). A warm Highland welcome awaits you at Hazeldean House. Free parking. Ten minutes walk to town centre. Ideal touring base for the Highlands. Very reasonable rates. STB ★★★. [🐕]
E-mail: mail@hazeldeanhouse.co.uk
Website: www.hazeldeanhouse.co.uk

Kincraig

Attractive Highland village close to Loch Insh and Glenfeshie, midway between Aviemore and Kingussie.

NICK & PATSY THOMPSON, INSH HOUSE GUESTHOUSE AND SELF-CATERING COTTAGES, KINCRAIG, Near KINGUSSIE PH21 1NU (01540 651377). B&B in 1827 Telford Manse and two timber s/c cottages in superb rural location. Ideal for many outdoor activities and good touring base.Dogs welcome. STB ★★★. [🐕]
E-mail: inshhouse@btinternet.com
Website: www.kincraig.com/inshhouse.htm

Kingussie

Tourist centre on the River Spey 28 miles south of Inverness.

COLUMBA HOUSE HOTEL & GARDEN RESTAURANT, MANSE ROAD, KINGUSSIE PH21 1JF (01540 661402; Fax: 01540 661652). Nestling in large grounds. Restaurant & Patio in walled garden offers superb Scottish cuisine. En suite bedrooms with mini-bar, TV, phone, tea/coffee. Romantic four-posters and family suite. Parking. AA ★★. [pw! 🐕]
E–mail: reservations@columba-hotel.co.uk

ARDEN HOUSE, NEWTONMORE ROAD, KINGUSSIE PH21 1HE (Tel & Fax:01540 6614369). Victorian Villa which retains many period features in a typical Highland town. Ideal base for touring, friendly and relaxed atmosphere and easy walking distance to centre of town.[🐕]
E-mail: ardenhouse@compuserve.com
Website: www.ardenhouse.org

Kylesku

Situated on Loch Cairnbrawn across from Ullapool

KYLESKU LODGES, KYLESKU IV27 4HW (Tel & Fax: 01971 502003). Self-catering holiday lodges in secluded location, convenient for bird-watching, hill walking and fishing. Open March to October. Colour brochure on request. [Pets £10 per week]
E-mail: info@kyleskulodges.co.uk
Website: www.kyleskulodges.co.uk

Lochcarron

Long inlet extending from Kyle of Lochalsh to foot of Glen Carron.

KRISTINE MACKENZIE, "BLACKWOOD", ARINACKAIG, STRATHCARRON IV54 8YN (01520 722296). Three properties in tranquil, secluded surroundings. Abundance of wildlife on working croft. Equipped to high standard, light, spacious with panoramic views. £100 to £300 inclusive.

Loch Ness

Home of "Nessie", extending for 23 miles from Fort Augustus to south of Inverness.

DAVID AND PATRICIA ALLEN, WILDSIDE HIGHLAND LODGES, WILDSIDE, WHITEBRIDGE, INVERNESS IV2 6UN. (01456 486373). STB ★★★ and ★★★★. Self-Catering. Cosy studio units built for two. Well appointed stone and cedar lodges for up to six. Open all year round, with free central heating. Mini breaks available and pets welcome. See our colour brochure or visit our web site. [Pets £15 per week].
E–mail: info@wildsidelodges.com
Website: www.wildsidelodges.com

Former croft situated 16 miles south of Inverness. Comfortable lounge, digital TV and open fireplace. Separate dining room. Fully equipped kitchen.Three bedrooms. Central heating. Pets welcome. For a colour brochure contact: ANDY AND ROSEMARY HOLT, ISLAND COTTAGE, INVERFARIGAIG, INVERNESS IV2 6XR (Tel/Fax: 01456 486631).
E-mail: rosemary@wildernesscottages.com
Website: www.wildernesscottages.com

Mallaig

Busy port at the end of the West Highland Railway line. Ferry port for Skye.

JILL AND TOM SMITH, SPRINGBANK GUEST HOUSE, EAST BAY, MALLAIG PH41 4QF (TEL & FAX: 01687 462459). STB ★ GUEST HOUSE. Overlooking the harbour and the Sound of Sleat to Skye. The house is fully centrally heated and double glazed. B&B from £16 to £18 per night. Evening meal by arrangement. Children and pets welcome. Phone for brochure. [🐕]

Newtonmore

Village on River Spey, 3 miles west of Kingussie. Holiday and Ski centre. Clan Macpherson Museum.

CRUBENBEG FARM STEADING, NEWTONMORE, INVERNESS-SHIRE PH20 1BE (01540 673566 Fax: 01540 673509) Beside River Truim surrounded by hills and woodlands. Sleep 2-5 guests. Children and pets welcome. Please contact Jennifer Graham for more information and brochure.
E-mail: enquiry@crubenbeg.com
Website: www.crubenbeg.com

Nethybridge

Popular Strathspey resort on River Nethy with extensive Abernethy Forest to the south. Impressive mountain scenery. Grantown-on-Spey 5 miles.

NETHYBRIDGE, STRATHSPEY. Choice of modern cottages or converted smithy. Linen and visitor laundry included. Septenber to May storage heating included. Good walking and touring area. STB ★★★/★★★★. Write or phone for brochure. MR AND MRS P. W. PATRICK, CHAPELTON PLACE, FORRES, MORAY IV36 2NL (01309 672505). [One dog free, thereafter £20 per week.]
E–mail: speyside@enterprise.net
Website: www.nethybridge.com/speysidecottages.htm

Onich

On shores of Loch Linnhe. Good boating, fishing. Fort William 10 miles.

THE INCHREE CENTRE, ONICH, FORT WILLIAM PH33 6SD (01855 821287).Situated midway between Ben Nevis and Glencoe. Fully Self-catering Chalets for 4-6 persons each. Sea and mountain views. Welcoming Bistro & Bar on site. Forest & waterfall walks nearby.Touring/walking guides provided. Discounts for couples. Open all year STB ★★[🐕]
E–mail: enquiry@inchreecentre-scotland.com
Website: www.inchreecentre-scotland.com

THE LODGE ON THE LOCH, CREAG DHU, ONICH, BY FORT WILLIAM PH33 6RY (01855 821582). Discover seclusion and serenity - enjoy one of the West Coast's finest panoramas. Choice of individual luxury rooms with many personal touches. Taste of Scotland. STB ★★★★ AA ★★★.
e-mail: reservations@freedomglen.co.uk
website: www.freedomglen.co.uk

Poolewe

Village lying between Lochs Ewe and Maree with the River Ewe flowing through.

MR A. URQUHART, CROFTERS COTTAGES, 15 CROFT, POOLEWE, ROSS-SHIRE IV22 2JY (Tel: 01445 781 268; 01445 781 704). Three traditional cottages situated in a scenic and tranquil area, ideal for a "get away from it all" holiday. Comfortably furnished with all mod cons.

Rhiconich

Locality at the head of Loch Inchard on west coast of Sutherland District.

RHICONICH HOTEL, SUTHERLAND, N. W. HIGHLANDS IV27 4RN (01971 521224; Fax: 01971 521732).She's your best friend so why leave her at home, bring her to Rhiconich Hotel, she'll be made equally as welcome as you will. A place where we put service, hospitality and really fresh food as a priority, but why don't you come and see for yourself? For further details contact Helen Fish.★★★[🐾]
e-mail: rhiconichhotel@cs.xom
website: www.rhiconichhotel.co.uk

Spean Bridge

Village on River Spean at foot of Loch Lochy. Site of WWII Commando Memorial.

Animal friendly holidays in the heart of the Scottish Highlands. EARENDIL, MUCOMIR, BY SPEAN BRIDGE PH34 4EQ (Tel & Fax 01397 712548).
E–mail: helen@dreamweavers.co.uk

MRS M. H. CAIRNS, INVERGLOY HOUSE, SPEAN BRIDGE PH34 4DY (01397 712681). Two spacious 4-berth luxury caravans, highest standard (fridge, shower, TV). 50 acre wooded estate, beautifully secluded overlooking Loch Lochy; beach, fishing, bird watching, lovely walks. Free gas and electricity. Discounts for two occupancy and two-week bookings. Controlled dog welcome. £180-£285 per week. Fort William & Lochaber Tourist Board, British Graded Holiday Parks inspected. SAE for details [🐾]

Tain

Small town in Ross & Cromarty district on south shore of Dornoch Firth. Invergordon 10 miles.

MANSFIELD HOUSE HOTEL, SCOTSBURN ROAD, TAIN IV19 1PR (01862 892052). STB 4 Star Hotel. Excellent restaurant accredited by Taste of Scotland with AA 2 Rosettes. Well-trained pets and owners welcome. [🐾]

Tongue

Village near north coast of Caithness District on east side of Kyle of Tongue.

BORGIE LODGE HOTEL, SKERRAY, TONGUE, SUTHERLAND KW14 7TH (Tel & Fax: 01641 521332). Set in a secluded highland glen lies Borgie Lodge. Try pony trekking, cycling and fishing. Jake and Sandy, Borgie Lodge pets, would like to make new friends.
e-mail: info@borgielodgehotel.co.uk
website: www.borgielodgehotel.co.uk

PLEASE MENTION THIS GUIDE WHEN YOU WRITE
OR PHONE TO ENQUIRE ABOUT ACCOMMODATION.
IF YOU ARE WRITING, A STAMPED,
ADDRESSED ENVELOPE IS ALWAYS APPRECIATED.

Biggar

Small town set round broad main street. Gasworks museum, puppet theatre seating 100, street museum displaying old shopfronts and interiors. Peebles 13 miles.

CARMICHAEL COUNTRY COTTAGES, CARMICHAEL ESTATE, BY BIGGAR ML12 6PG (01899 308336; Fax: 01899 308481). Our stone cottages nestle in the woods and fields of our historic family-run estate. Ideal homes for families, pets and dogs. 15 cottages, 32 bedrooms. STB ★★/★★★★ Self catering. Open all year. £180 to £480 per week. [pw! ✝]
E–mail: chiefcarm@aol.com
Website: www.carmichael.co.uk/cottages

WALSTON MANSION FARMHOUSE, WALSTON, CARNWATH, BY BIGGAR, ML11 8NF (Tel/Fax: 01899 810338). Situated in the peaceful village of Walston just five miles from Biggar, We are in an ideal place for touring the Clyde Valley and Scottish Borders. Pets by arrangement.
e-mail: kirby-walstonmansion@talk21.com

Harthill

Village 5 miles south-west of Bathgate.

MRS STEPHENS, BLAIR MAINS FARM, HARTHILL ML7 5TJ (Tel: 01501 751278; Fax: 01501 753383). Attractive farmhouse on small farm. Ideal for touring. Children welcome, babysitting offered. Bed and Breakfast from £16; weekly rates available. Reduced rates for children. Open all year. [pw! ⌖]
E-mail: heather@blairmains.freeserve.co.uk

Netherburn

Three miles north of Blackwood.

BROOMFIELD FARM, NETHERBURN, LANARKSHIRE ML9 3DH (01698 792929). Peaceful, non-smoking luxurious accommodation. All rooms have tea/coffee making facilites, TV. Full five-course Scottish breakfast. Two course Dinner from £8. B&B from £15. Family room £50 B&B. Pets welcome. Great food, great value, great atmosphere.

PERTH & KINROSS

Aberfeldy, Blairgowrie

STB ★★★★ Self Catering   Acharn, By Aberfeldy
Escape the rat race in comfort, peace and tranquillity.
Loch, farm and mountains on the doorstep.
Tel: 01887 830209   Fax: 01887 830802
www.lochtaylodges.co.uk

MACHUIM FARM COTTAGES

Well equipped houses on side of Loch Tay. Central for water sports, fishing, riding, walking and touring. All with electric central heating and wood burner/open fire. Bed linen for hire if required. Hotel within walking distance. Prices from £160 to £475 per week. Pets welcome at no extra charge.

Apply: Mr & Mrs J. H. Webb

★★★ / ★★★★
SELF-CATERING

**Machuim Farmhouse, Lawers, Aberfeldy,
Perthshire PH15 2PA. Tel: 01567 820670**

PERTHSHIRE AND CENTRAL HIGHLANDS

★ A choice of 1-3 bedroom self-catering Scandinavian-style chalets in 2 acres parkland, only 5 minutes' walk from shops and town centre.
★ OPEN ALL YEAR. Spring/Autumn Short Breaks welcome in warm, fully equipped, comfortable accommodation. Colour TV, Tennis, Children's amenities on site. ★ Ideal centre for touring in all directions. Golf (40 courses within an hour's drive), walking and fishing holidays. ★ Credit cards accepted.

For detailed brochure and bookings, please write or telephone:
ALTAMOUNT CHALETS, BLAIRGOWRIE, PERTHSHIRE PH10 6JN
Tel: (01250) 873324 • Fax: (01250) 872464 • Email : alastair@altamountchalets.co.uk • Website: www.altamountchalets.co.uk

Roslin Cottage Guest House
Lagrannoch, Callander, Perthshire FK17 8LE
Tel: 01877 330638 Fax: 01877 331448 e-mail: alifer@msn.com
Lynne and Alistair Ferguson   "Good Walkies Area"
Situated on the outskirts of Callander, the Gateway to the Trossachs. Roslin Cottage has recently been restored yet still retains many original features including stone walls, beams and an open fireplace in the lounge. We offer a varied Scottish Breakfast with Evening Meal on request. We use our own produce when available which includes eggs from our hens, ducks or geese, and honey from our apiary. We have three double, one twin and two single rooms, all with central heating, washbasin and tea/coffee maker. Bed and Breakfast from £16.50 per person per night; Evening Meal by arrangement. Single occupancy £18.50. Brochure on request. Ideal touring base, with sailing, fishing, walking, climbing, mountain biking etc., all on the doorstep.
Your dogs sleep in your room and are welcome in the lounge and in our large enclosed garden.
REDUCED WEEKLY RATES   DOGS ESPECIALLY WELCOME (and stay free)

INVERTROSSACHS COUNTRY HOUSE
CALLANDER, INVERTROSSACHS ROAD FK17 8HG
Relax in our lovely loch-side family home and grounds within the beautiful Invertrossachs Estate in stunning Perthshire. Family pets are most welcome and will enjoy the varied walks in our woodland, loch-side and hill trails. Your pets will be welcomed by ours and there will always be room for a few more at the log fire, after a great day out.
Tel: 01877 331126 • Fax:: 01877 331229 • website: www.invertrossachs.co.uk
See also Colour Advertisement on page 53

THE HIGHLAND HOUSE HOTEL
South Church Street, Callander FK17 8BN
Tel: 01877 330269; Fax: 01877 339004
e-mail: highland.house.hotel@lineone.net

This Georgian town house built around 1790 is now a private hotel run under the personal supervision of Lorna and Robert Leckie. All our nine bedrooms have en suite facilities and are tastefully decorated. Each room benefits from colour TV, hospitality trays and full central heating. Relax in our comfortable lounge, enjoy evening meals and why not sample a wee dram in our cosy intimate bar. Whatever your choice you will be assured of a friendly atmosphere and a warm welcome. B&B £20-£25 pp; Room only £17-£20 pp.

CRUACHAN FARM CARAVAN AND CAMPING PARK
Cruachan, Killin FK21 8TY (Tel: 01567 820302)
Family-run site of 10 acres adjacent to farm, set amidst beautiful Highland scenery. Ideal central situation for touring; walking, fishing and golf nearby. Licensed restaurant and coffee shop on site. Children and pets welcome. Open mid-March to October. Terms: (per night) touring caravans £7.50, motor caravans £7.00, car and tent £6.00, tents £5.00. Holiday caravans for hire, also Lodge House for self catering lets. Reduced rates off season. Brochure available.
E-mail: info@cruachan.killin.cu.uk   Website: www.cruachan.killin.co.uk

Wester Lix, near Killin, Perthshire, two cottages for groups of six or ten. Family run. Remote location set in nine acres with private Lochan. Excellent base for walking, hill climbing, mountain biking, and water sports, or touring and sight seeing. STB ★★ & ★★★
Gill & Dave Hunt, Wester Lix, Killin, Perthshire. FK21 8RD
Tel: 01567 820 990   *E-mail: gill@westerlix.co.uk   Website: www.westerlix.co.uk*

Please mention *Pets Welcome*
when enquiring about accommodation featured in these pages.

FHG

PLEASE MENTION THIS GUIDE WHEN YOU WRITE

OR PHONE TO ENQUIRE ABOUT ACCOMMODATION

IF YOU ARE WRITING, A STAMPED, ADDRESSED

ENVELOPE IS ALWAYS APPRECIATED

Ardoch Lodge

Tel/Fax: 01877 384666
E-mail: ardoch@btinternet.com
STB ★★★★
Dogs most welcome.
Free of charge

Exceptional walking and wildlife area - deer, red squirrels and a great variety of birds. Twelve acres of formal and informal gardens and grounds. Walk straight from the door through woodlands onto the hillsides or around the loch.

The two log cabins and cottage are well furnished, equipped and heated. Cleaned and beds freshly made for your arrival. All linen, towels and electricity included.

In the lodge all our bedrooms, which have outstanding views of the mountains, are spacious and have private bathrooms. Deliciously imaginative food using local produce plus a high level of service and comfort provides an excellent base from which to tour this beautiful part of Scotland.

Truly a place to unwind. Perfect for pets.

Yvonne & John Howes, Ardoch Lodge, Strathyre, Perthshire FK18 8NF
Visit our web site at www.ardochlodge.co.uk

Aberfeldy

Small town standing on both sides of Urlar Burn near its confluence with the River Tay. Pitlochry 8 miles.

LOCH TAY LODGES, REMONY, ACHARN, ABERFELDY PH15 2HR (01887 830209). Enjoy hill walking, golf, sailing or touring. Salmon and trout fishing available. Log fires. Pets welcome. Walks along loch shore from house. STB ★★★★ Self catering in village close to Loch. For brochure, contact MRS G. DUNCAN MILLAR at above address. [🐾]
Website: www.lochtaylodges.co.uk

MACHUIM FARM, LAWERS, ABERFELDY (TEL: 01567-820670) Well equipped houses on side of Loch Tay. Central for watersports, fishing, riding, touring and walking. Central heating. Prices from £160 to £475 weekly. Mr & Mrs J Webb.STB ★★★/★★★★ [🐾]

ALTAMOUNT CHALETS, COUPAR ANGUS ROAD, BLAIRGOWRIE PH10 6JN (Tel: 01250 873324; Fax: 01250 872464). Modern, fully equipped 1, 2 and 3 bedroom Scandinavian-style Chalets. Colour television. Centrally situated for touring Highlands. Children's amenities on site. Pets welcome. [Pets £1.50 per night, £10.50 per week]

Callander

Good base for walks and drives around the Trossachs and Loch Katrine. Stirling 14 miles.

LYNNE AND ALISTAIR FERGUSON, ROSLIN COTTAGE GUEST HOUSE, LAGRANNOCH, CALLANDER FK17 8LE (01877 330638; Fax: 01877 331448). Bed and good Scottish Breakfast from £16.50 per person. Evening Meal by arrangement. Comfortable accommodation in 18th century Cottage, historic features. "Good walkies area" – dogs are especially welcome. [🐾 pw!] e–mail: alifer@msn.com

INVERTROSSACHS COUNTRY HOUSE, CALLANDER FK17 8HG (01877 331126; Fax: 01877 331229). Relax in our lovely loch-side family home and grounds within the beautiful Invertrossachs Estate in stunning Perthshire. Family pets are most welcome. [🐾]
website: www.invertrossachs.co.uk

LORNA AND ROBERT LECKIE, THE HIGHLAND HOUSE HOTEL, SOUTH CHURCH STREET, CALLANDER FK17 8BN (Tel: 01877 330269; Fax: 01877 339004). Georgian town house built around 1790. Nine en suite bedrooms with colour TV, hospitality trays and full central heating. Comfortable lounge, evening meals, residents bar. B&B £20-£25 pp; Room only £17-£20 pp.
E–mail: highland.house.hotel@lineone.net

Killin

Village at confluence of Rivers Dochart and Lochay at head of Loch Tay.

CRUACHAN FARM CARAVAN AND CAMPING PARK, CRUACHAN, KILLAN FK21 8TY (01567 820302). Family run caravan and camping site; Ideally situated for touring, walking, fishing and golfing nearby. Licensed restaurant and coffe shop on site. Children and pets welcome.
E-mail: info@cruachan,killin.co.uk
Website: www.cruachan.killin.co.uk

GILL & DAVE HUNT, WESTER LIX HOLIDAY COTTAGES, WESTER LIX, KILLIN FK21 8RD (01567 820 9990). All cottages are decorated and equipped to a high standard. All cottages have washing machines, Freezers, oven etc. Well behaved pets welcome by arrangement. [🐾 PW!]
E-mail: gill@westerlix.co.uk
Web: www.westerlix.co.uk

Kinross

Town and resort on west side of Loch Leven, 9 miles north of Dunfermline.

THE GREEN HOTEL, 2 THE MUIRS, KINROSS, KY13 8AS (01577 863467; Fax: 01577 863180) Independent Country Hotel, ideally located in central Scotland. 46 spacious bedrooms, leisure complex with indoor pool, sauna, solarium, exercise facility, squash court and 2 golf courses (18 hole). Phone for brochure and tariff.
Website: www.green-hotel.com

Lochearnhead

Popular little touring centre on wooded Loch Earn, dominated by Ben Vorlich (3,244ft). Edinburgh 65 miles, Glasgow 50, Aberfeldy 30, Crieff 19, Crianlarich 16, Callander 14.

CLACHAN COTTAGE HOTEL, LOCHEARNHEAD FK19 8PU (01567 830247; Fax: 01567 830300). Well placed in central Scotland for touring. Excellent walking, mountain biking and fishing. Water-sports available from the hotel. Award winning "Taste of Scotland" restaurant.
website: www.clachancottagehotel.co.uk

MR ANGUS CAMERON, LOCHEARNHEAD HOTEL, LOCHEARNHEAD FK19 8PU (01567 830229). Small family-run hotel, restaurant and self-catering chalets at the West end of Loch Earn with lovely views across the loch. Excellent golf and touring centre with water ski-ing, sailing and windsurfing on our doorstep. Ample hill walking. STB ★★ AA ★. [Pets £1 per night, £7 per week]

Pitlochry

Popular resort on River Tummel in beautiful Perthshire Highlands. Excellent golf, loch and river fishing. Famous for summer Festival Theatre; distillery, Highland Games.

BALROBIN HOTEL, HIGHER OAKFIELD, PITLOCHRY PH16 5HT (01796 472901; Fax: 01796 474200). Scottish Country House Hotel. 15 en suite rooms, most with panoramic views, yet close to the town centre. Owned and run by the Hohman family at value-for-money prices. [🐾]

THE DUNALASTAIR HOTEL, KINLOCH RANNOCH, BY PITLOCHRY PH16 5PW (01882 632323; Fax: 01882 632371). Area of outstanding natural beauty. Hotel Fishing on Loch Rannoch and Dunalastair water. Great for outdoor pursuits including rafting and abseiling. Ideal touring base, yet far from the madding crowd. Friendly and professional staff. Hotel of unrivalled character with baronial dining room, elegant lounges, a sun lounge and delightful bar. All the good things Scotland has to offer in one great hotel!
E-mail: kids@dunalastair
Website: www.dunalastair.co.uk

KILLIECRANKIE HOTEL, KILLIECRANKIE, BY PITLOCHRY PH16 5LG (01796 473220; Fax: 01796 472451). Charming small Hotel set in 4 acres. Wonderful views. Superb food, high standard of comfort. Open Christmas and New Year. STB ★★★★ Hotel. AA ★★ Rosette. [★ pw!]

BONSKEID HOUSE, PITLOCHRY PH16 5NP (01796 473208; Fax: 01796 473310). Secure dog exercise area in walled garden. The house is ideally suited for families, individuals, and canine companions of all ages. A brochure is only a phone call away. Special weekend, weekly and Senior Citizen rates. Ring for details. [pw! ★]
E-mail: bonskeid@aol.com

JACKY & MALCOLM CATTERALL, "TULLOCH", ENOCHDHU, BY KIRKMICHAEL, STRATHARDLE PH10 7PW (01250 881404). Former farmhouse offers comfortable accommodation and good food. One family room with washbasin, one twin with washbasin; one en suite double room. All have tea/coffee making facilities and face open country to mountains beyond. Peace and quiet guaranteed. B&B £18; Dinner if required £10. Haven for wildlife and dogs. STB ★★★.

OAKBANK, 20 LOWER OAKFIELD, PITLOCHRY PH16 5DS (01796 472080; Fax: 01796 473502). Well appointed detached granite Victorian villa, overlooking beautiful Tummel Valley. Quality rooms, full Scottish breakfast. If you come by public transport we also provide car hire (discount to residents). We will meet you from Pitlochry train/bus station. Terms from £18 - £20. [★]

St Fillans

Village at foot of Loch earn, 5 miles west of Comrie.

FOUR SEASONS HOTEL, ST FILLANS PH6 2NF (Tel & Fax: 01764 685333). Ideal holiday venue for pets and their owners. Spectacular Highland scenery, walking, fishing, watersports. Wonderful food. Full details on request. STB ★★★ Hotel, AA ★★★ and 2 Red Rosettes, RAC ★★★ , Egon Ronay, Taste of Scotland.

Stanley

Pretty village on River Tay, 8 miles south-east of Dunkeld and 6 miles north of Perth.

MRS A. GUTHRIE, NEWMILL FARM, STANLEY PH1 4QD (01738 828281). On A9 six miles north of Perth. Lounge, sitting room. Twin and double en suite, family room with private facilities. Bed and Breakfast from £18. Evening meal on request. Reductions for children. Ideal for touring, fishing, golf. STB ★★★ B&B.
e–mail: guthrienewmill@sol.co.uk
website: www.newmillfarm.com

Strathyre

Village set in middle of Strathyre Forest, just off A84 north of Callander. Information centre and picnic area to south of village.

ARDOCH LODGE, STRATHYRE (01877 384666). Log cabins and cottage in wonderful mountain scenery. Comfortably furnished and fully equipped. Country house accommodation also available. Phone for brochure. Open all year. Pets most welcome. STB ★★★★. [★]

THE BEN SHEANN HOTEL, MAIN STREET, STRATHYRE FK18 8NA (Tel and Fax:01877 384609). Always a warm welcome. Single to family room, standard or en-suite. Car park. Open fields. Public and lounge bar. Wheelchair access. Open all year round. STB ★★ [Pets £3 per stay]
e-mail: bensheann@freeuk.com

Fintry

Village on Endrick Water, 5 miles east of Balfron

MRS MORRIS, NETHERTON COTTAGE, NETHERTON OF GLENBOIG G63 0YH (Tel & Fax: 01360 860242). Comfortable cottage on farm in scenic valley. Cosy lounge, woodburning stove. Beautiful views, lovely walks, enclosed garden. Ideal for relaxing, touring Edinburgh, Glasgow and the Southern Highlands.
e-mail: morrish2@aol.com

SCOTTISH ISLANDS

ISLANDS & HIGHLANDS COTTAGES. Awesome scenery,breathtaking sunsets, miraculous dawns and an abundance of wildlife to be found within the islands and highlands of Scotland. We have holiday properties to suit all tastes and pockets. Please send for our brochure. Islands & Highlands Cottages, The Isle of Skye Estate Agency, Bridge Road, Portree, Isle of Skye IV51 9ER (01478 612123).
website: www.ihc.ndirect.co.uk

ISLE OF LUING

ISLE OF MULL

Isle of Luing

Island lying between Seil and Scarba.

SUNNYBRAE CARAVAN PARK SOUTH CUAN, ISLE OF LUING, BY OBAN PA34 4TU (01852 314274). Escape from city life to the West Coast of Scotland. This beautiful island is a tranquil haven amid spectacular scenery. Call for Colour Brochure. [🐾]!

Dervaig (MULL)

Village 5 miles west of Tobermory

ARDBEG HOUSE, DERVAIG, ISLE OF MULL PA75 6QJ (Tel & Fax: 01688 400254). Comfortable country house. Four rooms are en suite, one has a private bathroom. Tea making facilities. Homely atmosphere. Situated in the picturesque village of Dervaig. Ideal for walking, fishing, birdwatching, boat trips, painting and photography; B&B from £25 pppn. AA ◆◆◆ [🐾 Pets £1 per night]. E-mail: iona@abnett.freeserve.co.uk

Gruline (Mull)

Locality at the head of Loch na Keal, 3 miles south-west of Salen.

TORLOCHAN, GRULINE, ISLE OF MULL PA71 6HR. (TEL: 01680 300380, FAX: 01680 300664). Situated in centre of Mull. Panoramic views over Loch na Keal. Working croft of 26 acres. Two Cottages, Two Log Cabins for self-catering and en-suite Bed & Breakfast. Friendly welcome awaits. "An Oasis in the Desert." Pets free of charge. [🐾]

ISLE OF SKYE

Dunvegan

Village at head of loch on north-west coast of Skye. Castle is ancient stronghold of the Macleods.

HARLOCH, NEAR DUNVEGAN, ISLE OF SKYE. Beautifully situated tradional crofthouse with panoramic views of the Cuillins and Loch Bracadale and within walking distance of the shore. Ideal for touring and walking. Tranquil. Relaxing with an enclosed garden. It is well equipped with two public rooms and two bedrooms and sleeps up to five people. TV, hi fi, washer, dryer, Pets welcome (maximum 2). Prices from £100 per week. For colour brochure contact - IRENE OR DONNIE MACDIARMID, 21 DUNROBIN AVENUE, ELDERSLIE PA5 9NW (Tel: 01505 324460)

Staffin

Crofting and fishing village on rocky coast around Staffin bay, 12 miles north of Portree.

C. M. BOOTH, GLENVIEW INN & RESTAURANT, CULNACNOC, STAFFIN IV51 9JH (01470 562248; Fax: 01470 562211). Traditional island house, ideally situated for exploring North East Skye. Comfortable en suite bedrooms. Restaurant renowned for traditional seafood, ethnic and vegetarian specialities. Dogs most welcome. STB ★★ HOTEL, Taste of Scotland, WHICH? Best B&B. [🐾] e-mail: valtos@lineone.net

ISLE OF ORKNEY

Westray

Part hilly, part low lying island

MOUNT PLEASANT, WESTRAY KW17 2DH (01857 677229). Relax on this beautiful island. Lovely sandy beach only 5 minutes' walk from caravans. Ideal for children. Indoor swimming pool. Bicycles and cars for hire. 3 caravans for hire. All linen provided. From £80-£85 per week. [🐾]

FOR THE MUTUAL GUIDANCE OF GUEST AND HOST

Every year literally thousands of holidays, short breaks and overnight stops are arranged through our guides, the vast majority without any problems at all. In a handful of cases, however, difficulties do arise about bookings, which often could have been prevented from the outset.

It is important to remember that when accommodation has been booked, both parties – guests and hosts – have entered into a form of contract. We hope that the following points will provide helpful guidance.

GUESTS: When enquiring about accommodation, be as precise as possible. Give exact dates, numbers in your party and the ages of any children. State the number and type of rooms wanted and also what catering you require – bed and breakfast, full board etc. Make sure that the position about evening meals is clear – and about pets, reductions for children or any other special points.

Read our reviews carefully to ensure that the proprietors you are going to contact can supply what you want. Ask for a letter confirming all arrangements, if possible.

If you have to cancel, do so as soon as possible. Proprietors do have the right to retain deposits and under certain circumstances to charge for cancelled holidays if adequate notice is not given and they cannot re-let the accommodation.

HOSTS: Give details about your facilities and about any special conditions. Explain your deposit system clearly and arrangements for cancellations, charges etc. and whether or not your terms include VAT.

If for any reason you are unable to fulfil an agreed booking without adequate notice, you may be under an obligation to arrange suitable alternative accommodation or to make some form of compensation.

While every effort is made to ensure accuracy, we regret that FHG Publications cannot accept responsibility for errors, omissions or misrepresentations in our entries or any consequences thereof.
Prices in particular should be checked because we go to press early. We will follow up complaints but cannot act as arbiters or agents for either party.

Aberdovey

Small resort on north shore of River Dovey estuary, 9 miles west of Machynlleth.

ABERDOVEY HOLIDAYS, DAVID & HILARY INMAN, HAFOD, CLAN DOVEY TERRACE, ABERDOVEY LL35 0EB (01654 767418). Attractive sea front flats, all have superb sea views, free car parking throughout the county. " Our guests just keep coming back".

Abersoch

Dinghy sailing and windsurfing centre with safe beaches. Pony trekking, golf, fishing and sea trips.

MR P. W. REES, "QUALITY COTTAGES", CERBID, SOLVA, HAVERFORDWEST, PEMBROKESHIRE SA62 6YE (01348 837871). Cottages set in all coastal areas, unashamed luxury, highest residential standards. Dishwashers, microwaves, washing machines. Log fires. Linen supplied. Pets welcome. [pw!]
Website: www.qualitycottages.co.uk

Bala

Natural touring centre for Snowdonia. Narrow gauge railway runs along side of Bala lake, the largest natural lake in Wales. Golf, sailing, fishing, canoeing.

MR & MRS LOOKE, RAFEL, PARC, BALA LL23 7YU (01678 540369). Delightful, cosy, well equipped cottage. Situated in tranquil, picturesque setting. £160 – £290 weekly inclusive of electricity, logs, bed linen. Open all year, short breaks available. [🐕]

TALYBONT ISA, Self-catering annexe. Twin bedded studio type with shower/bathroom, colour TV. Situated just two miles from Bala in beautiful country area. Ideal for walking, sailing, canoeing and fishing. Contact MRS G. SKINNER, TALYBONT ISA. RHYDUCHAF, BALA (01678 520234). [🐕]

MRS ANN SKINNER, TY GWYN BUNGALOW, RHYDUCHAF, BALA LL23 7SD (01678 521267). Bed and Breakfast, twin room and double room, ground floor situated in beautiful country area just near Bala Lake. Ideal area for walking, sailing, canoeing, fishing. Also six berth caravan with all mod cons to let self-catering. WTB ★★★ [🐕]

Barmouth

Modern seaside resort with two miles of sandy beaches, Surrounding hills full of interesting archaeological remains.

MR P. THOMPSON, LLWYNDU FARMHOUSE HOTEL, LLANABER, BARMOUTH LL42 1RR (01341280144). Historic farmhouse with friendly inhabitants waiting to wine and dine you in this stunning and still unspoilt part of Wales. Good food, wine, cosy atmosphere, en suite bedrooms, romance, relaxation. Situated on the Snowdonia coastline where the mountains join the sea.
e-mail: Intouch@llwyndu-farmhouse.co.uk
website: www.llwyndu-farmhouse.co.uk

LAWRENNY LODGE HOTEL, BARMOUTH LL42 1SU (01341 280466; Fax: 01341 281551). Quiet, family-run hotel overlooking harbour and estuary but only 5 minutes from town. Most rooms en suite, all with TV, tea/coffee making facilities and clock radio alarms. Restaurant menu includes vegetarian dishes. Residential licence. Large car park. WTB ★★ Hotel [🐕]

Beaumaris

Elegant little town dominated by castle built by Edward I in 13th century. Museum of Childhood has Victorian toys and music boxes.

MR P. W. REES, "QUALITY COTTAGES", CERBID, SOLVA, HAVERFORDWEST, PEMBROKESHIRE SA62 6YE (01348 837871). Cottages set in all coastal areas, unashamed luxury, highest residential standards. Dishwashers, microwaves, washing machines. Log fires. Linen supplied. Pets welcome. [pw!]
website: www.qualitycottages.co.uk

Betws-Garmon

Village 5 miles south-east of Caernarvon.

BEDDGELERT AT THE FOOT OF SNOWDON (07748 997820). Tiny cottage sleeping two in a picture post card village surrounded by wooded mountains, lakes and streams. Walkers (muddy boots) and pets welcome. Early booking advised. Cost £185 Weekly. Also mews cottagein Conwy and apartments near Beddgelert.

Beddgelert

Delightfully picturesque village in scenic landscape 4 miles south of Snowdonia.

COLWYN, BEDDGELERT, GWYNEDD LL55 4UY (01766 890276). Friendly 18th Century Cottage Guest House with beams and original stone fireplace. Most rooms en suite, one with four poster bed, all heated with fresh white linen and towels. The house is in the centre of the village overlooking the bridge. Bed and Breakfast £20 including 'walker's breakfast'. Wet pets and muddy boots welcome.WTB ★★.
e-mail: grey.wolves@virginnet.co.uk

Bodorgan

Town on the west side of the River Cefni estuary.

MRS J. GUNDRY, FARMYARD LODGE, BODORGAN, ANGLESEY LL62 5LW (01407 840977). Comfortable three-bedroomed house. Enclosed garden. Near beaches, common, forest. Fully equipped, bedding and electricity inclusive. Colour TV, microwave. Dogs and children welcome. WTB Graded 4 Dragons. [🐕]

Blaenau Ffestiniog

Good touring centre amidst dramatic scenery. Well-known slate quarries. Betws-y-Coed 12 miles. Ffestiniog 3.

OFFEREN COTTAGE, BLAENAU FFESTINIOG. Fully equipped 3-bedroomed centrally heated cottage. Sleeps 6 adults plus small child. 2 bathrooms. £89 to £285 per week. Brochure on request from: MR E.H. PRESTON, 14 SCOTT GREEN DRIVE, GILDERSOME, LEEDS LS27 7DA (Tel/Fax: 0113 252 1006 or Tel: 01766 830982). [🐕]

Bryncrug

Village 2 miles north-east of Tywyn.

IAN & WENDY JERVIS, GEUFRON FARM, BRYNCRUG, TYWYN, GWYNEDD LL36 9RW (Tel: 01654 711404). Cosy, comfortable character cottages; Two for couples only and two sleeping up to 4 so we are never over-crowded. Each cottage has lovely valley or sea views and panoramic walks from the doorstep. Short breaks available all year round. Please telephone for further details / brochure. Pets very welcome. [Pets £10 per week].

Criccieth

Popular family resort with safe beaches divided by ruins of 13th century castle. Salmon and sea trout fishing; Festival of Music & Arts in summer.

BRON RHIW HOTEL, CAERNARFON ROAD, CRICCIETH LL52 0AP (01766 522257). WTB Welcome Host - Gold Award. En suite facilities. Ironing facilities. Packed lunches. TV in all rooms. Hairdryers available. Special diets. Licensed Bar. Private parking.Telephone available. Switch/Credit cards accepted. Dogs welcome by prior arrangement. [🐕]

MRS A. M. JONES, BETWS-BACH, YNYS, CRICCIETH LL52 0PB (Tel and Fax: 01758 720047/01766 810295). Quality self-catering, traditional cosy cottages in an idyllic setting with oak beams, inglenook fireplace, log fires, antiques and lovely country furnishings. Some have four poster beds, own snooker table, sauna or jacuzzi. [🐕]
E–mail: cottages@rhos.freeserve.co.uk
Website: www.criccieth.co.uk/rhos

WERNOL CARAVAN & CHALET PARK, CHWILOG, PWLLHELI, GWYNEDD LL53 6SW (Tel & Fax: 01766 810506). Family-run park adjacent to farm. Cycle route, horse riding and golf courses nearby. Two or three bedroom chalets, and luxury caravans. Playing area, games room, pay-phone and laundry room. Colour brochure. WTB Grade 4. [Pets £10 per week.]
Website: www.wernol.com

MR P. W. REES, "QUALITY COTTAGES", CERBID, SOLVA, HAVERFORDWEST, PEMBROKESHIRE SA62 6YE (01348 837871). Cottages set in all coastal areas, unashamed luxury, highest residential standards. Dishwashers, microwaves, washing machines. Log fires. Linen supplied. Pets welcome. [pw!]
website: www.qualitycottages.co.uk

MRS LENA HUGHES JONES, TYDDYN HEILYN, CHWILOG, CRICCIETH LL53 6SW (01766 810441). Cosy, comfortably renovated Welshstone country cottage with historic features. Cardigan Bay sea views and mild Gulf Stream climate. Suitable parking and spacious garden. Three miles South Criccieth, on Llyn Peninsula and edge Snowdonia. Beautiful river walks amid wildlife, tree lined walks through farmland. Also Norwegian home to let, furnished. [🐾]

MRS M. WILLIAMS, GAERWEN FARM, YNYS, CRICCIETH LL52 0NU (01766 810324). Enjoy a break on a working farm in homely self-catering accommodation. Easy access by car to beaches, Inns, golfing etc. Short Breaks available. Pets welcome. [🐾]

Dulas Bay

On north-east coast of Anglesey, between Amlwch and Moelfre.

MRS G. McCREADIE, DERI ISAF, DULAS BAY LL70 9DX (01248 410536; Mobile: 077 21 374471). Beautiful Victorian Country House standing in 20 acres of woodland, gardens and fields. High standard of accommodation in two family rooms and one double all en suite. Pets welcome. Stabling available. ★★★. [🐾]
e-mail: mccreadie@deriisaf.freeserve.co.uk

Dwyran

Village on Anglesey 2 miles east of Newborough.

JUDY HUTCHINGS, TALY-Y-FOEL STUD FARM AND RIDING CENTRE, DWYRAN, ANGLESEY LL61 6LQ (01248 430377; Fax: 01248 430977) Waterfront location with spectacular views of Caernarfon Castle and Snowdonia. Farm en suite rooms with whirlpool baths. Private caravan. Riding and horse livery. Brochures and prices on application. WTB ★★★★ [🐾].
e-mail: riding@talyfoel.u-net.com
website: www.tal-y-foel.co.uk

Fairbourne

Bright little resort facing Barmouth across the Mawddach estuary. Safe spacious sands. A short distance inland is Cader Idris. Dolgellau 9 miles.

THE FAIRBOURNE HOTEL, FAIRBOURNE LL38 2HQ (01341 250203; Fax: 01341 250587). Views of Cardigan Bay from own grounds. Licensed. Private bathrooms. Bowls green. Games room. Car park. Open all year. Pets welcome. [🐾]

Harlech

Small stone-built town dominated by remains of 13th century castle. Golf, theatre, swimming pool, fine stretch of sands.

FRON DEG GUEST HOUSE, LLANFAIR, HARLECH LL46 2RE (01766 780448). Small Georgian cottage overlooking beach at Harlech. Pretty bedrooms. Central for unspoiled beaches and countryside, yet within easy reach of Porthmadog. Reasonable terms for Bed and Breakfast, also Dinner. [🐾]

MR P. W. REES, "QUALITY COTTAGES", CERBID, SOLVA, HAVERFORDWEST, PEMBROKESHIRE SA62 6YE (01348 837871). Cottages set in all coastal areas, unashamed luxury, highest residential standards. Dishwashers, microwaves, washing machines. Log fires. Linen supplied. Pets welcome. [pw!] website: www.qualitycottages.co.uk

Holyhead

Principal town on Holy Island. Passenger ferry terminal for Ireland

DAVID AND BARBARA PRICE, "OROTAVIA" GUEST HOUSE, 66 WALTHEW AVENUE, HOLYHEAD LL65 1AG (Tel and Fax: 01407 760259). A warm welcome to you and your pets in our guest house situated adjacent to park, beach and ferries to Ireland. Comfortable accommodation with first-class facilities. Welcome trays, colour TV and central heating in all rooms. Colour brochure available. WTB ★★★ Guest House, Welcome Host Gold Award. [🐾]

Llanddona

Village on Anglesey 3 miles north west of Beaumaris.

MR P. W. REES, "QUALITY COTTAGES", CERBID, SOLVA, HAVERFORDWEST, PEMBROKESHIRE SA62 6YE (01348 837871). Cottages set in all coastal areas, unashamed luxury, highest residential standards. Dishwashers, microwaves, washing machines. Log fires. Linen supplied. Pets welcome. [pw!] website: www.qualitycottages.co.uk

Llanfairfechan

Small resort on Conway Bay midway between Bangor and Conway.

YENTON, PROMENADE, LLANFAIRFECHAN LL33 0BY (01248 680075). Self-contained, seafront family apartments situated between the mountains and the sea. Fully-equipped, sleep two to six, sandy beach, scenic views, easy seaside or mountain walks. Good touring position. Relax in our beautiful, fragrant, award-winning garden. Pets Welcome. Ring Barbara Allix for brochure. Tourist Board Grade ★★★. [Pets £10 per week] E–mail: yenton@llan-holidays.freeserve.co.uk

Llangaffo

Village in Anglesey, 7 miles west of Menai Bridge.

ANN LAMB, PLAS LLANGAFFO, ANGLESEY LL60 6LR (01248 440452). Peaceful location near Newborough Forest and Llandwyn Bay with its miles of golden sands. Sheep, horses and hens kept. Free-range eggs and home-made marmalade for breakfast. Dinner optional. Tea/coffee making facilities. Horse riding available. [🐾]

Morfa Nefyn

Picturesque village 2 miles west of Nefyn.

MR P. W. REES, "QUALITY COTTAGES", CERBID, SOLVA, HAVERFORDWEST, PEMBROKESHIRE SA62 6YE (01348 837871). Cottages set in all coastal areas, unashamed luxury, highest residential standards. Dishwashers, microwaves, washing machines. Log fires. Linen supplied. Pets welcome. [pw!] website: www.qualitycottages.co.uk

Porthmadog

Harbour town with mile-long Cob embankment, along which runs Ffestiniog Narrow Gauge Steam Railway to Blaenau Ffestiniog. Pottery, maritime museum, car museum. Good beaches nearby.

MRS P. W. WILLIAMS, TYDDYN DU FARM, GELLILYDAN, NEAR FFESTINIOG, PORTHMADOG LL41 4RB (Tel & Fax: 01766 590281). Beautiful historic 17th century farmhouse situated in the heart of Snowdonia National Park. Cosy farmhouse bedrooms or superb stable and barn suites. WTB ★★★★★.[Pets £2 per night, £10 per week] e–mail: info@tyddyndu.co.uk website: www.tyddyndu.co.uk

MR P. W. REES, "QUALITY COTTAGES", CERBID, SOLVA, HAVERFORDWEST, PEMBROKESHIRE SA62 6YE (01348 837871). Cottages set in all coastal areas, unashamed luxury, highest residential standards. Dishwashers, microwaves, washing machines. Log fires. Linen supplied. Pets welcome. [pw!]
website: www.qualitycottages.co.uk

BLACK ROCK SANDS, PORTHMADOG. Private site, beach 150 yards.14 Caravans only. Fully equipped 6 berths. Own flush toilets. Showers and TVs. Shop and tavern nearby. APPLY: M. HUMPHRIES, 251 HEDNESFORD ROAD, NORTON CANES, CANNOCK, STAFFORDSHIRE WS11 3RZ (01543 279583).

Porth Neigel

Bay on south side of Lleyn peninsula, also known as Hell's Mouth.

Attractive cottage set in meadow near beach, quiet rural area. Sleeps 6, open fire, all comforts. Local carer. Near Abersoch. Details from MRS E.M. COOPER, 18 ST MARY'S LANE, LOUTH, LINCOLNSHIRE LN11 0DT (01507 604408 or 01472 825413).

Pwllheli

Popular sailing centre with harbour and long sandy beach. Golf, leisure centre, river and sea fishing.

MRS M. PARRY ROBERTS, "TY FRY", ABERDARON, PWLLHELI LL53 8BY (01758 760274). Modernised, fully furnished cottage with views over Aberdaron Bay. Two bedrooms sleeping five, cot, bathroom; large lounge, TV; kitchen/diner, cooker, fridge; metered electricity. Ample parking. Sandy beaches and coves, mountain walks nearby. Pets welcome. Booking March – October. SAE please.

Red Wharf Bay

Deep curving bay with vast expanse of sand, very popular for sailing and swimming.

MR P. W. REES, "QUALITY COTTAGES", CERBID, SOLVA, HAVERFORDWEST, PEMBROKESHIRE SA62 6YE (01348 837871). Cottages set in all coastal areas, unashamed luxury, highest residential standards. Dishwashers, microwaves, washing machines. Log fires. Linen supplied. Pets welcome. [pw!]
website: www.qualitycottages.co.uk

BRYN TIRION HOTEL, RED WHARF BAY, ANGLESEY LL75 8RZ (01248 852366; Fax: 01248 852013). Family-run Hotel with magnificent views. All bedrooms en suite. Large garden. Excellent restaurant. 20 minutes from Snowdonia. Ideal for touring North Wales. WTB ★★★ Hotel. [Pets £3 per night].

Trearddur Bay

Attractive holiday spot set amongst low cliffs on Holy Island, near Holyhead. Golf, sailing, fishing, swimming.

CLIFF COTTAGES AND PLAS DARIEN APARTMENTS, TREARDDUR BAY LL65 2TZ (01407 860789). Fully equipped holiday cottages, sleeping 4/8 plus cot. Near sea. Children's playground. Indoor and outdoor heated pools. Colour television. Choice of centrally heated apartments or stone-built cottages. Own private leisure complex with bowls, sauna, snooker, table tennis etc. Also tennis, croquet. Adjacent golf course. [🏌]

Talyllyn

Lake in course of River Dysynni, 2 miles south of summit of Cader Idris.

GWESTY MINFFORDD HOTEL TALYLLYN LL36 9AJ (01654 761665 Fax: 01654 761517). Small 17th century Drover's Inn at the base of Cader Idris, ideal for 'walkies' or as a centre for touring. Residential and restaurant licence; seven en suite bedrooms. WTB ★★★, AA ★★, Founder Member Taste of Wales, Good Food Guide 2000. [pw! 🏌]
e-mail: hotel@minffordd.com
website: www.minffordd.com

Tywyn

Pleasant seaside resort, start of Talyllyn Narrow Gauge Railway. Sea and river fishing, golf.

Fully equipped coastal house, close to sandy beach. 3 bedrooms, sleeps five. Gardens; garage. Pets welcome free of charge. APPLY – MR IAN WESTON, 18 ELIZABETH ROAD, BASINGSTOKE, HAMPSHIRE RG22 6AX (01256 352364; 01256 412233 evenings).

NORTH WALES

Betws-y-Coed, Colwyn Bay

SEASIDE COTTAGES

We have a large selection of self-catering seaside and country cottages, bungalows, farmhouses, caravans etc. offering superb, reasonably priced accommodation for owners and their pets. Our brochures contain details of all you need for a wonderful holiday – please telephone for your FREE copies now.

Mann's, Shaw's & Snowdonia Tourist Services.

01758 701702 (24 hours)

Edelweiss... a slice of countryside by the sea.
Conveniently located 2★ hotel.
• All rooms en-suite • Woodland gardens - pathway to beach & promenade.
• Good home cooking • Licensed bar • TV's & hospitality trays • Private car park.
Edelweiss Hotel, Colwyn Bay, North Wales. Tel: 01492 532314 - E-mail: edelweisshotel@hotmail.com

Bron-Y-Wendon Holiday Cottages

Wern Road, Llanddulas, Colwyn Bay LL22 8HG   Tel/Fax: 01492 512903   **WTB ★★★★★**
A farmhouse converted into luxurious, centrally heated cottages. Facilities include satellite TV, dishwasher, microwave and games room. All cottages have sea views and the beach is just a short walk away. Pets Welcome. Colour brochure available.   **Website: www.northwales-holidays.co.uk**

COLWYN BAY
NANT-Y-GLYN HOLIDAY PARK

WTB
★★★
★★★★
★★★★★

Cedarwood Chalets   Garden Cottages   Coach House
Situated in the exceptionally pretty, sheltered, Nant-y-Glyn valley, this unique development offers a high standard of self catering accommodation for 2-9 people. It is ideally situated for the town centre and the beach.
Pets Welcome. *For a colour brochure telephone: 01492 512282*
or visit our website at www.northwales-holidays.co.uk
Nant-y-Glyn Holiday Park, The Lodge, Nant-y-Glyn Road, Colwyn Bay LL29 7RD

The Golden Pheasant Country Hotel

Glyn Ceiriog, Near Llangollen LL20 7BB
Tel: 01691 718281 Fax: 01691 718479

This 18th Century Country Hotel situated in the beautiful
Ceiriog Valley is the ideal retreat for those wanting
comfortable accommodation, good food and a friendly
atmosphere. Surrounded by picturesque lanes, moorland
and forests it is perfect for those who love the countryside.
All 19 rooms en suite, colour TV and tea/coffee making
facilities. Traditional bar; lounges; restaurant; gardens and
patios. Dogs welcome in all rooms (except restaurant).
2 nights Dinner, Bed and Breakfast from only £85.00.

AA ★★★　　*WTB* ★★★

$\mathcal{S}unnydowns$ ✛lotel

WTB ★★★ *Luxury Hotel*

66 Abbey Road, Rhos-on-Sea,
Conway LL28 4NU
Tel: 01492 544256
Fax: 01492 543223
Web: www.hotelnorthwales.co.uk

(Proprietors: Mr & Mrs Mike Willington)

A warm, friendly welcome awaits you at the
Sunnydowns, just a two minute stroll from the
sea front. A perfect base for touring Snowdonia, the Isle of Anglesey and the famous
Castles of North Wales, or to enjoy golf, bowling, tennis, boat trips, fishing and water sports
nearby. There are also lovely walks for you and your dog to enjoy and Llandudno and
Colwyn Bay are only five minutes' drive away. The hotel has a lounge, bar, games
room, sauna and car park. Enjoy excellent cooking in our non-smoking restaurant (Thai
cuisine a speciality) or, by arrangement, eat in the Bar with your dog. Special diets can
be catered for. All bedrooms are en suite, with colour TV (video & satellite), tea/coffee
making facilities, hairdyer, mini-bar, refrigerator, direct dial telephone and baby listening
service. Dog sitting also available. We are open all year.

For further information, please phone or write for our colour brochure.

PUBLISHER'S NOTE

While every effort is made to ensure accuracy, we regret that FHG
Publications cannot accept responsibility for errors, omissions or
misrepresentations in our entries or any consequences thereof. Prices in
particular should be checked because we go to press early. We will follow up
complaints but cannot act as arbiters or agents for either party.

Betws-y-Coed

Popular mountain resort in picturesque setting where three rivers meet. Trout fishing, craft shops, golf, railway and motor museums, Snowdonia National Park Visitor Centre. Nearby Swallow Falls are famous beauty spot.

SEASIDE COTTAGES. MANN'S, SHAW'S AND SNOWDONIA TOURIST SERVICES (01758 701702). Large selection of self-catering seaside and country cottages, bungalows, farmhouses, caravans etc. offering superb, reasonably priced accommodation for owners and their pets. Please telephone for brochure.

SUMMER HILL NON-SMOKERS' GUEST HOUSE, BETWS-Y-COED LL24 0BL (01690 710306). Quiet location, overlooking river. 150 yards from main road and shops. En suite and standard rooms, tea-making facilities. Residents' lounge. TV. Ideal for walkers. B&B from £17.50. [Pets £1.50 per night.]

MRS MORRIS, TY COCH FARM-TREKKING CENTRE, PENMACHNO, BETWS-Y-COED LL25 0HJ (01690 760248). Hill farm in Wales. TV, teamaking, en suite. Set in National Park/Snowdonia. Very quiet and well off the beaten track. A great welcome and good food. Many return visits. [🐾]

Colwyn Bay

Lively seaside resort with promenade amusements. Attractions include Mountain Zoo, Eirias Park; golf, tennis, riding and other sports. Good touring centre for Snowdonia. The quieter resort of Rhos-on-Sea lies at the western end of the bay

EDELWEISS HOTEL, OFF LAWSON ROAD, COLWYN BAY LL29 8HD (01492 532314). Comfortable Country House Hotel set in own wooded grounds close to open parkland; ideal for dog owners. All rooms with en suite facilities. Well-behaved dogs welcome. [🐾] e-mail: edelweisshotel@hotmail.com

MRS L.J. DENT, BRON-Y-WENDON HOLIDAY COTTAGES, WERN ROAD, LLANDDULAS, COLWYN BAY LL22 8HG (Tel/Fax: 01492 512903). The ultimate in self-catering accommodation. Luxurious, centrally heated cottages with sea views. Facilities include satellite TV, dishwasher, microwave and games room. Beach just a short walk away. Pets welcome. Colour brochure. [🐾]

NANT-Y-GLYN HOLIDAY PARK, THE LODGE, NANT-Y-GLYN ROAD, COLWYN BAY LL29 7RD (01492 512282). Set in a peaceful, sheltered valley, Nant-y-Glyn offers cedarwood chalets, garden cottages and a coach house. 15 minutes' walk to the beach and town centre. Colour brochure available. WTB ★★★/★★★★/★★★★★ [Pets £8 per week].

Conwy

One of the best preserved medieval fortified towns in Britain on dramatic estuary setting. Telford Suspension Bridge, many historic buildings, lively quayside (site of smallest house in Britain). Golf, pony trekking, pleasure cruises.

THE LODGE, TAL-Y-BONT, CONWY LL32 8YX (01492 660766; Fax: 01492 660534; Freephone: 0800 9176593). Family-run Hotel with lovely en suite bedrooms. Enjoy peace and quiet, superb food and attention from friendly and efficient staff. B&B from £25 to £45; two days DB&B from £80 to £105 Pets welcome. [Pets £2 per night] E-mail: bbaldon@lodgehotel.co.uk Website: www.lodgehotel.co.uk

SYCHNANT PASS HOUSE, SYCHNANT PASS ROAD, CONWY LL32 8BJ (01492 596868). Sychnant Pass House is a lovely Victorian House set in two acres with a little pond and stream running through it. Step out of our garden and straight onto Snowdonia National Park land where you can walk for miles with your dogs. All rooms en suite. [🐾]

GLAN HEULOG GUEST HOUSE, LLANRWST ROAD, CONWY LL32 8LT (01492 593845). Victorian house close to historic town of Conwy and its Castle. All rooms en suite, TV and tea/coffee facilities. Convenient for many attractions. Children welcome. Car parking. B&B from £15. WTB ★★, AA ◆◆◆

Conwy Valley

Scenic area with many places of interest.

Secluded cottages with log fire and beams. Dogs will love it. Plenty of walks around mountains and lakes. For 2 - 7 people plus their pet(s). MRS WILLIAMS, LOW RISBY HOUSE, LOW RISBY, SCUNTHORPE, NORTH LINCOLNSHIRE DN15 0BX (01724 733990 or 0411 217 448) week lets only. [🐾]

"Saronfa", an attractive self-catering cottage in the beautiful Conwy Valley. Sleeps 4. Pets taken. Well equipped. Cosy log fire. Owner supervised. Snowdonia National Park, mountains, river, lakes. Terms £110 to £250. Winter Breaks from £16 per night. Free logs. MRS M.C. WADDINGHAM, "CEFN", TYN-Y-GROES, CONWY LL32 8TA (01492 650233; mobile: 077 74 860233). [🐾] e-mail: cottagenwales@supanet.com

Llandudno

Premier holiday resort of North Wales coast flanked by Great Orme and Little Orme headlands. Wide promenade, pier, two beaches; water ski-ing, sailing, fishing trips from jetty. Excellent sports facilities: golf, indoor pool, tennis, pony trekking, Leisure Centre. Summer variety shows, Alice In Wonderland Visitor Centre.

WARWICK HOTEL, 56 CHURCH WALKS, LLANDUDNO LL30 2HL (01492 876823). Friendly family-run hotel, all rooms en suite. Colour TV, hospitality trays. Superb discounts throughout the year. Private garden. 5 minutes' walk to town centre and pier. Pets welcome free of charge. [🐾]

TOM & CAROL LONG, HEN DY HOTEL, 10 NORTH PARADE, LLANDUDNO LL30 2LP (01492 876184). Experience the warm welcome extended by the proprietors of this charming Hotel, set opposite the Pier, with panoramic views. All rooms with central heating, TV, radio, teamakers; all en suite. Good food. Cosy bar. Tariff on request. WTB ★★ Hotel. [Pets £2 per night, £12 per week]

MR AND MRS J. WILLIAMS, DEVA, 34 TRINITY AVENUE, LLANDUDNO LL30 2TQ (01492 879518). Three top grade Self-contained Holiday Apartments for 2/3/4 adults. Central location. Car parking on premises. Short breaks early and late season. Highly Recomended Telephone for brochure. Well behaved dogs welcome.[🐾]

CLIFFBURY HOTEL, 34 ST. DAVID'S ROAD, LLANDUDNO LL30 2UH (01492 877224; Fax: 01492 873524) Pets and well behaved owners very welcome at our non-smoking hotel situated in a quiet area close to town centre and both beaches. Car park. En-suite rooms with TV and beverage making facilities. Please contact John or Rita for brochure. WTB ★★ Hotel. [🐾] e-mail: cliffbury@lineone.net website: www.cliffburyhotel.co.uk

Llangollen

Famous for International Music Eisteddfod held in July. Plas Newydd, Valle Crucis Abbey nearby. Standard gauge steam railway; canal cruises; ideal for golf and walking.

PEN-Y-DYFFRYN COUNTRY HOUSE HOTEL, NEAR RHYDYCROESAU, OSWESTRY SY10 7JD (01691 653700). Picturesque Georgian Rectory quietly set in Shropshire/ Welsh Hills. Ten en suite bedrooms, two with private patios. 5-acre grounds. No passing traffic. Johansens recommended. Dinner, Bed and Breakfast from £57.00 per person per day. AA/ETC ★★★. [🐾 pw!] E-mail: stay@peny.co.uk Website: www.peny.co.uk

BRYN DERWEN HOTEL, ABBEY ROAD, LLANGOLLEN LL20 8EF (01978 860583). Warm, friendly welcome for your pet in well-appointed hotel in picturesque Dee Valley. Super walking country, many tourist attractions including Llangollen Steam Railway. Special discounts for Pets Welcome! readers. [🐾] Website: www.city2000.com/tl/bryn-derwen-hotel.html

GOLDEN PHEASANT COUNTRY HOTEL, GLYN CEIRIOG, NEAR LLANGOLLEN LL20 7BB (01691 718281; Fax: 01691 718479). WTB/AA 3 Star. Situated in the beautiful Ceiriog Valley. All 19 rooms en suite, colour TV and tea/coffee making facilities. Dogs welcome in all rooms (except restaurant). 2 nights Dinner, Bed and Breakfast from only £85.00 p.p. [🐾]

Rhos-on-Sea

Popular resort at east end of Penrhyn Bay, adjoining Colwyn Bay to the north-west.

SUNNYDOWNS HOTEL, 66 ABBEY ROAD, RHOS-ON-SEA, CONWY LL28 4NU (01492 544256; Fax: 01492 543223). A WTB ★★★ luxury family hotel just 2 minutes' walk to beach & shops. All rooms en suite with colour TV, video & satellite channels, tea/coffee facilities and central heating. Hotel has bar, pool room and car park. [🅱 pw!]

Trefriw

Hillside village, popular as spa in Victorian times. Local beauty spots at Llyn Crafnant and Llyn Geironnydd. Woollen mill demonstrating traditional techniques.

MRS B. COLE, GLANDWR, TREFRIW, NEAR LLANRWST LL27 0JP (01492 640431). Large Country House on outskirts of Trefriw village. Good touring area with Llanrwst, Betws-y-Coed and Swallow Falls five miles away. Fishing, walking, golf, pony trekking closeby. Comfortable bedrooms, lounge with TV, dining room. Good home cooking. Parking. B&B from £18.

CARDIGAN

Aberaeron, Aberporth

Aberaeron

Attractive little town on Cardigan Bay, good touring centre for coast and inland. The Aeron Express Aerial ferry offers an exciting trip across the harbour. Marine aquarium; Aberarth Leisure Park nearby.

GILFACH HOLIDAY VILLAGE, LLWYNCELYN, NEAR ABERAERON SA46 OHN (01545 580288). Choice of modern Bungalows (4 persons) or luxury 2/3 person apartments. Fully equipped, linen, colour TV. Horse and pony riding. Tennis. Write or phone for brochure pack to the Manager. [Pets £15 per week.

Aberporth

Popular seaside village offering safe swimming and good sea fishing. Good base for exploring Cardigan Bay coastline.

MRS JANN TUCKER, PENFFYNNON, ABERPORTH, CARDIGAN SA34 2DA (Tel: 01239 810387; Fax: 01239 811401). Comfortable, self-contained, fully-equipped cottages adjacent to safe and sandy beaches. Dogs welcome by arrangement. Local attractions include water sports, Cardigan Bay dolphins and walking in the Presceli Hills. £150-£800per week. [🐾]
e–mail: tt@lineone.net

MR P. W. REES, "QUALITY COTTAGES", CERBID, SOLVA, HAVERFORDWEST, PEMBROKESHIRE SA62 6YE (01348 837871). Cottages set in all coastal areas, unashamed luxury, highest residential standards. Dishwashers, microwaves, washing machines. Log fires. Linen supplied. Pets welcome. [pw!] website: www.qualitycottages.co.uk

MISS M. ALLEN, YR YSGUBOR, PANTYFFWRN, ABERPORTH, CARDIGAN SA43 2DT (01239 810509). Sleeps 2. Delightful stone Cottage on beautiful, unspoilt West Wales coast. Quiet, comfortable; all amenities. Large dog-friendly garden. Ample parking. From £70 plus electricity. [🐾]

Ciliau Aeron

Village in undulating country just inland from the charming Cardigan Bay resorts of New Quay and Aberaeron. New Quay 12 miles, Aberaeron 6.

MR P. W. REES, "QUALITY COTTAGES", CERBID, SOLVA, HAVERFORDWEST, PEMBROKESHIRE SA62 6YE (01348 837871). Cottages set in all coastal areas, unashamed luxury, highest residential standards. Dishwashers, microwaves, washing machines. Log fires. Linen supplied. Pets welcome. [pw!] website: www.qualitycottages.co.uk

Lampeter

Small market town on River Teifi 20 miles from Carmarthen.

TYGLYN HOLIDAY ESTATE, CILIAU AERON, LAMPETER, CEREDIGION SA48 8DD (Tel/Fax: 01570 470684) Semi-detached self-catering bungalows, sleep 4-6. Bar and restaurant adjoining. Horseriding, golf, tennis, bowls, walking, swimming, ten-pin bowling, cycling, quad-biking and leisure centres - all nearby.
Website: www.tyglynholidaybungalows.co.uk

Llangrannog

Pretty little seaside village overlooking a sandy beach. Superb cliff walk to NT Ynys Lochtyn, a secluded promontory.

TYGLYN HOLIDAY ESTATE, CILIAU AERON, LAMPETER, CEREDIGION SA48 8DD (Tel/Fax: 01570 470684) Semi-detached self-catering bungalows, sleep 4-6. Bar and restaurant adjoining. Horseriding, golf, tennis, bowls, walking, swimming, ten-pin bowling, cycling, quad-biking and leisure centres - all nearby.
Website: www.tyglynholidaybungalows.co.uk

MR P. W. REES, "QUALITY COTTAGES", CERBID, SOLVA, HAVERFORDWEST, PEMBROKESHIRE SA62 6YE (01348 837871). Cottages set in all coastal areas, unashamed luxury, highest residential standards. Dishwashers, microwaves, washing machines. Log fires. Linen supplied. Pets welcome. [pw!]
website: www.qualitycottages.co.uk

PEMBROKESHIRE

Aberystwyth

Many of our top quality holiday properties accept pets.

PETS WELCOME

Cottages in Devon, Cornwall, Cotswolds, Pembrokeshire & the Heart of England.

COTTAGES
SHORT BREAKS AVAILABLE
For 120 page 2001 Colour Brochure
FREEPHONE 0800 378771 (24 hrs)
Powells Cottage Holidays, High Street, Saundersfoot, Pembrokeshire SA69 9EJ

TALBOT HOTEL

Newly refurbished Talbot Hotel is conveniently situated in the middle of town, near the shopping centre. All rooms are en suite we have a fully licensed bar, and can cater for parties and conferences. Only 2 minutes from the seaside. Free parking is available nearby. Open all year, TV in all rooms, full liquor licence. All pets welcome.
MARKET STREET, ABERYSTWYTH SY23 1DL (TEL: 01970 612575)

The
GOLF GUIDE
Where to Play
Where to Stay
2001

Available from most bookshops, the 2001 edition of **THE GOLF GUIDE** covers details of every UK golf course – well over 2500 entries – for holiday or business golf. Hundreds of hotel entries offer convenient accommodation, accompanying details of the courses – the 'pro', par score, length etc.

In association with 'Golf Monthly' and including the Ryder Cup Report as well as Holiday Golf in Ireland, France, Portugal, Spain, The USA, South Africa and Thailand .

£9.99 from bookshops or £10.50 including postage (UK only) from FHG Publications, Abbey Mill Business Centre, Paisley PA1 ITJ

POWELLS COTTAGE HOLIDAYS, HIGH STREET, SAUNDERSFOOT, PEMBROKESHIRE SA69 9EJ. Many of our top quality holiday properties accept pets. Cottages in Devon, Cornwall, Cotswolds, Pembrokeshire and Heart of England. For colour brochure FREEPHONE 0800 378771 (24 hours). [Pets £15 per week.]

Aberystwyth

Resort and small port at mouth of Rivers Rheidol and Yswyth on Cardigan Bay, 82 miles north-west of Cardiff.

MR E DAVIES, TALBOT HOTEL, MARKET STREET, ABERYSTWYTH SY23 1DL (01970 612575). Newly refurbished hotel, near shopping centre; all rooms en suite, fully licensed bar, only 2 minutes from the seaside, free parking and all pets welcome.

Bosherston

Village 4 miles south of Pembroke, bordered by 3 man-made lakes, a haven for wildlife and covered in water lilies in early summer.

MR P. W. REES, "QUALITY COTTAGES", CERBID, SOLVA, HAVERFORDWEST, PEMBROKESHIRE SA62 6YE (01348 837871). Cottages set in all coastal areas, unashamed luxury, highest residential standards. Dishwashers, microwaves, washing machines. Log fires. Linen supplied. Pets welcome. [pw!] Website: www.qualitycottages.co.uk

Broad Haven

Attractive little resort on St Bride's Bay in the Pembrokeshire Coast National Park. Superb sandy beach; National Park Information Centre.

MILLMOOR FARM COTTAGES AND ROCKSDRIFT APARTMENTS. Enjoy a relaxing and peaceful holiday only yards from safe sandy beaches and woodland walks. Personal supervision. Microwaves, fridge freezers, colour TV plus videos. Full central heating. Children's play areas, cots, high chairs. Brochure from HELEN MOCK (REF: PW01), MILLMOOR, BROAD HAVEN, HAVERFORDWEST SA62 3JH (01437 781507; Fax 01437 781002; FREEPHONE 0800 01 999 30). [Pets £12 per week.]

PEMBROKESHIRE NATIONAL PARK. Sleeps 6. Three-bedroom fully furnished Holiday House. Walking distance sandy beaches and coastal footpath. £120 to £300 per week. MRS L.P. ASHTON, 10 ST LEONARDS ROAD, THAMES DITTON, SURREY KT7 0RJ (020-8398 6349). [🐕] e–mail: lejash@aol.com

Croes Goch

Hamlet 6 miles north east of St Davids.

MR P. W. REES, "QUALITY COTTAGES", CERBID, SOLVA, HAVERFORDWEST, PEMBROKESHIRE SA62 6YE (01348 837871). Cottages set in all coastal areas, unashamed luxury, highest residential standards. Dishwashers, microwaves, washing machines. Log fires. Linen supplied. Pets welcome. [pw!] website: www.qualitycottages.co.uk

Croft

Village to the south-west of Cardigan.

CROFT FARM & CELTIC COTTAGES, CROFT NEAR CARDIGAN SA43 3NT (01239 615179). Featured in Daily Mail. Stone barn conversions with gym and recreation room, indoor heated pool, jacuzzi, and sauna . Orchard, colourful gardens, patio, BBQ and play area. WTB 5 Stars Award. Pets welcome. [Pets £15 per week] [pw!]

Haverfordwest

Administrative and shopping centre for the area; ideal base for exploring National Park Historic town of narrow streets; museum in castle grounds; many fine buildings.

PHILIP & HELEN THOMAS, NOLTON CROSS CARAVAN PARK, NOLTON, HAVERFORDWEST SA62 3NP (01437 710701 Fax: 01437 710329). Small, quiet, family park set in open countryside overlooking St Brides Bay. Ideal for touring. Luxury caravans for hire; short breaks available. Open March to November. WTB ★★★ Touring and Holiday Park. [🐕]

JEAN AND MAURICE GOULD, SCAMFORD CARAVAN PARK, KEESTON, HAVERFORDWEST SA62 6HN (Tel & Fax: 01437 710304). 25 luxurious caravans (shower, fridge, microwave, colour TV). Peaceful park near lovely sandy beaches. Super playground. Launderette. Five touring pitches, hook-ups. Modern shower block. [Pets £5 per week] E-mail: scamfordcaravanpark@talk21.com Website: www.scamford-caravan-holidays.co.uk

MRS C. REES, DUDWELL, CAMROSE, HAVERFORDWEST, PEMBROKESHIRE SA62 6HJ (01437 710324). Large house and stables in own grounds fully equipped, sleeps 10, close to beaches and pubs. Excellent riding country. Bring your own horse or hire nearby.

CLARE HALLETT, KEESTON HILL COTTAGE, KEESTON, HAVERFORDWEST SA62 6EJ (01437 710440; Fax: 01437 710840). Two fully equipped comfortable apartments sleeping 4/5 each, in a beautifully converted cottage with garden. Two-and-a-half miles from fabulous beaches. A short walk to our family run restaurant/bar. Open all year. Central heating, electricity and linen included.

Lawrenny

Village near River Cresswell estuary, 8 miles south-west of Narberth

MRS VIRGINIA LORT PHILLIPS, KNOWLES FARM, LAWRENNY SA68 0PX (01834 891221; Fax: 01834 891344). Come and relax with us. Spoil yourselves and your dogs while discovering the delights of hidden Pembrokeshire. Walk along the shores of the Estuary which surrounds us. Stunning coast within 15 minutes. Lovely South facing Farmhouse. B&B from £18, dinner on request. WTB ★★★ FARM. e–mail: ginilp@lawrenny.org.uk

Little Haven

Village on St Bride's Bay, 10 miles from Haverfordwest.

HAVEN COTTAGES, WHITEGATES, LITTLE HAVEN, HAVERFORDWEST, PEMBROKESHIRE SA62 3LA (01437 781552; Fax: 01437 781386). Cottages sleep two to twelve. On Coastal Path, 200 yards beach. Organic chicken and ostrich farm. Linen provided. B&B in fishing village. WTB ★★★ AA QQQQ. [Pets £12 per week]
E-mail: welshhaven@aol.com

Manorbier

Unspoiled village on South Pembrokeshire coast near Tenby. Sandy bay and fine coastal walks.

AQUARIUM COTTAGE, THE LOBSTER POT AND ORCHARD END, MANORBIER. Three pleasant country properties. Detached Cottage (sleeps 6). Ground-floor Flat (sleeps 4). Detached Bungalow (sleeps 6). All properties half-a-mile from the sea. Ample parking. Electricity, heating, bed linen and towels inclusive. Pets Welcome. Brochure available from: MRS J. HUGHES, ROSE COTTAGE, MANORBIER, PEMBROKESHIRE SA70 7ST (01834 871408). [🐾]
Website: www.aquariumcottage.co.uk

Newgale

On St Bride's Bay 3 miles east of Solva. Long beach where at exceptionally low tide the stumps of a submerged forest may be seen.

MR P. W. REES, "QUALITY COTTAGES", CERBID, SOLVA, HAVERFORDWEST, PEMBROKESHIRE SA62 6YE (01348 837871). Cottages set in all coastal areas, unashamed luxury, highest residential standards. Dishwashers, microwaves, washing machines. Log fires. Linen supplied. Pets welcome. [pw!]
Website: www.qualitycottages.co.uk

Newport

Small town at mouth of the River Nyfer, 9 miles south west of Cardigan. Remains of 13th-century castle.

MR P. W. REES, "QUALITY COTTAGES", CERBID, SOLVA, HAVERFORDWEST, PEMBROKESHIRE SA62 6YE (01348 837871). Cottages set in all coastal areas, unashamed luxury, highest residential standards. Dishwashers, microwaves, washing machines. Log fires. Linen supplied. Pets welcome. [pw!]
Website: www.qualitycottages.co.uk

Nolton Haven

Hamlet at head of inlet on St Bride's Bay. Fine coastal views.

J. CANTON, NOLTON HAVEN FARM, NOLTON HAVEN, HAVERFORDWEST SA62 6NH (01437 710263). Quality beachfront cottages 30 yards from Nolton Haven's sandy beach. Fully equipped, sleeping 4/6. Also nearby farm guest house offering Bed and Breakfast. [🐾 £5 per week self catering].
e-mail: pw@noltonhaven.com

FOLKESTON HILL HOLIDAY BUNGALOWS. A small group of bungalows in a sheltered valley which winds down to the sea. WTB Graded. Pets welcome – no charge. Brochure from JOHN & CERI PRICE, ST BRIDES BAY COTTAGES, NINE WELLS, SOLVA, HAVERFORDWEST, PEMBROKESHIRE SA62 6UH (01437 720027). [🐾]

St David's

Smallest cathedral city in Britain, shrine of Wales' patron saint. Magnificent ruins of Bishop's Palace. Craft shops, farm parks and museums; boat trips to Ramsey Island.

FELINDRE COTTAGES, PORTHGAIN, ST. DAVIDS, HAVERFORDWEST, PEMBROKESHIRE SA62 5BH (01348 831220). Well-equipped self catering cottages set in peaceful 8 acre location. Sea views. Away from main roads, safe for children welcome. One well-behaved dog welcome, except in August. Near sandy beaches, spectacular cliff walks and pub. WTB graded. [pw! £10 per week]
E-mail: steve@felindrecottages.co.uk
Website: www.felindrecottages.co.uk

RAMSEY HOUSE, LOWER MOOR, ST DAVID'S SA62 6RP (01437 720321). Mac and Sandra Thompson offer quiet relaxation exclusively for non-smoking adults. Superior en suite rooms with central heating, TV and tea makers. Traditional Welsh cuisine. Licensed bar. Parking. Open all year. Superb beaches and walks nearby – DOGS' PARADISE! WTB ★★★★ Guest House, RAC/AA ◆◆◆◆, DB&B £44 – £48. [🐾 - Maximum 2 dogs]

FFYNNON DDOFN, LLANON, LLANRHIAN, NEAR ST DAVID'S. Comfortable, well-equipped cottage with panoramic coastal views. Sleeps 6. Fully carpeted with central heating. Large games room. Open all year. Pets welcome free of charge. Brochure on request from: MRS T.A. REES WHITE, BRICKHOUSE FARM, BURNHAM RD, WOODHAM MORTIMER, MALDON, ESSEX CM9 6SR (01245 224611). [🐾]

MR P. W. REES, "QUALITY COTTAGES", CERBID, SOLVA, HAVERFORDWEST, PEMBROKESHIRE SA62 6YE (01348 837871). Cottages set in all coastal areas, unashamed luxury, highest residential standards. Dishwashers, microwaves, washing machines. Log fires. Linen supplied. Pets welcome. [pw!] Website: www.qualitycottages.co.uk

LOWER MOOR COTTAGES, ST DAVID'S. Beautifully restored stone and slate cottages. Panoramic views over coast and open countryside. Near coastal path and sandy beaches. Dishwashers, TV, games room, log fire, gas fired central heating. Open all year. Two to seven bedrooms; sleep four to sixteen. WTB Graded Five Dragons. Correspondence: T. M. HARDMAN, 140 CHURCH ROAD, EARLEY, READING RG6 1HR. Telephone: LILIAN MARLOW (0118 9266094).[pets £10 per week] E-mail: enquiries@lowermoorcottages.co.uk

Saundersfoot

Popular resort and sailing centre with picturesque harbour and sandy beach. Tenby 3 miles

VINE FARM, THE RIDGEWAY, SAUNDERSFOOT SA69 9LA (01834 813543). Former Farmhouse close to village and beaches. Central heating, log fires. All rooms en suite. Pets welcome – garden and paddock. AA Listed ◆◆◆◆. [pw! Pets £1-£2 per night.] Also available, one-bedroomed self -catering flat for 2.

MRS JOY HOLGATE, CARNE MOUNTAIN FARM, REYNALTON, KILGETTY SA68 0PD (01834 860 546). A warm welcome awaits you at our lovely 200-year-old farmhouse set amidst the peace and tranquillity of the beautiful Pembrokeshire countryside. Bedrooms have colour TV and all facilities. B&B from £17. [One dog free, second pet £1.00 per night.]

Solva

Picturesque coastal village with sheltered harbour and excellent craft shops. Sailing and watersports; sea fishing, long sandy beach.

MRS M. JONES, LOCHMEYLER FARM GUEST HOUSE, PEN-Y-CWM, NEAR SOLVA, ST DAVID'S SA62 6LL (01348 837724; Fax: 01348 837622). , Welcome Host Gold Award. 16 en suite luxury bedrooms, eight in the cottage suites adjacent to the house. All bedrooms non-smoking, with TV, video and refreshment facilities. Children Welcome. WTB ★★★★ Farm, RAC ◆◆◆◆ [pw! 🐾]

MR P. W. REES, "QUALITY COTTAGES", CERBID, SOLVA, HAVERFORDWEST, PEMBROKESHIRE SA62 6YE (01348 837871). Cottages set in all coastal areas, unashamed luxury, highest residential standards. Dishwashers, microwaves, washing machines. Log fires. Linen supplied. Pets welcome. [pw!] website: www.qualitycottages.co.uk

Tenby

Popular resort with two wide beaches. Fishing trips, craft shops, museum. Medieval castle ruins, 13th-century church. Golf, fishing and watersports; boat trips to nearby Caldy Island with monastery and medieval church.

MR P. W. REES, "QUALITY COTTAGES", CERBID, SOLVA, HAVERFORDWEST, PEMBROKESHIRE SA62 6YE (01348 837871). Cottages set in all coastal areas, unashamed luxury, highest residential standards. Dishwashers, microwaves, washing machines. Log fires. Linen supplied. Pets welcome. [pw!] website: www.qualitycottages.co.uk

Whitland

Village 6 miles east of Narberth. Scanty ruins of 12th century Cistercian house remain.

MARGARET & PETER GILDER, LLANGWM HOUSE, WHITLAND SA34 0RB (Tel & Fax 01994 240621). Fully modernised farmhouse set in its own 15 acres. En suite bedrooms with colour TV and tea/coffee making facilities. Licensed bar. No children under five. From £22. [🐕]
e–mail: llangwm.house@tesco.net

POWYS

Brecon

Brecon

Main touring centre for National Park. Busy market; Jazz Festival in summer. Brecknock Museum, ruined castle, cathedral of interest. Golf, walking, fishing, canal cruising, pony trekking.

THE BEACONS, ACCOMMODATION AND RESTAURANT, 16 BRIDGE STREET, BRECON LD3 8AH (Tel/Fax: 01874 623339). In the heart of the National Park. A recently restored Georgian townhouse with beautifully appointed standard en suite and luxury period rooms. Candlelit restaurant offering fine food and wines (5 nights). Clean, well-behaved pets with responsible owners welcome. WTB ★★★ Guest House, AA/RAC ◆◆◆. [Pets £2 per night] e–mail: beacons@brecon.co.uk website: www.beacons.brecon.co.uk

Builth Wells

Old country town in lovely setting on River Wye amid beautiful hills. Lively markets; host to Royal Welsh Agricultural Show.

MRS KATHERINE SMITH, CAER BERIS MANOR, BUILTH WELLS LD2 3NP (01982 552601; Fax: 01982 552586). Family owned country house hotel set in 27 acres of parkland. Free salmon and trout fishing; golf nearby, superb walking and touring. All rooms en suite. WTB/AA ★★★. [Pets £3.50] e-mail: caerberismanor@btinternet.com website: www.caerberis.co.uk

MRS LINDA WILLIAMS, OLD VICARAGE, ERWOOD, BUILTH WELLS LD2 3SZ (01982 560680). Situated in secluded grounds with glorious views of the beautiful Wye Valley. Attractive spacious rooms have double aspects, TV, drinks tray, wash basin. Guests own bathroom, separate WC. Bacon and sausage from local traditionally reared pigs, free range eggs and home made preserves for breakfast. WTB ★★★.

Crickhowell

Pleasant village in the Usk Valley at foot of Black Mountains. Fine Georgian houses, fragments of a castle, gateway of a long-vanished manor house, and 14th-cent church with elaborate tombs.

MRS P. LLEWELYN, WHITE HALL, GLANGRWYNEY, CRICKHOWELL NP8 1EW (01873 811155/840267). Comfortably furnished and well placed for exploring Black Mountains, Brecon Beacons, Big Pit Mine, Abergavenny and Hay-on-Wye. Double and twin-bedded en suite rooms with TV and tea-making. Restaurant dog friendly pub one mile. Terms from £15. WTB ★. [🐾]

Garthmyl

Situated on A483 between Welshpool and Newtown in unspoilt countryside.

Self-catering log cabins set in 30 acres of unspoilt woodland teeming with wildlife. Central heating, colour TV, microwave etc. Pets Welcome. From £175 – £615 per cabin per week breaks. Apply PENLLWYN LODGES, GARTHMYL, POWYS SY15 6SB or Tel/Fax 01686 640269 for colour brochure. [Pets £10 per stay] Website: www.selfcateringmidwales.com

Hay-on-Wye

Small market town at north end of Black Mountains, 15 miles north-east of Brecon.

PETER & OLWEN ROBERTS, YORK HOUSE, CUSOP, HAY-ON-WYE HR3 5QX (Tel/Fax: 01497 820705). Enjoy a relaxing holiday in this elegant Victorian Guest House quietly situated on the edge of Hay, "Town of Books". Excellent walking country for pets. AA ◆◆◆◆. [Pets £4.00 per visit.] website: www.hay-on-wye.co.uk/yorkhouse/welcome.html

MRS E. BALLY, LANE FARM, PAINSCASTLE, BUILTH WELLS LD2 3JS (Tel/Fax: 01497 851605). 17th century farm in rural Radnorshire, five miles Hay-on-Wye. Wonderful walking country. Self-catering apartments and Bed and Breakfast accommodation. A warm welcome for you and your pet(s).WTB ★★★. [🐾] e-mail: jbally@btclick.com

Llandrindod Wells

Popular inland resort, Victorian spa town, excellent touring centre. Golf, fishing, bowling, boating and tennis. Visitors can still take the waters at Rock Park Gardens.

THE PARK MOTEL, CROSSGATES, LLANDRINDOD WELLS LD1 6RF (01597 851201). In three acres, amidst beautiful countryside near Elan Valley. Luxury, self-contained, centrally heated Chalets. Licensed restaurant open all day. Swimming pool. Children's play area. Pets welcome. [Pets £1 per night, £5 per week]

Llanfair Caereinion

Small town on River Banwy, 8 miles west of Welshpool.

MRS ANN REED, MADOG'S WELLS, LLANFAIR CAEREINION, WELSHPOOL SY21 0DE (01938 810446). WTB 4 Dragons. Furnished bungalow designed for wheelchair access. Open all year. Also two six berth caravans, available April to November. Farmhouse B&B from £17 per person. [🐾]

Llangurig

Village on River Wye, 4 miles south-west of Llanidloes. Ideal walking countryside.

THE OLD VICARAGE COUNTRY GUEST HOUSE, LLANGURIG, MONTGOMERYSHIRE SY18 6RN (01686 440280). Charming Victorian house, ideal base for exploring the mountains and valleys of this unspoilt area. All bedrooms en suite. Warm welcome guaranteed. WTB ★★ [🐾]

MRS J. BAILEY, GLANGWY, LLANGURIG, LLANIDLOES SY18 6RS (01686 440697). Bed, breakfast and evening meals in the countryside. Plenty of walking locally. Prices on request.

Machynlleth

Small market town and tourist centre on River Dovey Valley. 16 miles north-east of Aberystwyth

PETS WELCOME at The Wynnstay Hotel in the historic Market Town of Machynlleth. This superb Johansens recommended hotel on the edge of Snowdonia National Park offers sandy beaches and glorious Welsh countryside perfect for long walks. Further details: 01654 702941.

website: www.wynnstay-hotel.com

Presteigne

Attractive old town with half timbered houses. Ideal for hillside rambles and pony trekking.

MRS R. L. JONES, UPPER HOUSE, KINNERTON, NEAR PRESTEIGNE LD8 2PE (01547 560207). Charming Tudor Cottage in lovely Border countryside. 2 miles from Offa's Dyke. Storage heaters, washing machine, microwave, colour TV, woodburner. Linen hire optional. Sleeps 5 plus 2 cots. Ample parking. Sun-trap garden. On working farm in peaceful hamlet. Children and pets welcome. WTB Grade 4. [🐾].

Rhayader

Small market town on River Wye north of Builth Wells. Popular for angling and pony trekking

OAK WOOD LODGES - SELF-CATERING LOG CABINS. Luxurious Norwegian log cabins with spectacular views of the Elan Valley and Cambrian Mountains. Walking, pony trekking, mountain biking, fishing and bird watching in idyllic surroundings. (01597 811422).

SOUTH WALES

Swansea, Wye Valley

Abergavenny

Historic market town at south-eastern gateway to Brecon Beacons National Park. Pony trekking, leisure centre; excellent touring base for Vale of Usk.

CHRISTINE SMITH, THE HALF MOON, LLANTHONY, NEAR ABERGAVENNY NP7 7NN (01873 890611). Friendly 17th-Century Inn. Serves good food and real ale. Enjoy wonderful scenery of Black Mountains. Good base. Walking, pony trekking. Dogs welcome. [🐾]

Gower

Britain's first designated Area of Outstanding Natural Beauty with numerous sandy beaches and lovely countryside to explore.

CULVER HOUSE HOTEL, PORT EYNON, GOWER SA3 1NN (01792 390755). Small, friendly Hotel with fabulous food and quality service. Peacefully situated, with superb coast and countryside. En suite, sea views. WTB ★★ Hotel, AA ★★. [Pets £2 per night.]

Llanmadoc

Village on Gower Peninsula, a secluded area with unspoilt beaches and many bird reserves

MRS A. MAIN, TALLIZMAND, LLANMADOC, GOWER SA3 1DE (01792 386373). Located near the splendid Gower coastline, surrounded by beautiful countryside. Tallizmand has tastefully furnished en suite bedrooms with tea/coffee facilities. Home cooking, packed lunches. Non-smoking. Pets by arrangement. WTB ★★★ Guest House [🐾] .

Mumbles

Seaside resort of Swansea to west and north west of Mumbles Head

MUMBLES & SWANSEA Holiday Homes, some with sea views. Flat locations. Well equipped, modern conveniences – carpets throughout. Convenient for beaches, countryside and town's amenities. Personally supervised. WTB Graded Three and Four Dragons. Cottage, Flat and Town house available. MRS JEAN GRIERSON, 112 MUMBLES ROAD, BLACKPILL, SWANSEA SA3 5AS (01792 402278). [🐾]

Pontypool

Town 8 miles north of Newport. Valley Inheritance exhibition centre in former Georgian stable of Pontypool Park House tells story of the valleys.

MRS S. ARMITAGE, TY'RYWEN FARM, TREVETHIN, PONTYPOOL NP4 8TT (Tel & Fax: 01495 785200). A very remote 16th Century Longhouse high in the Brecon Beacons National Park. Spacious en suite rooms, colour TV and beverage tray. Some four-posters. One room with jacuzzi. No smoking. No children. Light supper available. B&B from £20.00. We can also take horses. Stabling for two horses. Hill farm grazing, miles of unfenced riding. [🐾]

Swansea

Large town and part of Swansea Bay at mouth of River Tawe, 35 miles west of Cardiff. Remains of 14th century castle.

BEST WESTERN ABERAVON BEACH HOTEL, PORT TALBOT, SWANSEA BAY SA12 6QP (01639 884949). Modern seafront hotel. A warm Welsh welcome awaits you and your pets. 2 miles of flat promenade and an all year round pet friendly beach. Pets Paradise!! And for you..... comfortable rooms, fine cuisine, leisure centre and many local attractions. AA/RAC ★★★.[🐾]

Wye Valley

Scenic area, ideal for relaxation.

MR & MRS J. LLEWELLYN, CWRT-Y-GAER, WOLVESNEWTON, CHEPSTOW NP16 6PR (01291 650700). 1, 4 or more dogs welcome free. Self-catering, attractively converted stone buildings of Welsh Longhouse. 20 acres, super views of Usk Vale. Brochure. Three units (one suitable for disabled). Four Dragons Award. WTB ★★★ [🐾 pw!]

HOLIDAYS WITH HORSES

A selection of accommodation where horse and owner/rider can be put up at the same address – if not actually under the same roof!. We would be grateful if readers making enquiries and/or bookings from this supplement would mention *Pets Welcome!*.

Derbyshire

MRS J DICKINSON
MANIFOLD VIEW, TOP FARM, BUXTON SK17 0PR
(Tel: 01298 83271)

Barn conversion adjacent to the original farmhouse. Rural position in the Peak National Park. Many walks and rides from the cottage door. Brochure available, dogs welcome, ample parking. DIY Livery for horses

Devon

MRS J.COLTON
PEEK HILL FARM, DOUSLAND, YELVERTON PL20 6PD
(Tel/Fax: 01822 854808)

Good breakfast and comfy beds; TV, kettle in rooms. Views from Dartmoor to Bodmin. Picnics can be provided. Good walking; cycle hire. Pleasant stay guaranteed. Open all year except Christmas. 2 Crowns Commended.

DITTISCOMBE FARMHOUSE & HOLIDAY COTTAGES
SLAPTON, KINGSBRIDGE, DEVON TQ7 2QF
(Tel: 01548 521272; Fax: 01548 521425)

Riding, livery and stabling at the Dittiscombe Equestrian Centre. Take your horse to Dartmoor (12 miles), or hack across rolling Devon hills and lanes. Park your horse in the stables and enjoy the freedom of a comfortable self-catering cottage. Beaches nearby.

EAST DART HOTEL
POSTBRIDGE, DARTMOOR PL20 6TJ
(Tel: 01822 880213; Fax: 01822 880313)
Website: www.dartmoorhotels.com

Situated in the heart of beautiful Dartmoor. B&B from £24 ppp. Riding, falconry, shooting and hunting available. Enjoy fires, real ales and home cooked food. Beautiful walks all round, dogs very welcome.

JAYE JONES & HELEN ASHER,
TWITCHEN FARM,
CHALLACOMBE, BARNSTAPLE EX31 4TT
(Tel: 01598 763568)
E-mail: holidays@twitchen.co.uk • Website: www.twitchen.co.uk

Exmoor has 400 miles of bridlepaths! Explore heather moorland and wooded valleys. We offer excellent stabling, rider guide, route planning, good food and a hot bath!

MRS S. PLUMMER
LONG CROSS HOUSE
BLACK TORRINGTON, NEAR HOLSWORTHY EX21 5QG
(Tel: 01409 231219)

Edge of delightful village midway between Holsworthy and Hatherleigh. Children, dogs and horses welcome

Dorset

E. & S. HOWLEY
EYPE'S MOUTH COUNTRY HOTEL, EYPE, BRIDPORT DT6 6AL
(Tel: 01308 423300; Fax: 01308 420033)
Experience the tranquillity of Dorset. Situated in a secret spot, down a leafy lane, just a five minute walk from the sea. Restaurant with views over Lyme Bay.

Hampshire

JENNY MONGER,
LITTLE HORSESHOES, SOUTH GORLEY, RINGWOOD BH24 3NL
(Tel: 01425 479340)
E-mail: jenny@littlehorseshoes.co.uk • Website: www.littlehorseshoes.co.uk

Give your horse a holiday. Excellent DIY stabling and grazing, direct forest/heath access. Cosy, superior modern bungalow, enclosed garden and patio. Well behaved dogs welcome. BHS Standards. ETC ✿✿✿ Commended.

Lincolnshire

CAWTHORPE FARM
CAWTHORPE, BOURNE, LINCOLNSHIRE PE10 0AB
(Tel: 01778 426697; Fax: 01778 421536)
Welcomes guests for bed & breakfast. Stabling and grazing available. Hacking, hunting, Burghley Trails.

Norfolk

NICKY ST LAWRENCE
CHURCH FARM, NARBOROUGH, KINGS LYNN PE32 1TE
(Tel: 01760 337696/07801 641570; Fax: 01760 337858)
E-mail: nickystlawrence@ouvip.com
Relax in our chalk self-catering cottage overlooking your horses field/stable. Enjoy the woodburner and four-poster bed. Village shop/pub. Bridleways abundant. Horses £40 per week.

SCARNING DALE,
SCARNING, EAST DEREHAM NR19 2QN
(Tel: 01362 687269).
Self catering cottages (not commercialised) in grounds of owner's house. On-site indoor heated swimming pool and full-size snooker table. B&B for six also available in house. (sorry no pets in house). Grazing and Stables available .

Oxfordshire

JUNE AND GEORGE COLLIER
55 NETHERCOTE ROAD, TACKLEY, KIDLINGTON, OXFORD OX5 3AT
(Tel: 01869 331255; Fax: 01869 331670).
Bed and Breakfast in Tackley. An ideal base for touring, walking and riding. Central for Oxford, The Cotswolds, Stratford-on-Avon, Blenheim Palace. Woodstock four miles. Regular train and bus service with local Hostelries serving excellent food.ß

Shropshire

VIRGINIA AND ROBERT EVANS
CHURCH FARM, ROWTON, WELLINGTON, TELFORD TF6 6QY
(Tel: 01952 770381)
E–mail: church.farm@bigfoot.co.uk
B&B and self-catering in a quiet village yet equidistant from Shrewsbury and Ironbridge. Listed Grade II farmhouse; en suite rooms from £20pp. Self-catering barn conversion cottages sleeping 2-8 people. Ground floor bedroom from £160 per week.

Somerset

DAVID & JACKIE BISHOP,
TOGHILL HOUSE FARM, FREEZING HILL, WICK, NEAR BATH BS30 5RT
(Tel: 0225 891261; Fax: 01225 892128).

Luxury barn conversions on working farm 3 miles north of Bath. Each equipped to very high standard, bed linen provided. Stables.

BRYAN & JANE JACKSON,
HUNTERS MOON, EXFORD, NEAR MINEHEAD TA24 7PP
(Tel: 01643 831695)

Cosy bungalow smallholding in the heart of Exmoor. Good food (optional Evening Meal), glorious views, friendly atmosphere. Pets welcome free, stabling available. Open all year.

JULIA & JERRY BEGGS,
WESTERCLOSE HOUSE, WITHYPOOL TA24 7QR
(Tel: 01643 831302)

Two cottages and two bungalows on 10 acre estate overlooking Barle Valley. Dogs and horses welcome. Shop and pub 300 metres.

RALEGH'S CROSS INN, EXMOOR NATIONAL PARK, BRENDON HILL
SOMERSET TA23 OLN
(Tel: 01984 640343)

A warm friendly welcome in well-appointed Inn. DIY, part or full livery. Bar snacks, à la carte menu. "We're famous for our carvery". All rooms en-suite.

LEONE & BRIAN MARTIN
RISCOMBE FARM HOLIDAY COTTAGES, EXFORD, MINEHEAD TA24 7NH
(Tel & Fax: 01643 831480)
Website: www.riscombe.co.uk

Four self-catering stone cottages in the centre of Exmoor National Park. Excellent walking and riding country. Dogs and horses welcome. Open all year. ETC Rating: ★★★★

THE EXMOOR WHITE HORSE INN
EXFORD TA24 7PY
(01643 831229; Fax: 01643 831246)
E-mail: exmoorwhitehorse.demon.co.uk

Family-run 16th century inn situated in charming Exmoor village. 26 bedrooms all en suite, with colour TV and tea making. Fully licensed. Restaurant with varied menu.

East Yorkshire

MR ROBERTS
PAWS-A-WHILE, KILNWICK PERCY, POCKLINGTON YO42 1UF
(Tel: 01759 301168)
website: www.pawsawhile.net

Small family B & B set in forty acres pf parkland twixt York and Beverley. Fishing, golf, sauna, walking, riding. Pets and horses most welcome. Brochure available.

North Yorkshire

HIGH BELTHORPE
MEG ABU HAMDAN, BISHOP WILTON, YORK YO4 1SB
(Tel: 01759 368238; Mobile: 07720 651500)

BHS Approved Livery yard in lovely surroundings. Bring your horse to enjoy the most fabulous hacking over the Yorkshire Wolds, still unspoilt and quiet. Farmhouse B&B.

HOLIDAYS WITH HORSES

Borders

ALAN & CHRISTINE SWANSTON
FERNIEHIRST MILL LODGE & RIDING CENTRE
JEDBURGH TD8 6PQ
(Tel & Fax: 01835 863279)
A chalet style guest house set in grounds of 25 acres. All rooms en suite with tea/coffee making facilities. Licensed for residents. Well behaved pets (including horses) welcome by arrangement. STB, AA, RAC, ABRS, TRSS Approved.

Dumfries and Galloway

RUSKO HOLIDAYS,
RUSKO, GATEHOUSE OF FLEET, CASTLE DOUGLAS DG7 2BS
(01557 814215; Fax: 01557 814679)
Lovely spacious farmhouse and cosy, comfortable cottages near beaches, hills and forests. Use of tennis court. Loch and river fishing with tuition given, stabling and grazing available for your own horse, beautiful walking and riding country. Rates £150-£600. ★★ to ★★★

Isle of Mull

TORLOCHAN, GRULINE
ISLE OF MULL PA71 6HR
(TEL: 01680 300380, FAX: 01680 300664)
Situated in centre of Mull. Panoramic views over Loch na Keal. Working croft of 26 acres. Two Cottages, Two Log Cabins for self-catering and en-suite Bed & Breakfast. Friendly welcome awaits. "An Oasis in the Desert." Pets free of charge.

Anglesey and Gwynedd

JUDY HUTCHINGS,
TAL-Y-FOEL STUD FARM AND RIDING CENTRE,
DWYRAN, ANGLESEY LL61 6LQ
(Tel: 01248 430377; Fax: 01248 430977)
Comfortable waterfront WTB three star bed and breakfast and private caravan. Stabled livery. Open all year. Several miles of grass tracks and beach track riding, outdoor manege and cross country training course. Lessons. British Horse Society approved.

Powys/Hay-on-Wye (near)

MRS E. BALLY,
LANE FARM, PAINSCASTLE, BUILTH WELLS LD2 3JS
(Tel/Fax: 01497 851605)
E-mail: jbally@btclick.com

Self-catering and Bed and Breakfast accommodation. Nine good stables and ample grazing in the heart of rural Radnorshire with wonderful open riding. Some cross-country jumps.

The 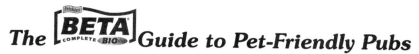 Guide to Pet-Friendly Pubs

Whenever you visit one of our public houses or hotels listed within the Beta Guide to Pet-Friendly Pubs you can be sure your four-legged friend will be more than welcome. He will find a fresh bowl of water, provided by the landlord to quench his thirst, and it's likely he will meet other canine visitors.

Beta Complete Dog Food
the best nutritional care at home and on holiday...

ENGLAND

BERKSHIRE

THE GREYHOUND (known locally as 'The Dog')
The Walk, Eton Wick, Berkshire (01753 863925).
Dogs allowed throughout the pub.
Pet Regulars: Harvey (Retriever), retrieves anything, including Beer mats. KIA - German Shepherd.

THE SWAN
9 Mill Lane, Clewer, Windsor, Berkshire (01753 862069).
Dogs allowed throughout the pub.
Pet Regulars: Ziggy and her family, Simba, Thumper and Cassy (Bichon Frise) – useful for keeping your lap warm; Taffy, who has a very waggy tail and who curls up and sleeps under a chair until closing time; Ben, a very friendly Alsatian who enjoys a drop or two of London Pride; Rupert, another Bichon, who calls in after his walks; Ben, the latest addition, a playful Springer Spaniel puppy.

THE TWO BREWERS
Park Street, Windsor, Berkshire (01753 855426).
Dogs allowed, public and saloon bars.
Pet Regulars: Harry (Pyrenean) and his mate Molly (Newfoundland) take up the whole bar, 'Bear' (Black Labrador), Tessa (Cocker Spaniel) and Charlie (Collie).

BUCKINGHAMSHIRE

WHITE HORSE
Village Lane, Hedgerley, Buckinghamshire SL2 3UY (01753 643225).
Dogs allowed at tables on pub frontage, beer garden (on leads), public bar.

CAMBRIDGESHIRE

YE OLD WHITE HART
Main Street, Ufford, Peterborough, Cambridgeshire (01780 740250).
Dogs allowed in non-food areas.

CHESHIRE

JACKSONS BOAT
Rifle Road, Sale, Cheshire (0161 973 8549).
Dogs allowed throughout on lead with the exception of the dining area.

CORNWALL

DRIFTWOOD SPARS HOTEL
Trevaunance Cove, St Agnes, Cornwall (01872 552428).
Dogs allowed everywhere except the restaurant.
Pet Regulars: Buster (Cornish Labrador cross) - devours anything.

JUBILEE INN
Pelynt, Near Looe, Cornwall PL13 2JZ (01503 220312).
Dogs allowed in all areas except restaurant; accommodation for guests with dogs.

THE MILL HOUSE INN
Trebarwith Strand, Tintagel, Cornwall PL34 0HD (01840 770200).
Pet Friendly.

THE MOLESWORTH ARMS HOTEL
Molesworth Street, Wadebridge, Cornwall PL27 7DP (01208 812055).
Dogs allowed in all public areas and in hotel rooms.
Pet Regulars: Thomson Cassidy (Black Lab), Ruby and Bertie (Golden Retriever).

THE WHITE HART
Chilsworthy, Near Gunnislake, Cornwall (01822 832307).
Dogs allowed in non-food bar, car park tables, beer garden.
Pet Regulars: Kai, Ben and Lawson (German Shepherds).

WELLINGTON HOTEL,
The Harbour, Boscastle, Cornwall (01840 250202).
Dogs allowed in bedrooms and on lead in pub.
Own private 10-acre woodland walk. Dogs welcome free of charge.

CUMBRIA

THE BRITANNIA INN
Elterwater, Ambleside, Cumbria LA22 9HP (015394 37210).
Dogs allowed in all areas except dining room.
Pet Regulars: Charlie (Collie cross), Annie (Retriever).

THE MORTAL MAN HOTEL
Troutbeck, Windermere, Cumbria LA23 IPL (015394 33193).
Dogs allowed throughout and in guest rooms.

STAG INN
Dufton, Appleby, Cumbria (017683 51608).
Dogs allowed in non-food bar, beer garden, village green plus B&B and cottage.
Pet Regulars: Toffee (cross between Saluki and Golden Setter); Willow (cross between Great Dane and an Old English Sheepdog); Kim (Weimaraner), best bitter drinker; Buster (Jack Russell), enjoys a quiet evening.

the best nutritional care at home and on holiday

WATERMILL INN

School Lane, Ings, Near Staveley, Kendal, Cumbria (01539 821309).
Dogs allowed in beer garden, Wrynose bottom bar.
Pet Regulars: Smudge (sheepdog); Gowan (Westie) and Scruffy (mongrel). All enjoy a range of crisps and snacks. Scruffy regularly drinks Blacksheep special. Pub dogs Misty (Beardie). Owners cannot walk dogs past pub, without being dragged in! Biscuits and water provided.

DERBYSHIRE

JINGLERS/FOX & HOUNDS

(A517) Belper Road, Bradley, Ashbourne, Derbyshire (01335 370855).
Dogs allowed in non-food bars, beer garden, accommodation for guests with dogs.
Pet Regulars: Benson (Springer), Hamlet (Pointer/Lab) – pedigree drinkers and Walkers crisps crunchers.

THE GEORGE HOTEL

Commercial Road, Tideswell, Near Buxton, Derbyshire SK17 8NU (01298 871382).
Dogs allowed in snug and around the bar, water bowls provided.

DOG AND PARTRIDGE COUNTRY INN & MOTEL

Swinscoe, Ashbourne, Derbyshire (01335 343183).
Dogs allowed throughout, except restaurant.
Pet Regulars: Include Mitsy (57); Rusty (Cairn); Spider (Collie/GSD) and Rex (GSD).

DEVONSHIRE ARMS

Peak Forest, Near Buxton, Derbyshire SK17 8EJ (01298 23875)
Dogs allowed in bar.
Pet Regulars: Fergie (Collie-cross), known as "The Fireguard".

WHITE HART

Station Road, West Hallam, Derbyshire DE7 6GW (0115 932 6069).
Dogs allowed in all non-food areas.
Pet Regulars: Archie, Chester and Brewser. Three cats: Itsy, Bitsy and Jasper.

DEVON

THE SHIP INN

Axmouth, Devon EX12 4AF (01297 21838).
A predominantly catering pub, so dogs on a lead please.
Pet Regulars: Cassie, Charlie, Digby and Beamish. Also resident Tawny Owls.

BRENDON HOUSE HOTEL

Brendon, Lynton, North Devon EX35 6PS (01598 741206).
Dogs very welcome and allowed in tea gardens, guest bedrooms by arrangement.
Pet Regulars: Jasmine (cat), self appointed cream tea receptionist. Years of practice have perfected dirty looks at visiting dogs.

THE BULLERS ARMS

Chagford, Newton Abbot, Devon (01647 432348).
Dogs allowed throughout pub, except dining room/kitchen. "More than welcome".

CROWN AND SCEPTRE

2 Petitor Road, Torquay, Devon TQ1 4QA (01803 328290).
Dogs allowed in non-food bar, family room, lounge. All dogs welcome.
Pet Regulars: 4 Jack Russell's - Sprocket, Scrappy Doo, Mouse and Minnie Mouse.

THE DEVONSHIRE INN
Sticklepath, Near Okehampton, Devon EX20 2NW (01837 840626).
Dogs allowed in non-food bar, car park, beer garden, family room, guest rooms.
Pet Regulars: Bess (Labrador), 'minds' owner; Annie (Shihtzu), snoring a speciality; Daisy (Collie), accompanies folk singers.

THE JOURNEY'S END INN
Ringmore, Near Kingsbridge, South Devon TQ7 4HL (01548 810205).
Dogs allowed throughout the pub except in the dining room.

PALK ARMS INN
Hennock, Bovey Tracey, Devon TQ13 9QS (01626 836584).
Pets welcome.

THE ROYAL OAK INN
Dunsford, Near Exeter, Devon EX6 7DA (01647 252256).
Dogs allowed in bars, beer garden, accommodation for guests with dogs.
Pet Regulars: Cleo

THE SEA TROUT INN
Staverton, Near Totnes, Devon TQ9 6PA (01803 762274).
Dogs allowed in lounge and public bar, car park tables, beer garden, owners' rooms (but not on beds).
Pet Regulars: Billy (Labrador-cross), partial to drip trays; Curnow (Poodle), brings a blanket and Buster (Mongrel).

THE WHITE HART HOTEL
Moretonhampstead, Newton Abbot, Devon TQ13 8NF (01647 440406).
Dogs allowed throughout, except restaurant.
Pet Regulars: Daisy (Collie).

DORSET

THE ANVIL HOTEL
Sailsbury Road, Pimperne, Blandford, Dorset DT11 8UQ (01258 453431).
Pets allowed in bar, lounge and bedrooms.

DURHAM

MOORCOCK INN
Hill Top, Eggleston, Teesdale, County Durham DL12 9AU (01833 650395).
Pet Regulars: Thor, the in-house hound dog, and Raymond, the resident hack, welcome all equine travellers; Gem (Jack Russell); Arnie (Ginger Tom).

TAP AND SPILE
27 Front Street, Framwellgate Moor, Durham DH1 5EE (0191 386 5451).
Dogs allowed throughout the pub.

ESSEX

THE OLD SHIP
Heybridge Basin, Heybridge, Maldon, Essex (01621 854150).
Dogs allowed throughout pub.

GLOUCESTERSHIRE

THE CROWN INN
Frampton Mansell, Stroud, Gloucestershire GL6 8JG (01285 760601).
Well behaved pooches welcome in our comfortable hotel.
Pet Regulars: Petra (Labrador), collects logs.

THE OLD STOCKS HOTEL
The Square, Stow on the Wold, Gloucestershire GL54 1AF (01451 830666).
Dogs allowed in the beer garden, accommodation for dogs and their owners also available.
Pet Regulars: Ben (Labrador) enjoys bitter from the drip trays and Oscar (Doberman) often gets carried out as he refuses to leave.

GREATER LONDON

THE PHOENIX
28 Thames Street, Sunbury on Thames, Middlesex (01932 785358).
Dogs allowed in non-food bar, beer garden, family room. Capability 2 Grading.
Pet Regulars: "Olly" (57 variety), Dixie (German Shepherd) and Monster (Shihtzu).

THE TIDE END COTTAGE
Ferry Road, Teddington, Middlesex (0208 977 7762).
Dogs allowed throughout the pub.
Pet Regulars: Chester, Golder Retriever – eats anything.

HAMPSHIRE

HIGH CORNER INN
Linwood, Near Ringwood, Hampshire BH24 3QY (01425 473973).
Dogs, horses and even goats are catered for here.

THE CHEQUERS
Ridgeway Lane, Lower Pennington, Lymington, Hants (01590 673415).
Dogs allowed in non-food bar, outdoor barbecue area (away from food).
Pet Regulars: Otto (Hungarian Vizsla), eats beer-mats and paper napkins. Likes beer but not often indulged.

THE VICTORY
High Street, Hamble-le-Rice, Southampton, Hampshire (023 80 453105).
Dogs allowed.
Pet Regulars: Sefton (Labrador), his 'usual' chew bars are kept especially.

HEREFORDSHIRE

THE GREEN MAN INN
Fownhope, Hereford, Herefordshire HR1 4PE (01432 860243).
Dogs welcome, but not in the restaurant.

HERTFORDSHIRE

THE BLACK HORSE
Chorly Wood Common, Dog Kennel Lane, Rickmansworth, Herts (01923 282252).
Dogs very welcome and allowed throughout the pub, on a lead.

THE ROBIN HOOD AND LITTLE JOHN
Rabley Heath, near Codicote, Hertfordshire (01438 812361).
Dogs allowed in non-food bar, car park tables, beer garden.
Pet Regulars: Bonnie (Labrador), beer-mat catcher. The locals of the pub have close to 50 dogs between them, most of which visit from time to time. The team includes a two Labrador search squad dispatched by one regular's wife to indicate time's up. When they arrive he has five minutes' drinking up time before all three leave together.

KENT

KENTISH HORSE
Cow Lane, Mark Beech, Edenbridge, Kent (01342 850493).
Dogs allowed in reserved area.

THE OLD NEPTUNE
Marine Terrace, Whitstable, Kent CT5 lEJ (01227 272262).
Dogs allowed in beach frontage.
Pet Regulars: Nut and Tory (Staffordshire Bull Terrier Crosses).

THE SWANN INN
Little Chart, Kent TN27 OQB (01233 840702).
Dogs allowed - everywhere except restaurant.

UNCLE TOM'S CABIN
Lavender Hill, Tonbridge, Kent (01628 483339).
Dogs allowed throughout.
Pet Regulars: Flossie, Pipa, Rusty. 10pm is dog biscuit time!

LANCASHIRE

ABBEYLEE
Abbeyhills Road, Oldham, Lancashire (0161 678 8795).
Dogs allowed throughout.

MALT'N HOPS
50 Friday Street, Chorley, Lancashire PR6 0AH (01257 260967).
Dogs allowed throughout pub.
Pet Regulars: Abbie (GSD), under-seat sleeper; Brandy (Rhodesian Ridgeback), at the sound of a bag of crisps opening will lean on eater until guest's legs go numb or he is offered a share; Toby (Labrador), valued customer in his own right, due to amount of crisps he eats, also retrieves empty bags; Mork – says please for bag of crisps and Zac - likes his pint of beer.

LEICESTERSHIRE

CHEQUERS INN
1 Gilmorton Road, Ashby Magna, Near Lutterworth, Leicestershire (01455 209523).
Dogs allowed in bar.
Pet Regulars: Suki – talking Samoyed.

LINCOLNSHIRE

THE HAVEN INN
Ferry Road, Barrow Haven, North Lincolnshire DN19 7EX (01469 530247).
Dogs allowed in the public bar, beer garden, and bedrooms on their own bed/blanket.
Pet Regulars: Jester the Collie.

THE BLUE DOG INN

Main Street, Sewstern, Grantham, Lincs NG33 5QR (01476 860097).
Dogs allowed.

Pet Regulars: The Guv'nor (Great Dane), best draught-excluder in history; Jenny (Scottie) shares biscuits with pub cats; Jemma (98% Collie), atmosphere lapper-upper. Spud and Nelson – Terriers.

MERSEYSIDE

AMBASSADOR PRIVATE HOTEL

13 Bath Street, Southport, Merseyside PR9 0DP (01704 543998).
Dogs allowed in non-food bar, lounge, guest bedrooms.

THE SCOTCH PIPER

Southport Road, Lydiate, Merseyside (0151 526 0503).
Dogs allowed throughout the pub.

MIDLANDS

AWENTSBURY HOTEL

21 Serpentine Road, Selly Park, Birmingham B29 7HU (0121 472 1258).
Dogs allowed.

Pet Regulars: Well-behaved dogs welcome.

NORFOLK

THE SPREAD EAGLE COUNTRY INN

Barton Bendish, Norfolk PE33 9DP (01366 347295).
Pet Regulars: Dirty Gertie, Pickles and Bosh.

MARINE HOTEL

10 St Edmunds Terrace, Hunstanton, Norfolk PE36 5EH (01485 533310).
Dogs allowed throughout, except dining room.

Pet Regulars: Many dogs have returned with their owners year after year to stay at The Marine Bar.

THE OLD RAILWAY TAVERN

Eccles Road, Quidenham, Norwich, Norfolk NR16 2JG (01953 888223).
Dogs allowed in non-food bar, beer garden.

Pet Regulars: Soshie (GSD); Annie (Labrador); and pub dogs Elsa (GSD). Elsa is so fond of sitting, motionless, on her own window ledge that new customers often think she's stuffed!

THE ROSE AND CROWN

Nethergate Street, Harpley, King's Lynn, Norfolk (01485 520577).
Dogs allowed in non-food bar, car park tables.

Pet Regulars: A merry bunch with shared interests – Duffy (mongrel); Tammy (Airedale); Dillon, all enjoy pub garden romps during summer and fireside seats in winter.

OXFORDSHIRE

THE BELL INN

High Street, Adderbury, Oxon (01295 810338).
Dogs allowed throughout the pub.

Owner's dogs; Bess and Elsa (Black Labradors).

SHROPSHIRE

THE TRAVELLERS REST INN
Church Stretton, Shropshire (01694 781275).
Well-mannered pets welcome - but beware of the cats!

LONGMYND HOTEL
Cunnery Road, Church Stretton, Shropshire SY6 6AG (01694 722244).
Dogs allowed in owners' hotel bedrooms but not in public areas.
Pet Regulars: Bruno and Frenzie; and owner's dogs, Sam and Sailor.

REDFERN HOTEL
Cleobury Mortimer, Shropshire SY14 8AA (01299 270395).
Dogs allowed in reception area and in guests' bedrooms.

SOMERSET

CASTLE OF COMFORT HOTEL
Dodington, Nether Stowey, Bridgwater, Somerset TA5 1LE (01278 741264).
Pet Friendly.

THE SPARKFORD INN
High Street, Sparkford, Somerset BA22 7JN (01963 440218).
Dogs allowed in bar areas but not in restaurant; safe garden and car park.
Pet Regulars: Holly (Jack Russell) and Stoner (Grizzly Bear)!

THE BUTCHERS ARMS
Carhampton, Somerset (01643 821333).
Dogs allowed in bar.

HALFWAY HOUSE
Pitney, Langport, Somerset TA10 9AB (01458 252513).
Dogs allowed.
Pet Regulars: Sam (Collie), Lotte (Otter Hound), Joe (Cocker Spaniel).

HOOD ARMS
Kilve, Somerset TA5 1EA (01278 741210)
Pets welcome.

THE SHIP INN
High Street, Porlock, Somerset (01643 862507).
Dogs allowed throughout and in guests' rooms.
Pet Regulars: Include Buster, Hardy (Jack Russell), terrorists from London; Bijoux (Peke), while on holiday at The Ship enjoys Chicken Supreme cooked to order every evening.

SUFFOLK

SIX BELLS AT BARDWELL
The Green, Bardwell, Bury St Edmunds IP31 1AW (01359 250820).
Dogs allowed in guest bedrooms and garden but not allowed in bar and restaurant.

THE COMPASSES INN
Wenhaston, Near Southwold, Suffolk IP19 9EF (01502 478319).
Dogs allowed throughout the pub and B&B (but not on the beds!). Bar open evenings only Tuesday to Sunday, and Sunday lunchtmes.
Pet Regulars: Raffles and Shadow (ex racing Greyhounds) who love all visiting dogs and crisps; Penny (Collie) and Cisco (young Doberman) who like to stand up at the bar.

SURREY

THE CRICKETERS
12 Oxenden Road, Tongham, Farnham, Surrey (01252 333262).
Dogs allowed in beer garden.

SUSSEX

THE FORESTERS ARMS
High Street, Fairwarp, Near Uckfield, East Sussex TN22 3BP (01825 712808).
Dogs allowed in the beer garden and at car park tables, also inside.
Owner's Dogs: Rascal and Sophie (Springer Spaniels).

THE INN IN THE PARK (CHEF & BREWER)
Tilgate Park, Tilgate, Crawley, West Sussex RH10 5PQ (01293 545324).
Dogs allowed in Patio area.

THE PLOUGH
Crowhurst, Near Battle, East Sussex TN33 9AY (01424 830310).
Dogs allowed in non-food bar, car park tables, beer garden.
Pet Regulars: Kai (Belgian Shepherd), drinks halves of Websters; Poppy and Cassie (Springer Spaniels), divided between the lure of crisps and fireside.

THE PRESTONVILLE ARMS
64 Hamilton Road, Brighton, East Sussex (01273 701007).
Dogs allowed in beer garden, throughout the pub (Pet Friendly).

QUEENS HEAD
Village Green, Sedlescombe, East Sussex (01424 870228).
Dogs allowed throughout the pub.

THE SLOOP INN
Freshfield Lock, Haywards Heath, West Sussex RH17 7NP (01444 831219).
Dogs allowed in public bar and garden.

THE SMUGGLERS' ROOST
125 Sea Lane, Rustington, West Sussex BN16 2SG (01903 785714).
Dogs allowed in non-food bar, at car park tables, in beer garden, family room.
Pet Regulars: Skip; Leo (Border Terrier), forms instant affections with anyone who notices him; Tim (King Charles Spaniel), quite prepared to guard his corner when food appears. The landlord owns a Great Dane and an Alsatian.

THE SPORTSMAN'S ARMS
Rackham Road, Amberley, Near Arundel, West Sussex BN18 9NR (01798 831787).
Dogs allowed throughout the pub.
Pet Regulars: Pippin, Spud Mollie and Nell.

WELLDIGGERS ARMS
Lowheath, Petworth, West Sussex GU28 0HG (01798 342287).
Dogs allowed throughout the pub.

WILTSHIRE

THE HORSE AND GROOM
The Street, Charlton, Near Malmesbury, Wiltshire (01666 823904).
Pet Regulars: P.D. (Pub Dog – Labrador).

THE PETERBOROUGH ARMS
Dauntsey Lock, Near Chippenham, Wiltshire SN15 4HD (01249 890409).
Dogs allowed in non-food bar, at car park tables, in beer garden, family room (when non-food).
Pet Regulars: Include Indy and Mac (West Highland Terriers).

Pet-Friendly Pubs ▬▬▬▬▬▬▬▬▬▬▬▬▬▬▬▬▬▬▬▬▬▬▬▬▬▬▬▬▬▬

THE THREE HORSESHOES
High Street, Chapmanslade, Near Westbury, Wiltshire (01373 832280).
Dogs allowed in non-food bar and beer garden.
Pet Regulars: Include Clieo (Golden Retriever), possibly the youngest 'regular' in the land - his first trip to the pub was at eight weeks. Westbury and District Canine Society repair to the Three Horseshoes after training nights (Monday/Wednesday). Five cats and four dogs in residence.

WAGGON AND HORSES
High Street, Wootton Bassett, Swindon, Wiltshire (01793 850617).
Dogs allowed throughout.
Pet Regulars: Include Gemma, a very irregular Whippet/Border collie cross. She likes to balance beer-mats on her nose, then flip them over and catch them, opens and shuts doors on command, walks on her hind legs and returns empty crisp bags. She is limited to one glass of Guinness a night.

YORKSHIRE

BARNES WALLIS INN
North Howden, Howden, East Yorkshire (01430 430639).
Guide dogs only

KINGS HEAD INN
Barmby on the Marsh, East Yorkshire DN14 7HL (01757 638357).
Dogs allowed in non-food bar.
Pet Regulars: Many and varied!

THE FORESTERS ARMS
Kilburn, North Yorkshire YO6 4AH (01347 868386).
Dogs allowed throughout, except restaurant.
Pet Regulars: Ainsley (Black Labrador)..

THE GREENE DRAGON INN
Hardraw, Hawes, North Yorkshire DL8 3LZ (01969 667392).
Dogs allowed in bar, at car park tables, in beer garden, family room but not dining room or restaurant.

NEW INN HOTEL
Clapham, Near Settle, North Yorkshire LA2 8HH (015242 51203).
Dogs allowed in bar, beer garden, family room.
Owner's dog: Time, (Rhodesian Ridgeback).

PREMIER HOTEL
66 Esplanade, South Cliff, Scarborough, North Yorkshire YO11 2UZ (01723 501062).
Dogs allowed throughout in non-food areas of hotel.

SIMONSTONE HALL
Hawes, North Yorkshire DL8 3LY (01969 667255).
Dogs allowed except dining area.
Pet Regulars: account for 2,000 nights per annum. More than 50% of guests are accompanied by their dogs, from Pekes to an Anatolian Shepherd (the size of a small Shetland pony!) Two dogs have stayed, with their owners, on 23 separate occasions.

THE SPINNEY
Forest Rise, Balby, Doncaster, South Yorkshire DN4 9HQ (01302 852033).
Dogs allowed throughout the pub.
Pet Regulars: Shamus (Irish Setter), pub thief. Fair game includes pool balls, beer mats, crisps, beer, coats, hats. Recently jumped 15 feet off pub roof with no ill effect. Josh; (Labrador) a guide dog. Indi and Jacques.

THE ROCKINGHAM ARMS
8 Main Street, Wentworth, Rotherham, South Yorkshire S62 7LO (01226 742075).
Dogs allowed throughout pub.

Pet-Friendly Pubs

Pet Regulars: Sheeba (Springer Spaniel), Charlie and Gypsy (Black Labradors). Kate and Rags (Airedale and cross-breed), prefer lager to coffee; Holly (terrier and pub dog), dubbed 'the flying squirrel', likes everyone, whether they like it or not!

THE GOLDEN FLEECE
Lindley Road, Blackley, near Huddersfield, West Yorkshire (01422 372704).
Dogs allowed in non-food bar, at outside tables.
Pet Regulars: "Holly", (Border Collie).

CHANNEL ISLANDS/JERSEY
LA PULENTE INN
La Pulente, St Brelade, Jersey (01534 744487).
Dogs allowed in public bar..
Pet Regulars: Dusty (Old English Sheepdog)..

WALES

ANGLESEY & GWYNEDD
THE GRAPES HOTEL
Maentwrog, Blaenau Ffestiniog, Gwynedd LL41 4HN (01766 590365).
Pet Friendly.

PLAS YR EIFL HOTEL
Trefor, Caernarfon, Gwynedd LL54 5NA (01286 660781).
Pet Regulars: We have both dogs and cats

THE BUCKLEY HOTEL
Castle Street, Beaumaris, Isle of Anglesey LL58 8AW (01248 810415).
Dogs allowed throughout the pub, except in the dining room and bistro.
Pet Regulars: Cassie (Springer Spaniel) and Rex (mongrel), dedicated 'companion' dogs, also Charlie (Spaniel).

NORTH WALES
THE WEST ARMS HOTEL
Llanarmon Dyffryn Ceiriog, Llangollen, North Wales LL20 7LD (01691 600665).
Welcome Pets.

POWYS
SEVERN ARMS HOTEL
Penybont, Llandrindod Wells, Powys LD1 5UA (01597 851224).
Dogs allowed in the bar, but not the restaurant, and in the rooms - but not on the beds

---

Please mention *Recommended Wayside & Country Inns*
when enquiring about pubs and inns featured in these pages.

SCOTLAND

ABERDEEN, BANFF & MORAY

THE CLIFTON BAR
Clifton Road, Lossiemouth, Moray (01343 812100).
Dogs allowed throughout pub.
Pet Regulars: Include Zoe (Westie), has her own seat and is served coffee with two lumps; Milo (Jack Russel), Murphy (Minature Daushound) and Bob (Collie).

ROYAL OAK
Station Road, Urquhart, Elgin, Moray (01343 842607).
Dogs allowed throughout pub.
Pet Regulars: Mollie (Staffordshire Bull Terrier) – food bin. Biscuits (from the landlady), Maltesers (from the landlord), sausages and burgers (from the barbecue).

ARGYLL & BUTE

CAIRNDOW STAGECOACH INN
Cairndow, Argyll PA26 8BN (01499 600286).
Pet Regulars: Our own dog Rocky is a Golden Labrador.

THE BALLACHULISH HOTEL
Ballachulish, Argyll PA39 4JY (01855 811606).
Dogs allowed in the lounge, beer garden and guests' bedrooms, excluding food areas.
Pet Regulars: Thumper (Border Collie/GSD-cross), devoted to his owner and follows him everywhere.

BORDERS

CULGRUFF HOUSE HOTEL
Crossmichael, Castle Douglas, Kirkcudbrightshire DG7 3BB (01556 670230).
Dogs allowed in family room, guest bedrooms, but must be kept on leads outside.
Pet Regulars: A cross-section of canine visitors.

HIGHLANDS

ARISAIG HOTEL
Arisaig, Inverness-shire (01687 450210).
Dogs welcome.
Pet Regulars. Regulars in the public bar include Luar (Lurcher), Cindy (Collie), Whisky (Terrier).

PERTH & KINROSS

FOUR SEASONS HOTEL
St Fillans, Perthshire (01764 685333).
Dogs allowed in all non-food areas.

𝔉𝔥𝔊 Diploma Winners 2000

Each year we award a small number of diplomas to holiday proprietors whose services have been specially commended by our readers. The following were our FHG Diploma Winners for 2000.

England

CUMBRIA

• Mr & Mrs Haskell, Borwick Lodge, Outgate, Hawkshead, Cumbria LA22 0PU (015394 36332).

• Mrs Val Sunter, Higher House Farm, Oxenholme Lane, Natland, Kendal, Cumbria LA9 7QH (015395 61177).

DEVON

• Jenny Fox, Highstead Farm, Bucks Cross, Bideford, Devon EX39 5DX (01237 431201).

DORSET

• Mr & Mrs Reynolds, The Vine Hotel, 22 Southern Rd, Southbourne, Bournemouth, Dorset BH6 3SR (01202 428309).

HAMPSHIRE

• Mrs Ellis, Efford Cottage Guest House, Milford Road, Everton, Lymington, Hampshire SO41 0JD (015906 42315).

KENT

• Pam & Arthur Mills, Cloverlea, Bethersden, Ashford, Kent TN26 3DU (01233 820353)

Wales

ANGLESEY & GWYNEDD

• Jim & Marion Billingham, Preswylfa, Aberdovey, Gwynedd LL35 0LE (01654 767239)

NORTH WALES

• Bob & Nesta Wivell, Pen-Y-Bont Fawr, Cynwyd, Near Corwen, North Wales LL21 0ET (01490 412663)

Scotland

ABERDEENSHIRE, BANFF & MORAY

• Garth Hotel, Grantown on Spey, Morayshire PH26 3HN (01479 872836)

PERTH & KINROSS

• The Windlestrae Hotel, The Muirs, Kinross, Tayside KY13 7AS (01577 863217)

HELP IMPROVE BRITISH TOURIST STANDARDS

Why not write and tell us about the holiday accommodation you have chosen from one of our popular publications? Complete a nomination form (see back of book) giving details of why you think YOUR host or hostess should win one of our attractive framed diplomas.

Index of Towns and Counties

Please also refer to Contents on page 67

FHG PUBLICATIONS

publish a large range of well-known accommodation guides. We will be happy to send you details or you can use the order form at the back of this book.

THE FHG DIPLOMA

HELP IMPROVE
BRITISH TOURIST STANDARDS

You are choosing holiday accommodation from our very popular FHG Publications.
Whether it be a hotel, guest house, farmhouse or self-catering accommodation, we think you will find
it hospitable, comfortable and clean, and your host and hostess friendly and helpful.

Why not write and tell us about it?

As a recognition of the generally well-run and excellent holiday accommodation reviewed in our
publications, we at FHG Publications Ltd. present a diploma to proprietors who receive the highest
recommendation from their guests who are also readers of our Guides. If you care to write to us
praising the holiday you have booked through FHG Publications Ltd. – whether this be board, self-
catering accommodation, a sporting or a caravan holiday, what you say will be evaluated and the
proprietors who reach our final list will be contacted.

The winning proprietor will receive an attractive framed diploma to display on his premises as
recognition of a high standard of comfort, amenity and hospitality. FHG Publications Ltd. offer this
diploma as a contribution towards the improvement of standards in tourist accommodation in
Britain. Help your excellent host or hostess to win it!

FHG DIPLOMA

We nominate ....

....

Because

Name ....

Address...

....

Telephone No...

ONE FOR YOUR FRIEND 2001

• •

FHG Publications have a large range of attractive holiday accommodation guides for all kinds of holiday opportunities throughout Britain. They also make useful gifts at any time of year. Our guides are available in most bookshops and larger newsagents but we will be happy to post you a copy direct if you have any difficulty. We will also post abroad but have to charge separately for post or freight. *The inclusive cost of posting and packing the guides to you or your friends in the UK is as follows:*

FARM HOLIDAY GUIDE
England, Scotland, Wales and Channel Islands.
Board, Self-catering, Caravans/
Camping, Activity Holidays.
£6.00 inc p&p ☐

SELF-CATERING HOLIDAYS in Britain
Over 1000 addresses throughout for
Self-catering and caravans
in Britain.
£5.50 inc p&p. ☐

**Recommended
COUNTRY HOTELS OF BRITAIN**
Including Country Houses, for the
discriminating
£5.50 inc p&p ☐

**Recommended
WAYSIDE AND COUNTRY INNS of Britain**
Pubs, Inns and small hotels.
£5.50 inc p&p. ☐

BRITAIN'S BEST HOLIDAYS
A quick-reference general guide for
all kinds of holidays.
£4.50 inc p&p ☐

**The GOLF GUIDE –
Where to play. Where to stay.**
In association with GOLF MONTHLY.
Over 2500 golf courses in Britain
with convenient accommodation.
Holiday Golf in France, Portugal, Spain,
USA, South Africa and Thailand.
£10.50 inc p&p ☐

B&B in Britain
Over 1000 choices for touring and holidays
throughout Britain. Airports and Ferries
Supplement.
£4.50 inc p&p. ☐

**The FHG Guide to
CARAVAN & CAMPING HOLIDAYS**
Caravans for hire, sites and holiday
parks and centres.
£4.50 inc p&p. ☐

BED AND BREAKFAST STOPS.
Over 1000 friendly and comfortable
overnight stops.
Non-smoking, Disabled and
Special Diets Supplements.
£6.00 inc p&p. ☐

**CHILDREN WELCOME!
Family Holidays and Attractions guide.**
Family holidays with
details of amenities for
children and babies.
£5.50 inc p&p. ☐

PETS WELCOME!
The unique guide for
holidays for pet owners
and their pets.
£6.50 inc p&p. ☐

**Recommended
SHORT BREAK HOLIDAYS in Britain**
'Approved' accommodation
for quality bargain breaks.
Introduced by John Carter
£5.50 inc p&p. ☐

Tick your choice and send your order and payment to
• •

FHG PUBLICATIONS, ABBEY MILL BUSINESS CENTRE, SEEDHILL, PAISLEY PA1 1TJ

TEL: 0141- 887 0428• FAX: 0141- 889 7204 • E-mail: fhg@ipcmedia.com

FHG

Deduct 10% for 2/3 titles or copies; 20% for 4 or more.

Send to: NAME...

ADDRESS ....

....POST CODE ....

I enclose Cheque/Postal Order for £...

SIGNATURE ....DATE ....

Please complete the following to help us improve the service we provide. How did you find out about our guides?:

☐Press   ☐Magazines   ☐TV/Radio   ☐Family/Friend   ☐Other

Walk it!

ee 32-page supplement
13 glorious walks to enjoy
around Britain

Along the Wye — page 30.

One of the greatest pleasures of owning a dog is getting out and exploring the great outdoors together.

This booklet, sponsored by BETA from Friskies, will provide you with inspiration. The walks featured will take you into some of the most beautiful parts of the country, from the cascading waters of Aira Force in Cumbria to the spectacular views across the River Wye in the Forest of Dean.

The relationship between dog and owner is unique — and there's no better way to celebrate it. So why not get out and enjoy yourselves this summer — happy hiking!

Sarah Wright

**Sarah Wright, editor,
Your Dog Magazine.**

Gowbarrow Fell and Aira Force — page 4.

Please remember...

when walking with your do
the country code. Keep to t
designated footpaths and r
take poop scoops with you
up as you go. Ensure your
close control at all times ar
on a lead around livestock,
or in game reserves.
● The information containe
booklet is correct at the tin
to press. Your Dog Magazir
can accept no responsibilit
changes or difficulties enco
any of the routes.

Sponsored by

ntents

Dolanog — page 12.

Hathersage — page 18.

rah Wright; **Art editor:** Shaun Smith;
Michael Parsons; **Artwork:** Andrew Mackintosh;
denburgh Reprographics, Peterborough, Cambs;
Heron Print, Maldon, Essex.

Gowbarrow Fell and Aira Force

BY MARY WELSH

The quiet, lonely summit of the Lake District's Gowbarrow Fell contrasts strongly with often crowded Aira Force. Both are visited on this pleasing five-mile walk.

Route planner

1 From the back of the car park, pass through two gates and on through the glade. Take the easily missed steps on your right to a footbridge over the Aira Beck. Climb the steps beyond and follow the path around to the left. By a dead tree beside the track, take the footpath on the right to a stile onto the open fell. Follow the grassy way as it bears right, with wonderful, ever increasing views of Ullswater. Remember to keep your dog on a lead if there are sheep about.

2 Continue climbing the path. After a short vertiginous stretch the way is fenced on the right and brings you to Yew Crag, with its memorial seat and cairn. Follow the path as it winds on, high above the lovely slopes. Cross a wooden footbridge spanning a deep gorge and continue to the ruins of an old shooting lodge; turn left here (do not go on to cross the wall).

3 The track rapidly becomes clearer and climbs steadily, with a wall away to your right. Carry on, across the peat, following the route as it swings steadily left, away from the wall, until you come to the north end of the tiny summit. Scramble upwards to the trig point.

4 After a pause here, take the wide track that sweeps across the moorland in the direction of the continuing wall, and then descends beside it. Soon Ullswater comes into view and ahead is remote Matterdale. Carry on down, walking beside mixed woodland to a ladder stile (some dogs might need help here).

5 Walk 90 yards on a permissive path to join the main track, where you turn left. This leads you into woodland with Aira Beck to your right, and lots of interesting smells for your dog. Pass High Force and follow any of the many tracks back to view Aira Force, best seen from the bridge at its foot. Return to the car park.

Aira Force has b
beauty spot sin
times.

FACT FILE

Distance: 5 miles.
Time: 3 hours.
Map: OS Outdoor Leisure 5.
Start/parking: The Aira
Force National Trust pay and
display car park on the A592
just east of the A5091; grid
reference 401201.
Terrain: Two high, narrow
paths on the way to the
hunting lodge; peaty paths
to fell top can be wet after
rain; steepish, long descent
from summit.
Nearest towns: Penrith,
Ambleside.
Refreshments: Aira Force
Tea Rooms close to the car
park; tables outside; good
choice in Penrith, Ambleside,
Glenridding and Patterdale.
Public transport: Stagecoach
Cumberland,
tel. (01946) 63222.
Stiles: Several; dogs may
need help over the ladder
stile.

BETA Tip
Brush up on your basic first aid. Dogs
are notoriously good at getting into
scrapes, particularly when out enjoying
themselves on long walks. Ask your vet
nurse for advice.

G THE WAY

rrow Fell (1,579ft)
the lesser heights
rom the shores of
vater. Its lower
e delightfully
nd it was here that
daffodils inspired
Vordsworth to
famous diary

● Above the trees, bracken
predominates and, higher
still, heather.
Aira Beck flows over the
meeting place between
Skiddaw slates and
Borrowdale volcanic rocks,
resulting in waterfalls that
were as popular with the
Victorians as they are today.

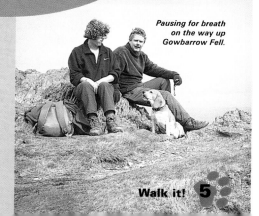

*Pausing for breath
on the way up
Gowbarrow Fell.*

Walk it! **5**

Clapham, Norber, Clapham

BY MARY WELSH

From the lovely Dales village of Clapham, this walk takes you into Crummack Dale, then returns below a fine limestone scar.

FACT FILE

Distance: 6 miles.
Time: 3 hours.
Map: OS Outdoor Leisure 2.
Start/parking: The pay and display car park at the Clapham Village National Park Centre; grid reference 745693.
Terrain: Generally easy walking but walking boots are recommended.
Nearest towns: Ingleton, Settle.
Refreshments: Good choice in Clapham, with outside tables.
Public transport: Rail enquiries tel. 0345 484950; all bus, train and coach enquiries tel. 0906 550 0000.
Stiles: Several; heavy dogs might need help over the ladder stiles. If you find the ladder stiles to the erratics (rocks carried by glacial action) too daunting, give the phenomenon a miss and continue down Crummack Lane to a cross of tracks where you turn right to return along Thwaite Lane.

Route planner

1 Turn right out of the car park and walk up through the village. At the church of St James, turn right following the signpost for Austwick. Follow the track, where your dog can have some freedom; this takes you through two tunnels and then divides. Turn left into Long Lane (a walled track), where your dog can continue to enjoy his freedom. As you pass, look left to where Clapham Beck issues from a cave, and the delightful Trow Gill, where long ago flocks and herds were hidden from marauders.

2 At the end of the walled way, take the right of two gates and climb the sheep pastures, with your pet on his lead, to a stile and then a cairn. Continue on the clear way that veers north-east (half righ by another cairn, the drar shape of Pen-y-ghent con view, and a bridleway joir the right.

3 Turn sharp right to w track. Follow the way route that passes west of Crummack Farm to join th narrow Crummack Lane, the dog a few romps. Ign left turn to Wharfe and th access track to Sowerthw Farm. Beyond the farm th swings right; leave it and the stile on the left (wher dogs might need a little h

4 Keep straight ahead; below Nappa Scars continue to the next stile gives access to the open Climb the next stone-ste

prber erratic.

Crummack
Dale

③

② Trow Gill

Crummack

Inglesborough
Cave

Clapham Beck

Thwaite

Flatt

④

Norber

⑤

Sowerthwaite
Farm

CLAPHAM P ①

⑥

B6480

Austwick

BETA Tip

Avoid letting your dog swim in any water that appears stagnant or unclean and make sure he doesn't try to drink polluted water which may cause stomach upsets.

Looking across to Robin Proctor's Scar.

walk on
wall to a
ed signpost (note the
of this as you return to it
rn right and climb the faint
ough many gritstone
. Continue on up the slope
for the best examples of
rratics to the right of the
th; return to the signpost.

right and continue to the
t stile below Robin
Scar. On his way home, a
roctor is believed to have
er the edge after indulging
uch of the village ale
rse died too. Follow the
t swings left to another stile
wall into Thwaite Lane.

right and follow the track
nce a busy highway
o Clapham.

ALONG THE WAY

● Several attractive bridges link Clapham's charming greystone houses which line both banks of Clapham Beck; dogs can have a drink here.

● Great gritstone boulders were carried by an ancient glacier from Crummack Dale and deposited on the much younger limestone of Norber. Rainwater erodes limestone faster than the gritstones leaving them standing on pedestals.

● The Farrer family acquired the manor of Clapham in the 18th century. In the 19th century they rebuilt Ingleborough Hall, the family mansion.

The two wide-walled tunnels you pass through at the start of the walk were built by the Farrers so they could reach their woodland without having to see the travellers on the once busy bridleway.

A nutritional breakthroug

BETA Complete BIOplus has revolutionised canine nutrition by using chicory — a natural pre-biotic.

In-depth research by Friskies' team of vets and nutritionists resulted in the use of chicory in the lifestage range. The vegetable has been proven to encourage the production of natural protective bacteria in the digestive system.

The benefits of feeding BETA Complete BIOplus can include a lively, more alert dog with a healthy skin and coat, while problems such as bad breath and flatulence may be reduced.

To understand the benefits of chicory and how a dog's digestive system works, Steve Andrews, MRCVS, Friskies' vet explains: "Food goes from the mouth to the stomach, which produces acids. This starts off the breakdown of food, but there is no absorption of nutrients.

"Next stop is the small intestine, where most of the digestion takes place. It's no longer such an acid

Your dog's diet is vital to his wellbeing.

environment and starts to become slightly alkaline. The food then moves into the large intestine which is the main site for bacteria involved in digestion."

We tend to think of bacteria as harmful b explains that some ar beneficial and some potentially harmful. " bacteria, like bifidoba

BETA Complete BIOplus is a complete lifestage range. Each of the nine products have been nutritionally balanced to meet a dog's needs whatever his age, breed, size or lifestyle. BETA is available only through specialist outlets such as g pet shops, pet superstores, breeders and country stores.

Don't forget that Friskies offers a helpline if you want to find out mor about the BETA range (see right).

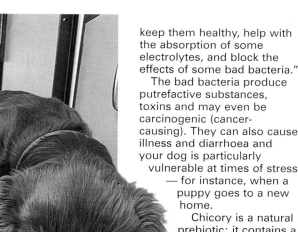

keep them healthy, help with the absorption of some electrolytes, and block the effects of some bad bacteria."

The bad bacteria produce putrefactive substances, toxins and may even be carcinogenic (cancer-causing). They can also cause illness and diarrhoea and your dog is particularly vulnerable at times of stress — for instance, when a puppy goes to a new home.

Chicory is a natural prebiotic: it contains a fibre called inulin which encourages good bacteria to grow and helps increase the absorption of beneficial nutrients.

"However, you won't get the same effect if you simply add fresh chicory to your dog's diet," adds Steve.

"You have to get the quantities and mix right. We use the chicory root, not the leaves, which is more difficult to source.

"The root has an altogether different taste from the chicory leaves we are accustomed to and seems to be enjoyed by dogs."

e B vitamins and omodulators une system helpers. y also produce nces which provide the gut cells to help

You're in good hands

If you need advice on caring for your pet or about the BETA range, why not call the Friskies Pet Care Team?

With a wealth of knowledge and experience in all aspects of pet care, from nutrition to pet behaviour and training, the team can be contacted Monday to Friday, 9am – 5pm, UK only.

In the last five years more than 250,000 pet owners nationwide have made contact for advice — so rest assured, you will be in good hands.

BETA has an active show schedule throughout the year, so if you are planning to visit one of the major country/ agricultural/dog shows why not visit the Friskies BETA stand?

Walk it! 9

Snape village walk

BY MARY WELSH

This well waymarked and maintained w
takes you along the green lanes and sa
tracks of the village of Snape. It passes
beside the River Alde and close to the
Maltings, famous for its music festivals

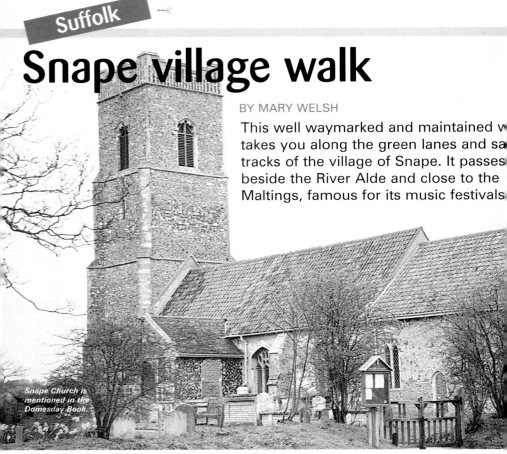

Snape Church is mentioned in the Domesday Book.

Route planner

1 From the parking area, close to the red pantiled church, cross the A-road and continue, south, for 100yds along the B1069. Turn left and stroll along a delightful green lane — offering freedom for your dog — that soon curves right and descends gently behind the village to join Priory Road. Turn right and walk straight on, watching for a wide sandy track which leads off to the left.

2 Follow this as it swings left again through pastures. At a deciduous copse, turn right to walk through trees to the side of the River Alde. Turn right here along the embanked path beside the river, where dogs can have more freedom. As you reach Snape Bridge you may wish to cross and visit the Maltings.

3 To continue the walk stroll right along Bridge Road and then take the left turn down an access track to Abbey Farm. Walk on ahead and then go right to join the very narrow Gromford Lane, which you leave, on your left,

after 20 paces. Now str
beside one of Suffolk's
arable fields and then b
right, along a narrow ro
crossroads.

4 From here you can
the continuing rou
stretching across the pa
Beyond a tiny strip of
woodland lies Wadd La
which you cross. Stride
a track to Croft Farm an
along the arrowed wide
track so typical of this a
Make a large curve on
these tracks, crossing f
A1094 and then the roa

Snape — a Suffolk village steeped in history.

FACT FILE

Distance: 5½ miles.
Time: 3 hours.
Maps: OS Pathfinder 1008 and 1009.
Start/parking: Close to Snape church; grid reference 395594.
Terrain: Level walking over good tracks and paths and along narrow roads, which are virtually traffic free.
Nearest town: Saxmunden.
Refreshments: The Plough and Sail at the Maltings; dogs are welcome at the tables outside where there is always a bowl of water for them.
Public transport: Bus enquiries tel. (01473) 253734.
Stiles: One.

ALONG THE WAY

● In the Little Domesday Book of 1085 Snape Church was valued at 16d. In the 17th century it had a thatched roof; by the 18th century it had been tiled. Today the church's simple unadorned interior is a haven of tranquillity.

● The Maltings at Snape, a complex of old industrial buildings, was once a thriving maltings with bargees plying their trade between the village and London. The buildings were converted by the composer Benjamin Britten in 1968. The walk takes you along the path beside the River Alde — the Curlew river in the composer's music.

BETA Tip

let your dog into fields of — not only may he damage but they may have been d recently; agrochemicals can be dangerous.

nden. Keep on to a cross s.

rn right and continue along e quiet way to the A1094 Cross and walk along the oposite. Take the path on t through pastures to ou back to the track taken utset of your walk. Turn return to the precincts of rch.

Dolanog

This walk is partly along Glyndwr's Way and partly along the Ann Griffiths' Walk. It takes you through gloriously contrasting countryside; you and your dog may wish to dawdle along the way!

The John Hughes chapel at Pontrobert.

The grassy path cuts through the bracken above Dolanog.

ALONG THE WAY

● Ann Griffiths composed hymns. She was born in 1776 on a small farmstead named Dolwar Fach, near Dolanog, a remote area in mid Wales. She died aged 29 following childbirth. Hers was an uneventful life and she never travelled from her home area. She was greatly influenced by the Calvinistic Methodist movement with its evangelical emphasis.

John Hughes, a preacher from Pontrobert, was her spiritual mentor and the recorder of her hymns.

● Glyndwr's Way is a 128-mile (206km) walking route that runs through some of the finest scenery in mid Wales. It is named after Owain Glyndwr, the Welsh warrior/statesman who fought a campaign for an independent Welsh nation in the early 15th century.

 Tip

Ensure your dog is wearing some form of identity disc during your walks. This is a legal requirement for all dogs in a public place.

FILE

:e: 7 miles.
 hours.
IS Landranger 239.
 arking: Small car
 posite the Ann
 s' Memorial Chapel,
 g; grid reference

: Woodland paths
 cks; field path;
 ads.
 t town: Welshpool.
 ments: The Royal
 ntrobert.
 ransport: Postbus,
 97) 826642.
 Three.

Route planner

 fore you set off from
 lanog, visit the
 ng memorial chapel to
 iffiths. Then with your
 the front of the
 walk right to a road
 n where you bear left
 ng Glyndwr's Way
 ragon waymarks).
 ne River Vyrnwy by its
 pedestrian bridge to
 of the road bridge.
 ie on the grass verge
 nain road (B4382), with
 r to your left, where
 is a spectacular
 ll. After 650m, take a
 gate on the left, cross

a field and climb another stile.

2 Bear right to cross a
    footbridge over a
tributary, where dogs can
drink. Walk on above the river
to your left and then through
woodland, which offers
freedom for your dog. Cross a
stile and move away from the
river along a farm track. Pass
a black and white house and
continue on the access lane
to a road. Turn left downhill,
then left again at a T-junction
to cross a bridge at
Pontrobert.

3 Ignore the left turn and
    walk straight ahead
along a narrow lane,
signposted John Hughes
Chapel (Hen Gapel). The
pretty whitewashed building
has been extensively restored
and is now a place where
pilgrims can worship.

4 Return down the lane
    and take the road on
your right, signposted
Llanfihangel; walk upstream.

At the Y-junction take the left
fork to pass through mixed
woodland, continuing up a
very narrow lane. At the top
of the hill, where the road
swings right and dogs can
come off the lead, turn left
and walk along a hedged
track, waymarked with the
bible logo of the Ann Griffiths'
Walk. At the Y-junction, take
the waymarked left fork.
Ignore any right turns and go
on through the plantation.
Continue on the gated
waymarked track, steadily
descending towards the wide
flowing River Vyrnwy. Cross
the feeder stream, Nant
Dolwar, where generations of
farmers have washed their
sheep (and dogs can have
another drink) at the foot of
the waterfall before the lively
stream enters the river.

5 After this the climbing
    way becomes hedged
and moves away from the
river. The track becomes a
road and leads back to the
car park at Dolanog.

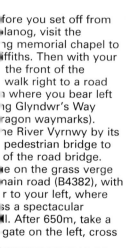

 fall where
 is of farmers
 eir sheep.

Walk it! **13**

Fairy Lochs

BY MARY WELSH

This is a delightful walk to the attractive Fairy Lochs, the site of a memorial plaque set on the side of a large rocky outcrop.

BETA Tip

Don't do too much walking on hot days. A leisurely stroll when the sun is shining is quite pleasant, but it is probably the worst time to give your dog intensive exercise.

FACT FILE

Distance: 3¹/₂ miles.
Time: 2 – 3 hours.
Map: OS Landranger 19.
Start/parking: In an old gravel pit opposite the Shieldaig Lodge Hotel; grid reference 807726.
Terrain: Easy walking but paths can be muddy.
Nearest villages: Badachro, Gairloch.
Refreshments: Shieldaig Hotel (evenings only); Badachro Inn (all day); dogs on leads in bars.
Public transport: Wester Bus, tel. (01445) 712255.
Stiles: None.

Route planner

1 Walk back, for 100yds, along the B8056 from the parking area, to take a cart track on the right, crossing a stream by a footbridge. Continue along the track, passing through woodland where your dog can enjoy some interesting smells. At the cairn and the signpost for the lochs, turn left up the hillside to follow a cairned path through glades of birch and then moorland. Just before the first loch look for the sign for the crash site — where an American plane came down in 1945.

2 Turn right and follow the lochside around by a steepish bank. Continue right across an open area and pass between some rocky spurs. Down to your left lie a few remains of the crashed plane.

On the rock face of a hi⸣ crag, overlooking the lo⸣ the poignant memorial ⸣ plaque, with the names young people killed. Thi⸣ quiet lovely hollow in th⸣ and a war grave, and as⸣ should be respected.

3 Carry on to the enc⸣ the loch below the⸣ wreckage to follow the ⸣ which take you down to⸣

ALONG THE WAY

dale. Join the good track
rn right. The large loch,
o your left, is surrounded
ssy slopes. Walk on
e Lochan Fuar. Beyond
e track takes you across
moorland, pungent with
yrtle and with craggy
ps on either side.

tride on to the B road
nd turn left to return to
rking area.

● In June 1945 an American Liberator
aircraft, carrying nine crew and six
passengers, returning home after a
long and bitter war, failed to clear the
summit of Slioch. The aircraft circled
as it descended, looking for a place to
land but plunged into the rocky spurs
about Fairy Lochs; no one survived.

Main picture:
The magical setting of Fairy
Lochs.

Above: Remnants of the
doomed Liberator still
remain in the water.

Walk it! **15**

Allen Banks

BY PADDY DILLON

Housesteads Roman Fort on Hadrian's Wall is one of the most popular visitor sites in Northumberland. Just to the south is the secret, hidden, wooded gorge of Allen Banks, where you can enjoy a quiet walk with your dog away from the crowds. There are two narrow suspension footbridges to cross, where you'd be advised to keep your dog on a short lead.

Left: The River All~ flows through an unspoilt rocky woodland gorge.

FACT FILE

Distance: 4 miles.
Time: 2½ hours.
Maps: OS Landranger Sheets 86 or 87.
Start/parking: Alongside Ridley Hall; grid reference 798641.
Terrain: Easy woodland and riverside paths, with short, steep ascents and descents; take care when crossing the suspension footbridges.
Refreshments: Off route at Haydon Bridge and Bardon Mill.
Public transport: Using buses and trains to reach Bardon Mill will add an extra two miles to the walking distance.
Stiles: None.

Route planner

1 Ridley Hall and Allen Banks are signposted from the main A69 road between Haltwhistle and Haydon Bridge. The car park for Allen Banks is in the former walled garden of Ridley Hall. A large information board points out the main paths and points of interest in the wooded gorge; it's a National Trust property. Follow the path away from the car park, upstream beside the River Allen. The way is well wooded and within half a mile you'll reach a narrow suspension footbridge.

2 Cross over the river using the footbridge, then walk straight up a flight of stone steps. The path leads throu~ oaks and beeches and you' pass stones marked with th word 'Tarn'. You'll reach M~ Tarn, which is no more tha~ small pool in a delightful b~ of larch and Scots pine. In summer there may be wat~ lilies growing on the surfac~

3 A wide path continues from the tarn, then it s~ round and begins to desce~ towards the river. There ar~ sorts of options, with path~ branching and branching a~ but aim to follow a good t~ path upstream, gradually

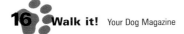

Keep your dog on a lead when crossing the suspension bridge at Allen Banks.

ALONG THE WAY

● The National Trust holds about 200 acres at Allen Banks and the walk is mostly on National Trust property, with the exception of Plankey Mill.

● Allen Banks is a well wooded area, with a great variety of trees and flowering plants, ferns, mosses and fungi. Ramsons fill the air with garlic scent. Look out for wood warblers among the trees and white-bibbed dippers in the river.

● The power of the river was once harnessed at Plankey Mill, but now you're more likely to see canoeists pitting their own power against the river, and offering plenty of entertainment to bystanders.

ding to the River Allen. Leave ods and walk through a meadow, passing a riverside the way to Plankey Mill.

oss over another narrow spension footbridge, then ght to follow the River Allen tream. If you remain fairly o the river, then you'll be led the first footbridge and ds to the car park. However, s a short detour you might like e on the way back to your car. left turn uphill to reach the Floor' viewpoint. The unusual derives from the use of sheep as a surfacing material at ot.

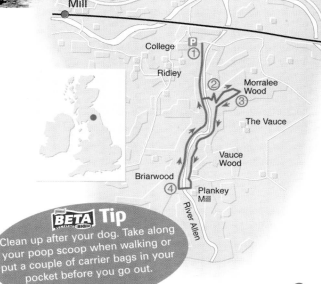

BETA Tip

Clean up after your dog. Take along your poop scoop when walking or put a couple of carrier bags in your pocket before you go out.

Hathersage

BY PAUL AND SANDY BIGGS

Romantics will adore Hathersage.
It is believed that Little John is buried In the churchyard while the area inspired Charlotte Bronte's writing of 'Jane Eyre'.

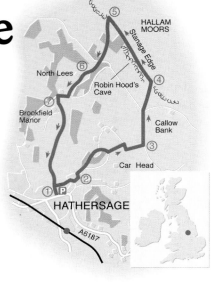

HATHERSAGE

Route planner

1 With the post office on your left, walk along the A625 to the Hathersage Inn. Turn left along Baulk Lane to a gate on the right. Go uphill to the church, passing through a number of gates.

2 Go to the left of the church then right by the old vicarage. A lane brings you to a stile where a grassy path leads to a wood. Walk by a stream to a bridge. Cross, and walk on through the trees to a white gate. Turn right, pass Moorseats Hall and join an access road. At Car Head, turn left, and take the very steep climb that brings you to a stile. Follow a track to the road.

3 Turn left, and walk along the uphill road to a road junction. Join a flagged path climbing up onto Stanage Rocks and turn left.

4 Walk along the top of the edge passing Robin Hood's cave. When reaching a large boulder on the right, turn left onto a distinct path.

5 Descend to a gate then pass through a plantation. Take the left-hand path of two through Hollins car park to the road. Turn left, then right at the public toilets to join a track. Continue ahead to North Lees Hall.

6 A pleasant walk from the hall brings you to a minor road. Turn right, then just past Bronte Cottage, turn left by a stream.

7 An obvious track leads to Brookfield Manor, passing to the left, and a short field path leads onto a track. At Lane End rejoin Baulk Lane. Follow the lane back past the cricket ground to return to the post office.

ALONG THE WAY

● The grave of Little John can be viewed in the churchyard of St Michael and All Angels. The church dates to 1831 although it is known that a church has stood on the site since 1281.
● Hathersage was known as Hereseige in the Domesday Book. This name is thought to have meant heather's edge.
● Charlotte Bronte stayed in Hathersage for three weeks in 1845. She visited many halls in the area, some owned by descendants of the Eyre family. Without a doubt the name Jane Eyre was borrowed from this famous family.

*Enjoying the superb
...nic views from Stanage Edge.*

*...ight: The grave of Little John
...chael and All Angels Church.*

FACT FILE

Distance: 5 miles.
Time: 3 hours.
Maps: OS Landranger 110,
Sheffield and Huddersfield
area; OS Pathfinder 743,
Hathersage.
Start: The post office,
Hathersage; grid reference
232815.
Parking: Small car park in
village or by roadside.
Terrain: Good footpaths
and tracks; some steep
climbs.
Nearest town: Sheffield.
Refreshments: Several
pubs in Hathersage; all
dog friendly.
Public Transport: Busline,
tel. (01332) 292200 or
National Rail Enquiries,
tel. 0345 484950.
Stiles: All easy for dogs.

BETA Tip

Before visiting a new area find out if
there are any restrictions on your dog.
For instance, some beaches have a
complete ban on dogs while others
allow them in specific areas only.

Hawkley

BY NICK CHANNER

Enjoy this glorious corner of Hampshire — and some of the most beautiful scenery the county has to offer.

*Rolling hills and v
paths are a feature of t.*

FACT FILE

Distance: 6 miles.
Time: 3 hours.
Map: OS Landranger 197.
Start/parking: The centre of Hawkley village; grid reference 746292. There's room to park near the church and the green.
Terrain: Field paths, tracks, woodland paths, and several stretches of quiet road. Undulating landscape with several steep ascents; muddy and wet in places after heavy rain.
Nearest town: Petersfield.
Refreshments: The Hawkley Inn at the start and finish of the walk welcomes dogs, as does The Trooper at Froxfield just off the route.
Public transport: Contact Hampshire County Council for a bus map of the county, tel. (01962) 846924.
Stiles: None.

Route planner

1 From the centre of Hawkley follow the road signposted Oakshott, Priors Dean and Wheatham. Take the first bridleway on the right and follow the path along the field edge to the corner. Enter the wood and bear left at the Hangers Way sign. The path forks after a few steps; keep to the right-hand, higher route and climb steadily through the trees. Further on, cut across a field to rejoin the woodland path, following it to the road.

2 Turn left and descend between trees, passing a footpath sign on the right. Keep going as far as a stony track on the right. Take th track and pass a cottage the left. Begin a long clin through the trees; the tra rough and rutted in place Pass a cottage and contin a metalled surface. The entrance to Warren Hous provides a lovely view o Hawkley Church. Pass La Stables and the entrance the Warren National Natu Reserve.

3 Follow the lane to re the road on a bend; left here. Pass some hou on the right and continu the last property, by an electricity transformer. T

ALONG THE WAY

● This lovely walk explores some of the most beautiful scenery in Hampshire — a rich blend of rolling hills, open downland and beech hangers.

● Hawkley village is famous in the area for its church, built in 1865 on the site of an ancient chapel. Its tall, distinctive tower can be seen from across the surrounding fields.

● High up on Shoulder of Mutton Hill is the sarsen Poet Stone, dedicated to the memory of the Edwardian poet Edward Thomas who was killed in the First World War. Thomas lived in the area and was greatly inspired by this glorious corner of Hampshire.

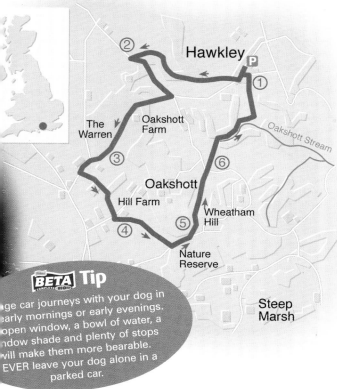

BETA Tip

...ge car journeys with your dog in ...arly mornings or early evenings. ...open window, a bowl of water, a ...ndow shade and plenty of stops ...vill make them more bearable. ...EVER leave your dog alone in a parked car.

ow a bridlepath ...n fields. Pass a trig ...n the right and make ...elt of woodland. Pass ...de the trees, go round ...ight in the field corner ...n turn left after a few ...ollow the path to the ...merging opposite a ...

rn right and walk ...ong to the junction ...d Litton Lane. To visit ...oper pub, go straight ...e next junction and ...ht; to continue the ...alk turn sharp left into ...on Lane. Continue ...when the lane becomes

a stony track running through a tunnel of trees. Turn left at the next junction and then bear right after a few yards to visit the Poet Stone, located on the upper slopes of Shoulder of Mutton Hill. Retrace your steps to the main track and turn right. Walk along to a stile.

5 Cross into the field and then head down through the trees, keeping the fence on the left. Follow Hangers Way down to a second and third stile and continue on the clear path as it follows the field edge. Pass a cottage on the right, cross a stile and turn

right to join a stony track. Follow it to the road and go straight over to the next stile, still following Hangers Way.

6 Cross an elongated field, with the Oakshott Stream on the left; cross a stile and a footbridge and continue over two more stiles before reaching a path junction in front of a house with a swimming pool. Turn left here and make for a stile. Follow the path between fields and woodland, swinging right to join a concrete track running through the trees. Merge with the road, go up the slope and return to Hawkley.

Blackdown

BY SYLVIE DOBSON

A stimulating walk visiting the highest point in West Sussex.

BETA Tip

Don't overestimate how far you'll want to walk if the weather is hot. Make sure there are some shady spots to rest along the way which will make the walk more enjoyable for both you and your dog.

*Below: The views [?]
Blackdown are s[?]*

*Main picture: Th[?]
highest point in [?]
Sussex.*

ALONG THE WAY

● At 919ft above sea level Blackdown is the highest point in West Sussex and on a clear day the views are superb. Nearby Aldworth House was once the home of Alfred, Lord Tennyson and it was here that he wrote 'Idyll of the kings'.

● The Sussex Border Path is a long distance path which traces as near as possible the inland boundary of the combined counties of East and West Sussex.

● Fernhurst was once a thriving village at the centre of the Wealden Iron Industry.

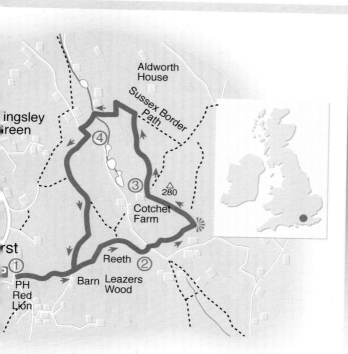

Sponsored by

FACT FILE

Distance: 4½ miles.
Time: 2½ hours.
Maps: OS Landranger 186;
OS Explorer 133.
Start/parking: Car park at
Fernhurst Recreation
Ground; grid reference
900285.
Terrain: Hilly.
Nearest town: Haslemere.
Refreshments: The Red
Lion Inn, where
well-behaved dogs are
welcome in the bar.
Public transport: West
Sussex Travel Information
Helpline, tel. 0345 959099.
Stiles: One — but
avoidable.

ute planner

Take the path by the side of the Red Lion
Inn and walk on ahead until you come to
ction by a barn. Go left and about 70yds
er on at another junction take the middle
(you return to this point at the end of the
. At Reeth House follow the drive to the
but be aware that there is a road ahead.

Walk right for a few paces before taking
the path on the left to climb steadily to
p of Blackdown. You will see a wooden
on your right; take the path on the right
ollow it to a T-junction. The viewpoint
emorial seat can now be found to the
To continue the walk go left and then
ain at the first junction. Follow the path
d to the right and continue down
lside.

t Cotchet Farm go right; ignore the
ath climbing up on the right and

continue ahead until you eventually come
to a wide crossing track. Go left along the
Sussex Border Path keeping left at a fork.
Descend to another crossing track and go left
again, still descending. Join the drive at what
was Wadesmarsh Farmhouse and then go left
by the side of a pond and continue to a lane.

4 Take the drive to Sheetlands, which you
will see to the left. At a 'Private' sign go
left up the bank before regaining direction.
Continue past the last of the houses and
onward through a plantation of young trees
to a fork. Go right ignoring any access tracks.
At the first obvious junction keep right and
then go straight ahead at a crossing track.
You soon reach what should be a familiar
junction from the start of the walk. Turn right
and remember to go right again at the barn
so that you can retrace your steps to the Red
Lion Inn.

Walk it! 23

Hambleden

BY ROBERT WILSON

Starting from the definitive English village, this walk leads through the woods towards Fawley, then returns through more Chiltern beechwoods back to Hambleden. As most of the walk is through woodland, it is ideal dogs as they can be let off the lead for much of the route.

ALONG THE WAY

● Hambleden is a classic English village and has been used for numerous film and TV settings. There is an excellent pub (which has a public bar where dogs are welcomed and a large garden), a shop within a row of brick and flint cottages and a cathedral-like church.

● The initial climb through the woods leads to a superb view across the Thames Valley, and there are further views across to Maidensgrove from the lane leading to Fawley. Being on the Chiltern chalk soil, the paths are usually not too muddy!

ture: Hambleden
itional English village.

eft: Your dog will enjoy
throughout this walk.

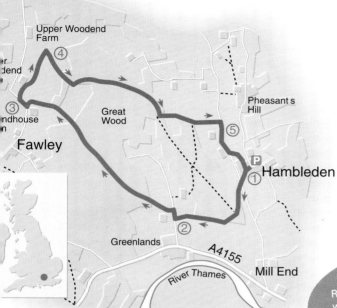

Upper Woodend
Farm

④

r
dend

③
ndhouse
n

Great
Wood

Fawley

Pheasants
Hill

⑤

P
Hambleden
①

Greenlands

②

A4155

River Thames

Mill End

ite planner

rom the car park, turn
eft to the village centre,
eft past the shop to
the road. Cross over
alk along the metalled
th opposite, past the
hool. On entering the
s, fork right uphill. At the
ntinue straight on down
her side. Turn right
a crossing track at the
edge.

urn right along a track,
hen turn left after the
ottage. Fork right uphill
e wood. Follow the
hrough the wood (there
termittent waymark
s to guide you).

Later the track leads between
a hedge and a fence to reach
a lane.

3 Turn right along this lane,
then right along the drive
to Lower Woodend Farm.
Continue past a converted
barn by a fence on your right.
Bear left over a stile (fence
now on left). Turn right across
the field to a stile in the
opposite hedge. The path is
usually well defined.

4 Turn right along this
track, which leads back
into the woods. Continue
straight on over a crossing

track in a dip. At the top, turn
right around a clearing, the
path leading to another track.
Turn right along this track,
then left at a T-junction. Bear
right into the trees and
continue the descent back
into Hambleden valley. On
leaving the woods continue
along the track to reach the
road by a white house.

5 Turn right along the road.
By a footpath sign turn
left across the meadow back
to the village and on past the
church. In the village centre
turn left past the pub back to
the car park.

Staithes to Port Mulgrave

BY MARY WELSH

This pleasing walk starts from the picturesque fishing village of Staithes. It continues along cliffs, part of North Yorkshire's Heritage Coast, and returns through glorious deciduous woodland where dogs can enjoy a romp and a good sniff.

Route planner

Map labels: Cowbar Nab, Old Nab, Cowbar, P, ②, ①, Staithes, Dalehouse, ⑤, A174, Piers, ③, Port Mulgrave, Borrowby Grange, ④, Borrowby Dale, Hinderwell

BETA COMPLETE BIO Tip

Groom your dog thoroughly after a walk. This will allow you to remove ticks before they have a chance to attach themselves.

1 Leave the car park and turn right downhill into the village. Explore the narrow alleys which are lined with white cottages topped with red pantile roofs. At the Cod and Lobster turn right along Church Street and climb uphill, following a coastal path sign.

2 At the end of the cobbles keep straight ahead on a narrow track, following the Cleveland Way signs. Pass the farm buildings and go over three stiles which take you through pastures to the cliff edge. Keep on the

cliff path and proceed with care — especially in high winds (dogs on leads). Join the road and walk into Port Mulgrave, looking down on the crumbling and long defunct piers of the tiny port. Walk through the little hamlet; turn right opposite the telephone box.

3 By the last building turn sharp left and cross the fields. Follow the path downhill to the A174. Cross into a lay-by and then go left over a stile. Follow the path downhill into the

wood, which offers freedom and glorious smells for your dog. Cross the footbridge and bear left up the path.

4 The path then swings sharply back on itself and soon leaves the woodland to cross open scrub. Continue downhill, past the caravan site; turn right over the bridge and join the track.

5 At the road, turn right uphill to the main road once more. Turn right and then left into Staithes.

FACT FILE

Distance: 3½ mile
Time: 2 hours.
Map: OS Outdoor 27.
Start/parking: Sta car park; grid refer 782185.
Terrain: Generally walking.
Nearest town: Wh
Refreshments: Sm shops and several Staithes with outs tables.
Public transport: I enquiries tel. (019 602146.
Stiles: Several but easy.
● Keep dogs on le near farm animals.

ALONG THE WAY

● The quaint fishing village of Staithes lies in a deep ravine between two rocky headlands. The tiny harbour is proud of its association with Captain Cook who, before going to sea, was an assistant to William Sanderson, a merchant in the village.

● The Cod and Lobster Inn takes a tremendous battering from the sea and, in the past, had to be tarred to keep out the wet when the sea broke over it. It has had to be rebuilt many times.

● During the 19th century, Port Mulgrave was an important centre for the extraction and shipment of ironstone. When the ironstone was worked out, another mine was opened near Boulby and the ore was brought along a tunnel in rope-hauled wagons on a narrow-gauge railway to the port.

us woodland
t playground for

The quaint fishing village of Staithes.

Carreg Cennen

BY JOHN NEEDHAM

Carreg Cennen Castle is probably the most spectacularly situated ruin in south Wales. Standing on a high limestone cliff, it dominates the Carmarthenshire landscape for miles around. Two fine, well waymarked walks radiate from it; this is the longer of the two.

ALONG THE WAY

● There was a Welsh stronghold here in the distant past, but the present castle was built by the English lord John Gifford who supported Edward I in defeating the Welsh in 1283. It was reclaimed briefly for Wales by Prince Owain Glyndwr in 1403, but demolished in 1462, locals being paid £28 5s 6d for the job.

● The artist Turner visited in 1798. He didn't paint Carreg Cennen from the best vantage point, but then he probably didn't do the dog walk!

● Admission charges are: adults: £2.50; others: £2; families: £7; unfortunately, no dogs allowed.

Route planner

1 Leave the car park and climb over a stile into a field near the entrance. Walk downhill, go through a gate and climb a stile onto a road. Go left and then over the stile at the second footpath you come to, which has a fingerpost bearing a castle symbol. Follow the yellow arrow signs, crossing two more stiles, and drop steeply downhill to a footbridge. Climb uphill to Llwyn-bedw Farm.

2 Turn right along a track. After crossing a shallow ford and the second of two cattle grids, climb a stile by another cas sign at a fork in the route. Go over two n stiles and then a further one out into a deliciously quiet and remote road. Turn l

3 Soon after a third cattle grid, leave t road again at a further castle sign. A gate, and another stile skirting a farmyar bring you alongside a fence, walking at a level with stupendous views of the castle cliffs across the valley. Cross a stile to dr downhill on a stony track. Go over a furt

A spectacular ruin — Carreg Cennen Castle.

FACT FILE

Distance: 4$\frac{1}{2}$ miles.
(the short walk is 1$\frac{1}{2}$ miles).
Time: 3 hours.
Maps: OS Landranger 159;
Explorer 186.
Start/parking: Castle car park.
Terrain: Farmland paths and tracks; a little walking on a very quiet road; two fairly stiff climbs; muddy in places after wet weather.
Refreshments: The tea/gift shop at Castell Farm (which also has ancient stocks and a magnificent peacock).
Nearest town: Llandeilo.
Public transport: None.
Stiles: 15, but four can be bypassed as can the cattle grids.

BETA Tip
COMPLETE BIO plus
Keep your dog on a lead around livestock, near farms or in game reserves.

Penhill Farm
P
① Castell

Trapp

Nature
Reserve
Hengrofft ④

②

Llwyn-
bedw

Pillow Mound ③

vards the castle, on a route
ids the next farmyard.

ntinue downhill, crossing
tile, to a footbridge, a stile
other footbridge. The last
e walk is up a long
ncline. At the top, pass
le entrance. Carry on
tarmac path to Castell
ith its tempting teashop,
rn to the car park.

Walk it! 29

Along the Wye

BY JOHN NEEDHAM

This four-mile walk in the north-west corner of the Forest of Dean follows the River Wye from Goodrich village to Symonds Yat, and takes in one of the most beautiful views in England. Add another mile and you can include the impressive ruins of Goodrich Castle.

ALONG THE WAY

● Symonds Yat Rock is 500ft high and is named after Robert Symonds a 17th century high Sheriff of Herefordshire; yat is local word meaning gate or pa

● Norman Goodrich Castle wa ruined during the Civil War; it i reputed to be haunted. Legend holds that on stormy nights th ghostly screams of two star-crossed lovers, Charles Clifford from a Royalist family, and Alice Birch from a Parliamentarian, who drowned the river, can be heard echoing from the Wye!

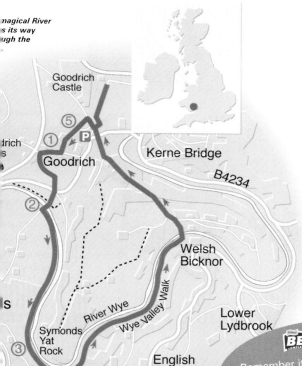

magical River
s its way
ugh the

Goodrich
Castle

⑤

P

drich
s

① Goodrich

Kerne Bridge

B4234

Welsh
Bicknor

②

s

River Wye

Wye Valley Walk

Symonds
Yat
Rock

③

④

English
Bicknor

Lower
Lydbrook

FACT FILE

Distance: 4 miles (5 to
include Goodrich Castle or
6½ for the circular walk).
Time: 3 – 4 hours.
Maps: OS Landranger
162; Outdoor Leisure 14.
Start/parking: Main street
in Goodrich village.
Terrain: Mostly level
paths; fairly steep climb at
Symonds Yat.
Refreshments: Picnic area
at Symons Yat Rock; also
pub at Goodrich.
Nearest town:
Ross-on-Wye.
Public transport: Red and
White, tel. (01989) 562319.
Stiles: None on short
walk; nine on longer
option.

BETA Tip

Remember it's dangerous to throw
sticks for your dog. If he likes to
play games take a toy with you
instead.

te planner

lk along the main village street until
u reach the pub. Enter a field and
footpath leading to a stile that
s you on the B4229. Take the minor
mediately opposite, going a short
e to a bridge over the Wye.

ss and take the obvious footpath
ng the riverbank on your left. This is a
ul stroll through lush water meadows.
ree-quarters of a mile follow the path
woodland cloaking the side of
m Hill.

a signpost indicating Symonds Yat turn
ht, zigzagging uphill past Wren's Nest
. Pass two further houses and emerge
oad. Continue uphill to the Yat Rock
ite. The prospect down to Symonds Yat

village is delightful, but wait until you see the
famous River Wye view! After perhaps visiting
the cafe, cross the footbridge to the main
viewpoint. The vista of the Wye looping away
into Herefordshire is magical.

4 To return to Goodrich simply retrace your
steps or if you want to make it a circular
route of 6½ miles, return to the Symonds Yat
signpost and turn right, following the river
eastwards to Welsh Bicknor. Cross the Wye at
a defunct, pedestrianised railway bridge and
return to Goodrich along a very quiet minor
road. See the OS map for details.

5 To visit the castle, walk along the main
street in the other direction, then turn
right and go over the crossroads to the
approach road.

Walk it! 31

 THE NATURAL WAY TO AID YOUR DOG'S DIGESTIO

 BETA Puppy – Optimal calcium and phosphorus – for healthy developmen bones and teeth. For puppies aged 1 – 6 months, also ideal for toy breeds.

 BETA Junior – Optimal calcium and phosphorus – for healthy developmen bones and teeth. Ideal for dogs from 5 – 6 months to adult maturity.

 BETA Pet – Contains essential fatty acids for a shiny coat. Ideal for family dogs with normal activity levels.

 BETA Chicken Recipe – Rich in chicken and rice for good digestibility. Off a tasty alternative for adult dogs.

 BETA with Fish and Rice – Optimal balance of Omega 6.3 oils to help maintain a healthy skin and glossy coat. Ideal for adult dogs.

 BETA Field – A high energy level food with additional Vitamin E for all hi active, working and sporting dogs.

 BETA Sensitive – Wheat gluten free for dogs with sensitive digestion.

 BETA Light - Low calorie recipe for less active dogs and those with a tend to gain weight.

 BETA Senior – Lower in phosphorus to help protect the kidneys of older c

If you would like further advice on caring for your pet, or BETA Complete BIOplus, call Friskies Pet Care Team, Freephone 0800 21 21 61.

Map 1

Map 2

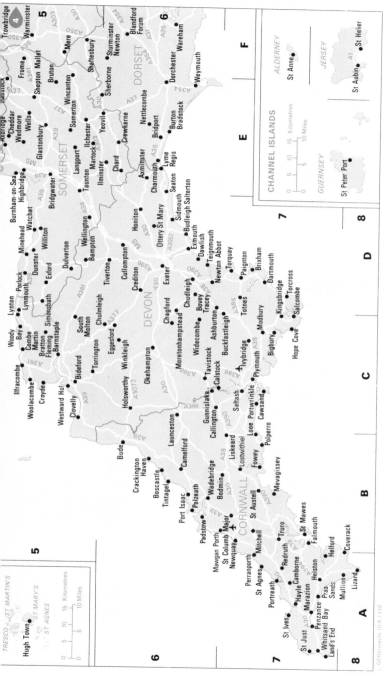

GEOprojects (UK) Ltd
Crown Copyright Reserved

Map 3

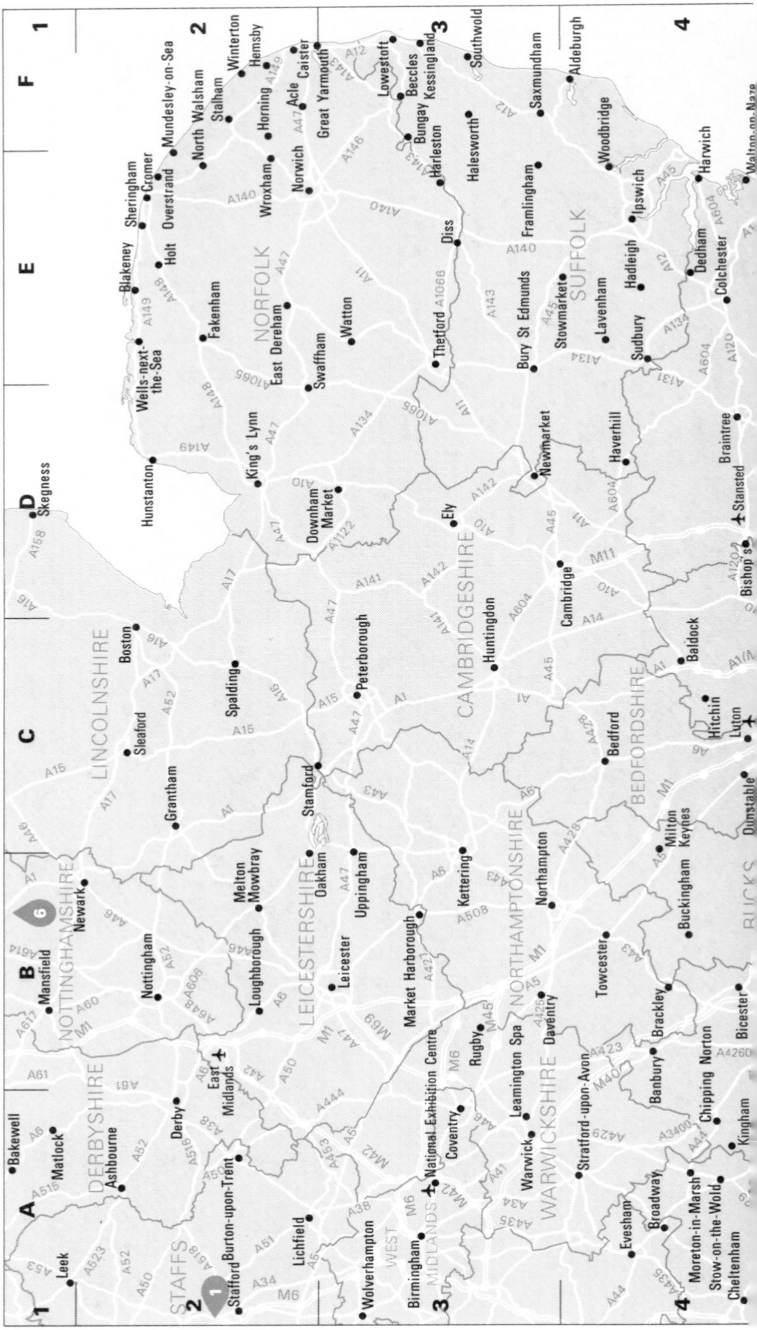
LINCOLNSHIRE
NORFOLK
SUFFOLK
CAMBRIDGESHIRE
BEDFORDSHIRE
NORTHAMPTONSHIRE
LEICESTERSHIRE
NOTTINGHAMSHIRE
DERBYSHIRE
STAFFS
WEST MIDLANDS
WARWICKSHIRE
BUCKS
Skegness
Boston
Sleaford
Grantham
Spalding
Stamford
Peterborough
Hunstanton
King's Lynn
Downham Market
Wells-next-the-Sea
Blakeney
Sheringham
Cromer
Overstrand
Holt
Fakenham
East Dereham
Swaffham
Watton
Thetford
Mundesley-on-Sea
North Walsham
Stalham
Winterton
Hemsby
Horning
Wroxham
Acle
Caister
Norwich
Great Yarmouth
Lowestoft
Beccles
Kessingland
Bungay
Harleston
Southwold
Halesworth
Diss
Saxmundham
Aldeburgh
Framlingham
Woodbridge
Ipswich
Harwich
Walton-on-Naze
Bury St Edmunds
Stowmarket
Lavenham
Hadleigh
Dedham
Colchester
Sudbury
Haverhill
Braintree
Newmarket
Ely
Cambridge
Huntingdon
Stansted
Bishop's
Baldock
Hitchin
Luton
Bedford
Dunstable
Milton Keynes
Buckingham
Northampton
Kettering
Towcester
Brackley
Bicester
Banbury
Chipping Norton
Kingham
Daventry
Rugby
Leamington Spa
Warwick
Stratford-upon-Avon
Coventry
National Exhibition Centre
Birmingham
Wolverhampton
Lichfield
Burton-upon-Trent
Stafford
Leek
Ashbourne
Matlock
Bakewell
Derby
East Midlands
Nottingham
Mansfield
Newark
Loughborough
Melton Mowbray
Leicester
Oakham
Uppingham
Market Harborough
Evesham
Broadway
Moreton-in-Marsh
Stow-on-the-Wold
Cheltenham

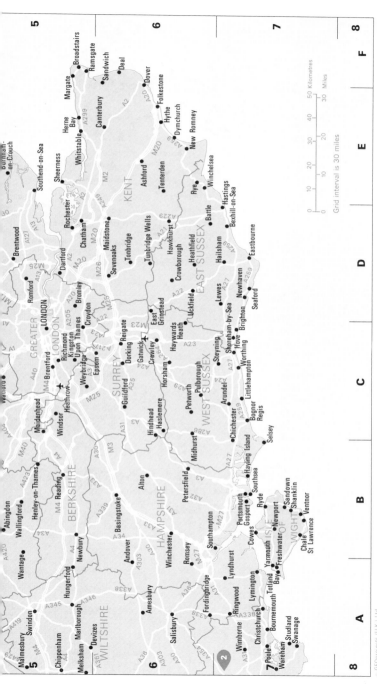

Map 4

Grid interval is 30 miles

50 Kilometres
30 Miles

Map 5

Map 6

E   F   G   H   1

Morpeth

BERLAND

A696

Whitley
Bay
Tynemouth
rbridge   A69   TYNE
Newcastle   South Shields   AND
upon-Tyne   WEAR
Sunderland

2

0   10   20   30   40   50 Kilometres
0   10   20   30 Miles
Grid interval is 30 miles

1. STOCKTON-ON-TEES
2. MIDDLESBROUGH
3. KINGSTON UPON HULL
4. NORTH EAST LINCOLNSHIRE

Durham

DURHAM   A690   A1(M)

HARTLEPOOL

Bishop Auckland   Redcar
dleton-in-Teesdale   Middlesbrough   Saltburn-by-the-Sea
A688   A68
Barnard Castle   REDCAR & CLEVELAND
A66   Darlington   Guisborough   Whitby
Stokesley   A171

3

Richmond

Leyburn   A684   Northallerton

Scarborough
Middleham   Thirsk   Helmsley   Pickering   Cayton Bay
A61   A170   Ayton   Filey

NORTH YORKSHIRE

Ripon   Castle   Malton   Flamborough
Howard   A64   A166   Bridlington
Grassington   Huby   Sledmere
A59   Driffield
kipton   Harrogate   York   A166   A163
hley   Ilkley   A64   A1079   Hornsea
Bingley   EAST RIDING
Bradford   Selby   OF YORKSHIRE   Beverley
eptonstall   WEST   A63   A614   M62
alifax   YORKSHIRE   M62   A63   Hull   Withernsea
Huddersfield   Goole

4

5

Barnsley   NORTH
A635   Doncaster   LINCOLNSHIRE
SOUTH   M18   Scunthorpe   Grimsby
Glossop   YORKSHIRE   A18   M180   Cleethorpes
A631   A46
Sheffield   Gainsborough   Louth
Worksop   A166   Mablethorpe
xton   A57   A158   Alford
Chesterfield   Lincoln
Bakewell   A60   Horncastle
Matlock   Skegness
DERBYSHIRE   NOTTINGHAM-   LINCOLNSHIRE
SHIRE   Newark
Ashbourne   A46   Sleaford   Boston
Trent   Nottingham   A17
Derby   A52   Grantham   A52
East   Spalding
ORDSHIRE   Midlands
Burton-upon-Trent   Loughborough   Melton
Lichfield   Mowbray
LEICESTERSHIRE   Stamford
Oakham   Peterborough
Leicester   Uppingham

6

7

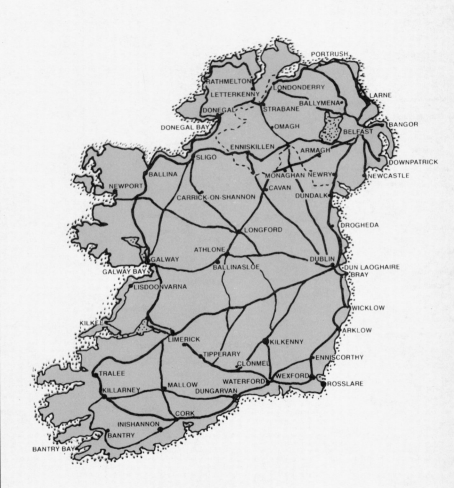